SAGE was founded in 1965 by Sara Miller McCune to support the dissemination of usable knowledge by publishing innovative and high-quality research and teaching content. Today, we publish over 900 journals, including those of more than 400 learned societies, more than 800 new books per year, and a growing range of library products including archives, data, case studies, reports, and video. SAGE remains majority-owned by our founder, and after Sara's lifetime will become owned by a charitable trust that secures our continued independence.

Los Angeles | London | New Delhi | Singapore | Washington DC | Melbourne

DECISION-MAKING

DECISION-MAKING
Concepts, Methods and Techniques

Shyama Prasad Mukherjee

Los Angeles | London | New Delhi
Singapore | Washington DC | Melbourne

Copyright © Shyama Prasad Mukherjee, 2022

All rights reserved. No part of this book may be reproduced or utilized in any form or by any means, electronic or mechanical, including photocopying, recording or by any information storage or retrieval system, without permission in writing from the publisher.

First published in 2022 by

SAGE Publications India Pvt Ltd
B1/I-1 Mohan Cooperative Industrial Area
Mathura Road, New Delhi 110 044, India
www.sagepub.in

SAGE Publications Inc
2455 Teller Road
Thousand Oaks, California 91320, USA

SAGE Publications Ltd
1 Oliver's Yard, 55 City Road
London EC1Y 1SP, United Kingdom

SAGE Publications Asia-Pacific Pte Ltd
18 Cross Street #10-10/11/12
China Square Central
Singapore 048423

Published by Vivek Mehra for SAGE Publications India Pvt Ltd. Typeset in 10.5/13 pt Adobe Caslon Pro by Zaza Eunice, Hosur, Tamil Nadu, India.

Library of Congress Cataloging-in-Publication Data Available

ISBN: 978-93-5479-107-9 (HB)

SAGE Team: Rajesh Dey, Syed Husain Naqvi and Aishna Bhatt

Dedicated to my wife Reba for her constant encouragement and support and for some insightful discussions on human behaviour.

Thank you for choosing a SAGE product!
If you have any comment, observation or feedback,
I would like to personally hear from you.

Please write to me at **contactceo@sagepub.in**

Vivek Mehra, Managing Director and CEO, SAGE India.

Bulk Sales

SAGE India offers special discounts
for purchase of books in bulk.
We also make available special imprints
and excerpts from our books on demand.

For orders and enquiries, write to us at

Marketing Department
SAGE Publications India Pvt Ltd
B1/I-1, Mohan Cooperative Industrial Area
Mathura Road, Post Bag 7
New Delhi 110044, India

E-mail us at **marketing@sagepub.in**

Subscribe to our mailing list
Write to **marketing@sagepub.in**

This book is also available as an e-book.

Contents

List of Abbreviations	xiii
Preface	xv

1	Introduction	1
	1.1. Prologue	1
	1.2. Decisions and Decision-making	2
	1.3. Ubiquity of Decisions	5
	1.4. Rationality and Bounded Rationality	9
	1.5. Hierarchy of Decisions	12
	1.6. Group Decisions	15
	1.7. Social Choice Decisions	16
	1.8. Decision-making and Problem-solving	17
	1.9. Descriptive and Normative Decision Theory	18
	1.10. Case-based Decision Theory	20
	1.11. Decision Theory and Decision-making	25
2	Decision-making Process	28
	2.1. Some Generalities	28
	2.2. Strategies	31
	2.3. States of Nature	33
	2.4. Criteria for Choice	34
	2.5. Utility and Its Measurement	36
	2.6. Regret	38
	2.7. Optimality Principle	40
	2.8. Establishing Trade-Offs	43
	2.9. Types of Decision Problems	45
	2.10. Elaborating Some Examples	49
	2.11. Sequential and Dynamic Decision-making	52
	2.12. Robustness of Decisions	53
3	Representation of a Decision Problems	55
	3.1. Decision Environment	55
	3.2. Decision Matrix	57

	3.3. Influence Diagram	59
	3.4. Decision Trees	62
	3.5. Influence Diagrams and Decision Trees	67
	3.6. Decision Analytic Network	68
	3.7. Gantt Chart	69
	3.8. Network Diagrams	71
4	Decisions under Certainty and Uncertainty	78
	4.1. Introduction	78
	4.2. Decision-making under Uncertainty	80
	4.3. Info-gap Decision Analysis	83
	4.4. Interval Programming Problem	86
	4.5. Decision-making under Certainty	88
	4.6. Unstructured Decision Problems	90
	4.7. Mathematical Programming	91
5	Decision-making under Risk	94
	5.1. Introduction	94
	5.2. Approaches to Decision-making under Risk	96
	5.3. Stochastic Optimization	97
	5.4. Stochastic Linear Programming	100
	5.5. Probabilistic Dynamic Programming	104
	5.6. Fuzzy Decision-making	105
	5.7. Prospect Theory	108
	5.8. Priority Heuristic	112
	5.9. Decision-making under Evidence Theory	113
6	Decisions under Competition	116
	6.1. Games and Decisions	116
	6.2. Matrix Games	117
	6.3. Solving Matrix Games	120
	6.4. Polymatrix Games	124
	6.5. The Prisoner's Dilemma	126
	6.6. Evolutionary Games	129
	6.7. Analysis of Meta Games	132
	6.8. Co-operative Games	135
	6.9. Stackelberg Games	137
7	Statistical Decision Theory	140
	7.1. Introduction	140
	7.2. Beginning from Classical Statistics	143

	7.3. Statistical Decision Process	144
	7.4. Some Examples	150
	7.5. The Optimality Principle	155
	7.6. Derivation of Minimax and Bayes Estimators	158
	7.7. Admissibility	160
	7.8. Completeness	162
	7.9. The Bayesian Paradigm	163
	7.10. Prolongation of the Bayesian Paradigm	175
	7.11. Multiple Decision Functions	179
	7.12. Sequential Decision Theory	185
	7.13. Design of Clinical Trials	189
	7.14. Robust Decision-making	192
8	Multi-criteria Decision-making	197
	8.1. Introduction	197
	8.2. Classification of MCDM Methods	200
	8.3. Essentials in MCDM	201
	8.4. VIKOR	202
	8.5. Analytic Hierarchy Process (AHP)	204
	8.6. Analytic Network Process (ANP)	207
	8.7. Data Envelopment Analysis	208
	8.8. TOPSIS	212
	8.9. Combinations of DEA, AHP and TOPSIS	214
	8.10. The Combined Compromise Solution (CoCoSo) Model	215
	8.11. OCRA	216
	8.12. PROMETHEE and GAIA	217
	8.13. MACBETH	220
	8.14. Multi-MOORA	223
	8.15. Stochastic Multi-criteria Acceptability Analysis	226
	8.16. Fuzzy MCDM	228
	8.17. Challenges Ahead	230
9	Social Choice Problems	232
	9.1. Introduction	232
	9.2. Distinctive Features of Social Choice	235
	9.3. Preference Aggregation	236
	9.4. Axioms and Arrow's Impossibility Theorem	238
	9.5. Consistency of Social Choice Functions	240
	9.6. Probabilistic Social Choice Functions	241

9.7. Social Choice and Social Network	245
9.8. The Nudge Theory	247
9.9. Computational Social Choice	249
10 Decision-making Models	**251**
10.1. Preliminaries	251
10.2. Approaches in Managerial Decision-making	255
10.3. Qualitative Decision-making Models	258
10.4. Models Using Quantitative Methods	267
10.5. Models for Problem-solving	272
10.6. Paired Comparison Analysis	274
10.7. Theory of Constraints	276
11 Alternatives and Constraints	**284**
11.1. Introduction	284
11.2. Issues in Optimization	286
11.3. Desiderata for Alternatives	288
11.4. Development of Alternatives	289
11.5. Pooling Expert Opinions	291
11.6. Domain Knowledge in Designing Alternatives	294
11.7. Probabilities as Alternatives	296
11.8. Alternatives in Evolutionary Algorithms	297
11.9. Rules or Procedures as Alternatives	301
11.10. Alternatives for Organizational Decisions	303
11.11. Constraints in Real-life Decisions	305
11.12. Using Infeasible Solutions	307
11.13. Figuring out States of Nature	311
11.14. Post-implementation Feasibility Check	312
12 Generation of Criteria	**313**
12.1. Introduction	313
12.2. Criterion versus Objective Function	314
12.3. Alternative-Criterion Interaction	316
12.4. Criterion versus Rule for Choice	317
12.5. Characteristics of a Criterion	318
12.6. Aggregate as a Criterion	320
12.7. Criteria in Group Decision-making	322
12.8. Points to Ponder	325
13 Paired Comparisons, Ranking and Scaling	**327**
13.1. Introduction	327

	13.2. Paired Comparison	329
	13.3. Aggregating Paired Comparison Results	330
	13.4. Ranking of Units	333
	13.5. Aggregation of Ranking Data	334
	13.6. Concordance in Multiple Rankings	335
	13.7. Consensus Ranking	338
	13.8. Scaling of Alternatives	343
	13.9. Rank Reversal	346
14	Role of Information	348
	14.1. Introduction	348
	14.2. Search for Information	350
	14.3. Value of Information	352
	14.4. Decisions in Fuzzy Environments	356
	14.5. Information to Identify Feasible Options	360
	14.6. Information in Social Choice Problems	361
15	A Peep into Gray Areas	364
	15.1. Are There Gray Areas?	364
	15.2. Impact of Uncertainty	365
	15.3. Concern for Computational Complexity	367
	15.4. Information Overload and Option Deluge	368
	15.5. Infirmities in Decision-making	371
	15.6. The Paradox of Choice	373
	15.7. Can We Conclude?	374

References and Suggested Readings   375
About the Author   396
Index   397

List of Abbreviations

AHP	Analytic hierarchy process
ATE	Average treatment effect
BADIR	Business question, analysis plan, data collection, insights, and recommendations
BCC	Banker, Charnes and Cooper
CBDT	Case-based decision theory
CCR	Charnes, Cooper and Rhodes
CI	Consistency index
CPM	Critical path method
DAN	Decision analytic network
DBR	Drum, buffer and rope
DEA	Data envelopment analysis
DMPs	Decision-making processes
DMUs	Decision-making units
D–S	Dempster–Shafer
ELECTRE	Elimination and choice translating reality
ENGS	Expected net gain due to sampling
EVPI	Expected value of perfect information
EVSI	Expected value of sample
FDP	False discovery proportion
FDR	False discovery rate
FWER	Family-wise error rate
GAIA	Geometric analytic interactive aid
GERT	Graphical evaluation and review technique
IvLP	Interval linear programming
LINEX	Linear exponential
LP	Linear programming
LSU	Linear set-up
MADM	Multi-attribute decision-making
MAE	Mean absolute error

MC	Markov chain
MCDM	Multi-criteria decision-making
MODM	Multi-objective decision-making
MOORA	Multi-objective optimization based on a ratio analysis
OCRA	Operational competitiveness rating
OODA	Observe, orient, decide, act
OP	Optimality principle
PCER	Per comparison error rate
PDCA	Plan-do-check-act
PERT	Programme evaluation and review technique
PHT	Poliheuristic theory
PROMETHEE	Preference ranking organization method for enrichment evaluation
PSCF	Probabilistic social choice function
Q-GERT	Queuing graphical evaluation and review technique
RI	Random index
SAW	Simple additive weighting
SD	Stochastic dominance
SELF	Squared error loss function
SMAA	Stochastic multi-criteria acceptability analysis
SMART	Specific, measurable, attainable, relevant and time-bound
SPRT	Sequential probability ratio test
SWOT	Strength, weakness, opportunity and threat
TDODAR	Time, diagnosis, options, decide, assign and review
TFNs	Triangular fuzzy numbers
TOC	Theory of constraints
TOPSIS	Technique for order preference by similarity to ideal solution
TU	Transferable utility
UDEs	Undesirable effects
VIKOR	VIekriterijumsko KOmpromisno Rangiranje
VSI	Value of sample information

Preface

Living beings have been engaged in decision-making for a wide array of objectives and in an amazing diversity of situations over eons of time. Decision-making, as an activity, differs from decision theory as a branch of knowledge. However, developments in decision theory or the theory of choice have admittedly contributed to improved decision-making. Quite in conformity with expectations, we find a plethora of published materials by way of books and articles on decision-making. On one hand, we come across volumes replete with philosophical concepts, mathematical models, statistical methods and computational techniques, and on the other hand, there are volumes that tend to minimize the role of quantification and focus on the roles of intuitions, creative thinking and experience.

The primary aim of this book is to present an integrative and more-or-less updated account of concepts, methods and techniques used in decision-making in a narrative format that avoids lemmas, theorems and corollaries along with their mathematical derivations but does not sacrifice rigour. The wide ambit of decision-making has not been overlooked, and an attempt has been made to present a unified viewpoint of the activity with the common ground covered more comprehensively rather than the distinctive methods and techniques used in different environments and for different purposes. The author would acknowledge, right at the beginning, that the vastness of decision theory and the richness of contributions by mathematicians, statisticians and social scientists, including economists, in particular, coupled with the fact that the author should not and does not claim anything beyond a modest acquaintance with the subject, a big decision-making problem had to be resolved first, namely to come up with a volume now or to continue learning more about the subject. Many considerations, including the anticipated short length of remaining life, eventually led to the first choice and the outcome is the present sheaf of papers on a subject that can easily justify a huge volume.

In no way, should a reader construe this volume as a text or a reference book on decision theory or decision analysis. No doubt, a general framework for decision-making embracing both the problems of choice and general optimization problems has been taken as the broad basis, but the depth of discussion may be found lacking. The idea behind this mode of presentation was its expected readability by a wide audience eager to know how decisions are made as well as how they should be made, not necessarily equipped to grasp mathematical and other intricacies sometimes involved.

Not a text on operations research or management science, this book does not attempt to cover systematic discussions on problems such as resource allocation, transportation and assignment, inventory or stock-building, queueing, replacement and maintenance, networks and the like. Such problems have been mentioned only as situations of decision-making with their respective distinctive features.

This volume is also not meant to be a text on optimization methods and techniques. In fact, issues related to the generation of alternative or candidate solutions to a decision problem, checking the feasibility of an alternative, how to handle an infeasible solution and what could be the appropriate optimality principle to adhere to are the issues which are focused here, rather than methods, tools and software to achieve optimal or near-optimal or even satisfactory solutions.

Statistical decision theory has been included as an important chapter. The content in its entirety takes care of many non-statistical decision problems. In fact, hints have been dropped, wherever felt necessary, to indicate the intricacies of problems which are unstructured or, at best, semi-structured. The material on Bayesian decision analysis may appear—not without any reason—to be just scrappy. The objective is to focus on the basic concepts as well as on the choice of priors and of loss functions but to avoid theorems on invariance or admissibility, which are amply discussed in several well-written texts. Similar is the case with sequential decision analysis, treated in a bit more detailed manner. A concise discussion on the Markov decision process has been added.

Social choice theory has not been left out of the purview. However, given the inadequate knowledge of the author and his intention to cover the wide spectrum of decision theory, the topic has been relegated to the content of a chapter. Important and distinguishing features of choice functions and their uses have been illustrated.

Discussions on topics such as social choice, statistical decision theory, games and decisions, multi-criteria decision-making and sequential decision-making have been far from comprehensive. In fact, comprehending any of these subjects and knowing about their diverse applications calls for the perusal of some well-written texts and reference books. The only justification for what has been attempted modestly in the present volume is to emphasize the common traits and the distinguishing features of these different aspects of decision-making as one of the most important and interesting engagements.

Circumscribed in its scope in the ways mentioned above, the present volume can modestly claim some unique features. Thus, the focus on alternatives, their identification and generation, the use of infeasible solutions in evolutionary algorithms and in ephemeral constraint optimization problems, the brief discussion on the role of information, the delineation of some decision models used to solve organizational decision problems, illustrations scattered throughout the book on non-traditional and emerging applications of decision analysis and lucid treatment of the subjects avoiding mathematical complexities are expected to single out this book from the many other publications which are quite rich in their content and are definitely worth reading.

A major part of the time during which the material for this volume was being firmed up, the world was in the grip of the COVID-19 pandemic, and only a few interactions with concerned members of the academic fraternity could take place, and that too, only on a virtual platform. Remaining indoors most of the time, my wife Reba continued to provide all the support in preparing the background and in firming up certain ideas relating to cognitive and affective aspects of human decision-making. Being not so adept at taking full advantage of digital devices, I had to approach my elder son Chandrajit off and on to help me out of some problem or the other. Indrajit, the younger son, also provided some technical guidance. Debangana (a granddaughter by relation) was a big help in incorporating the diagrams. I cannot but put on record the continuing help and support I received from Sri Rajesh Dey of SAGE Publications and his colleagues.

CHAPTER 1

Introduction

1.1. Prologue

I still remember the day during my second year of study at a college in which the first lecture on prosody was taken up by a widely respected teacher. He quoted verses written by several eminent poets, including some poet laureates, with accents to put stress on some syllables but without mentioning the phrase 'metrical structure'. We all enjoyed his recitations. In the second lecture (possibly the next day), he referred back to some of those verses, told us about the differences between them in terms of sequences of long and short syllables or syllables with stress and those with no stress and mentioned iambic, trochee, dactyl and anapaest as different metres in which verses are composed. Subsequent lectures on details, including some mnemonic verses, interested almost all of us. I had a friend studying at a different college and I gathered from him that their teacher had in the first lecture on prosody stated the different possible metric forms and provided illustrations from verses written by famous authors. These two teachers and a whole host of other teachers must have solved a decision problem—some knowingly, but most of them unconsciously—to choose one of the two alternatives, namely (a) mentioning the metric structures first and then providing illustrations and (b) considering verses written in different structures first and then mentioning the metric forms, referring to those illustrations. Most, if not all, teachers have solved this choice problem without any analysis but based on experience and intuition.

While exposing some topics in science, a decision is, implicitly or unconsciously, taken about whether to state general principles first, followed by examples, or to put forth examples first and to come up with general principles later, starting from the examples. It also remains true that the same teacher or exponent chooses one option on one occasion and the other option on a different occasion, depending on their perception of what would appeal most to the audience on each occasion.

Decisions can be—and they are quite often—situation-specific. Some simple and oft-used measures in statistics, for example, the standard deviation, can be explained as something as radius of gyration to a student with a physics or mathematics background, as the root mean square of current strength in an AC circuit to a student who knows about current electricity or just as the minimum root mean square deviation from some measure of central tendency to a student of statistics. The objective is to make the concept comprehended by the student group as easily as possible, and the exponent chooses one of these alternative ways to achieve this objective. The choice depends on the exponent's assessment of the background of the majority of students. Some political leaders depend more on logical reasoning than on facts and figures to make their points, while others refer to such facts and figures with a penchant for convincing their audiences. There could be others who would use both strategies. And they choose the alternatives (strategies) beforehand. Sometimes, the same leader may choose different strategies to drive their point home to different audience types.

1.2. Decisions and Decision-making

Decisions are made now—either instantaneously, on the basis of experience, intuition or alacrity and not involving any explicit analysis, or at the end of a due process of gathering and analysing pertinent information followed by the application of some logical or empirical principles—but are meant (in terms of implementation) for the future—immediate or near or remote. Exigencies may demand instant decisions, while planning requires well-worked out decisions. There could be a few exceptions where decisions are taken at the end of some implementation exercise to find out whether the objective(s) behind the implementation could be achieved or to what extent they could be achieved. (It may be rightfully argued that such an implementation exercise was preceded by a decision-making process.) Post-implementation decisions may also lead to identification of more effective and more efficient ways of implementation or even to scaling up or down the original objective(s). Such decisions are necessarily the outputs of due decision-making processes (DMPs), backed up by quantitative analysis and qualitative comprehension and support.

In some senses, decisions (preceding implementation) are like 'designs' for products or services. (One point of distinction may be borne in mind at this stage. Usually, many product/service units come out of the same design. However, even for repetitive actions of the same kind, decisions preceding these actions may change.) Just as 'quality of design', 'quality of conformance to design requirements' and 'quality of performance' are well-recognized facets of the quality of a product or a service, we can think of the 'effectiveness of a decision', 'effectiveness of implementing the decision' and 'effectiveness of a decision on implementation in meeting the original objective(s)' as three distinguishable entities. In fact, as in the case of a manufactured product or a service, we recognize the effectiveness of a decision to meet the original objective(s) only in terms of implementation being able to meet the objective(s). And in either case, we assume that during implementation there is no deviation from the 'design' or the 'decision'. It is possible to accommodate a question regarding any such deviation during the post-implementation decision-making process.

Decision analysis, theory of social choice, operations research, management science and related subjects are expected to deal with formulation, analysis and solution of decision problems faced by individuals, groups, organizations, states and even international bodies. However, looking at the content of many other disciplines, we come across many decision problems—not possibly mentioned and treated as such—which have become integral components of discourses in those disciplines. A close look at the following sample of decision problems will be convincing to some extent. These problems may all appear to be statistical in nature and may be discussed incidentally or in the usual course in standard texts and reference books on statistics. However, they cover various concerns faced by academics and professionals. Each one of them deserves to be comprehended fully as a decision-making problem with all its implications.

Decisions usually precede actions; decisions can also follow actions and their outcomes. The first type of decision is more important with outcomes associated with the available alternatives or options (features or attributes appearing in criteria for assessment/selection of alternatives) either known with certainty or known in terms of a probability distribution or to be observed after some simulation experiments or (small-scale) trial runs of actual experiments. These features may be observable/measurable right now (at the time of decision-making) or in the future over a certain fixed or random period. In some real-life situations, decisions precede actions, which are followed by decisions, which again are followed by decisions and so on, till a stopping rule— as a part of the decision-making process—enjoins a final decision.

Decision-making constitutes the core of management. It is a critical component of strategic management where we engage ourselves in fixing goals and priorities, working out a roadmap to achieve the goals and allocate resources for the different tasks to be taken up. Decision-making involves a blend of logic and intuition. This can definitely borrow strength from decision theory, and this theory has been being enriched by recent developments in data science.

Decision-making has been an area of interest for philosophers and scientists, economists and sociologists, executives and managers and a whole host of other not-so-explicitly-mentioned individuals and groups. Decision theory (as distinct from decision-making as an exercise that does not necessarily follow as a logical corollary of decision theory) that is more or less context-free as well as subject-free is comprehended in terms of decision rules to be followed to arrive at a 'good' decision, the interpretation of the word 'good' being left for further elaboration and confirmation. What has become far more important, especially to executives and managers, is decision-making in practice by individuals and groups in specific situations, combining in intricate fashions, subjective intuitions and instincts, domain knowledge and experience with objective rules applied to relevant information that is available. It is worthwhile to mention that operations research, which has been the primary motive behind the development of many models, methods and techniques as well as algorithms and software used in making and implementing as well as evaluating decisions in complex man-machine-material-environment systems, was defined by Miller and Starr (1973) as 'applied decision-making'.

It should be borne in mind that decision-making is not a monopoly of managers and executives (in the usual sense) only. Every one of us takes decisions all the time in our lives—to decide the course of studies to follow, to choose the profession or occupation to practise, to select the person to marry or remain single in life, to choose the place to live in, to visit the market every day or twice a week, to buy or rent a house or a car and so on. On some occasions, we take instant decisions, and on other occasions, we go on delaying a decision. In some cases, we collate all the relevant information before we reach a decision, while in some other situations, we simply use our ready wit to arrive at a decision. Of course, we calculate costs and benefits when we decide to invest in some properties or in some shares or stocks. Sometimes, we take decisions all by ourselves, and at other times, we consult somebody whom we trust as more knowledgeable or better informed to help us reach a good decision. Situations do exist when we find that decisions taken earlier have paid us well. At the same time, we also face situations when we regret such decisions.

1.3. Ubiquity of Decisions

A very common decision taken by medical professionals in countries where the healthcare delivery system is not adequate, particularly to meet exigencies thrown up by endemic or epidemic diseases, is to choose between some relatively cheap, less time-consuming and less sophisticated diagnostic tests to start treatment in the case of a 'positive' indication or to wait till the result of a more time-consuming, costly and confirmatory test is available. Consequences depend on the available relative frequencies of false-negative and false-positive cases reported for the two tests and the response to delayed treatment of a truly 'positive' case. It may be difficult to make general statements about these. Similarly, the healthcare administration or the state government itself may face a crucial choice problem between expenses to upgrade quite urgently facilities and manpower to meet any adverse eventuality at a high cost and spending less on this account to enable release of funds to help the marginalized sections of the people to augment public health measures, including sanitation and personal hygiene.

In a study of customer satisfaction with the existing brand of a certain product, it is important to gather information from customers about their levels of satisfaction/dissatisfaction and the reasons thereof. A direct question like 'are you satisfied with this product' may not beget a truthful response. Using a randomized response technique is an unjustified overdose of theory, and one may try to extract some information from answers to questions like 'how many friends and acquaintances do you have or do you recommend this brand for purchase?' or 'how many times have you purchased this brand in preference to others?' or similar questions. Which strategy is likely to provide us with reliable information about a subjective realization like customer satisfaction is a hard nut to crack.

In a chemical or pharmaceutical experiment to process several basic chemicals mixed in certain proportions for a certain time under a certain temperature using a catalyst (to be determined/chosen) to produce a certain compound with some desirable properties, the problem in designing and analysing the concerned response surface experiment is how to treat more than one response (properties of the output), say, yield and concentration. Do we consider those as equally important and set targets for each or prioritize those and optimize the more important or primary response subject to some lower/upper limits for the remaining response variables?

In designing a sample survey with a pre-determined sample size, say n from a population of size N, how do we allocate the total sample across say k strata with sizes $N_1, N_2, ..., N_k$ so that sub-sample sizes from the strata satisfy the conditions that these are all integral? $N_h > n_h > 0$, $\Sigma n_h = n$ and that the variance of the estimate of, say, the population mean is as small as possible.

For estimating an unknown population parameter, two estimators with some desirable properties already exist, and the need is to combine them to get a better estimate. Many options may exist, and the question is: How do we make a choice? Just to illustrate, we have the sample mean and the sample variance (with degrees of freedom as the divisor) as estimates of the Poisson parameter. How about a convex linear combination of the two or a suitably penalized sample mean as a better estimate? And how to find the penalty factor?

A manufacturer of some electronic devices has to demonstrate a specified reliability or probability that the device will continue to function satisfactorily for a stipulated period of time (reasonably large) and has to decide between two alternative test plans. They can put a random sample of units on test and find out how many survive till the stipulated time and, based on that number, estimate the reliability of the device. Alternatively, they can put a sample of units on test, record the time of failure for each item till a pre-specified test time and note the number of units surviving till the test time. Obviously, the test time is smaller than the specified life time. The first plan based on the number of failures (by a test time or by the mission-specified life time) will have cost consequences different from those involved in the second plan based on times to failure. Costs are in terms of the number of items completely used up, the number of items partly used up and still available for use, providing energy during the test to the units put on test, test time and computation of estimated reliability. A non-cost consequence of importance is the precision of the estimated reliability. The decision problem here is not just a binary choice between two test plans. Any test plan involves several decisions relating to sample size, test time and the like. Plans using censoring of different types call for more decisions.

In the context of poverty estimation, the national statistical system has to decide on a suitable measure or index of poverty, from among indicators such as the head count ratio, income gap ratio, Watt's index, Sen's index and several others. We should note that the decision should be related to the purpose or objective of using the measure to be finally chosen. And the purpose could be to estimate the total number of persons who should be provided with some resources or relief, irrespective of how poor they are. A different purpose could be to estimate the total amount of money required to lift the entire population below the poverty line to the non-poor level. A third objective could be to reduce inequality in the incomes of the poor and to ensure that none remain too poor. It is worthwhile to note that a related decision at a preceding stage is: How to determine the poverty line? Should it be based on disposable income or wealth in possession or productive assets in possession or consumption of necessities such as food, clothing, health and shelter? Should it take into account the distribution of income in the entire population?

There are several decision problems in the context of quality management which take recourse to general optimization methods and techniques, occasionally involving complicated objective functions and constraints, which are not directly considered as a distinct part of operations research or even of production management. Thus, the problems of designing a process control plan based on a Shewhart control chart or a cumulative sum control chart in terms of control limit factors or V-mask parameters, sample size and sampling frequency for various process parameters have been studied by quite a few investigators but are not recognized as contributors to decision analysis. Similar is the case with optimal design of a continuous sampling inspection plan characterized by the sampling interval and the length of a run of non-defective items. Even a binary decision to go for a control chart or a sampling inspection plan versus a scheme of complete inspection followed by necessary corrections may be of interest in short production runs as well as in slow production processes turning out critical units.

One decision problem faced by environmental management in state administration is, given an existing ecosystem like a large tract of marshy land not under cultivation or a large water body currently not in good shape or a patch of grassland adjoining a forest, which of the following decisions should be taken for implementation:

(a) conserving the ecosystem as it is, implying indirectly a gradual deterioration in its visibility and appeal, (b) intervening in the ecosystem to conserve it in a better form, adding at the same time to its commercial value by way of enhanced attractiveness to tourists and nature lovers; such an intervention will usually take care of any adverse impact of the existing state of affairs and of intervention activities on the wider environment and (c) converting the ecosystem into a new entity for commercial purposes or for meeting the needs of infrastructure development or to augment recreation facilities. The latter two alternatives will involve costs to be incurred now that can be more or less directly estimated. But the benefits are only to accrue in the future and, hence, are uncertain in nature and magnitude. It is only imperative to treat expenses to be incurred now and benefits to arise in the future as two sets of criteria. For a decision to be made now, benefits have to be duly discounted to yield the expected present net value. Coming to the 'cost' aspect, there have been suggestions to realize a part of the amount to be spent on conservation or enhancement (of the beauty and utility) of an ecosystem by the beneficiary 'public'. And we confront a social choice problem where members of society with diverse attitudes and perceptions about the underlying issues will have to decide on amounts 'willing to pay'. A similar decision to be made by members of society, in case an existing ecosystem has to be changed for the sake of some infrastructure development, concerns the amount 'willing to accept' as compensation. The latter may be sidelined in several situations. In fact, environmental management with too many players or stakeholders with diverse interests involved has been a hot topic for multi-criteria decision-making (MCDM) in modern decision analysis.

1.4. Rationality and Bounded Rationality

Decisions are taken, as they have to be taken, by all human beings, irrespective of their levels of knowledge and skill, their mental make-ups and interests. However, in the context of decision-making, it is generally assumed that every decision-maker is 'rational' and can make a sensible choice to satisfy their interests, and such a choice presumes quite a few attributes of the decision-maker.

Rationality assumption has been a matter of philosophical discussions and debates for a long time. As mentioned in the *Stanford Encyclopedia of Philosophy*, Aristotle attributed rationality to human beings, though Bertrand Russell admitted to having failed to find any evidence to support Aristotle.

The assumption of rationality that seeks a cause behind every action and stresses decisions based on logic may, in some extreme situations, lead to inaction in the absence of any rational decision, and such inaction may invite unfortunate consequences. This has been illustrated by Buridan in a somewhat veiled attack on Laplace's principle of equal ignorance (about the states of nature and thus about the outcomes) to justify equal probability. Buridan constructs a piquant situation in which a donkey stands exactly mid-way between two buckets of water, each full to the brim. The donkey is extremely thirsty but cannot decide which bucket to reach, since, speaking logically, it has no basis for preferring one bucket to the other. Indecision and inaction meant that the donkey died from dehydration. The lesson to be derived from this contrived example of Buridan's ass is that even in such situations where seeking more information to build up a preference relation is ruled out, people make decisions based on intuition and emotion. In fact, such decisions have been dubbed as context-specific and cognitively biased by some economists and psychologists, though they have been supported as quite valid by others.

The concept of rationality in the context of human behaviour, as is reflected in decision-making by economic agents, was modified to that of 'bounded rationality' by Simon (1957), taking due account of limitations on the part of decision-makers in accessing relevant and useful information, possessing adequate analytical capability and accessing requisite computational resources. Such decision-makers or economic agents who may not be found to act in a manner in which the expected utility is a maximum are sometimes characterized as 'cognitively limited' agents. Without complete knowledge of all possible options and accurate ideas about their outcomes under each likely state of nature, most decision-makers are cognitively limited. Intricate environments within which decision-makers have to operate may also pose limitations.

Bounded rationality—as distinct from classical 'rationality' assumed by economists earlier—offers an explanation for observed deviations in human behaviour from 'perfect rationality' or 'global rationality'. Thus, whenever a decision-maker placed in a competitive situation does not necessarily choose an option that just maximizes their expected utility or gain, even at the cost of huge losses to the competitors, and not acting in a completely selfish manner, at the same time not ignoring their own gain, we may notice a departure from classical rationality. 'Bounded rationality' does accommodate such behaviour.

Satisficing as an alternative to optimizing is a strategy adopted by a decision-maker who aspires to achieve a given level of performance for the option chosen (in terms of its outcome or impact). This may be the minimally acceptable option, preferred especially in situations where a search for the globally optimal solution may be quite demanding on mathematical knowledge and computing resources in identifying all possible alternatives, examining their feasibility otherwise, assessing the outcome of each alternative considered and locating the globally optimal alternative(s). A threshold level for the objective function is initially decided, and once we arrive at an option for which the objective function reaches or exceeds this threshold, we are satisfied, and we choose this option to form our decision. The principle of satisficing has often been advocated in dealing with multiple criteria. Thus, for just two criteria in respect of which each option considered should be evaluated, we may first decide on which criterion is more important and fix a threshold level for performance in respect of the other criterion. Here, we can search for an optimal solution in respect of the first criterion, subject to satisficing in respect of the second criterion. The search can start with the first criterion only, and once we arrive at the optimal solution, we can check if it satisfies the threshold level for the other criterion.

Satisficing has been criticized because of its possibility of missing the true or global optimum. Given a specification of what will count as a good-enough outcome, satisficing replaces the optimization objective from the expected utility theory of selecting an undominated outcome with the objective of picking an option that meets your aspirations. Ignoring the procedural aspects of Simon's original formulation of satisficing, if one has a fixed aspirational level for a given decision problem, then admissible choices from satisficing can be captured by the so-called ϵ-efficiency methods (Loridan, 1984; White, 1986).

1.5. Hierarchy of Decisions

Levels and types of decision-making depend on many factors, which are as follows:

- Status of the decision-maker—an individual or a collective body, responsibility held and authority enjoyed in relation to decision-based actions. The decision-maker is bound in some cases to consider just the given options, and in some others, they can generate or develop other alternatives.
- The entity about which the decision is being made—a system, an operation, a method, an experiment, a survey, a finding from a study and so on. Some are concrete; others are abstract, and abstract entities are used to model concrete ones.
- The environment in which the decision-maker is placed includes their access to pertinent resources, namely information bearing on the decision problem and required to solve it, as well as knowledge, experience and skills to process the information.
- Nature (representing externalities that influence the consequences of any decision alternative) and the measure of the outcome(s) of the decision and the impact(s) thereof on the system under consideration as well as on related systems or entities. Outcomes could be immediate in some cases and remote in others, related to a point in time in some cases and spread over a period of time in others, exactly or approximately determinable in some cases and only predictable with uncertainty in others.

Decisions can be categorized as strategic, operational and tactical depending on the status and constitution of the decision-maker, the length of the planning horizon to be kept in mind, the type of activities and their outcomes to be influenced and the impact(s) of the decision—when implemented—on the system within which the decision has been taken. From this point of view, a strategic decision usually relates to a long planning horizon of several years, sets out long-term goals and plans, is taken by people enjoying adequate authority and tasked with heavy responsibility, involves a lot of risk and uncertainty and needs thorough scanning and analysis of the external environment to collect and process pertinent information. Strategic decision-making lays down goals and objectives for tactical and operational decision-making. These decisions relate to problems like diversifying revenue streams or acquiring new businesses and their vertical integration with existing business verticals for a business organization. That way, strategic decisions influence many interest groups, and their outcomes have far-reaching consequences—beneficial or adverse—on the entire system and/or the environment within which it operates, even with international ramifications. A decision to link internal rivers flowing through a region or a country to derive full benefit from the total volume of water in these rivers during different seasons is a strategic decision that will have a continuing impact on the lives of people in the region in many ways. A decision that will entail a lot of expenditure and will occupy a considerable time period to be implemented is no doubt a strategic decision to be taken by the top functionaries in public life after a substantial amount of deliberations, consultations and computations. For an autonomous academic or a research organization, a decision, to open its programmes to international collaboration and funding or even hiring international faculty with an offer of attractive salaries and perks or introducing completely new areas of research or new courses for which resources, including manpower and laboratories, have to be substantially augmented, illustrates strategic decisions.

Tactical decisions are meant to translate strategic decisions into action plans in terms of decisions regarding acquisition/augmentation of technology, capacity, facilities and so on and their deployment. Senior and middle-level executives in business houses and bureaucrats in charge of implementation of national or state-level policies and projects are usually involved in developing tactical decisions for a medium-term horizon. The allocation of some national or state resources among several competing entrepreneurs interested in enriching the resource or, at a slightly lower level, the choice among alternative technologies by an entrepreneur for value addition to some such resource illustrates tactical decisions.

Operational decisions are usually taken by frontline decision-makers who are required to implement various tactical decisions into practice. These are short-term decisions regarding actual deployment and management of resources for carrying out different operations. It may be pointed out that most operational decisions—decisions preceding and succeeding operations—relating to production planning, job scheduling, machine sequencing, inventorying, replacing equipment, transporting finished goods from plant to stores or dealers, fixing the number of service counters and a host of similar other decisions constitute the bulk of discussions in a text on operations research. Preparation of class routines, conduct of tests, organizing placement services, holding special lectures, seminars and similar programmes and so on are examples of operational decisions within an academic institution.

A decision relating to recruitment and deployment of workers to meet the needs of the technology adopted and other interests and obligations of the entrepreneur can be treated as a tactical decision or as an operational decision, depending on the scale of operations.

It is sometimes argued that the hierarchy mentioned above is not that important. The categorization is somewhat context-specific and arbitrary. A decision dubbed as tactical may well be regarded as an operational decision, and an operational decision, in some cases, may well qualify to be considered as a strategic decision. For a given manufacturing or service organization, strategic decisions regarding different business processes—core and support—can be definitely distinguished from operational and tactical decisions taken by its management. This is why decisions are sometimes classified as meta-level, macro-level and micro-level. And meta-level decisions even within an organization may be called strategic. However, national-level public decisions are undoubtedly strategic in nature.

Meta-level decision-making affecting the social, economic and political systems, and their processes in a country has become more important than ever before. This has national and even international implications. During the 100th anniversary of the small city of Flint in Michigan, USA (2014), an international conference addressed the vexing decision problem for economic planners: 'Richer and more unequal or poorer and more equal—which is the better alternative?' The controversy around carbon emissions to reduce energy consumption or to augment the existing supply of energy continues unabated. Meta-level decision problems are difficult to formulate, not to mention the evasive nature of the solution. In the first example, the two alternatives have to be comprehended and concretised in terms of several actions/operations as well as in terms of the consequences that will follow in the socio-economic arena, since they are both alternative objectives as well as alternative courses of action. Actual application requires many actions to be taken at different levels to be planned optimally, taking care to avoid risks of sub-optimization.

1.6. Group Decisions

Groups of people, with varying intuitions and emotions, experiences and capabilities, preferences and indifferences, working in a group, a society or a business organization, have to take decisions on important issues. And within such a group, there could be some leaders and some expert advisors besides ordinary members. In such cases, several levels of decisions or decision-making situations have been pointed out by management scientists. These are as follows:

1. The leader alone decides—a single decision-maker who might have been interacting with others over time but not seeking or using any input from any others for making the decision in the present context.
2. The leader decides with inputs from key stakeholders, who may represent a mix of external interests as well as people within the group. The processing and eventual use of such inputs is left to the single leader.
3. The leader builds a consensus with input from a subgroup, retaining the final say in the matter. The choice of the subgroup is also left to the leader.
4. The whole group votes on a decision (which may be suggested by any of the above mechanisms) before its acceptance or the decision is delegated to someone else for a final say.

5. True consensus is built through discussions, consultations and compromises (whenever needed). This decision is the easiest to implement through wilful acceptance by all concerned.

While such steps can be visualized within a well-knit organization with defined roles and responsibilities of members, they may be difficult to realize within a loosely knit organization or in a society.

1.7. Social Choice Decisions

Important decisions are sometimes taken by groups or communities or societies, by noting and aggregating suitably preferences of individual members for different feasible (implementable) options or strategies, as well as their indifferences between some alternatives. The group could comprise just the husband and his wife willing to take a joint call on a particular issue at hand or the community of medical professionals interested in reaching a collective decision about the treatment protocol for a newly surfacing disease or residents of a city wanting to decide collectively on the best location for a recreation facility or a religious institution. Individual preferences and indifferences are not always explicit; alternatives may not be given or known in advance and may emerge during deliberations; members may not agree on the feasibility or otherwise of any alternative, and we may not have the advantage of applying some attractive optimization principles to arrive at a decision.

In a practical choice situation with a given set of alternatives S (based on a partial order among the alternatives), a decision-maker makes a personal assessment of what constitutes the best alternative when choosing one. Different decision-makers in the same situation and with the same set of alternatives may have different assessments of what constitutes the best alternative, and hence, their choices may differ. Each of them, however, may be able to justify the choice that was made. Even if the same choice was made by different decision-makers, their justifications could differ. Consider a subset X of the set of alternatives and let $C(X)$ be the set of alternatives chosen from this subset. If we examine the subsets of alternatives chosen by the same decision-maker based on different subsets of *X*, *we can develop some ideas about* what may be called a choice function used by an individual decision-maker. It is quite interesting to note that the number of possible choice functions for a set of alternatives with N elements is as large as $2^{2N(N-1)}$. With just three alternatives available to a decision-maker, the number of choice functions possible in theory is 4,096.

There have been several lines of development in social choice theory, the classical economists' social choice, behavioural social choice and computational social choice. From axioms and game theory to ranking and ordering and incorporation of empirical evidence, a variety of tools have been used to offer an engaging literature on the subject that has grown since the days of Arrow, in both depth and diversity. In fact, Arrow's impossibility theorem and subsequent attempts to overcome the impossibility can be regarded as the cornerstone of social choice theory in relation to decision theory.

1.8. Decision-making and Problem-solving

Decisions have to be taken to solve a problem encountered right now, like those involved in fighting a fire that has erupted on the upper floors of a high-rise residential or commercial building. The goal is to minimize casualties or serious injuries to human lives or severe and irreparable damage to documents, records and material goods. Constraints could arise in terms of the absence of a ladder to reach the floor engulfed by fire or/and inadequacy of water pressure in the water storage nearby or/and non-availability of foam to be sprayed and so on. States of nature could be no one living in the building or the floor, people living in the building and the like. The options available to the fire-fighting team include dousing the flames coming out of the affected floor first, evacuating any humans likely to be trapped inside first, entering the building and switching off all electrical devices first and the like. The team has some experience of fighting such a fire several times in the past.

Decisions have to be taken, with due analysis and care, to solve problems likely to be faced in the future or continuing to plague the concerned people. Thus, planners have to decide on measures to reduce levels of poverty in the country through possible economic measures. Social and political considerations may appear as constraints on implementing measures likely to affect some interest groups, like corporate houses. Possible measures (decisions) could include the imposition of higher rates of direct taxes payable by the affluent sections of the people, putting curbs or higher entry taxes on luxury goods, improving the collection of indirect taxes from retail outlets, enhancing spending on corporate social responsibility, improving the productive efficiency of manufacturing and service enterprises, emphasis on labour-intensive but efficient service enterprises and the like. The goal is to achieve a visible decline in the head count ratio of poverty.

Decisions may not be necessarily linked up with problem-solving in the sense illustrated above but to help those in pursuit of knowledge in different disciplines become more effective and efficient in their efforts. Thus, good decisions are required to design an experiment, which is rather costly, to cut down on time and cost as well as on likely failures. We have to choose factors for inclusion as well as their levels, along with all experimental conditions, to come up with an expected response(s) with minimum cost and the shortest time. The same is the need for decisions at every stage of any investigation into a new phenomenon or a new aspect of an existing phenomenon.

1.9. Descriptive and Normative Decision Theory

It may not be irrelevant to appreciate the difference between decision-making and decision theory—the latter providing or, better, meant to provide support to the former. Again, decision-making is focused on actions based on decisions and decision theory—as the very name implies—is concerned with concepts, methods and techniques that can be and are being used by decision-makers to arrive at effective decisions targeted at achieving some underlying goals and objectives.

Similarly, it is important to distinguish descriptive decision theory from normative decision theory. The former deals with discernible generalities behind how decisions are actually made by individuals and institutions, while the latter is concerned with principles and procedures which should be followed by decision-makers in reaching decisions, the way they should choose criteria to evaluate the outcomes of possible choices and the extent and nature of information they should seek for this purpose, as well as the type of analysis that should be carried out to decide on a choice and even to find out a means to assess the performance of a decision after its implementation. Descriptive decision theory is not just a dossier of decisions made purely subjectively, based on decision-makers' emotions and intuitions. Revealed preferences among alternatives in respect of their outcomes, previous experience in dealing with decision situations or problems bearing some similarity to previous situations and corresponding decisions, any consultations or deliberations held, any logical argument spelt out, possible explanations of the way a final choice was made from the standpoint of behavioural sciences, explanations that can beget some support from economic theory and other features are codified to build up what may be justifiably called a theory. Also, the 'theoretical' content of normative decision theory hardly needs any elaboration at this stage. Suffice it to say that the present volume is primarily devoted to several chosen aspects of normative decision theory.

The Poliheuristic theory (PHT) of decision-making was developed in the early 1990s to bring together the cognitive and rationalist traditions in analysis of foreign policy decisions to take due cognizance of both the process (the how) and the outcome (the why) in foreign policy decision-making. PHT looks upon the cognitive and rationalist approaches to foreign policy analysis as complementary rather than competitive perspectives on how leaders make foreign policy decisions, integrating them into a unified framework and drawing strength from both. On the one hand, the advantages of the cognitive approach in providing more descriptively realistic accounts of how foreign policy decisions are made by leaders are enjoyed, and on the other, the ability of the rationalist models to provide deductive explanations of foreign policy choices is fully incorporated.

In fact, PHT models foreign policy as a two-stage process that combines a heuristics-based and an expected-utility-maximizing stage of decision-making. In the first stage, actors use a range of cognitive shortcuts that may run counter to rational choice assumptions and serve to simplify the decision problem by quickly eliminating unacceptable alternatives from the choice set. Decision-makers reject alternatives outright that score below a cut-off value on what they have identified as the most important dimensions of the decision, instead of establishing trade-offs among different dimensions or attributes of the available options. To illustrate, in foreign policymaking, domestic political loss associated with any alternative is accorded a high priority, and an alternative that is unacceptable on this crucial dimension is discarded. In the second stage, a more demanding and thorough screening of the remaining alternatives is undertaken to identify the alternative(s) that maximizes expected utility. While PHT can be applied outside the regime of foreign policy analysis, it has not found wide acceptance.

Growing attention is being paid by executives and professionals to 'behavioural decision theory', which should not be taken as synonymous with a theory concerned only with intuitive or cognitive decisions. In fact, exponents of this emerging theory accord due role to the decision-maker and to both cognitive and affective aspects of the process. Some even talk of rule-based as well as role-based decision-making as distinct processes, recognizing the fact that people engaged in certain professions, like doctors, do and should decide their actions in a given situation on the basis of instincts or intuition or experience without waiting for what may be appropriately called 'rational'. Some authors on behavioural decision theory go to the extent of claiming descriptive, normative and prescriptive decision theory as three distinct constituents of behavioural decision theory, stretching it to include case-based decision theory (CBDT). There are others, of course, who do not subscribe to this all-pervasive exposition of the subject.

1.10. Case-based Decision Theory

Gilboa and Schmeidler (1995) put forth a whole theory of reasoning or making choices or decision-making that departs from the classical set-up dominated by expected utility. It is well-known that the classical theory is primarily based on deductive logic and probabilistic inference, without an explicit recognition of inductive logic. Gilboa and

Schmeidler argued that human decision-making takes into account behavioural data in terms of decisions or actions taken in similar decision problems recalled to the extent possible. This makes it possible to extend the scope of logical decision-making to situations where the classical framework in terms of states of nature, their probabilities of occurrence and utilities associated with possible alternative decisions (actions) cannot be used to comprehend and structure a decision problem. In fact, there exist problems where the states of nature are not given initially, nor can they be conveniently identified. Hence, all possible pay-offs for each alternative may not be known, and even in a state of nature initially incorporated, the pay-off may not be certainly known. However, such a decision problem might have been faced earlier by some decision-makers. The extent of similarity with those problems (that can be recalled by the present decision-maker) in terms of causes involved may be assessed by the present decision-maker, may be subjectively. The actions taken in those problems and the outcomes realized are better known. The concept of 'expected utility' may not be relevant. The set of problems with some similarity to the current problem, the set of actions taken to resolve those and the corresponding set of outcomes realized together constitute a 'case' in the language of Gilboa and Schmeidler, and with some axiomatization necessary to develop a theory, they have come up with what is known as CBDT, which has found interesting and useful applications in managerial decision-making.

CBDT cannot be regarded as a self-complete decision theory embracing general optimization problems besides choice problems. It was developed as an alternative to the Bayesian paradigm, which requires a prior probability measure over a large space containing states of nature, which are truth functions defined on all possible observations (and thus also on all possible observation-based rules). It avoids induction and does not suffer from any logical inconsistencies, since cases cannot be contradicted though rules can be.

As indicated above, a case here means a triplet of (problem, act result). Gilboa and Schmeidler refer to Hume (1748/1999) to justify the use of previously observed or narrated cases via analogies. Hume maintains that,

> All arguments from experience are founded on the similarity which we discover among natural objects, and by which we are induced to expect effects similar to those which we have found to follow from such objects. From causes which appear similar, we expect similar effects. This is the sum of all our experimental conclusions.

On this logic, we can solve decision problems by choosing acts which were successful in similar decision problems. It is clear that the focus in CBDT is on acts, rather than on decisions leading to these acts, and that acts chosen should be satisficing rather than 'optimal'. It is also true that the subtle distinction between decisions and acts (to implement decisions) is not that important unless we accommodate some likely deviation during implementation. And we are facing decision problems where an objective function cannot be conceptualized conveniently for the purpose of optimization.

The two key concepts in CBDT are those of *similarity* between decision problems and the *desirability* of an outcome/result. Similarity could be understood in terms of the 'nearest neighbour' technique, by possibly identifying key features of a decision problem. However, the most similar case which can be recalled by the decision-maker might have resulted in a major catastrophe or a very adverse result. Otherwise, besides the most similar case yielding a satisfactory result, some other acts in potentially similar cases might also have fared successfully and should be taken into account. Utility could be taken as the desirability measure for any result/outcome. We, of course, need to aggregate this utility over many cases to obtain an overall ranking of an alternative act.

In a formal statement of CBDT, we take the following as the given primitives:

P: A set of decision problems p
A: A set of available acts a
R: A set of possible results or outcomes r
M: A subset of P which can be recalled by the decision-maker, called memory

CBDT postulates the desirability of a result as its utility $u(r)$.

A decision-maker is characterized by a utility function that assigns real numbers to values of outcomes and a similarity function that assigns real numbers $s(p, q)$ to pairs (p, q) of problems. Faced with a new problem p, the decision-maker chooses the act a that maximizes the overall utility defined as: $U(a) = \Sigma s(p, q) u(r)$ summed overall $(q, a, r) \in M$.

According to CBDT, choose the act that maximizes U.

The memory has been defined in such a manner that (a) no problem is encountered more than once (apparently dissimilar problems may be really similar to the decision-maker) and (b) memory is a set. The order in which cases appear in a memory is immaterial. If the description of a problem includes a time parameter, the memory set is as informative as a sequence of information.

Gilboa and Schmeidler suggested the following variants of the above procedure.

- **Averaged similarity:** Where for each act, the similarity coefficients are normalized to sum up to unity.
- **Act similarity:** In which the result of an act is considered along with the results of similar acts in the past. Similarity judgements of acts and of problems may depend on each other. Thus, the similarity function is defined in the space of problem–act pairs, and an act is evaluated by the sum of products of similarity of product pairs and the result of each act, taking into account the results of similar acts.
- **Memory-dependent similarity:** It allows the decision-maker to learn that some features of problems are more or less similar or that some attributes of a problem are more or less important, based on past experience. In such a case, the similarity function is likely to evolve with memory or the subset of cases recalled, an entity that may change over time.

Usually, CBDT avoids rules. However, if the decision-maker takes into account all past cases, and these warrant the induction of a rule, the decision-maker would also act in accordance with this rule.

In expected utility theory, as also in CBDT, acts are ranked by weighted sums of utilities. Of course, in the expected utility theory, outcomes and corresponding utilities against different states of nature for any act or option are, at least in some situations, 'anticipated'. These are 'actual' outcomes and corresponding utilities achieved in the case of CBDT. However, several differences come up. In CBDT, each act is evaluated over a different set of cases. If acts a and b are such that $a < b$, then the set of elements in M summed over to get $U(a)$ is disjoint from the set used in $U(b)$. In fact, the first set may even be empty for some acts. On the other hand, every act in the expected utility theory is evaluated at each stage.

CBDT results in conservative or uncertainty-averse behaviour. If each act a, $\in A$ ever results in an outcome r_0, the decision-maker will only try new acts until they find one that yields $u(r_0) > 0$. Thereafter, they will try this act over and over again. They will be 'satisfied' with the reasonable act a and will not act to maximize their utility function. In some senses, this implies that the null point on the utility scale corresponds to their aspiration level. CBDT does not differentiate between 'certain' acts which lead to the same outcomes with certainty and 'uncertain' acts whose outcomes are not certainly known.

For operational purposes, CBDT requires a case library to be built up as a repository of cases along with the acts chosen to resolve the problems and the outcomes realized. The tasks involved in CBDT are (a) retrieval of the case that matches the current problem in terms of features or attributes to the best extent, (b) reuse of the previous case, namely the act, repaired if the proposed act does not solve the problem satisfactorily, (c) revise the act or solution evaluated for its appropriateness by comparing it with the confirmed target class and (d) retain the act finally chosen and the outcome realized in the library.

In its initial formulation, the generation of acts or possible solutions to the current problem was not a part of the case-based decision process; the authors themselves noted the importance of this activity and encouraged its adoption to enrich the case library.

1.11. Decision Theory and Decision-making

Decision theory is a composite body of knowledge derived from various disciplines, including philosophy, economics, mathematics, statistics and psychology, that has pushed the frontiers of research in political science and international relations, sociology, computer science and even cybernetics and cryptology. It integrates normative, descriptive and prescriptive aspects of how human decisions are made as well as how they should be made. Going by epistemological principles, decision theory embodies concepts, methods and techniques as well as tools like software to apply them in practice. The theory is growing fast and so are its applications in real life.

Decision-making is a task or an activity, not carried out aimlessly and without reference to a context. Decision-makers—called agents by some authors—are placed in some environments and are charged with the responsibility of achieving some goals or objectives, sometimes categorically and clearly spelt out and only vaguely or broadly indicated in some others, by making (or should we say, taking) decisions which are meant to be acted upon or implemented in the manner decided. If a decision-maker is needed to make a 'good' decision—as should be a natural requirement—a concomitant question awaiting an answer will be, 'what do we mean by "good"?' If 'good' is to imply a 'good' outcome, we have to wait for implementation or realization of the decision to find out if it was 'good' or not. If the implication is 'rational', the definition of rationality will dodge us. One may indirectly take it as 'consistent' and that again cannot be judged as a stand-alone decision. Should a cognitive or an 'affective' or a 'calculating' or an 'intuitive 'decision be considered as 'good'? One may get back to the issue of a 'good' outcome. Also, to be noted is the fact that cognitive and affective needs are often in conflict. Of course, decision-making by way of solving general optimization problems will mostly steer clear of such issues, since the alternatives and their outcomes are linked in terms of functional relations and outcomes can be directly observed or computed, exactly or approximately, without a wait for implementation. However, there could be complex optimization problems where assessment of the outcome of any alternative may involve simulation of the underlying system or running an experiment, and that may take some time.

Implementation may or may not be a responsibility of those who decide. However, those who decide have to be aware of the needs of implementation and—in many situations—be involved in assessing the extent to which the goals and objectives can be achieved eventually. Implementation is a generic term and may imply simulation, computation, comparison and integration.

The decision–action pair is so natural that in several decision-making procedures, these terms have been used interchangeably. There are decision problems in the conceptual world where implementation of any possible alternative yielding some choice measure forms the basis of deciding an alternative as optimal or as satisfactory.

Theory provides an important input to someone carrying out a task; the knowledge and experience of the decision-maker along with their intuitive and imaginative capabilities bring in more inputs. Theory mandates the availability of some information bearing on the decision problem, along with the attendant resource requirements. The relative weights placed on theory and on these other inputs depend a lot on the decision-maker, the goal or objective and the context or environment.

Individuals who have taken path-breaking decisions in difficult situations have embodied their decision-making exercises with varying inputs from decision theory in terms of certain models for decision-making which definitely deserve our attention.

As the title of this book suggests, the focus here is on decision-making aided and strengthened by decision theory in all its domains and dimensions, at the same time emphasizing the role of human behaviour in all its diversity. However, the well-established facet of decision theory dealing with general optimization problems, which is rich in quantitative methods and provides rather little scope for human interference except in some marginal roles, has been accorded its due place in the book. In fact, many models, techniques and results developed in the context of general optimization theory have found useful applications in practice, in conjunction with several aspects of cognitive and even affective decision-making, to yield 'good' decisions. Decision-making, in that way, has derived strength from advances in several branches of knowledge, including mathematics, computer science, behavioural economics, logic and related subjects.

CHAPTER 2

Decision-making Process

2.1. Some Generalities

A decision-making process is characterized by the pair (Ω, OP) where Ω is a set of alternatives and OP is an optimality principle (OP is different from optimality criteria). OP can be expressed by a choice function operating on any subset $X \varepsilon \Omega$. In a general decision-making problem, both these may be unknown, and information required to solve them is extracted during the decision-making process. With Ω known, we have a choice problem, and with both Ω and OP known, we have a general optimization problem.

It has been generally argued that in a choice problem (much discussed in the theory of social choice), the available options or decisions (and the corresponding actions) admit of qualitative description, while in a general optimization problem, they are in terms of values of some quantitative features. In fact, in the latter case, we speak of 'decision variables' as variable features (varying over alternatives) whose values or levels we are required to specify in the decision we make. A choice problem does not directly involve any such decision variable(s). As can be easily understood, in both the cases, decisions are based on the outcomes of actions (indicated by the decisions) or some suitable indicators based on these outcomes. And such outcomes can also be expressed mostly in quantitative terms, though there are situations where the outcomes are binary (yes/no) or are qualitative in character and can possibly be expressed in terms of categorical data, such as completely satisfied, satisfied, indifferent, dissatisfied and completely dissatisfied. Once we deal with qualitative (ordinal or nominal) outcomes, we face a problem in establishing preference relations among them. On the other hand, situations involving quantitative outcomes can be quite conveniently ordered to provide a decision input. In addition, if more than one decision-makers are involved, individual preferences are likely to vary among them, complicating any such ordering. Choice problems are mostly of the latter type and justify a distinct treatment.

Alternatives or options are sometimes called 'strategies'. At least some of the elements constituting different strategies must be different in terms of their values or levels or other implications. Such elements as vary from one strategy to another and as are to be determined through a choice among the alternatives under consideration by the decision-maker are usually branded as 'decision variables'. Let us consider the classical product mix problem to maximize profit by deciding on the number of units or quantities of several, say n, different product items that can be produced with the available resources.

The decision-maker has to decide on the number or quantity x_i of item i to be produced and the decision variables $X = (x_1, x_2, \ldots, x_n)$ represent a strategy.

Alternatives and their attributes (criteria) present a vast panorama. Take the case of several alternative designs for an engineering system whose performance measures can be found only through wet or dry simulations. In the case of selecting one or a few 'best' populations (of outcomes like yields of a crop variety) in terms of some unknown parameter, like the mean, one sometimes assumes a certain distribution of the outcome and takes a sample of actual observations to proceed. Of course, we deal with decision problems where the attributes can only be guessed or predicted at the time of decision-making and can be determined only when an alternative has been implemented. There are, however, many situations where the attributes are known with certainty right at the beginning. In the example just mentioned, one can take profit per unit of any item as known with certainty, though the same can be certainly when only the product is eventually marketed, beyond being produced as per the production plan.

Comprehending a decision problem in terms of spelling out the objectives to be achieved, assigning weights to indicate the relative importance of each objective, identifying possible alternatives and attributes for each alternative and assessing their values or levels as indicators of the extent to which any alternative satisfies any of the objectives and finally choosing an alternative as better than the others may be quite a daunting task, particularly in choice problems. In general optimization problems dealing with integer-valued variables involved in the alternatives, some of these problems do arise and pose difficulties.

The author used to take up the apparently trifling case of making a cup of tea to illustrate the nuances of a decision-making problem. Alternative ways of preparing tea could be characterized in terms of (a) sequences according to which constituent operations of boiling water, adding milk and tea leaves and sugar, (b) time for which water is heated or boiled and time between dipping tea leaves and straining made tea and (c) amounts of milk, sugar and tea leaves to be added. Just for the sake of example, one can add milk to water, boil the mixture for a few minutes and then add tea leaves, wait for a few minutes more and then use a strainer to get the cup of tea to which may be added some sugar. This can be visualized as a multi-objective decision-making (MODM) problem, with, say three objectives, namely tea should be tasteful, tea should have a good/aromatic flavour and it should have a pleasing colour. To most decision-makers, the first objective is the most important, followed by the two others. Some may attach a high priority to flavour. The big question is how do we judge any of these objectives? And none can be assessed before sipping the tea. Only some previous experience or some peer influence can be used to make a decision initially for a choice to be made. In addition, even the post-taste evaluation, especially for taste, is only subjective.

2.2. Strategies

The very basic element in decision analysis is the assumed existence of a set of alternatives or options out of which some (may be just one) will have to be chosen. The set must have at least two elements, and the elements may be given right at the beginning or may unfold over some period or may have to be generated by the decision-maker, with external assistance of experts or consultants if so needed. The options or alternatives may be concrete entities or objects, like candidates in a selection process for filling up some vacancies or may be just abstract entities like functions of sample observations to provide an estimate of an unknown parameter or the sequence in which certain jobs have to be processed on each of several machines subject to some specified orders in which each job has to pass through each machine. An alternative could be a single entity or a package like a portfolio or an algorithm involving steps indicating where to start, in which direction to move at each step and when to stop or a protocol for carrying out a clinical trial for a new drug.

Alternatives may be obvious and easily identifiable: They could be non-obvious and could require an effort for identification. Alternative rules or procedures or methods for carrying out a task for achieving some goal or objective in the perceptual or conceptual world are sometimes called 'strategies'—a term used during the early days of the development of operations research in the context of military operations.

'Strategies' are more often used in operations research than in the context of decision analysis. They are, of course, involved in discussions about games. Some authors liberally use the term 'strategy' to mean 'a course of action' or just an action available to a decision-maker. However, it would be better to maintain a distinction between the two in terms of a strategy being the manner in which a decision is to be put into action rather than the decision or the action implied by the decision. This is rather obvious from the fact that in a two-person game, say with player A having options or alternatives $A_1, A_2, \ldots, A_m$ and the opponent player B having options $B_1, B_2, \ldots, B_n$, a mixed strategy for player, which is really a probability vector $p=(p_1, p_2, \ldots, p_m)$ $1 \geq p_i \geq 0$ and $\Sigma p_i = 1$ where p_i is the probability that player A will choose option A_i in a particular play of the game, is to be interpreted as the manner in which player A will choose this strategy in terms of a random number drawn before they make their move. A pure strategy signifies that a particular option will always be chosen by the player concerned. A strategy, this way, is rather a 'move' made by a decision-maker and not just an option available to them.

2.2.1. Constraints

Hardly any decision-making process is a free-wheeling of ideas or a completely unbridled use of models, methods, techniques and software. Limitations are imposed in different ways in different situations on the strategies that can be considered, the quality and quantity of pertinent information that can be accessed, computational resources that can be committed, time by which a decision has to be reached, heterogeneity among members in a group involved in making a decision that cannot be ignored and a host of other checks illustrate the fact that a decision-making process must take into account factors which circumscribe the 'freedom' of the decision-maker(s), and such factors are generally referred to as 'constraints.' In general optimization theory, some complex but unconstrained problems do surface, but the majority of such problems admit of constraints of various sorts. As just mentioned, we may be constrained to using a less efficient method to solve a choice or an optimization problem because of constraints on resources available to us.

In the more restricted but usual case, the term 'constraint' applies to alternatives or strategies, implying that all conceivable alternatives cannot be considered as possible or probable solutions to the decision problem. Alternatives which satisfy the given constraints are termed as 'feasible'. There could be situations where we may have to deal with constraints which involve some uncertainty expressed in terms of probability. Thus, an inequality constraint to be satisfied by a solution vector of decision variables (a set of such variables being a strategy) may involve some random coefficients with a joint probability distribution—completely specified or otherwise—and we can only speak of the probability that a possible solution vector satisfies this 'chance' constraint. Then, this latter probability may be constrained to be at least as large as a specified value.

2.3. States of Nature

'States of nature' constitute an important element in the decision-making process. These are scenarios—meant to be mutually non-overlapping and possibly exhaustive—which are perceived by the decision-maker as characterizing the environment or context in which a decision is made (and a consequent action is taken) and through which the consequence of the decision (outcome of the action) is determined. These could be quantitative in nature, indicated by some value(s) or interval(s) of value(s) of some variable(s)—deterministic or random—or could be just nominal or, sometimes, ordinal in nature. These could be completely specified in some situations, like in games of chance where they are a part of the rules of the game. In many more cases, they could only be incompletely envisaged by the decision-maker, depending on the availability of and access to relevant information. These are, no doubt, beyond the control of the decision-maker.

A set of extraneous factors that influence the pay-off for a given alternative is sometimes referred to as the 'state of nature'. The state of nature is specified in terms of some relations connecting an alternative or option to its outcome or pay-off(s). Usually, the states of nature are beyond the control of the decision-maker, except in the Markov decision process, where actions chosen by the decision-maker at some stage can influence the states of nature in subsequent stages. In such cases, states of nature can also be understood as states in which the underlying system can be in successive stages of decision-making. However, in sequential decision-making or in games requiring multiple moves or choices of the participating players, states of nature before a particular move can be influenced by decisions taken earlier and, thus, change over moves. Even otherwise, states of nature which are usually affected by external factors may change over time, causing the 'expected' outcome of any action at the time of decision-making to differ from the outcome actually realized sometime later. For example, in the product-mix or resource allocation problem, the total cost or profit calculated at the time of decision-making with the cost or profit coefficients in the prevailing state of nature can well differ from the actual cost or profit computed at the end of production or at the time of marketing.

Corresponding to contextual information about states of nature, or the environment in which the decision-maker is placed, we often characterize decision-making as an exercise (a) under certainty (b) under uncertainty and (c) under risk.

In completely structured decision problems, alternatives or options available to the decision-maker(s), states of nature and outcomes of alternatives for each state of nature are all presented together, as in the case of a two-person zero-sum game. While we refer to states of nature as discrete usually, it is quite possible that such states correspond to values or intervals of values of certain variables which can vary continuously over some respective zones. In addition, as already pointed out, states of nature could well constitute the support of a probability distribution.

In statistical decision theory, states of nature are generally taken as possible values of some unknown parameter(s) or possible truths or unknown realities about some statements which are subjected to verification in the light of sample observations.

Exogenous to the decision-making process, states of nature have to be duly taken into account to arrive at optimal or satisficing solutions.

In some situations, states of nature (also called states of reality in certain contexts like multiple hypothesis testing) are not easily identifiable as distinct from the outcomes or pay-offs of any strategy associated with the states. The outcomes are directly identifiable and even measurable and can be attributed to possibly different states of nature. In such cases, outcome states are recognized as a combination for further development of a method or a technique for choosing among the alternatives.

2.4. Criteria for Choice

As is evident, decisions are taken by individuals or organizations to achieve some goals or objectives. The latter are related to certain operations or actions which are influenced and/or guided and directed by the decisions. Such objectives and goals can be classified as: (a) Those which are either achieved or not and the options are also binary, like carrying out the operation or not carrying it out. Even if there are multiple options or strategies, for each option or strategy, the objective or goal is either achieved or missed. (b) Those which admit natural and most often unique measures of the extent to which any objective or goal is achieved. Measures like cost or profit or time to complete an operation or number of people or machines required or some other appropriate measures can provide convenient yardsticks for comparing alternatives or options. (c) Those which do not admit natural or unique measures of the extent of achievement by any option and we have to develop some problem-specific measure in such cases.

The extent to which alternatives achieve a particular objective as indicated by some appropriate measures and in terms of which a choice can be made among the options or alternatives is called a criterion. Thus, a criterion is not just any feature of an option but refers to a measure by which one can assess the extent to which such a feature indicates the extent to which some objective behind the decision problem is achieved. In fact, some features which do not contribute to a yardstick for comparison will not be treated as criteria. For example, decisions to minimize the capital 'locked up' in inventory, purchase cost per unit (if it does not depend on the quantity ordered or purchased at a time) need not be considered in a situation where the total demand is known exactly and no shortage or excess is allowed. Only the order/set-up cost and the holding or storage cost are considered to find the total 'effective' cost as the criterion.

The measure(s) indicating the extent to which an alternative satisfies the objective may not be directly taken as the criterion for a choice among the alternatives. To allow the decision-maker's subjective evaluation of an alternative in terms of some such measure, we sometimes convert the measure to some 'utility' or ' pay-off ' in an objective or rule-based manner. Here also, different choices of the utility function exist, and ultimately, the decision-maker has to accept some form of the utility function with the coefficients or parameters involved assigned values based on experience or on expert advice or by personal preference.

In the ultimate analysis, a criterion is a function defined in the space of alternatives and is itself a variable. The nature of this function and its value for a specified alternative depends on the information available to the decision-maker in a given context. We may have complete and exact knowledge of the relation and can determine the unique value of the criterion variable for a given alternative. In some other cases, we may only guess some possible values of the criterion for any alternative corresponding to several sets of exogenous factors. As a subclass within this category, we may be able to assign probabilities to these various sets and, accordingly, work with a probability distribution of criterion values for a given alternative. Such a probability distribution of pay-off may be summarized by scalars, like the expected pay-off or the pay-off variance or the probability that the pay-off exceeds a specified value. For a choice among alternatives, any such summary measure may be taken as the criterion.

2.5. Utility and Its Measurement

The outcome of a decision/action alternative is often stated in monetary terms (and the term 'pay-off' has become quite natural to indicate loss or gain). In situations where the outcome is a cardinal measure other than monetary value, it may be conveniently and even uniquely converted to monetary terms. However, there exist situations where the different outcomes can only be put on a preference scale and cannot be quantified in the usual manner. In decision-making under risk, we associate different outcomes for a particular alternative with different states of nature, and we assign probabilities of occurrence to the latter. We proceed to speak in terms of expected values to make a choice among the alternatives. In fact, outcomes—binary or ordinal or measurable—as are known or as can be computed or even predicted from the available information at the time of decision-making, along with probabilities associated with the different states of nature, constitute the basis for decision-making under risk.

Decisions are taken by individuals in their personal capacities or as members of a group or an organization to achieve some objective(s), and decisions are not necessarily based on the pay-offs or outcomes directly; what is more important is the extent to which the decision-maker feels that the objective behind solving the decision problem has been satisfied. Had this feeling or perception been the same for different decision-makers, a comparison among the alternatives with regard to their ability to satisfy the objective could have been easier and person-free, especially when the objective could be directly related to loss or gain. It may be added that such perceptions will vary from one individual to another, as well as from one occasion to a second, even for the same individual.

In addition, this has led to the development and use of 'utility' as an indicator of the real worth of the outcome or pay-off of an alternative under a given state of nature, as a yardstick for comparison among alternatives by a decision-maker. Attempts to measure the utility of objects, events, states and their properties date back at least to Bentham (1989), though the later work of Neumann and Morgenstern (1953) provided the scientific basis for utility measurement. Utility being subjective, the utilities of different individuals cannot be compared. This subjectivity may not create a problem unless more than one decision-maker is involved, and especially when they act under competition—as in a game problem.

Different forms of utility function (of a physical or monetary amount x) have been proposed. As early as 1738, Daniel Bernoulli proposed $\log x$ in the context of maritime insurance. Buffon suggested $1/x$ while $x^{1/2}$ was offered by Cramer. All these are monotonic decreasing functions of x. The utility of a certain amount of money x to a decision-maker may also depend on the amount already in possession of the decision-maker, since the utility of an (additional) amount x to somebody already possessing a large amount is much less compared to that of another with little or no money in hand. In this argument, the gain in utility if you have y in hand and you get x has been taken as:

$$1/x - 1/(x+y)$$

Given any two outcomes, O_1 and O_2, we find their utilities in the following manner.

We establish a preference relation, and say O_1 is preferred to O_2 (an outcome with a greater magnitude will be preferred to one with a lower magnitude).

We now find a probability α such that the decision-maker is indifferent to $\alpha\, O_1$ and O_2 or has no preference between O_1 with probability α and O_2 with certainty.

In this case, we will take the utility of O_1 as $1/\alpha$, taking the utility of O_2 as 1. In the case of more than two outcomes with the preference ordering $O_1 > O_2 > O_3$, we first find α_1 such that $\alpha_1\, O_1 = O_2$ and next find α_2 such that $\alpha_2\, O_2 = O_3$. In this case, we set the utility of O_1 as $1/\alpha_1$ and that of O_2 as $1/\alpha_2$, treating the utility of O_3 as unity. It is also needed to check if $\alpha_3\, O_1 = O_2$ where α_3 is a probability. This procedure can be generalized to any number n of outcomes with $1+2+2+\ldots+(n-2)$ possible checks and initial evaluation.

The issue of the indifference of a decision-maker between a certain lower amount with certainty and a higher amount to be attained with some probability reflects the attitude of a decision-maker towards risk. If the certainty amount is equated to the expected value of the amount to be obtained with some probability, the decision-maker is categorized as risk-neutral, while a risk-taker will agree to be indifferent between a high amount with a small probability so that the expected value is smaller than the certainty amount, and a risk-averter will insist on a high probability for the uncertain amount so that the expected value exceeds the certainty amount. In fact, this provides the basis for the standard gamble for measuring utility. With the development of probability theory, the standard gamble method of determining utility has gained wide acceptance.

2.6. Regret

In the case of decisions made under uncertainty about the states of nature and, hence, about the outcomes associated with any decision/action, once a particular state of nature is found to take place sometime after a decision has been taken, it is quite possible that the outcome or pay-off actually received by the decision-maker in the face of uncertainty turns out to be smaller than the highest outcome or pay-off that could have been achieved had the realization of this state of nature been known. The emotional response to this lost opportunity is usually in terms of regret that the best decision had not been taken.

This opportunity cost or cost of lost opportunity has been taken as a measure of regret for a particular alternative corresponding to a given state of nature. Thus, we can convert a pay-off matrix to a regret matrix and then apply some optimality criterion to find the optimal decision under uncertainty. We should bear in mind that probabilities cannot be associated with the states of nature involved, since we are working in complete ignorance about the likely occurrences of these states. Of course, it can be argued that in such a situation, the outcomes of different strategies or alternatives are also likely to be uncertain, except for alternatives whose outcomes are relatively insensitive to states of nature.

Consider the following example where an investor has to decide the mode in which to invest and the pay-off matrix may be, in terms of likely rates of return—in three anticipated states of nature namely war, peace and depression given as:

	War	Peace	Depression	Minimum
Speculative stocks	20	1	−6	−6
High-grade stocks	9	8	0	0
Bonds	4	4	4	4

Going by the maximin pay-off criterion, the best decision is to invest in bonds. However, if one anticipates a war to really take place, the best decision would have been to invest in speculative stocks, and the pay-off losses with the two other decisions, namely going in for high-grade stocks and bonds would be 11 and 16 respectively. Thus, the anticipated 'regrets' could be put in a regret matrix with the following elements:

	War	Peace	Depression	Maximum
Speculative stocks	0	7	10	10
High-grade stocks	11	0	4	11
Bonds	16	4	0	0

It is quite natural for a decision-maker to opt for the minimax regret criterion and to invest in bonds so that the maximum regret would be the least, irrespective of which state of nature is eventually realized. At this point, it is worthwhile to observe that once a particular state of nature has been found to have occurred, the outcomes of the different alternatives under that state can be known almost certainly, and those may differ from the corresponding outcomes as anticipated when the decision was being taken. Accordingly, actual regrets might well differ from anticipated regrets, and the minimax regret criterion can only take into account the anticipated regret values. Just like risk-aversion as a human behaviour, regret aversion or rather regret minimization is also an aspect of intelligent human behaviour.

As remarked earlier, expected pay-off or expected utility cannot be worked out in the above context. Taking recourse to the logic that equal ignorance leads to equal probabilities, we may not need to find an alternative which is the 'best' among all such alternatives. Instead, we may work in terms of only one reasonable alternative suggested by intuition or by experience and may need to establish that this is 'satisfactory'. We may even play around with this alternative to suitably modify it and come up with an alternative that can be accepted as 'satisfactory'. In some such cases, we may have some 'aspiration' level, and a 'satisficing' solution is required just to meet this level. It is quite possible that this solution is not an 'optimal' one; the expected pay-off in the above problem would be maximized by the decision to invest in high-grade stocks, while applying the minimum expected regret criterion would also make the same investment decision the best. However, this is just a coincidence in this particular example and is not generally true.

2.7. Optimality Principle

The concept of optimality and of optimal solutions (decisions) have been inextricably linked up with decision theory. However, in a discussion of decision-making as distinct from decision theory, these concepts may not be at all involved in some situations. In fact, decisions may have to be made when all possible alternatives are not identified, and we may not need to find an alternative which is the 'best' among all such alternatives. Instead, we may work in terms of only one reasonable alternative suggested by intuition or by experience and may need to establish that this is 'satisfactory'. In some such cases, we may have some 'aspiration' level, and a 'satisficing' solution is required just to meet this level. It is quite possible that this solution is not an 'optimal' one. In fact, Schwartz (2004) has brought out sharply the distinction between decision-makers who are 'maximizers' and those who are 'satisficers'. The first group attempts to find the 'absolute' best option, while the second tries to find something that is good enough, without worrying that something better might be out there.

The optimality principle in a decision problem has to be chosen by the decision-maker to suit the context of the problem and the objective or goal to be achieved by solving the problem. The fundamental need is to compare alternatives against some criterion (criteria) to choose the 'best' or a subset of better-than-others alternatives within the identified set of alternatives under consideration. One can visualize a number of possible situations. The simplest case involves alternatives which are numerically expressed (in terms of values of decision variables) to be judged against some objective criterion (which could be numerically expressed or otherwise) yielding a unique measure or score (like pay-off or some form of utility or some extent of regret felt after the decision has been proved right or wrong) for each alternative. This ideal case corresponds to the criterion being a continuous function defined in the space of alternatives (often called the 'decision space'). Here, the numerical measure or score, subject to the constraints, admits to a 'maximum' (minimum) value. However, the procedure adopted by the decision-maker to scan the decision space may result in finding an alternative that gives the maximum value attainable by the search procedure, and this maximum attainable value (taken as the optimal) may not be the absolute maximum value.

We will restrict ourselves to scalar choice functions, n-round tournament choice functions, totally extremal choice functions, Pareto choice functions, Nash optimality, choice functions with reference to an ideal point, dynamic choice functions and the like.

A choice function $C(X)$ on S is said to be a general scalar function if there is a numeric function $g(x)$ $g: S-E_1$ such that $C(X) = \text{Arg Max } g(X)$ over X. It is called a scalar function if $g(x) = g(y)$ with $x = y$. A choice function C is a general scalar function if and only if it is generated by a strongly transitive anti-reflexive binary relation. The numeric function g could denote the pay-off or outcome of an alternative x.

There exists a sizeable volume of literature on choice functions and their development from relations, their properties, interrelations among different classes of choice functions and their use in decision-making. In fact, the theory of choice in mathematics has contributed a lot to the development of several methods used in MCDM or multi-objective programming. Of course, the explicit mention of an underlying choice function has been missing in the development of these methods. In the paragraphs that follow, an attempt will be made to present some definitions of choice functions and their uses very briefly. Some elaborations appear in the chapter on ranking and scaling alternatives but, again, without explicitly aligning the discussion with choice functions. We will restrict ourselves to scalar choice functions, n-round tournament choice functions, totally extremal choice functions, Pareto choice functions, Nash optimality, choice functions with reference to an ideal point, dynamic choice functions, and the like.

A choice function $C(X)$ on S is said to be a general scalar function if there is a numeric function $g(X)$ $g: S-E_1$ such that $C(X) = \text{Arg. Max } g(X)$ over X. It is called a scalar function if $g(x) = g(y)$ with $x = y$. A choice function is a general scalar function if and only if it is generated by a strongly transitive, anti-reflexive, binary relation. The numeric function g could denote the pay-off or outcome of an alternative x.

A choice function C on S is a Pareto choice function if there exist a series of numeric functions $g_1, \ldots, g_m$ such that:

$$C(X) = \{x | (y \in x) | g_I(y) \geq g_I(x) \ (I = 1, 2, \ldots, m)|\}$$

Pareto choice functions are important in multi-objective programming or MCDM. A choice function that is the union of scalar functions is said to be totally extremal. The implication of this new concept is that if we define r numeric functions (criteria) $g_1, \ldots, g_r$ and r choices are made from X, with the first one according to the first criterion, the second one according to the second criterion, etc., then a totally extremal choice function is the union of these r choices.

2.7.1. Tournament Choice Function

Suppose N players meet n times during a tournament, and the outcome of each game is either a victory or a defeat. The results of an n-round tournament can be represented by a $N \times n$ matrix T with elements t_{ij}=number of times ith player is defeated by player j. Obviously $t_{ij}+t_{ji}+n$ for all i and j (different from i) and $t_{ii}=0$ for all i. To identify the winner, we may use two different choice functions. On the one hand, we can recognize the number of defeats a player suffers and would like to minimize this. On the other hand, we can take into account the maximum number of defeats a player suffers with respect to each player as the choice function and like to minimize the same.

2.8. Establishing Trade-Offs

Having an interest in more than one objectives apparently of equal relevance and importance behind resolving a decision problem and finding it difficult to achieve all of them, we take recourse to establishing some trade-offs among these objectives. Similar is the case with several criteria which appear to reflect the attainment of a single objective or of multiple objectives. We sometimes go in for a trade-off among options or alternatives, though they seem to be equally appealing to us. Even when evaluating the alternatives in terms of the criterion (criteria), we tend to establish trade-offs among alternative methods. Thus, the concept and involvement of trade-offs has become an integral part of decision-making, and possibly, this is one reason why we do not reject the statement that 'economics is all about trade-offs.' In addition, decision-making pervades economics, and economics has stimulated developments in decision theory.

Economics teaches you that making a choice means giving up something. To quote Russ Roberts, the disregard of trade-offs and of opportunity costs (costs—direct or indirect—of lost opportunities) plays out in the same pattern again and again in our lives. Even if we try to find ways around fundamental constraints, the trade-offs show up somewhere.

One extreme implication of a trade-off, say between two entities, is to sacrifice one completely in favour of the other. However, trade-off generally means 'more of the more desired/wanted, accepting less of the less desired/wanted'. Of course, 'more' or 'less' are terms to be interpreted by the decision-maker, taken to be boundedly rational. In fact, in the general sense, a trade-off does not ignore any of the entities under consideration (objectives/criteria/alternatives/methods of evaluation, etc.) completely. Rather, it assigns weights or measures of 'relative' importance to each entity and, whenever needed to facilitate comparison, considers the weighted aggregate or average as a single entity.

Whenever we like to prioritize criteria and to assign weights to them as measures of their relative importance in a given context (and to eventually consider the weighted aggregate for a choice among the alternatives), we involve trade-offs—consciously or discreetly—and such trade-offs, reflected in the weights or the priorities, are bound to be subjective. Even if the individual decision-maker is 'rational', these will be influenced by their preferences/indifferences or personal value judgements. 'Value' itself is a personalized concept. Very rarely is this the uniquely determinable monetary value or the less directly measurable 'monetized' value. A rational decision-maker may, of course, try to assess the value of an alternative objectively without letting preferences play a role.

Identifying different possible entities, deciding which are more desirable/wanted than others, assessing to what extent an entity is desirable or otherwise or even putting different entities on a mental scale for desirability are all person-specific issues. How much must I give up to get a little more of what I want most? And this is where we face the issue of making value judgements. Win-Win is not a complete picture. It is true that objective, person-free approaches to yield some reasonable or approximate answers to such issues have been explored and used in recent times, and these efforts have definitely provided good inputs to the decision-making process. General applicability with success may be quite a difficult task to accomplish.

An imaginative trade-off exercise may broaden the vision of the decision-maker and consider options or alternatives which otherwise would not have entered the decision-making process. Thus, in a macro-level decision problem to meet increasing demand for energy through the generation of additional power and at the same time taking care of pollution caused by old and fuel-inefficient existing power plants, given a cap on the total investible amount, we may extend our vision from supply-side management to demand-side management as well. This means we can possibly invest a part of the money in promoting measures to reduce energy consumption through the installation of devices and equipment with low power demand and in campaigns to conserve energy and curb energy consumption. Again, within supply-side management, trade-offs can be established between actions to increase generation, on the one hand, and to reduce the impact of pollution, on the other. Thus, actions to build some new power plant(s) and close down all existing power plants and build new clean and efficient plants instead, may be balanced against actions such as purchasing scrubbers for old power plants and moving all power plant generation 'off shore'. Combinations of these two types of actions may also be thought of.

2.9. Types of Decision Problems

DMPs differ in several respects. In some, the initial set of alternatives is given, either in terms of a finite number of already identified alternatives or in terms of an infinite but identifiable alternatives with properties which can be determined exactly or approximately. In some cases, the whole set of alternatives may not even be imaginable at the beginning and may go on changing as we proceed. Some DMPs do not start with an initial set of alternatives. The identification or generation of alternatives may or may not be a part of the DMP itself.

Alternatives and their distinguishing properties or features (criteria) present a wide panorama. Some decision-making addresses just the choice of weights or importance measures to be assigned to different criteria for building up a single combined criterion to facilitate choice.

We have a set of probability distributions, and we want to select a subset based on some summary measure(s). Or we want to select one that provides the best fit to an observed set of data based on some criterion like AIC, BIC or CIC. We like to select a candidate for a given position through an interview, and on screening, we find a set of candidates who fulfil the 'essential' requirements.

We have to estimate in terms of a sample of observations an unknown parameter in a given model, based on some criteria such as bias, mean squared error and robustness. We cannot imagine and cannot at all identify all possible alternative estimators right in the beginning.

Of course, we have decision problems where we can surely enumerate a few feasible alternatives. But their properties could be only guessed initially and determined only in the future.

Decision problems traditionally discussed in operational research literature are usually 'structured' ones, and most of them are faced and resolved repetitively by organizations who are interested principally in achieving their own interests by maximizing benefits or minimizing costs or maximizing the benefit-to-cost ratio. It is true, however, that concepts, methods and techniques developed in operational research can be and have been gainfully applied to solve decision problems. Benefits derived and costs incurred by individuals and groups beyond those represented by the organizations making decisions are also accorded due importance. Thus, many problems in social choice are sometimes unstructured or only partly structured, involving stakeholders not easily identified, benefits and costs which are spread over different periods of time and subject to the impacts of unforeseeable external environments, the feasibility of options changes over time and even feasible options already chosen and being implemented become infeasible later on.

Operational research deals mostly with problems faced by manufacturing and service organizations to achieve some relatively well-defined goals and objectives. That way, decisions have to be taken in almost every area of operation, namely procurement of materials, machines, technology and finance; employment and of people and their deployment on different tasks and responsibilities; conversion of inputs to products, by-products and wastes (with commercial value); maintenance of equipment, facilities and utilities; pricing, distribution and warehousing, and selling of products and services. Evidently, decision problems associated with all these operations are too many and will occupy pages to enumerate a majority of them in necessary detail. We have a sprinkling of decisions which normally precede important industrial operations.

In the design arena, a very important and interesting problem is determining the amount of redundancy and its allocation over subsystems in designing a complex and critical system in order to maximize system reliability, subject to certain constraints on total cost or total volume or weight (especially in the case of airborne systems or systems to operate within limited space, like a sub-marine).

In the procurement arena, the decision problems include the following:

- Which brand of a machine for a specified process to select, given that there are at least two brands for which the providers give out some information about costs of acquisition, about energy consumption, about warranty period and useful life period, about maintenance costs, about salvage costs or reuse value, about safety and insurance related costs, about service quality offered and the like?
- Which vendor to approach for procuring a certain material? Which vendor rating index to use and what weights should be assigned to the three factors, namely quality, price and delivery? Which sort of staggered delivery to accept?
- When to buy some materials and how often during a planning period? How much quantity to order each time?

Decision problems in the production area include the following:

- What temperature to maintain during a conversion operation and for how much time?

- Which maintenance policy to go by—block replacement or age replacement? And what should be the replacement interval or age for planned replacement?

Coming to manpower management, decisions have to be made to address problems of the following sorts:

- How do we allocate different jobs to different possible candidates to achieve maximum overall efficiency?
- After how much of a retention period in a given position, should an employee be promoted to the next higher position?

Important marketing decisions relate to the following questions:

- How much price discount to offer against bulk purchase and what should be the time by which payment has to be made by the customer, once delivery has been completed?
- How best to react to customer complaints? Should customer education programmes be made compulsory? When and how quickly is a replacement of a product/service or a part thereof replaced?
- How many service counters operate in parallel to deal with potential customers?

Statistical decision theory opens up a huge variety of problems in which decisions have to be taken on the basis of observations of some random variable(s) denoting the response(s) in some experiments which could be physically carried out or could just be simulated. Going beyond the classical problem of estimating some unknown parameter(s) and testing some simple or composite hypotheses, we face problems of prediction and forecasting, discrimination and classification, as well as selecting the best or a subset of the best few among a set of populations or distributions or among alternative physical systems to be assessed for their performance. In that way, ranking and selection procedures have attracted a lot of attention from research workers, and by pervading all these areas, we find the application of Bayesian models and methods to account for certain uncertainties. Problems of multiple decisions and compound decisions and associated models and methods have contributed significantly to the substantive content of scientific investigations in many emerging areas.

In entering the realm of social choice or of governmental decisions that affect the entire population of a country or a state, cost-benefit analysis is the much-discussed mechanism for decision-making. Feasible alternatives are not easily identifiable and their features in relation to the objectives to be achieved in line with some declared policies are not easily measurable. A decision like whether a particular institution of higher education will provide some stipend to every student enrolled in a particular course, and if so, how much should the stipend be per month has to consider not only financial aspects but also its social aspect, by way of some discrimination being attempted between students getting admitted to this institution and those going to some other institutions where they will have to pay fees for their studies. For a state-funded institution, such a decision will have some likely impacts on other activities demanding money from the budgetary support from the state. How to evaluate the consequences of activities adversely affected by the decision to introduce or increase stipends?

To facilitate women to move out of their households and attend to jobs or tasks outside, should the state decide on a policy of free rides for women on public transport services? How to quantify the benefits of such a scheme? How to disentangle women's movement to discharge duties and responsibilities outside households from movements encouraged and enabled by the 'free ride' offer? How do we compute the loss in revenue, given the fact that the public transport system is currently gender neutral?

2.10. Elaborating Some Examples

The age-old practice of sampling inspection of units/items in a lot/consignment provides an effective illustration of a decision-making problem where a decision has to precede an action. Consider first the case of a single sampling inspection plan by attributes of the acceptance-rectification type. The alternatives are the pairs of decision variables (n, c) where n is the size of a random sample to be drawn from a lot of N items with an unknown fraction of defective p, and c is the acceptance number in the sense that the lot will be accepted if the number of defectives in the lot does not exceed c. The features associated with the finitely many alternatives (n, c) $1 \leq n \leq N-1$ and $0 \leq c \leq n-1$ are (a) the cost of inspection to be borne by the producer/supplier and (b) the risk of accepting a poor quality lot with a quality $p \geq p_t$ where p_t, the lot tolerance proportion defective, is the poorest quality the customer is prepared to tolerate. The optimality principle adopted is to simply take the probability of accepting a lot of quality p_t to be around 0.10 as a constraint and to minimize the average amount of inspection as a function of (n, c). A concrete optimization problem formulation would be to select integers n and c such that $I(p_0) = n + (N-n)$ Prob $[x > c | p_t]$ is a minimum subject to the condition $L(p_t) =$ Prob $[x \leq c | p_t] \approx 0.10$ (or some such pre-assigned small value), where x is the number of defectives observed in the sample and p_0 is the process quality (average fraction defective) maintained by the producer.

It may be noted that the two criteria—one appearing as a constraint and the other as an objective function—are contradictory in nature. Further, risk as the product of a probability multiplied by the cost consequence of accepting a poor quality lot could have been added to the expected cost of inspection to make up for a total cost function to be minimized or the two costs could be separately minimized, as in goal programming or compromise programming or reference point programming.

In the classical approach, with n and c being integers, it may not be possible to satisfy the constraint exactly and the consequences of departures from the specified consumer's risk on the two sides have different implications for the two stakeholders in the decision-making process. Considering the producer as the only decision-maker, we could possibly take the constraint as a '$\geq$' inequality. In any case, this becomes a chance-constrained non-linear integer programming problem, defying a convenient solution algorithm.

To illustrate how an innocent-looking optimization problem may be quite difficult to solve, we consider the secretary selection problem. There are n candidates who can be ranked according to some selection criterion (criteria) from 1 (best) to n (worst), and there is no tie. We interview i randomly selected candidates one by one and select the best of these i candidates. Let r be the rank of the selected candidate in the population of candidates. Let a be the over-head cost, k be the cost of interviewing a candidate and c be the constant in the cost of 'regret' that we could not select the best candidate and have selected one with an expected rank $E(r)$, which can be simply taken as $c\,[1-E(r)]$. Thus, the problem reduces to finding an integer $i<n$, such that the total cost $T(i)=a+k\,i+c\,[1-E(r)]$ is a minimum. We can make the formulation more acceptable by requiring that:

$$\Pr(|\,r-r_0\,| \geq m) \leq \alpha \text{ (pre-assigned small)}$$

Here, r_0 and m are very small integers.

This is a chance-constrained non-linear integer programming problem. A simple algorithm has been offered by Mukherjee and Mandal.

Assessing the extent of agreement among multiple rankings in the case of several judges ranking the interviewed candidates by using Kendall's coefficient of concordance or similar measures is not a big problem. However, the development of a consensus ranking (if there is sufficient agreement among judges) is a complex issue. Going by the Kemeny and Snell distance approach, this becomes a non-deterministic polynomial time or NP-hard problem. The problem becomes more complex if we have to work with time-dependent constraints, as in the case of some experts being available only intermittently to conduct interviews.

This problem may be looked upon from a slightly different angle. Given n alternatives which are found to be feasible (candidates who are found to be initially eligible for selection), we have to select one who is as close to the 'best' candidate as possible. However, information about the attribute to be associated with any candidate on the basis of which the decision-maker can make a choice is not currently available and has to be obtained only through a process of interview, assumed to correctly assess the relevant attribute for selection. Gathering this information means time and cost, the magnitude of which would depend on the number of candidates to be interviewed. In the absence of any information, one can choose any of the candidates at random, and this individual will have a rank, say m, in the whole group of n candidates. In this case, i candidates are interviewed, and we decide to choose the best among them (one with the lowest rank among these i candidates), and this rank is, suppose, r. Bringing in the concept of 'regret' or 'opportunity cost' for failure to select the candidate with rank 1, the value of sample information (VSI) comes out as: VSI $=(m-r)\,k$ and in repetitive decision-making, we have the expected value of sample (EVSI) information as:

$$\text{EVSI} = [(n+1)/2 - (n+1)/(n+i)]\,k$$

As expected, EVSI is always positive. We can thus get the expected net gain due to sampling (ENGS) as:

$$\text{ENGS} = \text{EVSI} - \text{Cost of sampling} + [(n+1)/2 - (n+1)/(n+i)]\,k - c\,i$$

One may now try to maximize ENGS to find the optimum value of i. ENGS is a non-linear function of the only decision variable i.

2.11. Sequential and Dynamic Decision-making

In sequential decision-making, the decision-maker makes successive observations on a process to gather additional information (obviously incurring some costs, implicitly or explicitly) before a final decision is made. The procedure for deciding when to stop getting further information or when to continue is called the 'stopping rule' or 'stopping strategy'. The objective is to find a stopping rule that minimizes losses or maximizes gains, taking due account of costs. Search problems, inventory problems, gambling problems and 'secretary-type' problems, etc., illustrate the wide variety of sequential decision-making situations. A classic example of sequential decision-making is reflected in the sequential sampling inspection of products and the associated cumulative-sum techniques for controlling quality during production.

Dynamic decision-making has been characterized by three features. First, a series of actions (following decisions) has to be taken over time to achieve some overall goals. Second, actions at different times are interdependent, implying that later actions and decisions depend on earlier actions. Third, the environment (in terms of states of nature) changes voluntarily as well as because of the consequences of earlier actions. Dynamic decision models describe the moment-to-moment deliberation processes that precede each action in a sequence of actions. Dynamic decision-making relates to the control of dynamic systems to achieve some goal. It does not necessitate a sequential search for information, though such information pertaining to changes in the decision environment may help reach better decisions.

2.12. Robustness of Decisions

Decisions—especially those made under uncertainty—using theoretical constructs or models are vulnerable to deficiencies caused by deviations in the actual decision situation (encompassing information about similar situations used in comprehending the present decision situation as well as consequences of actions chosen now, to be realized in due course, versus the goals and objectives), from those assumed and used in the construct or the model. Such unintended deviations may arise in situations where the decision-makers do not know or do not agree on the mechanism to represent fully and faithfully the features of the decision-making situations. In fact, decisions in terms of choices and their consequences are likely to be sensitive to such deviations from the model assumptions to varying extents, depending on the way choices are made. The intention is to devise procedures for decision-making which are sufficiently robust against deviations from the model assumptions, at least to a reasonable degree.

Constructs or models imply—in a generic sense—inputs to the decision-making process, and these inputs could be (a) prior probabilities of occurrence or realization of different states of nature, (b) outcomes or utilities associated with any alternative or (c) the distribution(s) of any underlying random variable(s). Decisions could be sensitive to some or all of the inputs. (Probability distributions are often referred to as 'models' in a somewhat restricted sense.)

Given that uncertainty cannot be totally avoided, what is desired is to arrive at decisions that are sufficiently robust to 'moderate' or 'tolerable' deviations of 'reality' from 'assumptions'. Delineating what is 'moderate' or 'tolerable' may not be an easy task and may often depend on the consequences of a decision that turns out to be not the best attainable one or even not the correct one. It is easier to understand and quantify 'sensitivity' of the decision to such deviations or departures. In fact, research workers tend to express the measure of sensitivity in terms of some measurable consequence of a decision as a function of the extent to which the actual situation in respect of some component of the input to decision-making deviates from the assumed situation.

CHAPTER 3

Representation of a Decision Problems

3.1. Decision Environment

Proceeding with this attempt to tackle the problem of ignorance, it is often argued that we deal only with decision-making under risk, subsuming decision-making under uncertainty as a particular case.

Decision-making under certainty refers to a situation where there is only one state of nature (that need not be explicitly mentioned) resulting in only one pay-off (outcome) against any alternative. This is, evidently, the simplest decision-making situation. Decision problems formulated in terms of (linear or non-linear) non-stochastic optimization exercises illustrate decision-making under certainty. For example, the classical product-mix problem or the classical inventory problem with known demand or the transportation problem and similar other problems studied in operational research belong to this category of decision paradigms.

Decision-making under uncertainty is discussed in a context in which we have multiple pay-offs associated with a given alternative, corresponding to multiple states of nature, and the decision-maker has no way to consider any one state of nature and hence any corresponding pay-off as more or less likely to be eventually realized compared to any other alternative. As a prolongation of decision-making under uncertainty, we have a situation where some information exists to assign (subjective) probabilities of occurrence to the different states of nature. These probabilities reflect the decision-maker's degree of belief about how likely it is for the different states of nature to be realized. Thus, decision-making under risk reflects partial knowledge about states of nature, while decision-making under uncertainty reflects the absence of any knowledge. In the case of decision-making under uncertainty, either these probabilities cannot be calculated or they are not known.

In a somewhat philosophical reference to the role of nature as a second decision-maker implicitly involved in the decision-making process through the states of nature (as if these are decided by nature), the above three decision-making situations are construed in terms of nature being 'passive' in the first case and 'interactive' in the remaining two. Some even argue that a two-person game can be recognized as a decision problem where nature plays the role of a second and equally wise decision-maker who tries to see that the first or original decision-maker or the statistician cannot get more than the worst pay-off for any alternative that they may choose. Thus, the role of nature in this case can be branded as 'counteractive'.

As indicated in the Chapter 2 and as can be easily envisaged, there will be many decision problems, including general problems of optimization, where the components of a decision problem, namely alternatives, states of nature and their associated probabilities, outcomes or pay-offs corresponding to each alternative, criterion for a choice among the alternatives and the optimality principle to be used for the purpose of making a choice, may not be spelt out clearly or even vaguely. Representation of such problems for convenient analysis and solution may be difficult. Of course, there will be many others which can be conveniently represented to grasp the nuances and to avoid to some extent computations which may appear—at least prima facie—to be a bit repelling. In this chapter, we present some simple tools frequently used to represent structured decision problems.

3.2. Decision Matrix

As pointed out earlier, the number of alternatives (of course, feasible) may be finite in some situations and infinite in others. Restricting ourselves to situations in which there is only a finite number of alternatives and a finite number of states of nature, we can have a convenient representation of a decision-making problem in terms of a decision (pay-off) matrix with rows as the alternatives (also called strategies), columns corresponding to states of nature and cells containing values of the outcome variable or the utility derived by the decision-maker from this outcome. In decision-making under certainty, we work with just one column and the matrix reduces to a vector.

Usually, states of nature are taken to be 'given' to the decision-maker and beyond their control. However, there exist situations in which a decision reached or an action taken at some stage may influence the states of nature and/or their occurrence probabilities, as in sequential decision-making or in the Markov decision process. Further, it may not be convenient in all cases to identify all the possible states of nature or to assign probabilities of occurrence to these states. However, it may be easier in most cases to identify the outcomes of any alternative that are associated with different states of nature. In fact, outcome–states as combined entities can be better determined. Even in situations where one is not able to identify all possible states of nature and believes that there could exist states of nature beyond those identified, all possible outcomes of a decision alternative can be determined or predicted. This motivates us to have an alternate representation of a decision problem in terms of a matrix where the rows still correspond to alternatives, but the columns represent outcome states and cell elements (which are pay-off or utility in the traditional representation) represent probabilities assigned to the outcome states. Since outcome–state combinations for all the alternatives taken together will always exceed the number of states in the traditional decision tree, the alternate representation will have more columns than the classical matrix. We can always transform a traditional decision matrix into a new one, though the converse is not true. The following example is expected to elucidate certain aspects of this transformation.

Example 3.1. Percentage rates of return on investment in three types of mutual funds under three different anticipated market conditions (as states of nature) appear as follows:

Type of Fund	Down Market	Moderate Market	Up Market
Utility	5	7	7
Aggressive growth	−10	5	30
Global	2	7	20
Probability of occurrence	0.1	0.5	0.4

It may be noted that the first alternative produces the same outcome, namely 7, under moderate market as well as up market conditions. We can transform this matrix to the following form with outcome states in columns and occurrences probabilities as cell entries:

Type of Fund	Outcome States						
	−10	2	5	7	8	20	30
Utility	–	–	0.1	0.9	–	–	–
Aggressive growth	0.1	–	0.5	–	–	–	0.4
Global	–	0.1	0.5	–	–	0.4	–

The comparison of expected values remains the same between the two representations, and this invariance of the comparison holds for the expected (usual logarithmic) utility values also. However, we may not be able to reconstruct the classical decision matrix from the second representation since we do not have information here about which state of nature produced a particular outcome for any alternative.

Influence diagrams and tree diagrams are widely adopted graphical representations of many decision problem situations. In fact, these simple devices are quite useful for modelling a decision problem and even for solving it (using the expected utility criterion).

3.3. Influence Diagram

An influence diagram (also called a relevance diagram) is a compact graphical-cum-mathematical representation that can be treated in some senses as a generalization of Bayesian networks. Developed in the mid-1970s with an intuitive, easy-to-understand semantic, this tool is directly applicable to team decision analysis, since it allows incomplete sharing of information among team members. This is also used in game theory as an alternative representation of a game tree.

An influence diagram is a directed acyclic graph that represents key alternatives, risks and outcomes, taking into account interconnections among these key variables and their sequencing. Several types of nodes and arcs connecting those are used and represented by symbols are not strictly the same in all expositions and applications of this tool to help analyse a static risky decision situation. The nodes and arcs generally involved are as follows.

Decision nodes: These are usually represented by squares or rectangles, one node for one decision or, sometimes, for a range of mutually exclusive decision alternatives which demand simultaneous consideration. By decisions, we include decisions to gather information, fundamental decisions affecting the final choice and outcomes, as well as decisions relating to the implementation of a possible decision.

Chance events or uncertainty nodes: Corresponding to each uncertainty like an uncertain outcome of an identified possible action, these are usually represented by ovals or circles.

(Sometimes a subtype of this type of node represents a special situation where the outcome is deterministically known, provided the outcome of some other related uncertainties is known, usually shown in terms of double ovals.)

Nodes corresponding to calculated or fixed inputs and outputs are usually drawn as rounded rectangles.

Outcome or value nodes: Corresponding to each component of additive, separable utility, usually represented by a polygon or even a triangle.

Arcs are used to connect nodes and, that way, key variables. Of course, nodes are connected only if there is a directional influence between them. Feedback loops are not generally considered in view of the fact that a static situation is under consideration. Arcs indicate relevance or sequence among nodes. A predecessor node corresponds to the independent variable, while the successor is the dependent variable. Arcs into nodes indicate sequencing. Arcs are primarily classified on the basis of the nodes into which they terminate. Thus, we have functional arcs that end in decision nodes, implying the influence of nodes at the tails on the value or some of its components. Conditional arcs correspond to situations where the uncertainty at their heads is probabilistically conditioned on all the nodes at their tails. These arcs obviously end in uncertainty nodes. In a second type of conditional arc, the uncertainty at the head of such an arc is deterministically conditioned on all the nodes at its tails. Finally, information arcs terminate at decision nodes and indicate that these decisions are made beforehand with the outcomes of all the nodes at their tails.

Alternatives in this graphical representation are collectively stated in decision nodes and information arcs. Information in terms of what is known along with deterministic/probabilistic interrelations connecting different information items are represented by uncertainty/deterministic nodes and incoming conditional arcs. Preferences are modelled by value nodes and functional arcs terminating therein.

It is to be noted that every node in this diagram is probabilistically independent of its successor nodes, given the outcomes of its immediately preceding nodes. Further, a missing arc between two non-value nodes A and B implies the existence of a set of non-value nodes C such that B is independent of A, given the outcomes of C.

With a due display of alternatives, information and preferences, an influence diagram does provide an effective yet simple tool for decision analysis.

A simple procedure for constructing an influence diagram to model the structure of a decision problem is stated in *Decision-making and Forecasting* by Marshall and Oliver (1995). These sequential steps are summarized as follows:

1. Create a preliminary list of decisions and random events (or quantities of interest) whose outcomes are believed to be important in the formulation of the problem. Identify the attributes and objectives that are to be used to measure the consequences of the decisions and outcomes.
2. Name each random quantity and decision. Represent each random quantity with a circular node and a decision with a square node. Draw them in order of occurrence from left to right.
3. Identify any influences or dependencies between random quantities and decisions. Insert directed arcs between nodes that influence one another with the direction corresponding to the natural influence believed.

The simple example given in Wikipedia and presented in Figure 3.1 is quite interesting. This relates to planning a vacation. There is one decision node (vacation activity), two uncertainty nodes (weather condition and weather forecast) and one value node (satisfaction). Two functional arcs ending in satisfaction, one conditional arc ending in weather forecast and one informational arc ending in vacation activity complete the influence diagram. Functional arcs ending in satisfaction indicate that satisfaction is a utility function of weather condition and vacation activity. Thus, satisfaction of decision-makers can be quantified if they know what the weather condition is likely to be and what their choice of activity is. (They do not value weather forecast directly.) The conditional arc ending in the weather forecast implies that this

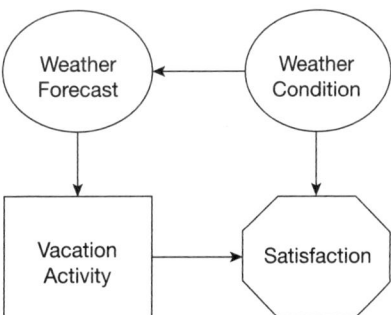

Figure 3.1 *An Influence Diagram*

forecast may depend on the weather condition, when making their choice. The informational arc ending in vacation activity indicates that they will only know the weather forecast when making their choice. In other words, the actual weather condition will be known only after they make their choice. And the only forecast is what they can count upon at this stage. It also follows that vacation activity is independent of weather condition given the weather forecast is known.

3.4. Decision Trees

Not too often do we find outcomes of different alternatives taking place right at the time of decision-making rather than at a later time, rendering the nature and magnitude of an outcome uncertain, affected by chance. There are situations where any choice among the alternatives now will lead to some actions or alternatives later, and we have to choose one, which again will lead us to a situation where we have to decide on some alternatives available at that stage.

Outcomes likely to be associated with the alternatives chosen at different stages depend on alternatives chosen and actions taken at earlier stage(s). We are really not taking decisions sequentially at different stages but visualizing the fallout of a single decision made right now. Thus, we are not in a sequential decision-making situation or a dynamic decision-making situation, dealing with a dynamical system. We are to take one single decision now, with an eye over the entire scenario that is likely to evolve in the future, to evaluate each of the alternatives currently available and finally choose one. In such situations, a decision tree is a simple graphical tool that has been widely used to represent the decision-making process.

The use of a decision tree tends to create an impression that it is a tool for sequential decision-making. Really speaking, a decision tree represents a non-sequential decision-making process where a decision has to be taken now at the end of an analysis of foreseeable scenarios in different steps by assigning different probabilities to each such scenario and carrying out a comparison of the expected utilities (derived from outcomes or values of the objective function) for each terminal decision point. We are not deciding and acting sequentially, as in a sequential decision-making process. The latter involves a chain of decisions, the decision at any stage depending on what is observed at that stage following the decision at the previous stage. In a decision tree, we do not observe any outcomes associated with the possible scenarios. We are simply visualizing those and assuming probabilities for their realization.

The use of a decision tree proceeds in the following several steps:

1. Building up the physical tree structure involves nodes, branches and leaves to represent states of nature, actions (including terminal actions) and decision points as well as outcomes
2. Assigning probabilities to various states of nature and values to the outcomes of different actions
3. Analysing the entire representation to decide on the optimal decision 'now' in terms of a course of action through different possibilities

The bare structure of a decision tree is made up of nodes, represented by small rectangles or circles and line segments connecting the nodes. Nodes can stand for some states of nature or some actions which can be taken or even possible outcomes of an action being taken. Line segments will join an action with each of its possible outcomes and an outcome with a subsequent action. Thus, all reasonable alternatives are visualized. Every alternative course of action represented in the decision will eventually end in some terminal action. Each sequence of nodes and segments ending in a terminal action is called a branch.

Marshall and Oliver (1995) provide a procedure for constructing decision trees once the set of random events and actions have been defined together with their sets of probabilities and respective utilities (cost/pay-off). Much like (sequence) influence diagrams, decision trees are constructed in chronological order and nodes are connected by branches. The steps include are as follows:

1. Draw a branch for each possible action from the first (leftmost or topmost) decision node. If it is a chance node, do the same, drawing a branch for each possible consequence.

2. Label each branch emanating from a chance node with a unique element from the set with the corresponding probability and consequence.
3. Label each branch emanating from a decision node and its respective loss or consequence.
4. Place the consequence values from the set on the terminal nodes at the end of each branch.

An interesting example of a decision tree to represent an investment decision problem was provided by Miller and Starr (1969). It is presented in the following example:

Example 3.2. A company has an option on the drilling rights on a particular property. The company may start drilling right away or it could first initiate a geological assessment survey and then decide whether to drill or to give up drilling. Alternatively, it could first have a seismic test and then decide whether to drill or to stay away. To be on sure footing, it could first have a geological survey followed by a seismic test and then decide whether to go for drilling or not. The following costs of these actions can be taken (in some monetary units):

Geological survey	5,000
Seismic test	25,000
Drilling oil	130,000

As against these costs, the value of oil (if found) would be 500,000.

The different variable outcomes (which essentially reveal the states of nature) can be indicated as follows:

G: Geological survey shows the presence of oil

G': Geological survey fails to show the presence of oil

S: Seismic test shows the presence of oil

S': Seismic test fails to show the presence of oil

O: Oil is present below the property

O': Oil is not present below the property

Probabilities which can be assigned (by the decision-maker to the two ultimate states of nature and conditional probabilities for the outcomes of some preliminary actions of survey and test, given either of these two states of nature) were taken as follows:

$$P(O)=0.2 \text{ and hence } P(O')=0.8$$

$$P(G/O)=0.7 \text{ and hence } P(G'/O)=0.3$$

$$P(G/O')=0.3 \text{ and hence } P(G/O)=0.7$$

$$P(S/O)=0.9 \text{ and } P(S'/O)=0.1$$

$$P(S'/O)=0.2 \text{ and } P(S'/O')=0.8$$

Symbols O, G and S stand for oil is present; geologic survey finds oil, and seismic test finds oil respectively, while their contrary situations are indicated by symbols O', G' and S', respectively.

This is a (non-sequential) binary decision problem involving a choice between two terminal actions (decisions), namely to start drilling immediately or to give up drilling. There are two eventual states of nature, namely oil exists and oil does not exist. There are several intermediate decision points and some outcomes are likely to follow some preceding decisions/actions, and all these are based on some probabilities taken as granted. In a way, the alternatives are: conducting a geologic survey and drilling if oil shows up, making a geologic survey and conducting a seismic test if oil shows up and drilling if the test confirms the presence of oil, taking the seismic test first and proceeding to drill if oil shows up, drilling right away or giving up if either the geologic survey or the seismic test fails to establish the presence of oil. There may be some other alternatives also.

This problem can be well represented by a decision tree as shown hereafter (Figure 3.2). For the analysis, we have to associate a probability with each of the line segments in the decision tree. At the end of several branches leading from a node, each of these receives a probability of 1. Since when only one line segment leads out of a node (decision point), it is certain what the next node will be. To each

66 Decision-making: Concepts, Methods and Techniques

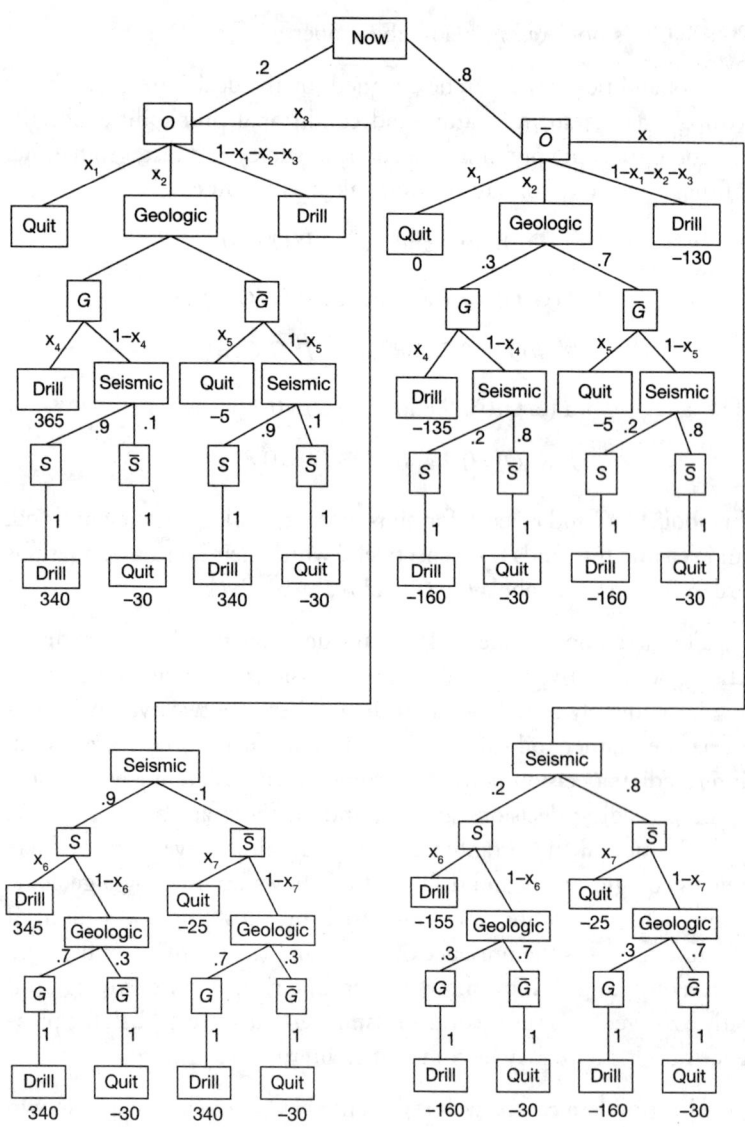

Figure 3.2 A *Tree Diagram Representation*

empty line segment, we will assign a probability x to be determined by following the rules:

1. The sum of all the probabilities on all the line segments leading out of a node must be 1, since one of these segments has to be followed.
2. In every case, the same probability x has to be assigned to corresponding segments in the parts of the tree emanating from O and O'. This reflects the fact that the decision-maker does not know which part of the tree they are on, so far as O and O' are concerned.

The analysis is rather simple. We calculate the expected value for each node as the sum of products of probabilities attached to all the line segments emanating from the node with the expected values of the nodes to which these segments lead. Doing this for each of the terminal nodes, we select the node with the highest expected value as the solution to the problem. In this problem, the highest expected value corresponds to the decision to first conduct a geologic survey and then to drill if the survey shows the presence of oil. This will result in an expected value of 365.000.

3.5. Influence Diagrams and Decision Trees

An influence diagram gives basic information, while a decision tree presents detailed information. This is one reason why the former is less messy, since the latter involves an exponentially increasing number of branches as we add more variables to the study. The influence diagram is more appealing as a graphical display, while the decision tree is often quite unattractive. The influence diagram has the advantage of revealing dependencies among variables, a desirable feature lacking in a decision tree. In fact, the two representations are sometimes looked upon as complementary to each other. Some argue that we should start with an influence diagram and then develop a decision tree. A decision tree cannot represent conditional independence and requires pre-processing of the probabilities involved in the problem.

Both the influence diagram as well as the decision tree provide representation of only symmetrical decision problems. Asymmetry in the context of decision problems may arise in two ways and give rise to (a) structural asymmetry in cases where the value taken by one variable restricts the domain of the other variables and (b) order asymmetry when several orderings of the decisions are possible. To deal with asymmetrical decision problems, we have the decision analytic network (DAN), outlined in the following section.

3.6. Decision Analytic Network

A DAN is a directed acyclic graph with chance nodes (represented by ovals), decision nodes (represented by rectangles) and a utility node (represented by a diamond). Arcs coming into decision nodes represent information that will be available when the decision is made, arcs coming into chance nodes represent probabilistic dependence and arcs coming into a utility node represent what the utility depends on. To augment the network features, we should provide the domain for each random variable as well as the domain for each decision variable. In the following diagram:

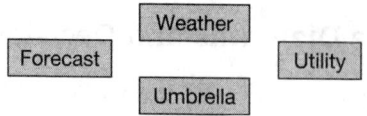

Utility depends on the weather (categorized as sunny and rainy, usually) and the decision to carry an umbrella or not (a dichotomy) based on the information provided by the forecast at the time when the decision to carry an umbrella or not is taken. Depending on the weather and on the decision taken, we will have a utility that could be categorical or even measurable.

In a DAN, a link like XY may imply:

1. Causal inference when Y is a chance node
2. Functional dependence when Y is a utility node
3. Temporal order when both X and Y are decision nodes

4. Revelation when X is a decision node and Y is a chance node
5. Restriction when X and Y are decision or chance nodes

The first three are common in an influence diagram, while the fourth corresponds to an information arc in the influence diagram.

3.7. Gantt Chart

For some relatively simple sequencing problems, Gantt charts have been used to find out the objective function value like the total elapsed time and even to determine the optimal job sequence on each of two machines to minimize this total time. Consider the two-machine, two-job problem in which each of the jobs J_1 and J_2 has to go through machine M_1 first and then machine M_2. Required processing times are indicated as follows:

	M_1	M_2
J_1	2	7
J_2	5	4

From the Gantt charts presented in Figure 3.3, we find the total time for completing the jobs as 13 units of time for the sequence J_1-J_2 and 16 for the sequence J_2-J_1. While we can use this chart to evaluate the time for completion of more than two jobs for each possible sequence, the number of possible sequences will increase exponentially.

Incidentally, there does exist a graphic technique for solving a two-job, m-machine problem. We consider the following a problem with Jobs 1 and 2 and Machines A, B, C and D:

Job 1	Sequence	A	B	C	D
	Time	2	4	5	1
Job 2	Sequence	D	B	A	C
	Time	6	4	2	3

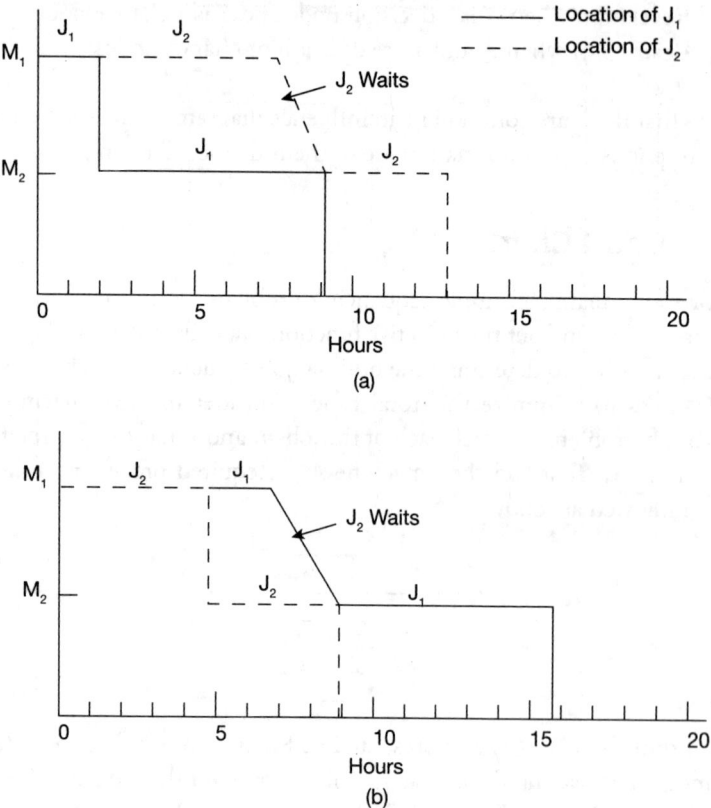

Figure 3.3 A Gantt Chart Representation

In the graph (Figure 3.4) representing the problem, cross-hatched rectangular blocks represent overlaps that must be avoided. A horizontal line corresponds to work on Job 1, while Job 2 remains idle. A vertical line corresponds to work on Job 2, while Job 1 remains idle. The equiangular line represents work on both jobs simultaneously. Consequently, the shortest line consisting of combinations of horizontal, vertical and equiangular lines from the origin to the goal represents an optimal sequence. In this case, it turns out that both jobs can be worked on simultaneously until Job 1 is completed, and then Job 2 is completed. Thus, the total elapsed time comes out at 15 units.

Representation of a Decision Problems 71

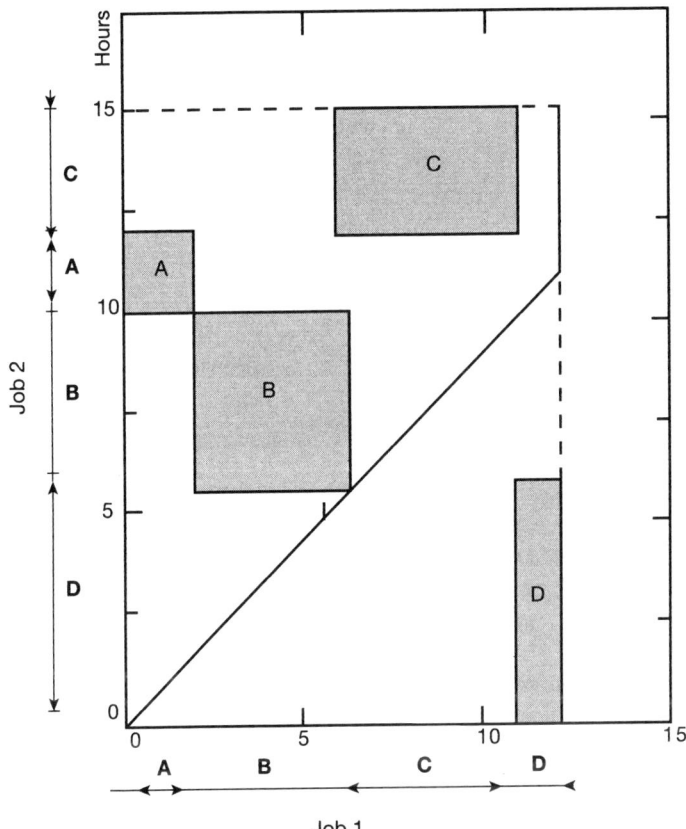

Figure 3.4 *Graph for the Gantt Chart*

3.8. Network Diagrams

Quite a few decision problems in real life can be modelled by networks of different types and solved by using appropriate network algorithms. These include the problem of finding the shortest route between two cities on an existing network of roads, determining the start and completion times for several interlinked activities which together constitute a project, determining the minimum cost flow schedule from oil fields to refineries through a pipeline network and the like.

A network is defined in terms of a finite set of nodes linked by a finite set of arcs or branches. Associated with each network is some type of flow. In general, the flow in a network is limited by the capacity of its arcs, which may be finite or infinite. An arc is said to be directed or oriented if it allows positive flow in one direction and no flow in the opposite direction. A network is directed if all of its arcs are directed. A path is a sequence of distinct branches that join two nodes regardless of the direction of flow in each branch. A path forms a loop or a cycle if it connects a node to itself. A directed loop or a circuit in which all the branches are oriented in the same direction. A connected network is such that every two distinct nodes are connected by at least one path. A tree is a connected network that may involve only a subset of all the nodes in the network, whereas a spanning tree links all the nodes in a network with no loops allowed.

3.8.1. Programme Evaluation and Review Technique (PERT) and Critical Path Method (CPM)

PERT and CPM are network-based methods to assist in the planning, scheduling and controlling projects. A project is a collection of interrelated activities, with each activity consuming time and resources. Activities in a project have to satisfy some precedence relations. And the problem is to find the optimum schedule of activities so that the total time or other resources consumed to complete the project are minimized. First, we have to define the activities in the project, their precedence relationships and their time requirements. Then, the project (and the associated decision problem) is presented as a network that takes care of the precedence relations among the activities. Finally, we carry out network-specific computations to facilitate development of the optimal schedule of activities. The two methods differ in the fact that CPM treats the activity durations as deterministic, while in PERT, we assume a probability distribution for each activity duration. In fact, a beta distribution has been generally assumed to yield the following expression for the expected activity at time T:

$$E(T) = 1/6 \text{ (maximum time} + 4 \times \text{modal time} + \text{minimum time)}$$

Here, the modal time is the time most often taken to complete the activity, while the maximum and minimum times are the pessimistic and optimistic times required. Similarly, the variance of activity time in PERT is estimated as:

$$\text{Var}(T) = (\text{Maximum time} - \text{minimum time})^2/36$$

Each activity in the project is represented by a directed arc (commonly known as an arrow) pointing to the direction of progress in the project. The nodes of the network (also referred to as events) establish precedence relations among the different activities. The following rules are followed to draw the network:

- Each activity is represented by one and only one arrow in the network.
- Each activity has to be identified by two distinct end nodes.
- Before adding an activity to the network, care has to be taken to note activities which must immediately precede this activity, which activities must follow this activity and which activities must run concurrently with the activity being added. Thus, the activity (i, j) can start as soon as all the tasks directed towards i have been completed.
- In order that (i, j) can represent a unique activity, if two or more activities start and the two real activities are labelled as (i, j) and (i, x). The following is the network representation for a project involving 12 activities $A-L$ with the following precedence relations: $A \wedge B, A \wedge C, B \wedge D, B \wedge G, B \wedge K, C \wedge D, C \wedge G, D \wedge E, E \wedge F, F \wedge H, F \wedge L, G \wedge L, G \wedge I, H \wedge J, I \wedge J$ and $K \wedge L$, where $X \wedge Y$ implies that X must be completed before Y can start.

3.8.2. Graphical Evaluation and Review Technique (GERT) and Queuing Graphical Evaluation and Review Technique (Q-GERT)

Project planning and management have taken the help of graphical tools such as PERT and CPM for representation and analysis of decision problems involved since the 1950s. However, these tools make

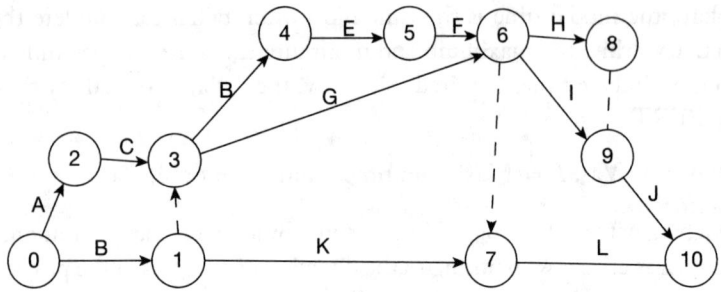

Figure 3.5 A Network Diagram

use of only one type of deterministic node (sinks) and do not accommodate some complex features of real-life projects, particularly in the context of planning and management of research and development projects. In such projects, both successes and failures occur for a project or/and its components, with probabilities that can be anticipated or otherwise incorporated into representing the project and simulating it. There could be feedback about the outcome of some activities, and such feedback may necessitate repetition of the activity. Eventually, we have to deal with a stochastic network for both network logic analysis and for activity time estimation.

In this context, GERT and its modified version, Q-GERT, have been found to be quite useful, especially for R&D projects as well as for other projects where some of the above-noted features appear. The technique was first described by Pritsker and Happ in 1966 (Pritsker, 1979). Subsequent development included Q-GERT, which allows the user to consider queueing (waiting) within the system. The major drawback of GERT is the relatively complex programming (Monte Carlo simulation) required to model the GERT system. However, GERT has been used pretty widely in other contexts, like in reliability modelling.

As mentioned in Wikipedia, GERT uses activity-on-arrow notation only. Nodes are used to connect activities as well as to determine the type and condition of relations between them. Relations concerning activities emanating from node can be (a) deterministic, every activity coming out has probability equal to 1, implying that it will be performed, and (b) each such activity has some probability of appearance. In that way, each task or activity has two parameters, namely duration and probability of appearance.

There are three logical operators in GERT which concern activities coming into a node. These are: XOR—alternative (only one path/activity possible), OR—alternative (one or more paths can be performed) and AND—alternative (all paths have to be performed). The most common is AND, implying that every activity has to happen before an emanating activity can start.

PERT and CPM do not provide alternative paths or activities. They do not allow loops since no activity can be repeated. No decisions are provided in the diagram for PERT or CPM. These do not allow any scaling to replace some detailed groups of activities with one summary task. In PERT, activity times are usually taken to follow the beta distribution over the range (optimistic time, pessimistic time). GERT is free from these limitations, though at the cost of some added complexity.

In Q-GERT, queueing is allowed in front of nodes where more than one path (activity) ends and can route items through servers based on established decision rules.

Consider the case of an R&D project comprehended in terms of five phases or activities, namely (a) formulation of the concrete research problem, (b) research activity to find a solution, (c) proposed solution, (d) prototype development and (e) solution implementation. With a dummy start, the project is initiated with Activity 3–4 which results in the formal statement of the problem to be taken up by the research team. At Node 4, we have to reckon with two different possibilities, namely (a) the problem was not adequately defined and hence originated Activity 4–3, which means the first activity has to be repeated, and (b) the project proceeds through Path 4–5 to the next phase or task. Completion of Activity 5–6 may lead to four alternative outcomes, namely (a) it may be found out that the problem was incorrectly defined to start with, not allowing a viable solution proposal to be developed, (b) research done to develop the proposed solution was found to be insufficient to cause the loop indicated by Path 6–4 to repeat the process of research into the problem, (c) analysis may reveal that no implementable solution does exist; this is a typical outcome leading to Path 6–7 referred to as project washout or failure, and (d) when the proposed solution has been found to be implementable, we proceed on Path 6–8 to develop the prototype. Execution of this task leads to two possible outcomes, namely (a) successful project completion at Node 9 and (b) redevelopment of the prototype is felt necessary, causing Loop 8–8. If a satisfactory prototype is developed, the solution is implemented on Path 8–9. (Node 9 is the second network 'sink' corresponding to project success, while Node 7 represents another 'sink' implying project termination without success.) Figure 3.6 provides the diagrammatic representation.

Whenever more than one outcome is envisaged, the probability of occurrence of each outcome has to be estimated. As in PERT, we have to provide an estimated duration for each activity in terms of the minimum, maximum and mode (most likely value). Similarly, estimates of fixed and variable costs have also to be worked out. Some of the activities may not involve any costs in some projects. For activity duration, we may specify the distribution as either beta, as in PERT, or we may assume the duration to be constant.

With these inputs, the GERT model can be simulated a large number of times. We can find out the probabilities of the terminal events of project washout and project successful completion, as well as the corresponding estimated expected time and expected cost.

The network itself can be modified to reflect the impacts of alternative strategies. GERT networks are usually sensitive to outcome probability changes. However, the network is not as sensitive to activity time changes as node branching probability changes. Information about the probability of project washout may be vital to project management in assessing the impact of resource and technology input options so that this probability can be minimized. Also, an early indication of this probability may alert management to a quick diversion of project manpower to other projects.

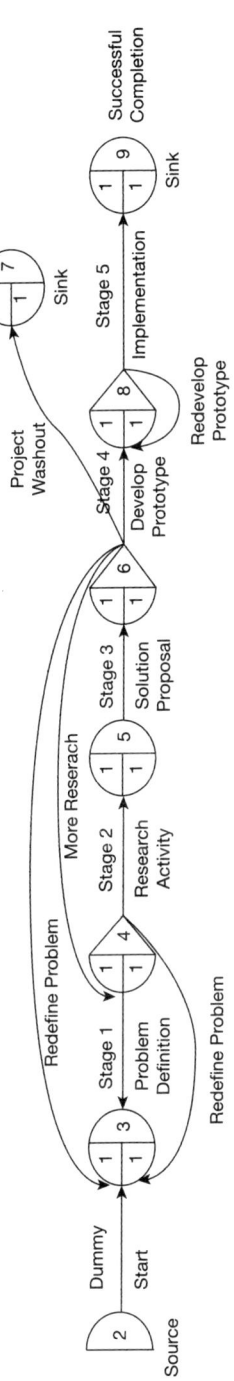

Figure 3.6 Showing a GERT Representation of an R&D Project

CHAPTER 4

Decisions under Certainty and Uncertainty

4.1. Introduction

Decision-making under certainty is not necessarily a simple job. In the context of general decision or choice theory and dealing with the general optimization problem, we may face a host of situations where the data pertaining to the alternatives or options, including constraints imposed on them, outcome functions and objective(s) to be achieved by solving the decision problem, are all known to us completely, and we take decisions—in a relatively straightforward manner or through a complicated exercise—under certainty. The point to be emphasized is that 'certainty' here does not always imply 'simplicity', and we come across a variety of problems as well as a variety of solution approaches to such problems.

We will first consider decision problems under uncertainty, which can be represented appropriately by a pay-off matrix and then discuss the different procedures to get the optimum or 'best' choice among the alternatives, using different optimality principles. The concepts of pay-off, utility and regret have been explained in the first chapter.

Such problems may not sometimes fit into a matrix representation and except for portraying a reference situation, these problems have lost their pristine importance. Uncertainty in decision-making may extend to situations where we do not have adequate information about the number and nature of alternatives or about the possible states in which the underlying system could be or when we do not exactly know the outcomes of a particular alternative in any possible state of nature.

In the second part, we proceed to hint at the very wide range of optimization problems which can be clubbed as problems of decision-making under certainty. A lot of variations should be recognized in this context in terms of the number and nature of objective functions which work as the criteria for choice. It may be pointed out that some such problems may involve complex and even covert statements, and in some cases, the alternatives are not explicitly recognized. Indeed, the entire gamut of decision problems which are represented by (deterministic) mathematical models and solved by using classical optimization tools or mathematical programming algorithms, even going beyond the traditional programming formulations, can be treated under the caption 'decision-making under certainty', and this characterization is a clear indication of the vastness of the subject and of the synoptic nature of the presentation contained in this chapter.

As is pretty well known, mathematical programming (focusing only on deterministic aspects) has grown into a vast arena for academic activities and for applications in real-life decision-making. Numerous facets of the subject have been dealt with by a whole host of authors—economists, mathematicians, statisticians and social scientists—to produce a deluge of expository, research and review articles published in a wide array of periodicals. Mathematical programming in its entirety cannot be discussed adequately in a single book, howsoever voluminous and well written. Even presenting an overview is a problem, and what has been attempted in this chapter is a collection of brief expositions of some selected topics pieced together just to indicate the roles of various optimization methods in the context of decision-making under certainty, though not avoiding conceptual and computational complexity.

Before we close the canvas for this chapter, we add that interval programming illustrates decision-making under uncertainty, where uncertainty about coefficients involved in the objective function and/or in the constraints is expressed by giving an interval of values for any such coefficient. The lower and upper bounds for the interval are derived from historical data. The methodological problem lies in the existence of several partial orderings in the set of intervals, giving rise to several types of solutions. This approach to dealing with uncertainty has been primarily applied to linear objective functions, though some work has been reported in the area of fractional linear programming (LP). Sengupta and Pal (2009) refer to the advantages of using intervals to represent uncertain or imprecise measurements over fuzzy set theoretic or probabilistic approaches for solving real-world decision-making problems.

4.2. Decision-making under Uncertainty

Consider the problem faced by a farmer who likes to decide on the use of their farmland during the coming sowing season. Based on past experience and other relevant information, they can be helped to formulate their problem in terms of a simple matrix.

Use of Land	Pay-Off (Gain) in Some Monetary Unit			
	Adequate Rain	Moderate Rain	Light Rain	Drought
Grow paddy	50	40	30	0
Grow wheat	35	60	40	−5
Grow soyabean	−50	100	45	−10
Grazing	12	15	15	10

There have been four optimality principles or rather different criteria, based on different logical propositions and proposed by different scientific workers to choose the best possible option or alternative. The resulting choices are quite likely to differ among themselves, except in some pay-off matrices, which reveal some special features.

4.2.1. Laplace's Maximum Average Pay-Off Criterion

Laplace argued that in the absence of any knowledge about the likelihood of realization for any state of nature, we should take them as equally likely and consider the maximum average (arithmetic mean) pay-off against an alternative as the criterion for choice. Simple to compute, this procedure led to Laplace being characterized as 'rational'. In philosophical terms, nature does not favour any particular state in preference to any other.

In this problem, average pay-offs come out at 30, 32.5, 21.25 and 13 respectively for the alternatives in the order listed in the table above. Thus, growing wheat is the best choice.

4.2.2. Wald's Maximin Pay-Off Criterion

Wald, who made the initial contribution to statistical decision theory, has been portrayed as a 'pessimist' who remains prepared for the worst, arguing that nature will be most unfavourable and will not allow any outcome better than the minimum for any alternative. Thus, the best choice is the one for which the minimum pay-off is the maximum. In the example considered, the minimum pay-offs are 0, −5, −50 and 10 respectively, and the maximum of these minima corresponds to the option to allow grazing animals on the land.

4.2.3. Hurwicz Criterion considering both Minimum and Maximum Pay-offs

Hurwicz is not a pessimist outright, nor does he believe that nature will be most favourable to yield the maximum pay-off for any given option. However, the decision-maker may use their own belief in either of these two extreme positions and consider a weighted average of the maximum and the minimum pay-offs corresponding to each option for the purpose of choosing the best option. In fact, the criterion makes use of the 'expected' pay-off obtained as α max pay-off $+(1-\alpha)$ min pay-off, where α, reflecting the degree of belief of the decision-maker in nature being most favourable, is referred to as the coefficient of optimism. This coefficient may vary from one decision-maker to another, yielding possibly different optimal choices. It is, of course, possible that the same choice remains true over a certain range of α values and that would make the choice a robust one. Hurwicz has been mentioned as an 'adventurist' in the annals of decision-making.

With a coefficient of 0.80, the expected pay-offs are respectively 40, 47, 70 and 10, and the best choice would be to grow soyabeans. However, if we take a coefficient of 0.4, the expected pay-offs become 20, 21, 10 and 3 respectively, so that the best choice would be to grow wheat.

4.2.4. Minimax Regret Criterion of Savage

Savage, also known for his contributions to statistical decision theory, introduced the concept of regret, explained in Chapter 1. He looks at the likely impact of a decision or choice made in the face of uncertainty on the emotional satisfaction or otherwise of the decision-maker when some state of nature is eventually realized, and the decision-maker finds that either the decision was correct or it was wrong. The extent of dissatisfaction that arises later with a wrong decision, resulting in the loss of opportunity to achieve some higher pay-off under the state of nature observed later, as the regret associated with the decision under a state of nature can be estimated now—at the time of decision-making—by converting the pay-off matrix to a regret matrix and then applying the minimax regret criterion for choosing the best option. Because of this cautionary approach, Savage has been accepted as 'a bad loser'.

The regret matrix, in our case, works out as follows:

Use of Land	Regret			
	(Rainfall Amount)	Adequate	Moderate	Light Drought
Grow paddy	0	60	15	10
Grow wheat	15	40	5	15
Grow soybean	100	0	0	20
Allow grazing	38	85	30	0

The maximum regrets are 60, 40, 100 and 85, and going by the minimax regret criterion, we should accept 'growing wheat' as the best choice.

To sum up, we note that different criteria can identify possible different choices as the optimal ones in a decision problem. Each criterion has a logical basis, and it is quite relevant for the decision-maker to note the logical basis behind the criterion they may choose.

4.3. Info-gap Decision Analysis

Sometimes, we have to reckon with situations where we are uncertain not merely about the parameters in a parametric model used in the decision analysis but also about the shape of the functional relation or the functional form. Such situations which have not been addressed successfully through probabilistic methods or fuzzy numbers and fuzzy relations have often been referred to as 'severe uncertainty' or 'deep uncertainty' situations.

Before we venture into this difficult situation of severe or deep uncertainty, let us just recall Wald's maximin principle that underlies what is called 'worst case analysis' and prepares the decision-maker for the worst possible state of the system. To be even simpler, we consider the possible (decision, state) pairs and for each we find out the extent to which a decision alternative satisfies the constraint associated with that state, as well as the outcome or the pay-off yielded by the pair. It is quite possible that uncertainty about states of nature causes uncertainty about pay-offs corresponding to each of the alternatives, as well as uncertainty about the feasibility or ability of each alternative to satisfy relevant constraints, and in some situations, constraints could be state-specific. Thus, a comprehensive account of uncertainty should consider both the pay-off and feasibility aspects of each alternative. In Section 4.2.2, we mentioned the use of the maximin principle to take care of only pay-off uncertainty. To illustrate the wider perspective, we look at the following example given by Sniedovich (2016).

Example 4.1. In the following table, the symbol (p, V) represents the pay-off for an alternative that satisfies all the constraints, while the pair (p, x) stands for pay-off for an alternative that fails to satisfy some of the constraints. The pair (d, s) represents the (decision-alternative, state). As in optimization theory, the maximin principle also gives precedence to constraint satisfaction over pay-off, implying that the outcome (p, V) is preferred to the outcome (p', x) irrespective of the values p and p'.

(Decision, State)	State 1	State 2	State 3	State 4	State 5
d_1	(55, x)	(43, V)	(18, V)	(63, V)	(37, x)
d_2	(38, V)	(22, V)	(11, V)	(12, V)	(10, V)
d_3	(85, V)	(83, x)	(23, x)	(72, V)	(50, x)

According to Wald's principle, as stated above, the worst cases yielding the minimum pay-offs are (37, x), (10, V) and (23, x) respectively for d_1, d_2 and d_3, and the best alternative is d_2. If we consider only the feasible (alternative, state) pairs, the minimum pay-offs are 118, 10 and 72 so that d_3 is the maximin alternative. Furthermore, if the feasibility condition is just ignored (as in Section 4.2.2), the minima would be 37, 10 and 23 respectively, and the first alternative would be the best.

While the maximin principle is hailed as quite logical and acceptable in the face of uncertainty, there are genuine difficulties associated with the principle. Implementation of this principle quite often mandates radical changes in the existing environment and may be quite costly. Further, the worst case may be extremely rare, and the opportunity costs for some of the feasible and better alternatives may be high. Also, a rather sticky philosophical question is raised about the implicit assumption in the maximin principle that 'nature'—as if playing the role of an equally wise decision-maker—tries to act as an adversary, minimizing the decision-maker's pay-off for whatever alternative the latter may choose. In some cases, an important question is: How bad is worst? If the 'worst' is substantially poorer than the next best, should we go out to guard ourselves against that worst scenario?

Ben-Haim (2001, 2006) offered the information-gap (popularly mentioned as 'info-gap') decision theory in this context. This theory has been applied to a wide variety of problems in biological conservation, homeland security, medicine, engineering, economics, etc. Of course, some of its pitfalls have been pointed out by Sniedovich (2006) and a few others.

Briefly, in the words of Ben-Haim, the info-gap decision theory is a non-probabilistic method for prioritizing alternatives and making choices and decisions under deep/severe uncertainty. An info-gap is the disparity between what is known and what is wanted for a responsible decision. The info-gap analysis does not presume a worst-case analysis (the basis behind Wald's maximin principle) or reliable probability distributions. Info-gap decision theory offers two new concepts, namely robustness and opportuneness. The robustness of an alternative is the greatest horizon of uncertainty up to which the alternative satisfies critical outcome requirements. On the other hand, the opportuneness of a decision alternative is the least horizon of uncertainty at which the decision enables better-than-anticipated outcomes. The robustness strategy sacrifices the outcome and maximizes the immunity to errors or surprises. This differs from outcome optimization. The robustness function demonstrates the trade-off between immunity to error and the quality of the outcome. It shows that knowledge-based predicted outcomes have no robustness against uncertainty in that knowledge. In an innovation dilemma, the decision-maker must choose between two alternatives, where one is putatively better than the other but is more uncertain.

The minimax (maximin) and info-gap analysis both require prior judgements by the decision-maker. Either identify a model or contingency (worst-case analysis) or specify the worst tolerable outcome (info-gap analysis). These prior judgements are different and, thus, corresponding alternative selections may not agree in the two cases.

Equalling order quantity, with or without shortages and excesses being allowed, involves a single decision variable, like order quantity (in the case of purchase inventory) or production lot size (in case of production inventory), and we usually have a problem with decision-making under certainty. There could be generalized models allowing different quantities to be procured for different reorder intervals and allowing reorder intervals to be of different lengths or incorporating quantity discounts into price, etc. Similarly, an asset replacement problem like finding the time (age) at which an equipment should be replaced by a new one, given the costs of usage and maintenance as functions of age, salvage value at a particular age and rate of discount on money illustrates a problem of decision-making under certainty. The discounted present net value at any age may be taken as the criterion to find the optimal replacement time.

4.4. Interval Programming Problem

Interval programming models decision problems where the parameters (coefficients in the objective function or/and in the constraints) are not exactly known, nor are they estimated or approximated but are allowed perturbations within closed intervals. Usually, LP problems with such parameters have been discussed, though the method has been applied to multi-objective as well as fractional LP problems also. Unlike classical LP problems, interval linear programming (IvLP) problems are not amenable to convenient transformations to desired forms to impose non-negativity restrictions on decision variables or to convert some inequality constraints into linear equations because of the dependence problem in interval analysis. Combining some values (not necessarily the bounds) from the intervals for coefficients defining constraints, the solution space could be infeasible or unbounded. Similarly, with coefficients in the objective function given as intervals, we get infinitely many solutions. Chinneck and Ramadan (2000), Hladik (2009), Luo and Li (2013), among some others, discuss various aspects of IvLP and solutions thereof.

IvLP has been applied to capital budgeting, production planning, plastic limit analysis of structures, mixing and blending problems, etc.

To optimize an interval objective function, we need to have an order relation over close intervals, and we do not have any unique one. Saocheng (1994) formulated two LP problems, one with the largest possible feasible region and providing the most favourable version (with single values of the coefficients chosen from the respective intervals) of the objective function to yield the 'best' optimum solution and the other with the smallest feasible region leading to the 'worst' optimal solution. Thus, we get a range of objective function values that again speaks of the uncertainty about the actual optimum value. Inuiguchi and Sakawa (1995) considered an IvLP problem with objective function coefficients in closed intervals and proposed the closest single solution, namely the minimax regret solution, by minimizing the maximum difference between the values of the objective function for any two versions of the objective function.

A second type of interval programming problem is illustrated by an LP problem in which the linear inequality constraints have both lower and upper bounds. Thus, the problem to minimize $z = C'X$ subject to $U \geq AX \geq L$, $X \geq 0$ is an interval programming problem in which L and U are constant column vectors. We now define the slack vector $Y \geq 0$ such that $AX + Y = U$. Thus, the problem under consideration is equivalent to the problem:

Maximize $z = CX$ subject to $AX + Y = U$, $U - L \geq Y \geq 0$, $X \geq 0$

Luo and Li (2013) consider optimal solutions to IvLP problems from a unified framework, proposing weak and strong feasibility as well as weak and strong optimality of solutions and providing a means to check these properties of solutions. Allowing coefficients in the objective functions, constraint matrix and resource (right-hand side) vector to lie in intervals, IvLP can be looked upon as a family of linear programmes written in the form:

Min $c'x$ subject to $x \in M(A, b)$

Here, $A = [A_1, A_2]$ $A_2 \geq A \geq A_1$ and $b = [b_1, b_2]$ $b_2 \geq b \geq b_1$

Similar is the case with vector c. One of the following three forms of $M(A, b)$ is usually assumed:

$$M(A, b) = [x : Ax = b \; x \geq 0]$$
$$= [x : b \geq Ax]$$
$$= [x : b \geq Ax, x \geq 0]$$

The following example cited by them illustrates a small part of the above discussion.

The IvLP problem is to minimize:

$$[-1, 0]\, x_1 + [-2, 0]\, x_2 + [-1, 2]\, x_3 \text{ subject to}$$

$$3 \geq x_1 + 2 x_2 + [-1, 1]\, x_3$$

$$[4, 5] \geq x_1 + [-1, 3]\, x_2 + [1, 2]\, x_3$$

$$x_1,\, x_2,\, x_3 \geq 0$$

It can be easily seen that $x^* = (1, 1, 0)'$ is a strong, feasible solution to this IvLP. It can also be shown that this solution is a weak optimal solution to the IvLP since it can be easily verified to be an optimal solution to the following LP problem. To minimize:

$$-x_1 - 2x \text{ subject to } 3 \geq x_1 + 2x_2 \text{ and } 4 \geq x_1 + x_2 + x_3 \quad x_1\, x_2\, x_3 \geq 0$$

4.5. Decision-making under Certainty

As indicated earlier, quite a few problems in decision-making covered under operations research can be put under this category. For example, inventory problems with known demand, known and constant (may be zero) lead time and supply exactly equalling order quantity, with or without shortages and excesses being allowed, involve a single decision variable like order quantity (in the case of purchase inventory) or production lot size (in the case of production inventory), and we usually have a problem with decision-making under certainty. There could be generalized models allowing different quantities to be procured for different reorder intervals and allowing reorder intervals to be of different lengths or incorporating quantity discounts into price, etc. Similarly, an asset replacement problem like finding the time (age) at which an equipment should be replaced by a new one, given the costs of usage and maintenance as functions of age, salvage value at a particular age and rate of discount on money illustrates a problem with decision-making under certainty. The discounted present net value at any age may be taken as the criterion to find the optimal replacement time.

Unlike the above problems, which do not require the use of any programming algorithm, there are decision problems which are usually considered within the ambit of mathematical programming. The transportation problem in which quantities of a material/entity are available at several sources, quantities required at several different destinations (warehouses or stores or distribution centres) and the unit cost of transportation from each source to each destination are all known constants. We are required to decide on the quantity to be transported from each of the sources to each of the destinations so that the total cost of transportation is minimized. Constraints like demands at destinations to be exactly met (if the total quantity available does not pose a problem) may have to be satisfied. In this case, an alternative or a strategy consists of a set of quantities specified by the source × destination combination. This problem is generally formulated as a LP model and solved accordingly. A similar problem is known as the assignment problem, in which some jobs have to be assigned to the same number of persons in such a way that the overall performance effectiveness is maximized, given the effectiveness of each person on each of the jobs.

In fact, many problems of decision-making under certainty are better recognized in terms of the procedures—mostly mathematical programming methods—adopted to solve them. These problems vary in respect of (a) the nature of alternatives along with the constituent decision variable(s) as well as the nature and size of the space occupied by the alternatives—in some cases, the alternatives admit of ready identification, while in certain others these have to be identified following some procedure, (b) the nature of constraints to be satisfied by the alternatives to qualify as being 'feasible'—in some problems these are just minor and obvious restrictions on the decision variable(s) like non-negativity or lying in a bounded interval, while in certain others constraints could be in terms of some equations or inequalities, (c) the nature and number of objective functions—most problems may deal with a single objective function, while multiple objectives may be involved in some others, and the objective function(s) may be linear or non-linear of various forms or even step functions and (d) the number of decision-makers involved, not in a competitive situation, but in a complementary framework.

In the subsequent sections, we provide brief expositions of some selected solution methods for problems of the above kinds, stating the types of decision problems that are amenable to these methods for their solution.

4.6. Unstructured Decision Problems

Decision problems faced by an individual or an organization may not necessarily involve any uncertainty about the outcomes of different options or alternatives, as they are affected by the states of nature. However, all possible alternatives may not be certainly known or one may be in doubt about all possible states of nature that may arise during implementation. In such situations, we may not be fortunate enough to have a structured representation of the decision problem. The alternatives could be nominal or even ordinal in character and the outcomes could also be just ordinal, amenable to ranking in some order of priority.

Dealing with the problem of estimating an unknown population parameter (may be a vector) based on a sample of observations on a random variable whose probability distribution involves the parameter, we may regard different possible rules or methods for generating estimates as the decision alternatives, like the method of moments, the method of maximum likelihood, the method of least squares or the method based on quantiles. One can think of other methods, and it may be difficult to get an exhaustive set of such methods. Going further, we note that within each such method we have ample choice of some decision variables. For example, in the method of moments, the order(s) of the sample moment(s) or in the case of the method based on quantiles, the order(s) of the quantile(s) or the choice of the function to be minimized in the method of least squares, etc., can be decided by the statistician, and there seems to be no end. Sometimes, we consider convex linear combinations of two different estimators as our estimators, and there exist infinitely many such combinations. Fortunately, once an estimator is chosen, its outcome or pay-off in terms of properties like bias or sampling variance can be computed exactly or approximately. In fact, a good amount of research continues in search of newer and newer estimators, and we can only have a limited choice of an alternative within a pre-specified class of alternatives.

In the burgeoning area of market research, market segmentation based on different criteria, like considerations of price, quality and service, besides demographic differentials, is often recommended for making a strategic decision to launch a new product or service initially in one segment for the purpose of assessing the need for a change. If the objective is to choose one segment for the launch that will yield a fair idea about demand for the product or service, each segment can be treated as an alternative and pay-off, or outcome figures will have to be collected for a comparison across segments. There is no unique segmentation principle and no exhaustive set of segments in general. All that can be claimed in such a context is the choice of a specified segmentation approach adopted.

The third form of uncertainty is associated with pay-offs or outcomes of an alternative, as can be associated with a given state of nature. This is quite expected if the outcome of a choice can only be assessed after its implementation, and it is pretty difficult to predict the outcome or pay-off, especially in situations where implementation can invite many uncertainties and cause many deviations from the expected path.

4.7. Mathematical Programming

As remarked earlier, deterministic optimization embodied in mathematical programming is usually concerned with constrained optimization. We have a set of decision variables, and the possible sets of their values correspond to the options or alternatives. Constraints are generally imposed on these variables, like requiring them to be (a) non-negative or (b) bounded on either sides(s) or (c) integers or just binary or a combination of both. Additional constraints may be in terms of given relations (equations or inequalities) connecting decision variables with available resources. There will be one objective function or several such functions which have to be maximized or minimized. The objective function(s) could be linear or non-linear, including ratios of linear and non-linear functions, polynomials or posynomials or even non-regular step functions. In fact, a lot of discussions have been held about the mathematical nature of the objective function(s).

Alternatives can be easily identified in some problems, while it may be difficult and even unnecessary to identify all of them initially in some other problems. Verification of constraints to establish feasibility or otherwise of alternatives may be a straightforward task in most cases and may be quite problematic in some.

Dynamic programming opens up a new chapter, and it makes a valuable contribution to sequential or multistage decision-making. As a method of optimization, it is involved in formulating and solving decision problems under probabilistic uncertainty represented by the Markov decision process. Mathematically, being a bit different from other single-stage optimization methods, dynamic programming, introduced by Bellman in the 1950s, finds wide applications in diverse fields. A discussion of deterministic as well as stochastic dynamic programming methods and their applications has been an essential part of any text on mathematical programming. We intend to include a very brief account of deterministic dynamic programming in this section, and we postpone a reference to stochastic dynamic programming to the next chapter on decision-making under risk.

A second area of interest—both in academic research and in practical applications—is the topic of integer programming in view of the fact that, in many applications of LP, in particular, the decision variables are bound to be integers, like the number of batches or lots to be produced, the number of workers to be assigned a task or the orders in which several tasks are to be performed. Fractional programming has become quite a prominent topic in the context of data envelopment analysis (DEA) as well as in dealing with stochastic optimization problems. One of the earliest problems of this type (though not formally mentioned as a fractional programming problem) arose as the equilibrium model for an expanding economy in which the growth rate is the maximum of the smallest of several output–input ratios.

A class of optimization problems that have led to the development of several heuristics for solving the computationally complex problems of combinatorial optimization. To mention a few, the knapsack problem, the graph colouring problem, the travelling salesman problem, the sequencing problem, the vehicle routing problem and the set covering problem have been studied by many investigators who continue their search for more efficient solutions to these and similar problems.

Not to make this section too long and too heavily loaded with mathematical details, we avoid discussing—even briefly—a few topics such as fractional programming, multi-objective optimization, multi-level programming and goal programming, along with compromise programming. Separate sections could also have been devoted to dynamic programming with sub-sections dealing with deterministic and stochastic decision-making problems as well as to combinatorial optimization involving integer decision variables but have not been attempted. However, interested readers can easily access well-written texts and reference books as well as review articles (cited at the end) on these and related topics.

CHAPTER 5

Decision-making under Risk

5.1. Introduction

Decisions are often taken in situations where we are uncertain about the pay-off corresponding to a feasible alternative. The pay-off depends on the state of nature likely to prevail when the pay-off is to be realized, and we know, at best, the probabilities with which different states of nature will be realized. Such probabilities are less likely to be data-based and/or objectively calculated and usually reflect the decision-maker's subjective degrees of belief in the realizations of the different states, looked upon as random. Thus, a part of our information is an assumed probability distribution (discrete or continuous) over the set of all possible or imaginable states of nature, and this distribution induces a distribution of pay-offs associated with any feasible alternative.

A somewhat different situation may also be covered by decision-making under risk. There could be a single state of nature, known for certainty. However, constraints could involve random variables as coefficients in linear or non-linear relations connecting the decision variables. As a result, the feasibility or otherwise of an alternative becomes a probabilistic event, and we have to account for this in our search for the optimal.

Stochastic optimization deals with a class of structured decision-making problems under risk, though developments in stochastic optimization were not necessarily motivated by the need to arrive at optimal or good decisions under risk.

While probabilities take care of randomness associated with pay-offs, lack of precise knowledge or the presence of ambiguity about the outcomes has been sometimes treated as a somewhat different phenomenon and recourse has been taken to fuzzy sets to analyse such situations. In fact, fuzzy decision-making, including a large component of fuzzy mathematical programming, has grown rapidly over the years to embrace new developments in fuzzy set theory, like intuitionistic fuzzy sets.

Looking outside the realm of general optimization problems, decision-making under risk has taken into account something called a reference point in converting the outcomes or pay-offs to any option or alternative under any particular state of nature that takes into account the decision-maker's current situation in terms of assets, wealth or welfare, since the latter tends to influence the choice among the options. The concept and use of utility introduced by Neumann and Morgenstern (1944) laid the basis for expected utility as the basis for choice under risk. Some years later, the prospect theory based on actual behaviour of participants in some financial bets or gambles motivated Kahneman and Tversky (1984) to develop the prospect theory to explain the actual human decision-making process using the concept of a value function and the weighting of probabilities given in the problem.

The present chapter is devoted to a discussion of Stochastic optimization in some details, along with some illustrations of how the expected utility theory and the prospect theory have been used in the context of decision-making under risk. Some recent developments in the field have also been considered briefly. This was followed by a rather short presentation on fuzzy mathematical programming and fuzzy decision-making outside the ambit of mathematical programming. Incidentally, decision-making under the Dempster–Shafer (D–S) theory of evidence has also been illustrated. Furthermore, as mentioned earlier, an attempt has been made to familiarize the reader with the essentials of prospect theory and the related concept of priority heuristic.

5.2. Approaches to Decision-making under Risk

Several different approaches for analysis and resolution of decision problems under risk have emerged over time and can be broadly categorized as expected utility (money value) theory, prospect theory, risk-sensitivity theory and heuristics theory by taking into account economic 'rationality' as well as empirical evidence bearing on human behaviour in risky situations. The expected utility theory and the risk-sensitivity theory are normative, while the prospect theory and the heuristics approach are descriptive. A basic differentiation can be made in terms of the criterion used to choose the 'optimal' solution. Utility and its measurement have been discussed in Chapter 1, and prospect theory and the use of heuristics, along with a brief explanation of risk sensitivity, will be discussed in the current chapter. Each of these approaches has invited criticism on some count or the other. For the risk-sensitivity theory, empirical support is still not adequate.

5.2.1. Risk-sensitivity Theory

This theory was proposed by Caraco et al. (1980) based on some experimental evidence on the food foraging behaviour of a certain type of bird that revealed risk preference and risk-aversion of the animal depending on his energy budget. (This prompted the authors to argue that decision-makers shift from risk aversion to risk preference in situations of need, where need is defined as the disparity between the decision-maker's present state and the desired state or goal). This disparity varies from one environment or time to another. In fact, it is theorized that decision-makers do not just maximize some desirable outcomes, but they avoid decisions that fail to satisfy their needs. In that way, this approach to decision-making is aimed at 'satisficing' rather than 'optimizing'. One of the major problems with applying this theory is the difficulty of identifying and even quantifying the 'need' for an individual decision-maker in a given situation. The 'environment' in which alternatives exist delineates the risks associated with the latter, and the 'need' assessment relative to the outcomes leads to preferences or aversions.

The issues in testing the applicability of this approach (through a specific model to suit a particular decision-making situation) include the manner in which the decision-maker evaluates an option to satisfy their need based on the information available to predict the mean outcome as well as the variability (indicated by the variance, say) in outcome corresponding to an option or alternative. The need could be multidimensional and may involve both qualitative and quantitative aspects, like a reward (or loss) amount, the delay in its realization and its convertibility to some other entity related to the need or the energy budget of the decision-maker. Aggregation of the different dimensions of need using appropriate weights after due normalization may pose interesting problems. Past information about the outcome and its behaviour may not be adequate for the purpose of prediction, especially when all of it may not be duly recalled by the decision-maker and resources may not allow new information to be collected and processed. A second issue could be created by indifference in terms of the mean-variance criterion among quite a few options. In such cases, what is 'fit' for the decision-maker may have to be operationalized in terms of some other criterion.

These and other related issues have, in some sense, circumscribed the use of this theory in real-life decision-making situations. Some of these limitations have been mentioned in the works of Kacelnik and Bateson (1996), while a good account of the theory can be found in the works of Mishra (2014).

5.3. Stochastic Optimization

Stochastic prescriptive (optimization) models represent several phenomena studied in operations management which involve probabilities associated with different possible outcomes of any alternative or action corresponding to different states of nature (usually depending on the actions or alternatives). As, in other cases, an alternative or a strategy may involve a number of (non-random) decision variables, there could be several possible states of nature, each specified in terms of a set of values or levels of some factors and the outcome or pay-off associated with an alternative for a given state of nature may be characterized by several consequences, all of which possibly can be expressed in monetary units. All the variables involved in the alternatives, the states of nature and the outcomes could be continuous. (It is important to note that out of the variables in the state of nature which determine the outcome of any alternative, only one or a few can vary from one state to another, while the other can remain the same as known constants.) Some models could be relatively simple, others could be quite complicated. However, classical calculus, along with the use of Lagrange multipliers—whenever needed—provides the solutions or 'best' alternatives.

Thus, in a stock-building operation, different quantities to be procured (against purchase orders or production plans) represent alternatives, demands that may arise are states of nature and shortages or excesses with their cost consequences stand for pay-offs or outcomes. Constraints on the alternatives are known and non-random. Demand is random with a known or assumed probability distribution. The objective function is thus random, and we have to find the optimal order quantity or quantity to be produced. Outcomes could be further affected by random lead times or/and by random variations in quantity delivered or produced against an order quantity or a planned quantity. In the classical newsboy problem, demand X has a distribution with a distribution function $f(x)$, and for an order quantity q, the total expected inventory cost (involving only excess and shortage costs of c_1 and c_2 respectively per unit) works out as: $T(q) = c_1 f(q-x) f(x)\, dx + c_2 f(x-q) f(x)\, dx$, which directly yields the optimal order quantity as $q_0 = F^{-1}(c_2/(c_1+c_2))$.

A plethora of probabilistic inventory models with strategy vectors defined in terms of order quantity, order preponement time, credit period, rate of discount offered, etc., and states of nature described by demand, fraction of defectives in supply, lead time, rate of decay during storage, and the like have been studied by a whole host of research workers with usually a single objective, namely the expected total cost.

Similarly, in a waiting-line problem, alternatives could be different numbers of servers provided by a service system to render service at random times to customers who arrive at random instants of time. Assuming all joining customers are patient and the holding capacity is sufficiently large to accommodate all incoming customers, the number of customers waiting for service at any time or the number of servers remaining idle at any time are random outcomes, again with their (direct and indirect) cost consequences. The decision problem could be to find the number of servers to be provided such that the total cost of customers waiting for service and servers remaining idle in a stationary state is at minimum.

An important operation in maintenance management is the replacement of equipment to arrest its increasing operational costs and in the case of an item which fails at a random point in time. Thus, two types of replacement, namely on failure and in anticipation of failure, have to be carried out to ensure uninterrupted service by the system with the stochastically failing item. One replacement policy is to replace an item at times $T, 2T, 3T, \ldots$, or at intervals of time T in anticipation of failure and on failure whenever it occurs. The cost of a unit replacement in anticipation of failure or of a planned replacement per unit is C_p, while that for a failure replacement is C_f, usually larger than C_p. WE assume that the probability distribution of failure time for the item has an increasing failure rate. The optimal value of the decision variable T has to be worked out by minimizing the expected total cost of replacement per unit time. This comes out as:

$$F(T) = 1/T \text{ [expected no. of failures in } (0, T) \times C_f + n\ C_p]$$

$$= 1/T\ [n\ F(T)\ C_f + n\ C_p]$$

where n is the number of items in operation with independently and identically distributed failure times. Here again, we do not need any programming algorithm to find the optimal value of planned replacement time T.

We can just go on illustrating such situations in which decisions under risk have to be taken. What is generally done in such cases is to reduce the problem to one of decision-making under certainty by considering the expected cost and then minimizing it. In a sense, we make use of the expected utility theory.

5.4. Stochastic Linear Programming

Leaving aside these problems, which normally do not involve any algorithm to solve, we have a relatively huge area covered by stochastic or probabilistic programming, with an emphasis on stochastic LP. It may not be out of place here to mention that most such problems will also eventually be formulated as (deterministic) mathematical programming problems. Of course, there will be some problems which call for the use of metaheuristics to solve them, including some in which the optimality of the solution has not yet been proved theoretically.

It would be wise to start with the simple LP (resource allocation) problem, namely to minimize the following objective function to bring out the diversity of stochastic programming problems (which arise in real-life contexts) and corresponding solution approaches:

$$z = C'X \text{ subject to } AX \geq b, X \geq 0$$

Three different situations can be thought of, which are as follows: (a) only the vector of coefficients C is random, inducing randomness in the objective function (outcome of choosing any alternative x) z which will have a distribution induced by the (multivariate) distribution assumed for elements of the vector C for each feasible solution x, (b) only the matrix A or the vector b is random or both these are random, implying chance constraints which are to be satisfied with some specified probability and (c) only the strategy or set of decision variables X is assumed to be random, not as a part of the original formulation of the problem but to yield a better expected value for the objective function.

There could be complex situations involving randomness in all these three respects.

5.4.1. Random Objective Function

Here, we deal with a random objective function having a distribution depending on the joint distribution of the coefficients in C. The situation is amply illustrated by the popular product-mix problem as a simple yet motivating example of a LP problem. The objective is to maximize profit by producing the optimal number of units of different feasible product types with the available resources. The total profit is assumed to be a linear function with coefficients which represent the (anticipated) profit per unit of the product of a given type. We should note that the total profit which will be actually realized when a set of units of the product types are sold in the market may well differ from the anticipated amount. In fact, the time gap between product planning and product marketing may be characterized by many unexpected factors that make the actual profit coefficients random variables, and we can only speak of the expected total profit. Market intelligence may provide us with some ideas about the random behaviour of market prices and, hence, of profit coefficients.

If we assume C to have a multivariate normal distribution, for a given solution X, Z will be univariate normal with $E(z)=\mu' X$ where μ is the mean vector of the coefficients C. Further, $\text{Var}(z)=\Sigma' X \Sigma$, where Σ represents the variance–covariance matrix. If the coefficients are independent of one another, we simply consider the variances and further simplification may result if we assume these variances to be the same. We take μ and Σ to be known constants.

We can have the following equivalent deterministic problems which can be solved by appropriate programming algorithms.

1. **LP:** Minimize $E(z)=\mu'X$ subject to $AX>bX\geq 0$
2. **Quadratic programming:** Minimize $\text{Var}(z)$****
3. **Quadratic programming:** Minimize the variance (s.d.) penalized mean $E(z)-k\,[\text{Var}(z)]^{1/2}$ for some given value of k
4. **Fractional programming:** Minimize the coefficient of variation of z {s.d. $(z)/E(z)$}
5. **Fractional programming:** Minimize the probability of exceedance $\Pr\{z>r\}$ for given $r>0$
6. **Fractional programming:** Minimize $z0$ the quantile of z such that $\Pr\{z>z0\}=\alpha$ given small value

The same formulations remain valid even when C has some distribution other than the multivariate normal. Obviously, solving such deterministic optimization problems will be quite difficult, especially when the univariate distribution of z is not easily derived and/or not conveniently invertible.

One can imagine similar formulations of optimization problems involving quadratic or polynomial or even posynomial objective functions, though such formulations have not been studied so far.

In all the above formulations, we try to reduce the probability distribution of the random objective function to a single summary measure or a combination of two such measures. In fact, some authors tend to emphasize the use of mode for this purpose as the most probable value of the objective function to be realized. For a symmetric distribution, the expected value equals the modal value, but the two will differ in other cases. However, it may be easier to work out the expected value rather than the mode.

Theoretically, it seems better to establish the dominance of one distribution (indexed by one solution X) over other distributions, in which case the index of the dominating (or dominated) solution becomes the optimal solution. And it is well known that stochastic dominance (SD) implies expectation dominance but is not implied by the latter.

Denote the distribution function of z for a given X by $F_x(t)$. Then, if for some X', $F_x'(t) > F_x(t)$ for all $t > 0$, then X' should be taken as the optimal solution. The corresponding value of z is the stochastically smallest value of z.

It is quite difficult, however, to find such an X' even in simple situations.

5.4.2. Chance-constrained Programming

In the case of chance-constrained programming problems, we may face the following several different situations:

1. Minimize z subject to $\Pr\{A_i X \geq b_i\} = \alpha_i$

    $i = 1, 2, \ldots, m$ or $\Pr\{A_i X \geq b_i, i = 1, 2, \ldots, m\} = \alpha$

Here, α and αi are pre-specified small values (aspiration levels), and A_i and b_i are the ith row of A and the *i*th element of b respectively, and only b is a random vector.

Assuming the elements of b are independently (and most often) identically distributed, and that these distributions, say F_i's are invertible explicitly, these constraints can be restated as: $A_iX = H_i(\alpha_i)$, where H_i is the inverse of F_i, $i=1, 2, ..., m$, and a similar relation holds for the overall aspiration level. If we have a common cumulative distribution function F for all b_i, $H = F - 1$.

2. In the same constraints, elements of A can only be random, not those of b. The treatment of the chance constraint poses similar problems as in Case 1.
3. We can have randomness in both A and b. Constructing deterministic equivalents of chance constraints may be quite involved, except when the distributions assumed are too simple. Chance-constrained programming with multiple deterministic objectives can be tackled in terms of goal programming or fuzzy programming. Of course, probability distributions of available resources should be amenable to inversion in closed form.

Generally speaking, there are two broad approaches to solving stochastic LP problems, namely:

- **Here and now (active):** In this, the decision-maker has to make a decision based on the assumed probability distributions and no data.
- **Wait and see (passive):** In this, we wait to use some realized values of the random variables involved. In this context, we can simulate such values and reduce the problem to a deterministic optimization problem.

Let us look at the following problem to minimize $C'X$ subject to $\Pr\{AX \leq \} \geq \alpha$, $X \geq 0$.

This chance-constrained stochastic LP problem can be reformulated as to minimize f such that $\Pr\{f \geq C'X\} \geq \beta$ subject to $\Pr\{AX \leq b\} \geq \alpha$, $X \geq 0$. This really means that f (called the target function) is the quantile of order β in the distribution of $z = C'X$.

5.4.3. Case of Random Decision Variables

In a somewhat theoretical framework, a few attempts have been made to allow decision variable(s) to be random and to derive the optimal distribution(s) of such variable(s) that will ensure a better value for the objective function (mostly the expected value of a random objective function). This problem is quite complex even with simple discrete and partly known distribution assumed for the decision variable(s). Most such attempts have dealt with a single decision variable or at most two.

Consider the classical newsboy problem and imagine that a random quantity is ordered on each occasion by drawing a random number from a probability distribution to be determined. Assume, for the sake of simplicity, that the possible order quantities are $q_1, q_2, ..., q_k$. We have to find out probabilities with which these values will be ordered, say $\Pi_1, \Pi_2, ..., \Pi_k$ such that the overall expected cost, $T(q, \Pi) = \Sigma T(q_l) \Pi_l$, is a minimum over the set of probabilities ($T(q)$ being the expected total cost for the given demand distribution and q as the order quantity) subject to the constraint of non-negativity and a unit sum. It follows from Jensen's inequality that this minimum is smaller than the minimum in the constant order quantity situation. This becomes a LP problem in k variables subject to only one linear constraint. This will imply a degenerate most favourable distribution, adding little significance to the entire procedure. However, we can work out some other constraints like the expected order quantity equals the expected demand to result in a two-point most favourable distribution. Other reasonable constraints can also be thought of. These days, ordering quantities determined through random sampling from a distribution is quite convenient.

5.5. Probabilistic Dynamic Programming

As pointed out in Chapter 4, dynamic programming is a very useful and widely applied tool for multistage decision-making under risk. To explain this point, let us consider an investment decision problem. An individual wants to invest up to a certain amount C in stocks over the next n years. We assume a simple investment plan to buy stocks at the beginning of a year and to sell them off at the year's end. Accumulated money may be reinvested (wholly or partly) at the start of the next year. The return on investment is affected by unpredictable market conditions, Condition I yields a return r_i with a probability p_i, where $i=1, 2, ..., m$, say. The problem before the investor is how the money should be invested to realize the highest accumulated return at the end of n years.

Let x_i = Amount available for investment at the beginning of year i, $x_1 = C$

Y_i = Amount actually invested at the beginning of year i, $x_i \geq y_i$
A dynamic programming formulation of the decision problem will recognize each year as a stage, alternatives at stage i as y_i and state at stage i as x_i

Let $f_i(x_i)$ = Maximum expected amounts accumulated for years i, $i+1, i+2, ..., n$, given x_i at the beginning of year i.

Corresponding market condition k, we get:

$$x_{k+1} = (1+r_k) y_i + (x_i - y_i) = r_k y_k + x_k$$

The dynamic programming formulation can now be written as:

$$f_i(x_i) = \text{Max} (\Sigma_k p_k f_{i+1} [x_k + r_k y_k]) \text{ maximum over } x_i \geq y_i \geq 0$$

where $f_{n+1}(x_{n+1}) = x_{n+1}$ since no investment can be made after year n. Thus,

$$f_n(x_n) = x_n \Sigma p_k (1+r_k) \quad k=1, 2, ..., m$$

This is a function linear in y_m and hence attains its maximum at $y_n = x_n$

This problem could be formulated in a different way to maximize the probability of achieving a certain level of return after n years.

5.6. Fuzzy Decision-making

Fuzzy preferences, fuzzy ranking and rating method, fuzzy constraints, fuzzy criteria and fuzzy input data characterize some of the many aspects of complex decision problems under 'uncertainty' or 'risk' treated in terms of fuzzy logic. Interesting and useful applications can be found in many areas. Apart from the general concepts of membership functions, ranking fuzzy sets using cardinal utilities (Baldwin & Guild, 1979), ranking and rating method (Bass & Kwakernaak, 1977), ranking fuzzy sets by maximizing and minimizing sets (Chen, 1985) and several other methods are among recent contributions to this subject. Besides, the use of fuzzy linguistic variables or intuitionistic fuzzy variables and similar other concepts have enriched the content of fuzzy decision-making mathematically quite rich.

Bellman and Zadeh (1970) suggested a fuzzy model for decision-making which accommodates fuzziness in the goal and in the constraint. These are treated as fuzzy sets with membership functions $\mu_C: X$ to $[0, 1]$ and $\mu_G: X$ to $[0, 1]$ where X is the set of all conceivable alternatives. The objective function f is a mapping from X to the outcome space Y and we generate a fuzzy goal defined on a set Y to induce a fuzzy goal G on the set X with a membership function defined by the relation $\mu_G(x) = \mu_G(f(x))$. A fuzzy decision is then defined as the choice that satisfies both the goal G and the constraints C and this can be modelled by the intersection of G and C with the membership function $\mu_D(x) = \text{Min}\ [\mu_G(x), \mu_C(x)]$ where $x \in X$. This definition of intersection, however, does not allow any interdependence, interaction or trade-off between the goals and the constraints under consideration. An alternate fuzzy set intersection or aggregation operation should be used to reflect a situation in which some degree of positive compensation exists between the goals and the constraints.

Once we have found a fuzzy decision, we may need to choose the best crisp single alternative from this fuzzy set. This can be directly obtained as the alternative x which attains the maximum membership grade in D. One drawback to this procedure is that we ignore information about the other alternatives. This leads to a choice of the centre of gravity of the fuzzy set D.

The method can be extended to multiple goals and multiple constraints by introducing corresponding weighting coefficients and taking a convex combination of weighted goals and weighted constraints to define the fuzzy decision D by the relation:

$$\mu_D(x) = \Sigma u_i \, \mu_{Gi}(x) + \Sigma v_j \, \mu_{Cj}(x)$$

Here, the first sum is over the goals and the second over the constraints.

A simple example given in Klir and Folger (1993) may be found interesting.

Example 5.1. Suppose the goal of a problem of choosing among four possible jobs is to derive a high salary, given the constraint that the job is interesting and within a close driving distance. The salaries for the four jobs, a, b, c and d, are indicated by the function f as:

$$f(a) = 30{,}000 \; f(b) = 25{,}000 \; f(c) = 20{,}000 \text{ and } f(d) = 15{,}000$$

The first constraint of interest value is represented by the fuzzy set C_1 defined over the universal set of four alternative jobs is given by:

$$C_1 = 0.4/a + 0.6/b + 0.8/c + 0.6/d$$

And the second constraint relating to driving distance is defined by the fuzzy set C_2 as:

$$C_2 = 0.1/a + 0.9/b + 0.7/c + 1.0/d$$

The fuzzy goal G is defined by the membership function:

$$1 \text{ for } x > 40{,}000$$

$$\mu_G(x) = -0.00125 \, (x/1{,}000 - 40)^2 + 1 \text{ for } 13{,}000 < x < 40{,}000$$

$$0 \text{ for } x < 13{,}000$$

The corresponding goal G' defined over the alternatives is given by:

$$G' = 0.875/a + 0.7/b + 0.5/c + 0.2/d$$

Taking the standard fuzzy set intersection of these three fuzzy sets, we get the fuzzy decision D given by:

$$D = 0.1/a + 0.6/b + 0.5/c + 0.2/d$$

Finally, we take the maximum of this set to obtain b as the best alternative. We should note that in this approach, the goal and the constraints are symmetric concepts and are dealt with similarly.

We may consider another example from the operations area. Three maintenance strategies, namely corrective, preventive and predictive (based on condition monitoring), have been compared according to eight maintenance decision criteria, namely low-maintenance cost, improved reliability, improved safety, high product quality, minimum inventory, acceptance by labour and enhanced competitiveness with linguistic ratings or weights as very important, critically important, critically important, critically important, moderately important, very important, moderately important and very important respectively have been considered by Verma et al. (2007) by using several methods for selection of the best strategy.

5.7. Prospect Theory

This far, we have used the expected utility (arising from the different states of nature with their associated probabilities) to the decision-maker as the yardstick for comparison of alternatives. As noted earlier, the theoretical framework for this was proposed by Neumann and Morgenstern in 1945. This normative theory has been widely accepted as a model for the decisions which perfectly rational decision-makers (agents) are expected to make. Thirty-four years later, Kahneman and Tversky came up with their prospect theory to argue that the choice among alternatives is made by a decision-maker based on their perception of the value of each alternative. Prospect theory, as explained in their seminal paper in *Econometrica* (1979) entitled 'Prospect Theory: An Analysis of Decision under Risk', laid the foundation stone of behavioural economics based on experimental findings. Initially confined to observations of human behaviour in the context of financial bets and gambles, the theory has since been applied in many fields, including economics, software development, law, international relations, etc. The theory was revised by Kahneman and Tversky in 1992 to remove some of its deficiencies.

The theory moves around the primary finding that 'losses hurt more than equal gains please.' This is why some people refer to this theory as the loss-aversion theory. Decision-making is essentially concerned with establishing a trade-off among the values of different alternatives, as perceived by the decision-maker.

It is true that both the utility and value of the additional amount of gain are considered in relation to the context in which the decision-maker is placed. But while in utility, it is the amount already in possession of the decision-maker that counts, in prospect theory, the value depends on the level of aspiration of the decision-maker or some social comparison which they have in mind that is important. In both, the relative and not the absolute outcome of an alternative under a given state of nature determines the choice. A second distinctive feature of the value function is derived from the fact that people tend to be more risk-averse when in a domain of gains, avoiding alternatives that offer higher pay-offs with lower probabilities. They are more risk-takers when placed in a domain of losses, tempted to accept risks from alternatives with high pay-offs in the hope of recouping previous losses, and unlike in utility theory, negative and positive gains of equal magnitude are not considered as having equal impact (in reverse directions though) in prospect theory.

A prospect can be understood as a set of outcomes or pay-offs x_i, where $i = 1, 2, ..., n$, with respective potential/declared/subjective probabilities p_i, where $i = 1, 2, ..., n$, of being realized or achieved. Thus, a prospect corresponds to one option or bet or strategy and decision-making under risk involves the choice of one (some) among the given options or prospects. Let $u(x_i)$ be the utility of the outcome x_i with the reference point w (asset/wealth/welfare currently possessed by the decision-maker) in terms of a chosen utility function. Then, the three tents of the expected utility theory are as follows:

1. **Additivity (expectation):** The overall expected utility of a prospect is:

$$U(x_1, x_2, ..., x_n; p_1, p_2, ..., p_n) = p_1 u(x_1) + p_2 u(x_2) + ... + p_n u(x_n)$$

2. **Asset integration:** The prospect is acceptable if: $U(x_1+w, p_1, x_2+w, p_2, ..., x_n+w, p_n) > u(w)$ with an obvious implication of utility augmentation through the prospect.
3. **Risk aversion:** The utility function u is concave so that $u'' < 0$.

Kahneman and Tversky came up with experimental findings from different bets and patterns of decisions by participants to show that the three tents of the expected utility theory are not met in practice. Some of these examples were based on the Allais paradox (1953), which is not explained by the expected utility theory.

Example 5.2.   Option A   Option B

$2,400 with probability 0.33   2,400 with certainty
$2,500 with probability 0.66
Nil with probability 0.01

Among 72 participants, 82 per cent voted in favour of Option B and the remaining 18 per cent in favour of Option A, though the expected utility of Option A is slightly higher than that of Option B.

Example 5.3.   Option A   Option B
$4,000 with probability 0.2 $3,000 with probability 0.25
Nil with probability 0.8   Nil with probability 0.75

Among 95 participants, only 20 per cent voted in favour of A with an expected utility of 3.200, larger that the utility of Option B voted by the majority.

Example 5.4.   Option A   Option B
A tour of England,   A tour of England
France and Italy with a   with certainty
probability of 0.5

Only 22 per cent of the participants voted in favour of Option A.

The above examples illustrate what may be called the *certainty* effect, while two other phenomena, the *reflection* effect and the *isolation* effect were also explained by Kahneman and Tversky.

Alternatives or options are evaluated in terms of an overall expected utility of the outcome to the individual computed according to the formula:

$$V = \Sigma \prod(p_i)\, v(x_i)$$

Where x_i is the ith potential outcome of the option and p_i is the respective probability, v is a value function assigned to an outcome, and $\prod$ is a probability weighting function that takes account of the fact that people tend to over react to small probability events and under react to large probabilities. It measures the impact of the probability of an event on the desirability of a prospect.

The value function passes through the reference point and is s-shaped and asymmetric. The probability weighting function is not well-behaved near the end points, 0 and 1. Although the values of the function at these points are 0 and 1 respectively, changes in probability near these points have disproportionate effects on the evaluation of prospects. The function has a slope 1 except at the end points and between 0.10 and 0.15 over-weighting shifts to under-weighting. In fact: $\prod(p) + \prod(1-p) < 1$.

Let (x, p, y, q) be a prospect with three outcomes, namely x with probability p and y with probability q and nothing with probability $1-p-q$. It is a regular prospect, that is, if $p+q<1$ or $x \geq 0 \geq 0$ or $y \geq 0 \geq 0$, then:

$$V(x, p, y, q) = \prod(p)\, v(x) + \prod(q)\, v(y)$$

However, if $p+q+1$ and either $x>y>0$ or $x<y<0$ then

$$V(x, p, y, q) = v(y) + \prod(p)\,[v(x) = v(y)]$$

Using prospect theory in decision-making involves two phases, namely (a) the editing phase in which the alternatives or options are characterized in terms of their features, presented in a desired order and using desired descriptions and (b) the evaluation phase in which an appropriate value function is introduced, taking effective note of the reference points. This theory states that decision-making depends on choosing among options that may themselves be based on biased judgements about their feasibility or potential desirability. For this reason, during the editing phase we have to take due care of 'framing effects' which can be attributed to certain tendencies in human behaviour. These tendencies could be further analysed as (a) segregation, giving more attention to factors that stand out at hand as relevant to the problem, (b) coding, tendency to categorize outcomes as gains or losses, rather than in terms of eventual states of wealth or welfare, (c) combination, tendency to add probabilities of choices that present identical outcomes, (d) cancellation, tendency to ignore common parts in different outcomes, (e) simplification or discarding very unlikely alternatives and (f) dominance from discarding alternatives that provide less valuable outcomes than others on each dimension.

An advancement over the prospect theory was suggested by Brandstätter et al. (2006) by proposing a 'priority heuristic' that can be used to make choices among options without trade-offs.

5.8. Priority Heuristic

Brandstätter et al. (2006) in their article on 'Priority Heuristic: Making Choices Without Tradeoffs' gave a comprehensive and insightful account of the expected utility (normative) theory as well as the prospect (descriptive) theory of decision-making under risk. They also provided a simple strategy, namely the priority heuristic, taking a cue from Rubinstein's work (1998), that could explain the Allais paradox, along with the certainty effect, the reflection effect and the possibility effect, as well as the fourfold pattern of attitudes towards risk analysed by Brandstätter and his co-authors, at the same time being pretty simple.

For a choice between bets or gambles in which all the outcomes are positive or zero, this heuristic involves the following three steps:

1. **Priority rule:** Go through the reasons in the order of minimum gain, chance of maximum gain and maximum gain.
2. **Stopping rule:** Stop examination if minimum gains differ by more than or equal to 1/10 of the maximum gain, otherwise stop if chances differ by more than or equal to 10 per cent.

3. **Decision rule:** Choose the bet with the more 'attractive' gain (chance) for the higher gain and the lower chance for the minimum gain.

The authors provide some two-bet examples with the percentage of responding participants preferring a particular bet. Consider the following cases:

- A 4,000 with a probability of 0.8 and 0 with a probability of 0.2
- B 3,000 with certainty
- C 6,000 with a probability of 0.45 and 0 with a probability of 0.55
- D 3,000 with a probability of 0.9 and 0 with a probability of 0.1

As many as 86 per cent of respondents voted in favour of D.

In a bid to explain the four-fold pattern of attitudes towards risk, the authors considered the median certainty equivalent gains or losses in bets to develop the following matrix-like structure:

Probability	Gain	Loss
Low	$C(100, 0.05) = 14$	$C(-100, 0.5) = -8$
	Risk-seeking	risk-aversion
High	$C(100, 0.95) = 78$	$C(-100, 0.95) = -84$
	Risk aversion	risk-seeking

Note: $C(100, 0.05) = 14$ stands for the case where the median certainty equivalent of a bet with a probability of 0.05 of winning 100, and winning nothing with a probability of 0.95 was found to be 14. Although the probability of winning is low, the amount is not that high. People settle for an amount of 14—greater than the expected amount of 5—and accept risk by voting in favour of the bet.

5.9. Decision-making under Evidence Theory

The theory of evidence was proposed by Dempster and Schafer to take account of partial ignorance due to incomplete or otherwise impaired information, leading to partial uncertainty in situations where fuzzy sets were not involved. Basic to this theory (also known as D–S theory) are concepts of belief and plausibility measures (one can be derived from the other), focal points, basic probability assignment and rules, like the rule for combining evidence from two or more sources. Unlike the membership function for finding the degree to which an (ambiguous) element belongs to several each of several sets with boundaries which overlap, belief measures are introduced to assign an element (or a subset A of the universal set X) with incomplete information to one of several sets with sharp boundaries.

For any set A, $m(A)$ is interpreted as the degree of evidence or belief supporting the claim that a specific element of X belongs to the set A alone and not to any special subset of A or as the degree to which we believe such a claim is warranted. Every set A for which $m(A) > 0$ is usually called a focal element of m. Focal elements are subsets of ion which the available evidence focuses. Belief or $Bel(A)$ represents the total evidence or belief that the element belongs to A as well as to the various special subsets of A. Plausibility of A denoted as $Pl(A)$ represents not only the total evidence or belief that the element in question belongs to A or to any of its subsets but also the additional belief or evidence associated with sets that overlap with A. Hence, $Pl(A) \geq Bel(A)$. It can be shown that $Pl(A) = 1 - Bel(A)$. Further, $Pl(A) \geq Pr(A) \geq Bel(A)$ where $Pr(A)$ stands for the usual probability measure for the set A. Use of the D–S theory has often been made by treating the belief measure and the plausibility measure for a subset as lower and upper probabilities for the subset.

To illustrate the application of the D–S theory in decision-making under uncertainty (eventually treated as a problem under risk), we consider the problem of deciding which of several paintings to be presented to an awardee so that the expected value or expected utility of the painting selected is the highest. Each of these paintings is supposedly drawn by a famous artist, and we do not have complete information on this. There are, say, three possible states of nature, namely A—the painting is an original one by a famous artist, B—the painting is an original one by a disciple of the famous artist and C—the painting is a counterfeit one by the famous artist (it may be by some other person). An expert gives their opinion about the specimen under consideration belonging to one of these four categories in terms of their belief measure, providing incomplete evidence about the state of nature. The results can be shown as follows:

Focal Element	m	Bel
A	0.10	0.10
B	0.15	0.15
C	0.12	0.12

One can take these belief measures as probabilities for the states of nature to evaluate each of the alternatives for a final choice. If opinion is sought from more than one expert, we can combine their belief measures by the rule proposed by Dempster and use the combined measure. There have been exercises to combine D–S theory with prospect theory to solve some real-life decision problems.

CHAPTER 6

Decisions under Competition

6.1. Games and Decisions

In an earlier chapter, we referred to games as problems of decision-making under competition, involving two or more decision-makers, assumed to be equally wise, working under complete uncertainty about decisions being taken by one another or having partial knowledge of the same. In the simplest case, the game ends as soon as each decision-maker has taken a decision. However, in many more situations, decision-makers may be required to continue taking decisions until the rules of the game lead to its natural end. Of course, in some cases, depending on decisions taken by the participants, the game may be over earlier than its natural end. The set of alternatives available to each of the decision-makers changes and is specified by the rules defining the game before each move or choice by a decision-maker. Each decision-maker, usually referred to as a 'player', gets a pay-off at the end of the game. The total of all pay-offs received by all the players may add up to zero, in situations where some players are required to give some amount to some other players and the total amount available to the players at the beginning of the game remains the same: only it gets re-distributed among the players. There are other situations where all the players can gain some amounts or some may lose and some may gain, but the total pay-off may not be zero. Accordingly, there are zero-sum and non-zero-sum games. And a game could be a two-person game or a multi-person game. In the latter case, multiple players may form blocks or groups.

In non-zero-sum games, players may not be stuck with the idea of inflicting losses on other players, since the goal of maximizing one's own gain may not run counter necessarily to large gains by other players. Of course, in some highly competitive situations, a player may be more interested in stopping an opponent from gaining much, even by adopting a strategy which holds them back from maximizing their own gain. However, intentions on the part of players in a game about how best to choose their strategies do not explicitly enter decision-making by the players. In fact, participating players may explicitly decide to consult one another before choosing individual strategies or may decide to adopt co-operative strategies or may decide to form interest groups. Usually, the role of intentions or emotions in decision-making under competition has not been discussed much. A recognition of this role may lead to changes in strategies over repetitive plays in a game. In this context, evolutionary game theory has grown as a subject of recent interest to policymakers.

6.2. Matrix Games

Important aspects of decision-making under competition, including situations where the decision-makers involved are not necessarily guided by mutually conflicting interests, though primarily interested in maximizing their respective gains in utility or welfare (or pay-offs), can be discussed in terms of only two players or decision-makers and their pay-off matrices, usually of finite dimensions corresponding to finitely many actions (options) available to each player. A decision rule is a probability distribution over the action space (a finite set) and the expected pay-off resulting from this distribution is the entity in which a player is interested. Such a distribution is often called a mixed strategy, while a pure strategy corresponds to a degenerate distribution which implies the same action being chosen every time the game is played.

Not necessarily restricted to the case of two players only, games or competitive decisions are categorized as zero sum and non-zero sum. These two types of games have their own distinctive features, which are briefly mentioned as follows.

The fundamentals of a zero-sum game where the pay-offs to the different players taking part in the game, some gaining and some others losing, add up to zero at the end of a play can be quite conveniently understood in terms of a two-person game, though a multi-person game presents some interesting and, at the same time, complicating aspects. Each player tries to maximize their gain in a spirit of competition against others. Players do not and are not allowed to communicate with one another before taking individual decisions. Thus, whichever decisions come out to be optimal will be adopted if the game is repeatedly played. Let us denote the pay-off to the players: if Player I chooses an action, then $A_i (i=1, 2, ..., m)$, and if Player II chooses an action, then $B_j (j=1, 2, ..., n)$, by p_{ij}. Then the expected pay-off to Player I (if they choose the mixed strategy), $X=(x_1, x_2, x_m)$, and their opponent, that is, Player II, chooses the mixed strategy, $Y=(y_1, y_2, ..., y_n)$, comes out to be $X'PY$ where P is the pay-off matrix for Player I. As mentioned earlier, the pay-off matrix for Player II is just the negative of P, so that P can be regarded as the loss matrix for Player II. The expected pay-off to Player I (also called the maximizing player) is called the value v of the game. A value $v=0$ implies the game is fair, while a value $v>(<) 0$ implies that the game is biased in favour of (against) Player I.

While zero-sum games, particularly those involving two persons or decision-makers with mutually opposed interests, acting in complete absence of the choice made by each other, have been largely studied, documented and applied, non-zero-sum games present interesting problems and are more generally applicable. Unlike in a zero-sum game, pay-offs or corresponding utilities for all the players for a strategy (involving a choice by all of them) do not add up to zero, so that even in a two-person case, both players can win or both can lose. They can communicate with one another, though in some cases, such communication may be denied. In the first case, they can adopt a joint strategy. These games are non-strictly competitive, since some complementary interests are generally involved, along with some mutually conflicting interests. A common form of a non-zero sum game is a bi-matrix game with two different pay-off matrices, one for each player.

6.2.1. Optimality Principle

Optimality (of a strategy pair) is ensured by Wald's maximin gain criterion for Player I and minimax loss for Player II. In a non-zero-sum game, the maximin criterion will be generally applied separately by the two players. In the case of any $m \times n$ game, the optimal mixed strategies or probability vectors can be found by solving the corresponding LP problem and its dual to derive the maximin (minimax) expected gain (loss). It is of interest to note that the number of non-zero elements in the two mixed strategies or probability vectors has to be the same.

Alternatively, we seek equilibrium (pure or mixed) strategies as optimal strategies. A Nash equilibrium point or strategy pair is one such that neither of the two players can improve their pay-off by moving away from this point if the other player sticks to their equilibrium strategy. In fact, if both players can declare their strategies, neither has an incentive to move away from their declared strategy. The equilibrium points or solutions have been generally spoken of in the context of non-zero-sum games. In a two-person zero-sum game, it can be proved that a minimax solution is an equilibrium point. In the case of a non-zero sum game involving two players, it can be proved (Nash) using the fixed point theorem that there exists at least one mixed strategy pair that is in equilibrium. In fact, Nash (1950) proved that for every pair of pay-off matrices, there exists an odd number of (mixed strategy) equilibria. Most non-zero sum games do not admit to Nash equilibrium in pure strategies. Example 6.4 deals with a simple game that has two pure strategy pairs in equilibrium with different pay-off pairs.

Example 6.1 illustrates this point with a pair of pure strategies being both a minimax and an equilibrium solution.

When strategies are formed from the observer's angle, whose main aim is to wish the best outcome for every player, that is, when strategies are formed from a socially balanced viewpoint, the outcome is called a Pareto outcome. A Pareto optimal strategy set is such that there does not exist any other set (solution) that is better for all the players, and at least one player strictly chooses the strategy over the others. All the outcomes are essentially Pareto optimal in a zero-sum game. Example 6.3 illustrates the notion of Pareto optimality.

6.2.2. Stability of a Solution

Just as chemical equilibrium is the state in which both the reactants and the product do not have a tendency to change with time, a set of actions or a solution is deemed stable when no player would change their action choice given the opportunity in repeated plays of the game. Stability defines both Nash equilibrium in strategic games and the core in co-operative games. It remains closely related to certain other properties, such as dominance, rationality and balance. In fact, stability selects subsets of the set of Nash equilibria which have these desirable properties.

It is obvious that in zero-sum games admitting at least one saddle point, the saddle point becomes a stable strategy, while in the case where such a saddle point does not exist, each player usually adopts a different action in each repetition of the game.

6.3. Solving Matrix Games

As expected, the maximin (expected) gain leads to the usual optimal strategy for a zero-sum game and an equilibrium strategy pair is commonly sought for a non-zero-sum game. In fact, existence of both these solutions (in mixed strategies) has been theoretically proved.

Among other solution concepts for a non-zero-sum game, mention may be made of the competitive solution where Player I will work out a maximin strategy in the pay-off matrix with elements $(a_{ij} - b_{ij})$ where a and b correspond to pay-offs to Player I and II respectively, and

Player II will work out their maximin strategy in the matrix $(b_{ij}-a_{ij})$. There is also the concept of a 'vindictive' solution, where each player is interested in inflicting the heaviest loss on their opponent, rather than maximizing their own gain. Here, Player I derives the maximin strategy in the matrix with elements $(-b_{ij})$ and Player II works with the matrix with elements $(-a_{ij})$. As opposed to these solutions, which reveal a spirit of competition, there could be a co-operative solution as well, derived by the two players from the single pay-off matrix with elements $(a_{ij}+b_{ij})$. Pay-off or expected pay-off pairs corresponding to the different solutions may not be the same, and no optimal strategy will be accepted.

Different types of solutions for some simple but interesting two-person games are provided in the examples as follows.

Example 6.1. Let us consider a simple two-person zero-sum game played by two children, each showing one or two fingers on the right hand and guessing on the left hand what the other child is showing (independently and in ignorance), showing one or two fingers. The rules of the game are such that if both children are correct or if both are incorrect (in guessing what the other child has shown), the score of each child will be zero: If only one child is correct and the other is wrong, then the child who makes a correct guess gets an amount equal to the sum of the fingers they have shown. And what is gained by one child is lost by the other. The pay-off matrix for any child with the four alternatives, namely (1, 1), (1, 2), (2, 1) and (2, 2), along with their pay-offs, are as follows. The first number within each parenthesis is shown by the right hand and the second figure is the guessed figure for the number of fingers shown by the other child.

	(1, 1)	(1, 2)	(2, 1)	(2, 2)
(1, 1)	0	2	−3	0
(1, 2)	−2	0	0	3
(2, 1)	3	0	0	−4
(2, 2)	0	−3	4	0

This is a skew-symmetric matrix and the strategy (1, 2) is the maximin strategy for this player with a pay-off of −2 and can be easily shown to be optimal for the other child. This may appear to be somewhat strange. Also, this strategy is also an equilibrium point in the sense that if one child moves away from this strategy unilaterally with the other child sticking to their strategy, then no child can improve his gain. Thus, we have found a particular strategy as the optimal one and this situation is known as one yielding a pure strategy pair solution or a saddle point solution.

Example 6.2. As distinct from the simple game above, consider a game with the following pay-off matrix to Player A, the negative yielding the pay-off matrix for Player B.

	B_1	B_2	B_3	B_4
A_1	2	2	3	−1
A_2	4	3	2	6

Here, there is no saddle point or a pure strategy pair solution and we talk about determining optimally the relative frequencies or probabilities p and $1-p$ with which Player A will adopt the two actions A_1 and A_2 and also probabilities q_1, q_2, q_3 and q_4 (summing up to unity) with which Player B will decide to choose actions B_1, B_2, B_3 and B_4 respectively. It can be graphically shown that the optimal value of p is 1/2 and Player B should play action B_3 with probability 7/8 and action B_4 with probability 1/8 and they should not play the other two actions at all. Thus, we have (1/2, 1/2) and (0, 0, 7/8, 1/8) as the two optimal mixed strategies.

Example 6.3. Let us take the pay-off pair matrix:

		Player II	
		a	b
Player I	A	(1, 2)	(0, 3)
	B	(2, 1)	(−1, 0)

The strategy pairs (A, a) and (B, b) are the two Nash equilibria with respective pay-off (value) pairs (1, 2) and (−1, 0).

Example 6.4. Consider the bi-matrix game with A and B as the actions available to Player I (named Susan) in Luce and Raiffa (1958) and a and b as the actions which Player II (named Bob) can choose with pay-offs:

	a	b
A	(1, 2)	(3, 1)
B	(0, −200)	(2, −300)

It can be easily shown that the competitive solution will be the pure strategy pair (A, a) with a pay-off pair (1, 2). The co-operative solution derived from the sum of the two pay-off matrices works out as the pair (A, b) with a pay-off pair (3, 1), while the vindictive solution (B, b) gives the pay-off pair (2, −300).

Let us now examine the effect of a possible communication allowed between Bob and Susan. If Susan and Bob cannot communicate with each other, no one can threaten the other. The strategy pair (A, a) is the equilibrium solution, since neither player can improve their pay-off by drifting away from this strategy unilaterally while the other sticks to this strategy. However, if they are allowed to communicate, Susan can threaten Bob by saying that she would play strategy B unless he commits himself to playing strategy b. If Bob submits, Susan will win 2 and Bob will lose 1, as opposed to Susan gaining 1 and Bob gaining 2 when communication was not allowed. Threat solutions are taken recourse to by the stronger player with a larger initial amount in possession, so that the incremental utility of the additional unit of money is less. If the game is played only once, players do not have fear of retaliation from their opponents, and they may behave differently than they would in a game played repeatedly.

Example 6.5. The Coordination Game
Imagine two persons walking along the same pavement from opposite directions. If both stick to their respective right or left, it will

be smooth for both. If either deviates from their choice, a chance of collision arises. This can be shown by the pay-off matrix, which is as follows:

	Left	Right
Left	(1, 1)	(0, 0)
Right	(0, 0)	(1, 1)

The strategies (Left, Left) and (Right, Right) are Pareto optimal.

6.4. Polymatrix Games

As noted earlier, the maximin (usually mixed) strategies—which can be easily computed using LP—lead to unique Nash equilibria. However, these equilibria are hard to compute in general, even for two-person non-zero-sum games and for three-person zero-sum games. In that way, the applicability of Neumann's minimax theorem seems to be quite limited. In this section, we will consider a class of multi-person zero-sum games where Nash equilibria can be conveniently computed by a direct generalization of the LP formulation of a two-person zero-sum game.

A polymatrix game or a separable network game can be defined in terms of the following:

- A finite set $V = (1, 2, \ldots, n)$ of players, denoted by nodes on a graph with a finite set E of edges, which are taken to be unordered pairs (i, j) of players (j, j)
- A finite set of strategies S_i for each player $i \in V$
- A two-person zero-sum game for each edge (i, j) between players i and j with strategy sets S_i and S_j respectively, resulting in a pay-off p_{ij} to player i

For each player i and strategy profile $s = (s_1, s_2, \ldots, s_n)$, the pay-off to player i under s is $p_i(s)$ as the total of their pay-offs in all the games with other admissible players (along adjacent edges).

Such a game is a zero-sum game if for all strategy profiles s, the pay-offs to all players come to zero.

Zero-sum polymatrix games can model situations in which players interact pairwise and take decisions, and the flow in and flow out of pay-offs beyond the system is not allowed. Furthermore, one easy way to conceptualize such a situation is to have only zero-sum games along the edges. Consider a game in which some evaders and some inspectors are the players and several exit points are the strategies. The network is a complete bipartite graph. Each evader can choose an exit point, and each inspector can choose to inspect any exit point within their jurisdiction. If the evader's exit point is not inspected, they win one unit. And for each exit point used by an evader which is inspected, the inspector wins one unit. All other pay-offs are zero. It can be verified that, for any strategy profile, the total pay-off is the total number of (eventual) evaders. Thus, this game is a constant-sum game and can be reduced to a zero-sum game by subtracting this amount from the pay-off of each player. It must be noted that the zero-sum nature of this game is global and not local, in the sense that there exist constituent games which are not zero-sum games.

It is not difficult to prove that the optimal mixed strategies for the players in a zero-sum polymatrix game can be obtained by the LP formulation of the problem in the case of a zero-sum two-person game. It can be further shown that if the LP problem has a solution, then a Nash equilibrium exists and conversely. The following four properties are true for a two-person zero-sum game:

1. Each player has a unique pay-off in all Nash equilibria, known as the value of the game.
2. Equilibrium strategies are max–min strategies.
3. Equilibrium strategies are exchangeable, that is, if (x_1, x_2) and (y_1, y_2) are equilibria, then so are (x_1, y_2) and (x_2, y_1). In fact, the set of equilibrium strategies is convex and the set of equilibria is the corresponding product set.
4. There are no correlated equilibria whose marginals with respect to the players do not constitute a Nash equilibrium.

It can be shown that only the last property holds for the polymatrix games. The following example shows how a zero-sum polymatrix game can have different equilibria with different player pay-offs. A strategy for three players a, b and c is (H, T, H) and the pay-offs are $(-1, 0, 1)$. It is directly seen that (H, T, H) is an equilibrium. Now, consider $(H, 1/2\ H + 1/2\ T, H)$. The pay-offs of the players are now $(0, 0, 0)$. It can be again argued that this is an equilibrium.

6.5. The Prisoner's Dilemma

Formulated by Tucker as a two-person game initially (though framed nearly 70 years back in RAND Corporation), this is a well-studied problem in game theory that brings out the fact although decisions by players in such a game—be it zero-sum or otherwise—are taken by individually rational interest to maximize one's own gain (as ensured by Nash equilibrium point solutions), it is possible in some cases that both the players get better pay-offs by choosing on the basis of an implicit co-operative instinct. In the classical context, we have two persons, A and B, arrested for suspected involvement in an offence who are put up in separate rooms in a prison-house with no opportunity to interact and to decide what they will do on being questioned about their involvement in the offence. The prosecutors offer a bargain to each prisoner separately, either to remain silent or to testify that the other committed the offence. The pay-off matrix, in terms of the amount of punishment (indicated by a negative pay-off) in years is as follows:

	B Remains Silent	B Denies
A Remains Silent	(−1, −1)	(−3, 0)
A Denies	(0, −3)	(−2, −2)

It can be easily verified that the strategy pair where each denies their involvement is the equilibrium solution, since none of the prisoners can lessen their punishment by unilaterally moving away from this strategy, while the other prisoner sticks to this strategy. And this is the strategy pair that is justified by individual rational self-interest. At the same time, it is clear that both prisoners could win (lessen their terms of imprisonment) by both remaining silent, intuitively co-operating with other for the sake of joint interest. In fact, in RAND, the secretaries who were first interested in this game 'trusted' each other and worked together for the best common outcome.

It may be added here that the strategy of co-operation where both the prisoners remain silent is not an equilibrium point and hence will not be accepted by either player acting in rational self-interest. Similarly, the strategy pair where each player denies the allegation is not Pareto optimal, while the three remaining pairs are. Further, if we consider the so-called 'co-operative solution' in terms of minimax loss for either player with a single common pay-off matrix by pooling corresponding elements in the two pay-off matrices, the optimal strategy of both players remaining silent does not work out to be the best solution. Further, if this game is repeated on a finite number of occasions (number known in advance to the two players), the same strategy, which is a strong Nash equilibrium point solution, will be adopted by the players. However, played infinitely many times where the players can make use of the choices being made by their opponents in determining their subsequent choices, no stable strategy may exist. In such situations, various other strategies, such as tit for tat, win–stay, lose–switch and the like, may be recommended.

The prisoner's dilemma has been extended to more general formulations for multi-player situations and has been applied in many domains, such as international politics, environmental negotiations, sports tournaments, economics and psychology.

The *Stanford Encyclopedia of Philosophy* offers an insight into this interesting problem, often called a 'puzzle' in game theory, that brings out the superiority of group rationality over individual rationality. It says that the contradiction thrown up lies in the fact that, whatever the other player chooses, each is better off confessing than remaining silent. However, the outcome obtained when both confess is worse for each than the outcome they would have obtained had they remained silent. This illustrates a conflict between individual and group rationality. A group whose members pursue rational self-interest may end up worse off than a group whose members act contrary to rational self-interest. If the pay-offs are not regarded as indicators of self-interest, a group whose members rationally pursue any goals may end up worse off than if they had not rationally pursued their goals individually. The prisoner's dilemma and its multi-player generalizations can be viewed as models to represent situations in which it is difficult to get rational, selfish agents to cooperate for their common good. Much of the contemporary literature has focused on identifying conditions under which players would or should make a 'cooperative' move corresponding to remaining silent.

It is also plausible to look upon this game as a model to represent a choice between selfish behaviour and socially desirable altruism. The move corresponding to confession benefits the actor, no matter what the other does, while the move corresponding to silence benefits the other player, no matter what that other player does. Benefiting oneself is not always wrong, of course, and benefiting others at the expense of oneself is not always morally required, but in the prisoner's dilemma game, both players prefer the outcome with the altruistic moves to that with the selfish moves.

The prisoner's dilemma can be generalized to two players with two options for each, namely co-operate or defect, with the following pay-off matrix in the canonical form:

		Player II	
		Co-operate	Defect
Player I	Co-operate	(R, R)	(S, T)
	Defect	(T, S)	(P, P)

For the prisoner's dilemma, the pay-offs must satisfy the condition.

$T > R > P > S$ with the implication of $R > P$ that mutual co-operation is superior to mutual defection and of $P > S$ that defection is the dominant strategy for each player. A special case is the 'donation game', where co-operation corresponds to offering the other player a benefit at a personal cost. Defection implies offering nothing. The donation game finds interesting examples in marketing strategies.

6.6. Evolutionary Games

As in sequential decision-making, we may be interested in deciding on an optimal strategy or policy for a game in several successive stages (time periods) in a way that the expected return over the finite planning horizon is maximized. We have a finite number of states of nature with which are associated certain probabilities and a finite set of actions available to the decision-maker at each stage and the action decided on at a particular stage (including the decision to quit) depends on the (random) outcome of the previous stage. Such a decision problem whose solution is a sequence of decisions/actions, one for each stage (often referred to as a policy), is usually formulated in terms of a probabilistic dynamic programming problem.

A typical example of such a game is linked to the Russian roulette wheel. The wheel is marked along the perimeter with n consecutive numbers, 1, 2, 3, ..., n. It is known that the wheel will stop at number I after one spin is p_i. A player has to pay a sum of ₹ x to get the opportunity to spin the wheel up to m spins. The resulting pay-off to the player is double the number shown in the last spin. We can structure the decision problem as:

Stage i corresponds to spin I of the wheel $i=1, 2, ..., m$.

Alternative decisions/actions at each stage are spinning the wheel once more or quitting the game.

The state of the system at Stage I is represented by one of the numbers obtained in the last spin. (The numbers shown in a spin do not depend on the number shown in the previous spin.)

Let $f_i(j)$ = maximum expected return given that the game is in Stage i and that j is the outcome of the last spin. Then, we have:

Expected pay-off at Stage I given that the last spin's outcome was j

$\qquad = 2j$ if game ends

$\qquad = \Sigma_k\, p_k f_{i=1}(k)$ if the game continues

The recursive equations may then be written as:

$$f_{m+1}(j) = 2j$$

End: $2j$

$$f_i(j) = \text{Max}$$

Spin: $\Sigma_k p_k f_{i+1}(k)$

$$F_1(0) = \Sigma_k p_k f_2(k)$$

The recursive equations start with f_{m+1} and terminate with $f_1(0)$.

Expected net return is: $f_1(0) - x$.

Example 6.6. Let us take the example considered by Taha (1999) with $n=5$ and probabilities $p_1=0.3$, $p_2=0.25$, $p_3=0.2$, $p_4=0.15$ and $p_5=0.1$. Furthermore, $x=5$ for a maximum of four spins.

It is obvious that $f_5(j) = 2j$ where j could vary from 1 to 5, with the decision to quit. In Stage 4, after Spin 3, we get:

$$f_4(j) = \text{Max}\ (2j)$$

Spin 3 Outcome	Expected Return		Optimum Solution	
J	End	Spin	$f_4(j)$	Decision
1	2	5	5	Spin
2	4	5	5	Spin
3	6	5	6	End
4	8	5	8	End
5	10	5	10	End

In Stage 4 at the end of Spin 3, we have for $j=1, 2, 3, 4$ and 5 expected returns if the game ends as 2, 4, 6, 8 and 10 respectively, as in the previous case. And if we continue to spin, the expected return will be:

$$f_4(j) = \max\ [2j,\ p_1 f_5(1) + p_2 f_5(2) + p_3 f_5(3) + p_4 f_5(4) + p_5 f_5(5)]$$

$$= \max\ [2j, 5]$$

Spin 3 Outcome	Expected Return		Optimum Solution	
J	End	Spin	$f_4(j)$	Decision
1	2	5	5	Spin
2	4	5	5	Spin
3	6	5	6	End
4	8	5	8	End
5	10	5	10	End

Similarly, for Stage 3, we get:

$$f_3(j) = \max\,[2j,\, 8.15]$$

We can construct a table like the one above for Spin 2 outcomes. To get $f_2(j) = [2j,\, 6.8125]$, we can repeat these steps for stages 2 and 1 to finally come up with:

$$f_1(0) = 7.31$$

The only option in Stage 1 is to spin.

Thus, the optimal policy or strategy for this game is indicated as follows:

Spin Number	Optimal Decision
1	Game starts, spin
2	Continue if Spin 1 produces 1, 2 or 3, else quit
3	Continue if Spin 2 produces 1, 2 or 3, else quit
4	Continue if Spin 3 produces 1 or 2, else quit.

The expected net return for the game is $7.31 - 5.00 = 2.31$.

Some distinctive features of this game as a decision problem may be noted as follows.

Alternatives to this problem are alternative policies or strategies, applicable to the entire game spanning the overall planning horizon, unlike alternatives (actions or decisions) available at each stage. A feasible policy is a sequence of decisions/actions, one for each stage. The action at any stage depends on the observed outcome of the previous stage. Outcomes at any stage occur with the same probabilities. The expected net return (reward) for the entire planning horizon or the game is the objective function to be maximized over a finite (may be large in some cases) set of policies. For each policy, the objective function can be evaluated right now and the optimum policy worked out.

6.7. Analysis of Meta Games

A real problem with the acceptance of results from normal game theory analysis is that game theory tries to convert the inherent uncertainty under which the players decide their strategies into certainty by assuming certain 'rational' behaviour for the players, namely that the players are guided by the expected utility maximization principle, which leads the assumption that in a two-person game, the opposite player always tries to minimize their maximum loss or maximize their minimum gain. This 'rationality' and the corresponding 'stable' solution have been challenged by some game theorists themselves. The latter argue that players should not and, in fact, do not act according to this principle. Instead, each player tries to predict what the strategy of the other player(s) could be before deciding on one's own strategy. Some may succeed in this prediction exercise, while others may fail.

Howard, in a series of publications, introduced the concept of meta games in which he augmented the given strategies with some more, assuming that each player knows the other player's strategy, and we search for equilibrium points in the augmented pay-off matrix. Analysis of meta games provides a unifying way for solving both cooperative and competitive solutions to non-zero-sum games and has received a lot of attention from a wide spectrum of workers applying game theory to explain several economic and social phenomena. In fact, the prisoner's dilemma discussed in an earlier section that can represent quite a few phenomena in marketing can be a good starting point to explain the workings of meta games. Indeed, any competitive situation that involves some attempt by each player or decision-maker to use some intelligence input about the strategies likely to be adopted by decision-makers with their interests thriving either at the cost of others' interests or jointly with other decision-makers brings out the contribution of meta games. We can conveniently make use of the example in Ackoff and Sasieny (1968) as follows. Two large companies, A and B, currently have the same price for their principal competitive products. Each is contemplating reducing its price to gain an increase in market share and hence in profit. The situation can be represented in the following diagram:

	B maintains price	B reduces price
A maintains price	Status quo (3, 3)	B gains market share and profit (1, 4)
A reduces price	A gains market share and profit (4, 1)	Both retain market shares but lose profit (2, 2)

It is obvious that (2, 2) is the only equilibrium point, resulting in the loss of profit to both. Now imagine that B knew or believed to be able to correctly predict what A was going to do. Then B could have formulated four different strategies, as shown in the following table:

	B's Possible Strategies				
	1 Regardless	2 Regardless	Tit-for-Tat	Tat-for-Tit	A
1	(1)=3, 3	(2)=1, 4	(1)=3, 3	(2)=1, 4	
2	(1)=4, 1	(2)=2, 2	(2)=2, 2	(1)=4, 1	

It may be noted that in this extended game matrix, we also have the same equilibrium point (2, 2). Now, suppose A believes or claims that they can exactly predict which of the four strategies will be adopted by B. Hence, A can formulate 16 possible strategies to yield a more extended game matrix in which we will find 3 equilibrium points, including (1, 1) and (2, 2), and (1, 1) clearly dominates (2, 2).

We find that A's Strategy 14 (2, 2, 1, 2) is the rational strategy, since it maximizes A's gain for each of B's strategies. One may argue for the sake of natural inquisitiveness as to what would happen if A now formulates a further matrix with knowledge about which of the 16 strategies would be adopted by B. Fortunately, Howard has shown that further extension of the game matrix beyond n levels, where n=number of players, will not yield any further equilibrium points. We also note that if A adopts strategy 14 and B plays tit-for-tat, they cannot be certain whether A is adopting Strategy 14 or Strategy 5. If B predicts that A is playing Strategy 5, they will shift to '2 regardless' and thereby increase their gain to 4. This would, in turn, drive A to Strategy 16 and a pay-off pair (2, 2). Here lies the role of communication between the two players. In experimental plays of non-zero-sum games with or without communication between the two players, games allowing communication generally have a higher probability of reaching stability and of reaching it sooner.

Analysis of meta games identifies equilibrium points missed by classical game theory. It also identifies equilibrium points in games where classical theory finds none. Examples can be easily built up to illustrate this advantage of meta game analysis.

	A's Possible Strategies	B's Possible Strategies			
		1 Regardless	2 Regardless	Tit-for-tat	Tat-for-tit
1	1, 1, 1, 1	3, 3	1, 4	3, 3	1, 4
2	1, 1, 1, 2	3, 3	1, 4	3, 3	4, 1
3	1, 1, 2, 1	3, 3	1, 4	2, 2	1, 4
4	1, 2, 1, 1	3, 3	2, 2	3, 3	1, 4
5	2, 1, 1, 1	4, 1	1, 4	3, 3	1, 4
6	1, 1, 2, 2	3, 3	1, 4	2, 2	4, 1
7	1, 2, 1, 2	3, 3	2, 2	3, 3	4, 1
8	2, 1, 1, 2	4, 1	1, 4	3, 3	4, 1
9	1, 2, 2, 1	3, 3	2, 2	2, 2	1, 4
10	2, 1, 1, 1	4, 1	1, 4	2, 2	1, 4
11	2, 2, 1, 1	4, 1	2, 2	3, 3	1, 4
12	1, 2, 2, 2	3, 3	2, 2	2, 2	4, 1
13	2, 1, 2, 2	4, 1	1, 4	2, 2	4, 1
14	2, 2, 1, 2	4, 1	2, 2	3, 3	4, 1
15	2, 2, 2, 1	4, 1	2, 2	2, 2	1, 4
16	2, 2, 2, 2	4, 1	2, 2	2, 2	4, 1

An equilibrium point that dominates all others in the meta game matrix appears to be one that most players in experimental as well as real-life conflict situations seem to select. Departures from such a dominant equilibrium point are also being investigated.

Howard refers to an altruistic equilibrium point as an equilibrium point that results from each player's trying to maximize the minimum gain of their opponent. Howard claims that such an altruistic equilibrium point, if it exists, will be fully acceptable to all the players and hence will be capable of producing long-run stability.

6.8. Co-operative Games

In some cases, players in a game may decide to co-operate with one another through mutual discussions, adoption of joint or correlated strategies and agreement on sharing the total pay-off or amount of utility resulting at the end of a play in a bid to enhance the wealth or welfare of each. Players may even decide to form groups or coalitions which become the ultimate decision-making units (DMUs). In fact, n-person games with transferable utility (called by the acronym TU games) were studied quite early in the development of game theory. In such games, each coalition S, as a non-empty subset of the set of players N, will be assigned a value $v(S)$ representing the total pay-off or utility amount that the members can jointly guarantee themselves that can be transferred without loss among the members of S.

A co-operative game with conflict is bargaining. The seller of a product or service, for instance, wants to sell it at a higher price while the buyer prefers a lower price. But each of them cooperates with the other to reach at a final decision, which may be social welfare maximization. A co-operative game without a conflict is illustrated by a group of workers forming a union.

Co-operative game theory assumes that groups of players, called coalitions, are the primary units of decision-making and may enforce co-operative behaviour. Consequently, co-operative games can be seen as a competition between coalitions of players, rather than between individual players. One of the main research questions in cooperative game theory is how to allocate in some fair way the pay-off of the grand coalition among the players. The answer to this question is related to a solution concept which, roughly speaking, is a vector that represents the allocation to each player. Different solution concepts based on different notions of fairness have been proposed in the cooperative game theory literature.

One assumption that has been made in connection with TU games is that any two disjoint coalitions, when acting together, can get at least as much as they can when acting separately. This is the super-additivity assumption that has been questioned. Aumann and Dreze (1974) argue that 'acting together may be difficult or costly or even illegal or the players may for various personal reasons not wish to do so.'

Coming to coalition games, the two questions which solicit decisions by players are as follows:

1. Which coalitions are likely to be framed?
2. How will the players in a coalition actually formed apportion their joint profit?

The second question has been answered by considering coalitions as being exogenously given. The other approach of forming coalitions endogenously based on preferences of the individual players (as decision-makers) by using such criteria as value and stability has been more widely discussed and accepted. However, the assumption of transferability of utility has not been included. Such an NTU coalition game can be regarded as involving two stages, namely the formation of coalitions by the players in the first stage and a non-cooperative game among the coalitions in the second stage.

Let N be the set of players, i, a coalition S is a non-empty subset of N, a partition, $\prod$, divides N into disjoint coalitions, and $\prod(i)$ is a coalition containing Player i. Players have preferences over which groups they belong to. Each player ranks all the coalitions before they decide to join one. (If Player I ranks only coalitions which include i, we have a hedonic game.) Coalition S blocks $\prod$ if all players belonging to the coalition strictly prefer being in S to being in the current coalition i.

Partition Π is said to be core stable if there is no blocking coalition. It is strongly core stable if there is no weakly blocking coalition (implying no player is worse off, at least one player is better off).

Consider the three-player game with the following preference patterns:

$$\text{Preference of player a: } ab > ac > a > abc$$

$$\text{Preference of player b: } bc > ab > b > abc$$

$$\text{Preference of player c: } ac > bc > c > abc$$

We note that partition abc is not core stable, since a blocks it. Partition ab is also not core stable since bc is a blocking coalition. Partition c is not core stable because bc is a blocking coalition. Thus, this game does not admit of a core stable partition.

6.9. Stackelberg Games

These are strategic games in which players operate at two levels of a hierarchy. In some sense, one of the players—in a two-person game—is called a leader who has the authority to pre-commit a strategy, while the other, called the follower, makes a response taking into account the leader's strategy. The leader need not play first but has to make their strategy known to the follower. However, even if their mixed strategy in terms of probabilities of choosing the available alternative strategies is known to the follower, the strategy (option) actually played in real time by the leader remains unknown. The leader chooses their strategy by predicting the best response that the follower can make. Finally, the leader updates their strategy to minimize the total game cost. Both players want to maximize their gains. With three players, A, B and C, we can think of three different possibilities, namely (a) A leads while B and C follow, (b) A and B lead and C follows and (c) A leads, B follows and B leads with C as a follower. In this n-person non-zero-sum game, the strategies of one player are known to the other players as well as the corresponding pay-offs, and the players do not co-operate. Thus, the Stackelberg games (introduced by Stackelberg in 1934 in the context of market duopoly) are asymmetric games, in which strategies of each player are known to the other(s).

Solutions to these games are called Stackelberg equilibrium points. Under suitable conditions, these games attain equilibrium, and the equilibrium point may not be identical with the Nash equilibrium point. (Incidentally, a Nash equilibrium may not be accepted as a solution to the game if it is Pareto non-optimal, even if it is the Nash equilibrium.) Furthermore, assuming certain conditions, it can be shown that the Stackelberg equilibrium is not worse than the Nash equilibrium. As a theoretical explanation of duopoly and also oligopoly, Stackelberg games are well recognized in economic theory. However, the Cournot equilibrium in economics has a different explanation.

A strong Stackelberg equilibrium strategy assumes that the follower breaks ties with the leader, implying that they choose their optimal strategy, which is also optimal from the leader's perspective. A weak Stackelberg strategy assumes that the follower chooses the worst strategy from the leader's perspective. In a finite game with two players, there is always a Stackelberg equilibrium in pure strategies. A two-person Stackelberg game can be taken as a bi-level LP problem and solved, usually by using the Karush–Kuhn–Tucker conditions. When both the players have conditionally independent private types, conditioned on action and previous state that evolve as controlled Markov processes, we have a stochastic version of the Stackelberg game.

Starting with applications in economics, these games have later found useful applications in security, dealing with defenders (in the role of leaders) and attackers (in the role of followers). The attackers, knowing the strategy declared by the defenders, try to dodge the former to escape. Loud administrators and local cloud service providers are potential real-life players in such games. Interest has grown these days in Bayesian analysis of Stackelberg games. Coming to the case of one leader and multiple followers, with the leader not knowing which follower will eventually appear, except in terms of prior probabilities. Bayesian games can be transformed into normal-form games, as shown in Example 6.6.

Example 6.6. For two followers, each of the players has two strategies with pay-off-matrix shown in terms of c and d for follower Type 1 and c' and d' for follower Type 2. The probabilities that follower Types 1 and 2 will be active are respectively α and $1-\alpha$.

The transformed game with a single follower having (2,2) strategies is as follows:

And we can work out an equilibrium in pure strategies for this transformed problem.

Several different modifications of the Bayesian Stackelberg security games have been formulated under different scenarios and reported in the literature. Global optimization problems for Stackelberg security games can be represented usually as mixed-integer linear programmes or mixed-integer quadratic programming problems. As such, these problems are NP-hard. For an interesting discussion, one can refer to Wilczynski et al. (2016).

Table 6.1 *Pay-off Matrix for Leader along Rows and Follower along Columns*

	c	d	c'	d'
a	2.1	4.0	1.1	2.0
b	1.0	3.2	0.1	3.2

Table 6.2 *Pay-off Matrix for Leader along Rows and Follower along Columns*

	cc'	cd'	dc'	dd'
a	$2\alpha+(1-\alpha)$	2α	$4\alpha+(1-\alpha)^2$	$4\alpha+2(1-\alpha)$
b	$\alpha(1-\alpha)$	$\alpha+6(1-\alpha)^2$	$6\alpha^2+(1-\alpha)$	6

CHAPTER 7

Statistical Decision Theory

7.1. Introduction

Three major paradigms pervade statistical thoughts and procedures, namely data analysis, classical statistics (also called frequentist or Neyman–Pearson statistics) and Bayesian analysis, which emerged almost in this order over the years. Sometimes, the first two are clubbed together. However, it is useful to remember that in data analysis, we may not use any stochastic models, like the pre-Gaussian least squares analysis, whereas in classical statistics, we routinely use stochastic models to represent the data and the models contain some unknown parameters which are not regarded as random variables. The restricted application of probability only in repeatable cases is inherent in the frequentist view of probability. In the Bayesian context, both the data and the parameters in the model are treated as random variables.

Wald's theory of statistical decision functions significantly expanded the scope of the concepts of confidence intervals and hypothesis testing and continued to keep the statistics fraternity engaged in its serious pursuit for some decades. Beyond the classical problems of parameter estimation and hypothesis testing, several other decision problems which could be solved in terms of data-based decision rules were brought under the umbrella of statistical decision theory. Thus, problems of classification and discrimination of subset selection of variables in regression analysis or ranking of populations with unknown parameters on the basis of sample observations and the like could all be considered in terms of decision rules, which involve implicitly an element of optimization relative to the context.

Statistical decision theory relates to decisions which precede actions and make use of information contained in sample observations as well as non-sampling information, like information about prior probabilities. Thus, decisions here are based on observed values of some random variable(s) assumed to follow a probability distribution which is either completely unspecified or only incompletely specified. The possible probability models from which the data at hand have arisen or unknown true values of the parameter(s) in an otherwise specified probability model or the classes/populations with their corresponding probability distribution to which the data belong are possible states of nature. In some sense, decision variables are parameters of the unknown population(s) involved in the decision-making problem and the decision-making process usually takes advantage of all relevant information available a priori. Eventually, decision functions or rules based thereon will be the decision alternatives on which we will apply some optimality principle to obtain the optimal rule and, subsequently, the optimal action. Such decisions lead to actions such as computing an estimate of some unknown population parameter, accepting (rejecting) a hypothesis regarding the value(s) of some parameter(s), choosing one out of several probability models that fit the observed data, classifying a given individual (set of observations) into one of several likely populations wherefrom it could arise and the like. Problems recognized as parameter estimation or hypothesis testing or classification or selection and the like illustrate statistical decision problems. To find out if the number of pavement dwellers in a particular city has increased by 20 per cent over the last 10 years, to estimate the relative potency of a new drug being developed, to classify an incoming patient in a healthcare facility as suffering from one of several distinct diseases or to find out who among a certain number of candidates should be selected on the basis of performance in a sample of tasks, can all be treated as statistical decision problems.

Decision alternatives could be possible different functions of the observed data that could be accepted as estimates of some unknown parameter, different critical regions leading to acceptance or rejection of a given hypothesis, alternative probability models that could possibly fit the observed data set, possible classes to which a given individual with observed values of some features (random variables), etc.

Decisions are generally made in a repetitive context and are yielded on a given occasion by following a decision rule applied to the observations available on that particular occasion. These rules, which dominate the study of statistical decision theory, can also be treated as decision alternatives quite justifiably. The search is for optimal decision rules, and these rules involve (statistical) decision functions and regions based on such functions. In this context, we may note that decision rules sharing some common properties are sometimes grouped into classes and such classes can be looked upon as alternatives. Some concepts, such as admissibility, completeness and the like, are typical properties of these classes of rules. As mentioned earlier, the role of prior information is quite important in this theory.

Statistical decision theory has been developed from several perspectives in several different directions, not only to find applications in several different areas of scientific investigation but also to enrich the substantive content (not merely the technical content) of research works in several real-life situations, from genomics, on the one hand, to systems engineering, on the other. Volumes have been written on this expanding subject and, by no means, this chapter is meant to provide anything beyond a broad idea of statistical decision theory, without entering into mathematical intricacies. In fact, many complex computational aspects, along with the algorithms to handle them, have been generally ignored. Even coverage of all important aspects is not being claimed. Keeping in view the expanding scope for application of Bayesian decision methods and procedures to enrich the substantial content of scientific studies in several emerging areas, a relatively greater emphasis has been laid on a discussion of the Bayesian paradigm and its prolongations. Similarly, one may find the section on multiple decision functions too sketchy, and an attempt has been made to expose the problem of robust decision-making.

7.2. Beginning from Classical Statistics

Classical statistics provide an interesting platform for decision-making under uncertainty. It may be added right here that parameter estimation and hypothesis testing (that way, choosing an appropriate stochastic model for the observed data) were the major concerns of decision-makers in classical statistics. Although decisions were based on the observed data, the performance of the decision alternative was judged by considering (averaging or integrating over) the entire sample space (encompassing all possible data). Thus, in the parameter estimation problem, the performance criterion for a possible estimate (regarded as an estimator or a random function of the observed data) was bias or sampling variance or both, and for a particular state of nature or true value of the parameter, we would calculate the expectation and/or the variance of an estimate by taking into account the entire sample space and going for an estimate with a minimum difference from the true parameter value or computing the sampling variance and choosing the minimum variance estimate. We would combine both the performance criteria and go for the minimum variance unbiased estimate. We could look beyond a particular state of nature and look for an estimate which would have a uniformly minimum bias among possible estimates, considering all possible states of nature. Thus, we would seek uniformly minimum variance unbiased estimates. Similarly, in the case of hypothesis testing, we will take the probability of committing a Type II error (of not rejecting the null hypothesis when the latter is not true and a certain deviation is the true state of nature) as the criterion of performance for a test and will seek the most powerful or even uniformly most powerful tests.

Contributions by Wald (1950) and Savage (1954) made a remarkable departure from this practice in the sense of introducing concepts of loss associated with each state of nature for each of the decision alternatives and the related concept of 'regret', focusing attention only on the data at hand and considering minimaxity as the optimality principle for choosing a decision alternative. One may note that 'loss' and 'regret' are essentially linked up with pay-off or utility advocated as outcomes of different options or alternatives under different states of nature in decision theory. (While economists focus attention on positive outcomes, like pay-off or gain in utility, statisticians are usually cautious to avoid loss as much as possible.)

As stated by Brown (2000), Wald viewed his theory as a codification and generalization of the theory of tests and confidence intervals already developed by Neyman and Pearson. The tools developed by Wald and subsequently by others survive as essential building blocks in contemporary research. In fact, Brown asserts that the minimax principle has been an essential foundation for advances in many areas of statistical research, such as hierarchical models, robust estimation, optimal design and non-parametric function analysis.

7.3. Statistical Decision Process

Let us recall at this stage—at the cost of some redundancy—the distinctive features of the statistical decision-making process before we proceed further. The constituents of this process may be comprehended as a set of states of nature, $\mu \in M$, which are generally in terms of some parameter (scalar or vector) in the distribution of the observed random variable(s) in the experiment or investigation to provide information and reduce the extent and impact of uncertainty, the parameter value being unknown to us. Sometimes, we may assume some probability distribution over this set, reflecting degrees of our belief that the individual states will be realized in practice.

A set of experiments or, better, experimental designs, $e \in E$ which we adopt to collect information about the unknown states of nature, reduce the extent of uncertainty in decisions. The design could be in terms of some decision variables, such as the number of observations to be collected or the stopping time or the type of controls to be exercised in collecting the observations. While the decision-making process, in its entirety, should take due account of the nature and boundary of E, in most decision problems, we start with a known set or even with just one known design e.

A set of outcomes $X \in S$ (the sample space) of the experiment, usually a set of random variables (affected by chance causes over and above assignable causes) which are observed (measured) during the experiment e.

A set of decision functions $d(x)$ based on the observed outcome x. It could be the value(s) of some statistic(s) computed from the observed x. Quite often, the decision function is in terms of a partition of the sample space or of the space of some statistics computed from the observed x. In the case of a single statistic computed from the observed x (which could be multidimensional), the decision function could be a partition of the real line representing possible values of the statistic. Decisions follow from the use of some decision rules applied to the decision functions. For example, accept a hypothesis if the value of the statistic lies in some specified interval on the line or assign a subject to a particular class/group if the statistic value belongs to a particular interval. Thus, the decision rule $\delta(x) \in D$ may be looked upon as a decision alternative.

A set of actions $a \in A$ which are indicated by the corresponding set of decisions. Actions could be 'accept, reject and continue to collect more information', 'assign a new individual to class or Group j ($j=1, 2, \ldots, m$, say)', 'select some population(s) as the best or the k "best" among $m > k$ populations', etc.

Thus, we deal with three spaces, namely the outcome space S, the decision space D and the action space A.

The problem in statistical decision theory and its scope in its classical set-up may be summarized as follows. Let $\{f_\mu, \mu \in\}$ be a family of probability density (mass) functions—univariate or multivariate—indexed by the unknown parameter μ (may be a vector) and let $(X_1, X_2, \ldots, X_n)$ be a set of values observed from f. A decision function d maps any point X in the sample space (of all observable values) to the set of decisions d (leading through a decision rule δ to corresponding actions) a. Thus:

$$\delta(X) = a \in A \text{ (the action space)}$$

If A contains only two elements, namely a_1 (accept the null hypothesis) and a_2 (reject the null hypothesis), the decision rule is to divide the sample space into two parts based on the observed value X, with action a_1 if the observed set belongs to the first part, otherwise the second action is taken. This corresponds to the problem of testing a statistical hypothesis and the actions correspond to rejection of the hypothesis and its acceptance (failing to reject). If A is the entire real line (space) or a delineated part thereof, we have the problem of estimation of parameter μ. If several groups within the family f are to be recognized as relevant, the action based on the decision function places the observed set into one of these groups. This is the problem of classification.

A considerable part of our discussion in this chapter has been in terms of the problem of estimation, and in that context, the differentiation between the decision function d and the corresponding decision rule δ does not matter much. Even though we do not need to bring in the notion of an action, a, that can also be dispensed with, our focus boils down to $d(X)$.

An important element in statistical decision theory, somewhat interpreted as a negative concept of utility or pay-off as the outcome of any action (based on a decision), is that of a loss function, L. The loss incurred by the statistician (decision-maker) if, based on an observed set X, a decision $d(X)$ leads to an action a, when the true value of the parameter is μ, is indicated by the loss function $L(\mu, d(X))$. This is a random variable with a distribution induced by the random variable X. The expected value of this random loss is called the risk associated with the decision function d when the true value of the parameter is μ, denoted by the symbol $R(\mu, d)$. In fact, this risk is the outcome of repeated decision-making of adopting the decision function (rule) d when the true state of nature is the value of μ. To illustrate, if d stands for an estimator of μ, the squared error loss, $L = E(d(X) - \mu)^2$, which is the mean squared error and is the sampling variance of the estimator d when d is taken to be an unbiased estimator.

While the squared error loss has been very widely used, other forms of loss functions have also found applications in some real-life applications. Thus, a very simple loss function appropriate in some cases is the $0-1$ loss function, in which an action based on an estimate of the state of nature equals the true state and does not cause any loss, while a unit loss (which can be suitably scaled up) occurs if the true state could not be found by the decision rule. Similarly, one can use the absolute error loss or the exponential loss or the linear exponential (LINEX) loss or the logistic loss or some generalized loss. A detailed discussion of loss functions appears in Section 7.4.

In the case of testing a hypothesis H_0: $\mu = \mu_0$ against the alternative H_1: $\mu \neq \mu_0$, a natural loss function associated with a decision rule ð is given by:

$$L(\mu, ð) = 1 \text{ if } \mu = \mu_0 \text{ and } a = a_2$$

$$= 1 \text{ if } \mu \neq \mu_0 \text{ and } a = a_1$$

$$= 0 \text{ otherwise}$$

The risk function takes the values $R(\mu, ð)$ which are known as the probabilities of incurring Type I and Type II errors respectively.

The problem in statistical decision theory can now be stated as: Given a decision function, $d \in D$, a loss function, $L(\mu, d)$, and the payoff or risk function, $R(\mu, d)$, how to choose a decision function $d(X)$ or a rule based thereon such that it has a risk that never exceeds the risk associated with any other decision function, whatever the unknown parameter value, and the 'problem' is that such a function does not generally exist. It may be added here that a decision rule based on a decision function d will usually involve computation of some statistic(s) from the observed value of X, some constants or parameters and some statement(s), and to find an 'optimal' rule will have to address these three aspects of the problem.

7.3.1. Decision Rules

A decision rule has been generally taken as a map from the observed outcome to an appropriate action a, and for this purpose, a decision rule stated as a logical proposition, namely 'if' (condition), 'then' (action), can involve some parameters, besides including some decision variable(s) in the experimental design. If the 'then' part is definitely given, we have a non-randomized rule. If, on the other hand, the decision rule maps an observed outcome to a probability distribution over the action space or associates a probability with each of the actions in

A, then the rule is said to be 'randomized'. Hence, the consequences of adopting a randomized decision rule, based on a given observed value of the outcome *x* of the experiment, will be a probability distribution of the consequence variable(s) induced by the probability dp distribution corresponding to the decision rule.

A simple way to state a randomized decision rule is to start with several, say k, decision rules δ_i, $i = 1, 2, \ldots, k$, to associate probabilities p_i with rule δ_i and finally to adopt the (randomized) decision rule $\delta_0 = \Sigma \delta_i p_i$. If we can develop a mechanism to select one of the rules using these probabilities, say δ_j, then compute $\delta_j(x)$ to choose the appropriate action.

Randomized decision rules extend the decision space D to D^* the space of probability distributions on D. The loss of a randomized decision rule (like an estimate) δ^* is defined as the average loss:

$$L(\mu, \delta^*(x)) = \int L(\mu, a) \, \delta^*(x, a) \, da$$

where $\delta^*(x, a)$ is the probability density on D. This extension, ix, required for the study of minimaxity and admissibility. Incidentally, for every prior distribution, the Bayes risk on the set of randomized estimates is the same as the Bayes risk on the set of non-randomized estimates. In finite decision problems, randomized decision rules define a risk set which is the convex hull of the risk points of the non-randomized decision rules.

To illustrate a randomized decision rule, let us consider the following simple hypothesis testing exercise:

Example 7.1. Let the sample observation X have a binomial, $B(n, p)$, distribution and suppose we have to develop a test for the null hypothesis, $H_0 : p < p_0$, against the alternative, $H_1 : p \geq p_0$, with the requirement that the size of the test or the probability of Type I error is a pre-specified value α. Consider the following class of randomized decision, δ, based on the decision function $d(X) =$ Sample total T.

Action Reject H_0 if T/n with probability

Some research workers classify decision rules as under, though such a classification is not a bad necessity. Here, we have the following categories of decision rules (Thomas & Thomas, 2006):

- **Crisp, exact:** Here, the 'then' part is univocal.
- **Crisp, approximate:** Induced from an inconsistent part of a data set, identified using the rough set theory. The 'then' part specifies several possible decisions that cannot be reduced to a single one due to inconsistent information.
- **Possible:** Covering entities that may belong to the class suggested in the 'then' part, entities that belong to a class are identified through rough set theory as entities belonging to the so-called upper approximation of the class.
- **Fuzzy:** Where each action in 'then' has a certain grade of membership for being appropriate.
- **Probabilistic:** Where 'then' covers entities which really belong to a class but also entities from other classes, with a requirement that entities from the first class outnumber those from other classes.

Decision rules which take into account observations of several variables, some with a positive utility and others with a negative utility, map the set of observed variable values or categories to a single element in the action space. In doing this, we may have compensatory rules that lead to the best action by balancing good and bad or positive and negative observations, like ratings by consumers on a particular brand of a product before taking a decision to purchase that brand or not. There are also non-compensatory rules and the three forms of them are as follows:

Non-compensatory and disjunctive: Where at least one good or positive data part is required to lead to the action 'purchase'.

Non-compensatory and conjunctive: Where a decision to purchase is made only when the data observed contains no negative value or rating.

Non-compensatory and lexicographic: Where the decision is based only on the observed values for the most important variables or ratings.

7.4. Some Examples

Before we proceed to discuss the optimality principle and subsequently details of the minimax and Bayes decision rules as well as further developments in statistical decision theory, let us illustrate some statistical decision problems which are widely known and can be conveniently delineated without much of a mathematical complexity. In the following sub-sections, we take up a few such problems.

7.4.1. Problem of Sampling Inspection

Reverting to the problem of single sampling inspection by an attribute mentioned earlier, we recognize the following elements:

The experiment e consists in inspecting a number n (to be determined as a decision variable) and classifying each item inspected as either defective or non-defective. The outcome space consists of n elements, which are 0 (for a non-defective item) and 1 (for a defective item). The decision function is $d(X) =$ number of defectives x observed, and this follows a binomial distribution $Bin(n, p)$ where p is the unknown probability of an item being defective. The decision rule states that: if $x > c$ (a specified number), reject the lot; otherwise, accept the lot. The parameters (n, c) are elements of the decision rule and have to be determined by the decision-maker. (To be noted is the fact that d and δ are different and that the decision rule is really given in terms of two variables, namely n and c. Hence, the pair (n, c) can be regarded as a decision alternative.) States of nature or parameters in the family of distributions from which the observations arise are values of 'p'. Only the trivial rule characterized by $(N, 0)$ can perform better than all others, whatever be p.

Here, performance of a non-trivial decision rule takes into account a feasibility requirement besides a pay-off function (or the risk function). The feasibility requirement is that the customer's risk defined as $\text{Prob}(c > x | p_t)$ where p_t is the highest tolerable proportion of defects specified by the customer is pre-specified (usually at 10% level). The risk function in this case (allowing complete inspection of a lot of N items rejected on the basis of sampling)—which can allow a comparison among alternative decision rules—does not explicitly involve a loss function and is given in terms of the 'average amount of inspection': $R(p; n, c) = n + (N-n) \text{Prob}[x > c]$.

The loss function of an acceptance rejection type plan where all items found during inspection are removed, satisfying the requirement of a customer's risk of close to 10 per cent, can be formulated in terms of cost of inspection (a per item), cost of wrongly rejecting a good quality item (b per item) and cost of accepting a poor quality item (k per item) and stated as:

$$L(p; n, c) = n \cdot a + (Np - x) \cdot k \qquad \text{if } x < \text{or} = c$$
$$= n \cdot a + b \cdot N(1-p) \qquad \text{if } x > c$$

The expected loss or risk assuming a binomial distribution of x becomes:

$$R(n, c) = n \cdot a + (N-n) p L(p) \cdot k + N(1-p)[1-L(p)] b$$

One can now introduce a prior distribution for p like the beta $B(m, n)$, with m and n known to work out the Bayes risk. The form of the loss function in an acceptance rectification plan and subsequent developments will change.

With the risk function stated above, it is well-nigh impossible to find the minimax risk solution corresponding to the least favourable distribution.

To sum up, we note that the decision-making process involves non-sampling prior information about p_0 and p_t besides as also the customer's risk besides the sample information X.

Hald (1981) discussed Bayesian sampling inspection plans most comprehensively. A considerable lot of literature has grown around Bayesian analysis of sampling inspection plans and their variants. In some of these contributions, the objective function to be minimized (with respect to the plan parameters) is not just the total system cost, but the ratio between this cost and the probability of correct detection. In this context, we should note that the focus is risk/expected cost minimization and not to work out the Bayes estimate of the unknown fraction defective in a lot. (Indirectly, this estimate is linked to the plan parameters, no doubt.) Some authors have studied the posterior distribution of the unknown fraction defective to find the probability that the posterior estimate exceeds the acceptable quality level. This probability may be incorporated in a feasibility constraint. While the beta prior has been most often used to represent likelihoods of different states of nature, other priors have also been studied. In some investigations, errors in inspection are taken care of. However, one important element in this broad problem remains in terms of the plan parameters (of which Bayes risk is a function) being positive integers.

7.4.2. Problem of Classification

Let us consider the problem of assigning an individual to any one of k classes or groups to which the individual may belong on the basis of a set of observed characteristics (to be regarded as random variables). Such a problem may arise when a newly found plant or animal has to be identified as belonging to one of several phenotypes or when an anatomist is required to identify the sex of a new born baby that is buried under the earth or when a medical practitioner has to find out whether a particular treatment should be undertaken for a particular patient presenting certain symptoms. There could exist situations where the observed individual does not belong to any of the already identified groups, as is the case when the concerned scientist discovers a new group or class.

Let X denote the measurements of an individual and S the sample space representing all possible values of X based on the observation x. A decision has to be taken about which group the individual belongs to. A non-randomized decision rule consists of partitioning the sample space into k mutually exclusive regions $w_1, w_2, \ldots, w_k$ and assigning an individual with measurements x to the ith population if $x \in w_i$. (In this case, the hypothesis is accepted.) The expected loss in applying this rule assigning an individual truly belonging to group i to group j is:

$$L_1 = f_{w1}\, r_{i1}\, P_1(x)\, dx + \ldots + f_{wk}\, r_{ik}\, P\, P_1(x)\, dx$$

where r_{ij} is the loss incurred in wrongly assigning a member of the ith population to the jth population.

A randomized decision rule, on the other hand, determines a vector with elements $\lambda_i(x)$, $i = 1, 2, \ldots, k$ with the stipulation that an individual with measurements x will be assigned to group I with probability $\lambda_I(x)$. After we get the observation x, we carry out a random experiment with k possible outcomes $1, 2, \ldots, k$ with probabilities $\lambda_1, \lambda_2, \ldots, \lambda_k$, and if the outcome turns out to be i, the individual is placed in group i. There will be infinitely many non-randomized or randomized decision rules.

Mis-classification results in loss in this problem. The loss function for a non-randomized rule, when the individual really belongs to group i, can be expressed as:

$$L_I = \int_{w_i} r_{i1} P_I(x)\, dx + \ldots + \int_{w_k} r_{ik} P_I(x)\, dx$$

Where r_{ij} is the loss incurred in assigning an individual belonging to group I to group j and $P_I(x)$ is the probability density at x for the distribution in group i. We can similarly define a loss for the randomized decision rule. In both cases, we have a loss vector which, as expected, plays a significant role in making a decision.

7.4.3. Problem of Prediction

The problem of classification does involve prediction of the label or class to which an individual belongs, on the basis of current observations of some features (random variables) using a decision rule based on available past (training) data on the features. A prediction problem implies the prediction of a measured quantity. Here, the predicted value(s) will be compared with the corresponding value(s) to be realized in the future to assess the performance of the prediction function.

Some investigators distinguish prediction from forecasting, some others do not. Prediction of the value(s) of some variable(s) of interest may be based on the value(s) of other variable(s) which influence the former, currently observed. Forecasting uses current values to guess values in the future and, in that way, is commonly considered in the context of time series analysis.

In both prediction and forecasting, we have to decide on the choice of variables used to predict or time points, as well as variables to be used for forecasting, besides the type of relations assumed between the variable(s) to be predicted and the predictor(s) or between the current value(s) and value(s) at past points of time. Whether the observed values or some suitable transforms should be involved in the analysis is also a decision issue.

7.4.4. Ranking and Selection Problem

Considerable attention of statisticians and decision theorists was focused on ranking and selection during the second half of the last century and a huge volume of published materials on the subject present a wide swathe of real-life decision problems and procedures to resolve them. There are a few classes of R&D problems corresponding to different objectives. Thus, we have the problem of selecting the system with the largest or smallest expected performance measure. One formulation of this type is the Indifference zone formulation. These procedures are designed to select the system with the highest true mean or a system with a true mean within less than δ of the highest true mean with probability $(1-\alpha)$. The second type of problem concerns selection of the system most likely to perform best in a single trial with a specified probability of correct selection guaranteed. Some problems may relate to complex systems, and we need to simulate their performance to rank the alternative systems and select the best. In situations where there is a limit on the budget for computation, we may proceed along Bayesian lines with some prior information.

An informative review of ranking and selection procedures is by Gupta and Panchapakesan (1984). Incidentally, these two authors, along with their co-workers, figure prominently among those who have contributed significantly to the relevant literature.

Let us consider a set of $k \geq 2$ normal populations with unknown means μ_i, $i=1, 2, ..., k$, and a common known variance σ^2. Our goal is to select a subset of size at most $m(1 \leq m \leq k-t)$ so that at least one of the populations with the $t(1 \leq t \leq k-1)$ largest means is included in the selected subset with a minimum guaranteed probability of P^*, whenever the difference between two consecutive ordered means is at least δ^* where P^* and δ^* are pre-specified. Several investigators have developed rules for subset selection under different assumptions about the populations and using concepts of preference zones and indifference zones, applied to samples of the same size from each population. Sequential procedures have also been studied. The special case of $t=1$ has been of interest in many DMPs. For the normal case, variance has been considered as the measure of performance by some authors, while the procedures for non-normal distributions have also been worked out. The case of any distribution (having some specified properties) has been solved by Mahamunulu (1967) with mean as the measure of performance or the criterion using a common fixed sample size from each population by calculating statistics from the samples and assuming that these are stochastically increasing in the corresponding means for each fixed sample size.

7.5. The Optimality Principle

Given the risk matrix (which could be infinite dimensional) where rows correspond to decision rules (and corresponding actions) $d(X)$ and columns correspond to states of nature (μ), we have three criteria to find what may be called the optimal rule. These are the uniformly minimum risk criterion, the minimax risk criterion and the minimum expected risk criterion. For the third criterion, we require a probability distribution over the parameter space M. Most often, no rule satisfying the first criterion can be found, unless we restrict the class of rules by imposing conditions, like unbiasedness. In the discussion that follows, we consider problems of parameter estimation only, without losing any generality.

The frequentist approach is not reductive enough to yield a single optimal solution, though the Bayesian paradigm does offer a unique optimal decision. Two optimality principles have been discussed in the former approach, namely minimaxity and admissibility. The minimax criterion was introduced as an insurance against the worst case, aiming at minimizing the expected loss (risk) in the least favourable case. From the Bayesian point of view, it is like putting a prior concentrated on the worst cases. States of nature which correspond to the largest loss situations are, in fact, very unlikely to occur. The first oil-drilling platforms were designed according to a minimax principle. In fact, they were supposed to withstand the combined action of the strongest gale and the strongest storm, at the minimal record temperature. Such a strategy gives a comfortable margin of safety but at a huge cost. Engineers took into account the distribution of such extreme weather phenomena in designing more recent platforms to reduce production costs.

The minimax rule associated with a loss function L is the value:

$$R^* = \inf_{\delta \in D^*} \sup_\mu R(\mu, d)$$

And a minimax decision function (possibly randomized) δ_0 is such that:

$$\sup_\mu R(\mu, \delta_0)$$

Example 7.2. Let X be Bernoulli $(1, p)$ and let p have two distinct values only, namely 1/4 and 1/2. The set of decision rules includes four elements, namely $d_1(0) = d_1(1) = a_1$; $d_2(0) = a_1$, $d_2(1) = a_2$; $d_3(0) = a_2$, $d_3(1) = a_1$, and $d_4(0) = d_4(1) = a_2$. Let us assume the following loss function values for the actions a_1 and a_2: $L(1/4, a_1) = 1$; $L(1/4, a_2) = 4$; $L(a_1, 1/2) = 3$, and $L(1/2, a_2) = 2$

The risk matrix can now be shown as:

Decision	p=1/4	p=1/2	Max Risk
d_1	1	3	3
d_2	7/4	5/2	5/2
d_3	13/4	5/2	13/4
d_4	4	2	4

Thus, the minimax decision rule is d_2 with a maximum risk of 5/2.

An important problem affecting minimaxity is that a minimax estimator does not necessarily exist. Risk is a convex function of the decision rule and the supremum of a convex function is convex. The infimum of this convex supremum may not always exist, and if it does, it may be intractable computationally. A minimax strategy exits when the state space is finite and the loss function is continuous. Towards this, we get the theorem due to Blackwell and Girshick (1954), which states: If the decision space is a convex compact set, and if the loss function is continuous and convex as a function of d for every $\mu \in M$, *there exists a non-randomized minimax estimator.*

There may be several minimax estimators and some of them may even perform uniformly better than others. It then becomes necessary to introduce a second (and more local) criterion to compare minimax estimators and to find estimators which perform 'globally' well.

The Bayes risk of a decision function d associated with a loss function is defined as:

$$R(\Pi, d) = E_\Pi R(\mu, d)$$

A decision function rule based on the d^* is known as a Bayesian rule if it minimizes the Bayes risk, that is, if:

$$R(\Pi, \delta^*) = \inf_\delta R(\Pi, \delta)$$

Sometimes, the Bayes estimate may not exist because the infimum of Bayes risk may not be attained by any decision rule. In such a case, we can find for some $\epsilon > 0$ a rule δ_ϵ such that $R(\Pi, \delta_\epsilon) < m_x + \epsilon$, and this rule will be called an ϵ-Bayes decision rule. If further, a rule δ is ϵ-Bayes for every $\epsilon > 0$ with respect to some prior (which may not be the same for different values of ϵ), then the rule is called extended Bayes.

The conditional distribution of μ, given $X=x$, is called the posterior distribution of the random variable μ, given the sample. It can be easily shown that the posterior mean, namely $E(\mu|X=x) = d(x)$ is the Bayes estimate of μ if we take the squared error loss. This is illustrated for the case of estimation of the Binomial parameter p as under:

Example 7.3. Assume X to have the binomial distribution with parameters n and p. Suppose we take a uniform prior for p over the support $0 < p < 1$ and the loss function as:

$$L(p, d) = [p - d(x)]^2$$

In this case, the posterior distribution of p comes out as:

$$H(p|x) = [{^nC_x} p_x (1-p)^{n-x}] / [\int^n C_x p^x (1-p)^{n-x} dp]$$

It follows that $E(p|x)=(x+1)/(n+2)$ which is the Bayes estimate.

The Bayes risk works out as: $1/[6(n+1)]$

Example 7.4. Let X be distributed as a normal $N(\mu, 1)$ variate and let us take the prior for μ as $N(0, 1)$. We assume the squared error loss to find the Bayes estimate of μ. It can be shown that the posterior distribution of μ given x has the p.d.f:

$$h(\mu|x)=[2\Pi/(n+1)]^{-1/2} \exp[-(n+1)/2\{\mu-\Sigma x(n+1)\}^2]$$

Hence, the Bayes estimate of μ works out as: $d^*(x)=E(\mu|x)=\Sigma x/(n+1)$ with the Bayes risk as: $r(\Pi, d^*)=1/(n+1)$.

7.6. Derivation of Minimax and Bayes Estimators

A decision rule δ is called an equalizer rule if $R(\mu, \delta)$ is the same for every value of the parameter in the state space. An equalizer rule that is extended Bayes must be minimax. In fact, one way to derive a minimax estimator is to work out the Bayes estimator and then to find if there exists a prior distribution that can render the Bayes risk a constant, independent of the parameter being estimated. In such a case, the Bayes estimate is evidently a minimax estimate. This is indicated by the following theorem: Suppose an estimate d^* is a Bayes estimate corresponding to a prior distribution Π on the parameter space. If the risk function $R(d^*, \mu)$ is a constant on M, then d^* is a minimax estimate of μ.

Example 7.5. Let $X \sim b(n, p)$. We want a Bayes estimate of p in the form $\alpha X + \beta$, using the squared error loss function (SELF). This implies that the risk of this linear estimate is:

$$R(p, d) = E_p([\alpha - np] + \beta + [\alpha n - 1] p)^2$$
$$= ([\alpha n - 1]^2 - \alpha^2 n) p^2 + (\alpha^2 n + 2\beta[\alpha n - 1]) p + \beta^2$$

To make this a constant, we set the coefficients of p and p^2 as zero to get:

$$(\alpha n-1)^2 - \alpha^2 n = 0 \text{ and } \alpha^2 n + 2\beta(\alpha n - 1) = 0 \text{ to yield}$$

$$\alpha = 1/[n^{1/2}(1+n^{1/2})] \text{ or } 1/[n^{1/2}(n^{1/2}-1)] \text{ and}$$

$$\beta = 1/[2(1+n^{1/2})] \text{ or } -1/[2(n^{1/2}-1)]$$

Since p lies between 0 and 1, we discard the second set of roots for both α and β so that the Bayes estimate with a constant risk becomes:

$$D^*(X) = X/(n^{1/2}[1+n^{1/2}]) + 1/(2[1+n^{1/2}])$$

Now, it can be shown that this linear estimate is a Bayes estimate for a prior with p.d.f.

$\prod(p) = [B(\alpha', \beta')]^{-1} p^{\alpha'-1}(1-p)^{\beta'-1}$, which yields the posterior expectation of p, given X, as $d^*(X)$ provided $\alpha' = \beta' = n^{1/2}/2$. This results in the minimax estimate $d^*(X)$ with a constant risk:

$$R(p, d^*) = 1/(4[1+n^{1/2}]^2)$$

Comparing this with the minimum-variance unbiased estimator (UMVUE; which is also the maximum likelihood estimate), namely $d(X) = X/n$, we find that the minimax estimate has a lower risk for small n, the reverse being the case with large n.

Going in a slightly different way, we can assume the least favourable distribution to be the beta distribution $B(\alpha, \beta)$ so that the Bayes estimator of p comes out as:

$Đ_\wedge(X) = (a+x)/(a+b+n)$ with the risk function for quadratic loss as:

$$RR(p, ð_\wedge) = (\alpha^2 + [n-2\alpha\{\alpha+\beta\}]p + [\{\alpha+\beta\}^2-n]p^2)/(\alpha+\beta+n)^2$$

For this to be a constant independent of p, we should have:

$$(\alpha+\beta)^2 = n \text{ and } 2\alpha(\alpha+\beta) = n$$

Which have a solution $\alpha = \beta = n^{1/2}/2$ giving the Bayes estimate:

$$ð_\wedge(x) = (x + n^{1/2}/2)/(x + n^{1/2})$$

This is the unique Bayes estimate, and hence, this is also the unique minimax estimate.

However, if we consider ∧ to be any arbitrary distribution over (0, 1), we can have more than one Bayes estimate with the same risk for priors which differ in respect of the first $n+1$ moments, and we do not have a unique minimax estimate.

7.7. Admissibility

If the losses for one decision rule dominate those for the second, the second rule is obviously better. However, if for some states of nature (in this case, groups), one rule involves greater losses than another, while a reverse behaviour is observed for the remaining states, then the two decision rules are not comparable. To choose between two such rules, we bring in the additional criterion of admissibility.

Using 'risk' as the criterion, the optimality principle for comparing alternative decision functions cannot be for a given state of nature or a value of μ. Decision-making under certainty makes little sense here, since we are primarily interested in estimating the unknown parameter directly or otherwise. Hence, the optimality principle in general decision problems makes use of an ordering among the alternatives in respect of a 'criterion' based on some pay-off or utility measure. Thus, taking risk as a criterion, a decision rule d dominates another decision rule d' if and only if $R(\mu, d') \geq R(\mu, d)$ for all μ, with strict inequality for some μ. The dominance relation is not a strict relation and establishes a partial order among the alternatives. With the additional requirement of being transitive as well as acyclic, the dominance principle corresponds to a strict ordering of the set of alternatives.

A decision rule is said to be admissible (with respect to a loss function) if and only if no other rule dominates it; otherwise, it is inadmissible. Thus, an admissible rule is a maximal element with respect to the dominance principle. An inadmissible rule is not usually considered. Admissibility, as a concept, is not an analogue of 'feasibility' of an alternative rule. However, inadmissible rules may be left out of the search for optimal decision rules. In fact, admissibility is something like weak optimality or Paretian efficiency. We have to find out which rules among the admissible ones perform better than others. If the class of admissible rules consists of a single member, we have an optimum solution. But generally, the class is quite wide and no two decision rules in the admissible set are comparable.

Wald took the stand that the decision-maker should be prepared for the worst situation, may it be a state of nature which results in the maximum risk, when the performance of a given decision function is considered against all possible states of nature. Branded as a 'pessimist' in the annals of management science, Wald proposed the 'minimax regret' criterion as the optimality principle.

The application of the minimax regret principle to choosing the optimal decision rule poses the computational problem of evaluating risks associated with possible states of nature (values of μ) for each of the rules under consideration. The latter could be quite considerable in the general set-up. It is true that in some real situations, we should incorporate only small number of states of nature and limit our choice to only a handful of alternative decision functions. In such situations, by constructing the risk matrix and applying the minimax principle, we can conveniently find out the optimal rule.

The other principle corresponds to decision-making under uncertainty or better risk, where we assign probabilities of realization to each possible state of nature. In fact, we treat the state of nature or the unknown parameter value as a random variable with an assumed probability distribution, denoted by $\prod(\mu)$ quite often taken to be continuous. This distribution is taken as a part of the 'information' provided to the decision-maker a priori and is commonly called a prior distribution. Further, we now argue that the risk associated with a decision function when the true value of the parameter is specified, that is, $R(\mu, d)$ is the conditional expected loss, given μ, and we can work out the unconditional risk by taking into account the prior distribution to arrive at what is generally called the Bayes risk, namely $ER(\mu, d)$, expectation over $\prod$. Subsequently, we can use minimum expected risk (unconditional risk) as the optimality principle. This gives us what is called the Bayes rule relative to the prior $\prod$. There may be several Bayes rules, and the choice of the prior is quite relevant.

In the Bayesian approach to decision-making, the observed value of X is taken as fixed, and loss is averaged over states of nature. Thus, the Bayesian would consider the expectation $E_{\Pi(\mu/x)} L(\mu, d(x))$ as the criterion. The frequentist would go by the previous formulation of allowing the observed value of X as random. A rule that minimizes the expected loss given the sample observations is called a generalized Bayes rule. In most cases, the Bayes rule and the generalized Bayes rule are identical. It can be shown that, under very mild conditions, every admissible rule is a generalized Bayes rule with respect to some prior—sometimes an improper prior. Conversely, Bayes rules with respect to proper priors are virtually always admissible, though generalized Bayes rules with respect to improper priors may yield inadmissible rules.

7.8. Completeness

In situations where the prior probabilities are not known or even not relevant, we have to find a way to choose among alternative decision rules. For this purpose, we may first try to reduce the extent of our search to what may be called minimal classes of rules from which a choice has to be made. This brings us to the concept of completeness. In fact, we define a class of decision rules C as complete if corresponding to a decision rule d outside the class, there exists a member of the class C which performs better than d. Further, a complete class which does not contain a complete subclass is called a minimal complete class. The following are some of the characterizations of complete and minimally complete classes of decision rules:

1. A necessary and sufficient condition for the existence of a minimally complete class is that the class of admissible decision rules is complete.
2. The class of loss vectors corresponding to all decision functions is a closed convex set in the k-dimensional Euclidean space.
3. The class A of all admissible decision rules is a minimally complete class.
    As can be easily made out, the third proposition is a vital step in our search for optimal decision rules. Now we come to the Bayes decision rules in this connection to note some further results.

4. Every admissible rule is a Bayes rule with respect to some prior distribution.
5. The class of all Bayes rules B is a complete class.
6. The Bayes rule with respect to any prior Π is admissible if all the components of this prior distribution are positive.

The latter three results go to strengthen the focus of decision-makers on Bayes rules. However, proposition 4 does not militate against some decision rules developed without considering the posterior risk to be admissible. Thus, in some situations, the minimax decision rules proposed by Wald may be identified as admissible. Incidentally, a minimax decision rule is one whose maximum component in the loss vector (considering the different states of nature as the components) has a minimum value. If we restrict ourselves to the class of admissible decision rules and try this principle, we may find a minimax rule which will obviously be admissible. It is interesting to note that if we have a vector of positive probabilities and if the components of the loss vector are all equal, the Bayes decision rule with respect to this prior (sometimes called the least favourable prior distribution) can be shown to be a minimax rule. Anyway, such situations are a bit pathological and can be generally left out of our discussion.

Concepts of admissibility and of completeness, coupled with minimal completeness, can be taken as the optimality principle in the context of statistical decision theory.

7.9. The Bayesian Paradigm

Several factors motivated statisticians to adopt the Bayesian approach to decision-making, which really takes us to decision-making under 'risk' in the sense that we assign probabilities to states of nature and thereby incorporate the prior distribution in formulating the decision problem and solving it by using a performance criterion that does not involve the entire sample space. The approach rests on the posterior distribution of the observed data to absorb any information that the decision-maker feel is pertinent. The optimality principle is in terms of admissibility of the decision rule (or the class of such rules) and invariance under certain types of transformation is another desideratum. Ghosh and Samanta (2002) provide a good account of the reasons why we should prefer the Bayesian route to decision-making. Besides foundational flaws of the classical approach, they point out situations where a performance criterion like the sampling variance may be computationally absurd or may require restrictive assumptions regarding the underlying stochastic model. Arguments in favour of the Bayesian approach include the fact that we have theorems which show that unless a decision procedure is based on a prior or a sequence of priors, it would be inadmissible. Further, we also have theorems to tell us that a class of decision procedures is complete (in the sense that given any procedure outside it, there is a procedure with lower risk within the class) if it is the closure of Bayes procedures.

7.9.1. Choice of Loss Function

An important element in statistical decision theory concerns the choice of an appropriate 'loss' function that reflects the performance of any decision rule. Usually, such functions have been chosen in the context of estimation problems, and we get a rich variety of loss functions to suit different decision-making situations. Consideration of the ease of computing posterior 'risk' is no longer a hindrance to the use of problem-specific, non-traditional loss functions. Once we go beyond the problem of estimating an unknown population parameter to problems of prediction and classification through procedures like regression analysis, artificial neural network or support vector machines, we find loss functions which are more appropriate than the classical squared error loss. In fact, some exponents of Bayesian decision analysis argue that the design of a loss function for a given decision-making problem with its distinctive features is a task in itself, different from the choice of any loss function from the known basket. Some commonly used loss functions have been briefly outlined in the following sub-sections.

7.9.1.1. The Quadratic Loss

The commonly used quadratic error loss or SELF does not discriminate between overestimation and underestimation of the true value of a parameter under consideration. This convex loss function was proposed nearly 200 years ago, penalizes large deviations heavily and excludes randomized estimators. However, this has the advantage of simplicity and yields intuitively sound Bayesian solutions. In fact, the Bayes estimates associated with this loss are just the posterior means. It may be noted that loss functions leading to posterior means, such as Bayes estimates, are called proper losses, and there exist loss functions other than SELF which are 'proper'.

The quadratic loss is quite interesting in the context of bounded parameter spaces, where the choice of a more subjective loss cannot be thought of. In such a case, the quadratic loss is tractable and the approximation error is negligible.

7.9.1.2. Absolute Error Loss

Not to over-penalize large but unlikely deviations or errors, we can introduce an absolute error loss which is also convex, namely $L(\mu, d) = |\mu - d|$. A more general form given by Laplace (1773) is a multi-linear form, namely:

$$L(\mu, d) = m(\mu - d) \text{ if } \mu > d$$

$$= n(d - \mu) \text{ if } \mu < d$$

This mixed loss increases more slowly, compared to the squared error loss and attaches different importance measures to overestimation and underestimation. Huber (1964) proposed a mixture of the absolute error loss and the squared error loss to keep a quadratic penalty around zero by taking:

$$L(\mu, d) = (d - \mu)^2 \text{ if } |d - \mu| < k$$

$$= 2k |d - \mu| - k^2 \text{ otherwise}$$

This convex loss slows down the progression of the squared error loss and has a robustifying effect. However, no explicit derivation of the Bayes estimate with this loss exists. In fact, an interesting result in this direction is the following: A Bayes estimate associated with the prior distribution Π and the linear loss suggested by Laplace is the quantile of order $m/(m+n)$ in the posterior distribution $\prod(\mu/x)$. In particular, when $m=n$, the posterior median becomes the Bayes estimate.

7.9.1.3. The '0–1' Loss

This is a non-quantitative loss used mainly in the context of hypothesis testing. Thus, if we are testing the hypothesis H_0: $\mu \in M_0$ against H_1: μ is not in M_0 and the decision space D consists of only two elements, 1 standing for acceptance of H_0 and 0 implying rejection of the null hypothesis, then the '0–1' loss is given by:

$$L(\mu, d) = 1 - d \text{ if } \mu \in M_0$$

$$= d \text{ otherwise}$$

The associated risks are Type I and Type II error probabilities respectively.

7.9.1.4. LINEX Loss Function

In situations where positive and negative errors in decisions have different consequences, justifying different amounts of loss incurred, we require asymmetric loss functions. One such asymmetric loss function used by Varian (1975) and studied by Zellner (1986) is the LINEX loss function, written as:

$$L(\eth, c) = (\exp[c\eth] - c\eth - 1)$$

Here, c is the non-zero shape parameter (can be both negative and positive), and $\eth$ is the difference between the ratio of the estimate to the true value and unity or just the difference. This is a convex loss function that rises exponentially on one side of zero and approximately linearly on the other and has been used for both underestimation and overestimation situations.

7.9.1.5. Intrinsic Loss Functions

In situations where interest lies in the distribution of the observed random variable, for example, in the prediction set-up, we can directly compare the unknown distribution (assuming the p.d.f. exists) $f(x|\mu)$ with the estimated one $f(x|d)$ and take the loss function as some measure of divergence or distance between the two. Entropy loss is defined as: $L(\mu, d) = E[\log(f(x|\mu)/f(x|d)]$ and the Hellinger distance loss given by $L(\mu, d) = 1/2 \, E[\{f(x|d)/f(x|\mu)\}^{1/2}]$ are the two functions usually chosen. For example, in case of a normal $(\mu, 1)$ density, these two work out as $1/2 \, (d-\mu)^2$ and $1 - \exp\{-(d-\mu)^2/8\}$ respectively.

The Hellinger distance always exists and is bounded above by 1. However, Bayes estimates cannot be conveniently and explicitly obtained with these loss functions, except in some special cases.

7.9.1.6. Adaptive Loss Functions

To meet the need for robustness, Barron (2019) proposed a general loss function which involves a shape parameter that can enable the function to cover many common loss functions as special cases and can be adapted during use. The general form is given as:

$$F(x; \alpha, c) = |\alpha-2|/\alpha \, ([\{x/c\}^2/|\alpha-2|]+1)^{-\alpha/2} - 1$$

Here, the shape parameter α controls robustness and the shape parameter c controls the size of loss in the quadratic bowl at loss $x=0$. Removing singularities at $\alpha=0$ and 2, the loss function can be written as:

$$f(x; \alpha, c) = 1/2 \, (x/2)^2 \quad \text{for } \alpha = 2$$

$$= \log[1/2(x/c)^2 = 1] \quad \text{for } \alpha = 0$$

$$= 1 \exp[-1/2 \, (x/c)^2] \quad \text{for } \alpha = -$$

$$= |\alpha-2|/\alpha \, [(x/c)^2/(|\alpha-2|+1)^{-\alpha/2} - 1] \quad \text{otherwise}$$

An adaptive loss alignment technique discussed by Huang et al. (2019) automatically adjusts the loss function parameters to directly optimize the evaluation metric on a validation set. This is quite useful for machine learning algorithms.

7.9.1.7. Other Loss Functions

The general entropy loss function has also been used in some cases and is specified as:

$L(ð; b, c) = b(ð^c - cð - 1)$ where ð stands for the relative deviation, $b > 0$ and c is non-zero. If $c = 1$, we get the entropy loss.

For prediction and classification algorithms, we need to consider some 'error' functions, which are essentially loss functions for training of the underlying machine learning procedure. Some of the loss functions are meant to take account of outliers or/and inliers present in the data and may involve some hyperparameter which has to be numerically specified.

The Huber loss (also called the smooth mean absolute error [MAE]) is less sensitive to outliers in the data than the MAE. In fact, it is essentially the same as MAE, becoming quadratic when the error is small. In terms of the predicted value $y' = f(x)$ for the observed value y, this loss function having a parameter ð is defined as follows:

$$L_ð(y - f(x)) = 1/2 \, (y - f(x))^2 \text{ for } |y - f(x)| < ð$$

$$= ð \, |y - f(x)| - 1/2 \, ð^2 \text{ otherwise}$$

The log-cosh loss is almost like the mean squared error loss and is given by: $L(y, y') = \Sigma_I \log \cosh(y_i' - y_i)$ without any hyperparameter.

The loss functions suggested for prediction through regression (where a quantity is to be predicted) include mean squared error, MAE, mean squared logarithmic error (when the target value has a wide spread), Huber loss, log-cosh loss and quantile loss.

While for the binary classification problem (where a label like 0 or 1 has to be predicted), we have the following loss functions: binary cross-entropy, loss, hinge loss and squared hinge loss.

The binary cross entropy loss is in terms of a score that summarizes the difference between the actual and the predicted distributions for predicting Class 1. The score is to be minimized and the perfect score is zero. This requires that the output layer be configured as a single layer and a sigmoid activation function be used to predict the probability of Class 1.

The hinge loss is primarily used with the support vector machine and the focus is on the sign of the difference between them. The target values are modified to lie in the set (−1, 1). The squared hinge loss is easier to work with. This function is as follows:

$$L_\lambda(y, y') = (\lambda - 1) \Sigma |y - y'| + \lambda \Sigma |y - y'|$$

Here, the first sum is over y's less than corresponding y' values and the second sum is over values of y greater than corresponding values of y'.

For the multi-class classification problem, the multi-class cross-entropy is often used as a loss function. It is based on the average difference between actual and predicted probabilities for all classes in a given problem.

7.9.2. Choice of Priors

The use of a 'prior' distribution of probabilities over the space of all likely states of nature is implicit in decision-making under risk. Such a distribution is assumed or developed right at the time of decision-making, based on available information embodied in the decision-maker's belief and intuition, knowledge and experience. In case observations are available on some random variable (may be a vector) whose probability distribution depends on the state of nature, decisions are usually based on the posterior distribution of the underlying parameter(s)—characterizing the state of nature—to incorporate any additional information that may be contained in the observations. The choice of a suitable prior plays a pivotal role in statistical decision theory. As indicated here, the prior may be suggested by an expert or by the decision-maker without looking at the observations or can be developed after the observations are available and taken into consideration.

The extreme view that a completely subjective prior with no regard to sample observations does not contain any information about the states of nature and their realization probabilities, leading to the nomenclature 'non-informative' for such purely subjective priors, has been generally discarded. As Poincare stated. It is not usually realistic to expect that one would be able to elicit more than a prior mean or a prior variance or a prior mode from a purely subjective prior. On some occasions, prior information about covariance can be derived from such a prior. It thus becomes customary to choose or derive priors in a non-subjective way, incorporating as much prior information as has been elicited. Unfortunately, purely non-subjective priors do have low information in terms of Shannon's missing entropy. And these tend to yield mostly data-dependent posteriors.

Ghosh and Samanta (2002) provide a comprehensive and informative discussion on the topic, adding their own contributions and interpretations of relevant works by others. According to them, one should use one of the following alternatives to develop a non-subjective prior that is not non-informative and not purely subjective:

1. Define a uniform distribution that fits the topology of the parameter space for a suitable topology induced by the Hellinger metric or Riemannian metric arising from the Fisher information matrix.
2. Maximize a suitable measure of entropy (or minimize information in this sense).
3. Choose a prior with some form of frequentist validation, since the use of a prior with little information should lead to the same sort of inference as what a frequentist would do.

The uniform distribution comes in handy as a prior but has a few limitations. It is not invariant under one transformation of μ, while one normally seeks a prior where one can pass from one prior $\Pi_1(\mu)$ for μ to the prior $\Pi_2(\eth) \; \eth(\mu)$ for any smooth one–one function $\eth(\mu)$ of μ by the usual Jacobian formula:

$$\Pi_1(\mu) = \Pi_2(\eth(\mu)) \; |d\eth/d\mu|$$

Further, the uniform distribution seems to maximize the Shannon entropy:

$$H(p) = -\int p(\mu) \log p(\mu) \, d\mu$$

In fact, the uniform prior reveals a situation that can be put in a somewhat crude and unfair manner as one of equal ignorance about the different states of nature. This is no doubt not a non-informative prior. Bernardo (1979) considered the change from the prior to the posterior distribution as indicating the additional information contained in the sample to find out how informative it is. He took the Kullback–Leibler divergence measure, namely:

$$K\{p\,\mu|X),\Pi(\mu)\} = E\,[\log p(\mu|X)/\Pi(\mu)]$$

He argued that if a prior is already quite informative, say degenerate at some point, then the posterior is the same as the prior and $K=0$, data providing no additional information. An asymptotic maximization of K yields Bernardo's reference prior. Ghosh and Samanta provide an algorithm for the purpose. They also show that under suitable regularity conditions, Jeffreys improper prior:

$\Pi(\mu) = \{\det. I(\mu)\}^{1/2}$, where $I(\mu)$ is the Fisher information matrix. Under suitable regularity conditions, the Jeffreys prior is a reference prior.

In case information on prior moments or quantiles is available, one can minimize with respect to the prior the Kullback–Leibler functional appropriately defined. Sun and Berger (1998) derived reference priors for multi-parameter cases when some information is available for some of the parameters.

More recently, attention has been paid to developing what are called 'probability matching priors' by equating posterior and frequentist probabilities. Ghosh and Mukherjee (1992), and quite a few others have contributed a lot to this topic. The basic idea can be explained in terms of the following example. Suppose $X_1, X_2, \ldots, X_N$ are independently and identically distributed random variables with a common normal distribution $N(\mu, 1)$ Let $\Pi(\mu)$ be the improper uniform prior for the parameter. Then the following is true:

$$\text{Prob}\,[\mu \in (X - z_{\alpha/2}/n^{1/2}, X + z_{\alpha/2}/n^{1/2}|\alpha] = 1 - \alpha$$

$$\text{Prob}\,[\mu \in (X - z_{\alpha/2}/n^{1/2}, X + z_{\alpha/2}/n^{1/2}|X] = 1 - \alpha$$

The first is the classical frequentist probability, which holds for many repetitions of samples, while the second has a Bayesian meaning and defines what is sometimes called a credibility interval for the parameter, given the sample mean. The improper uniform prior is a probability matching prior. It may be added that the limit theorem stating that, in large samples, the sample mean is approximately normally distributed, validates the first statement in a more general set-up.

The task of determining a probability matching prior involves solving a second order partial differential equation in the prior, which, in the case of $N(\mu, \beta)$ with μ as the parameter of interest, turns out to be an equation which is satisfied by any prior proportional to $1/\beta$:

$$\partial/\partial\mu \, [2^{1/2} \, \beta^2 \, \Pi(\mu, \beta)/(\mu^2 + 2\beta^2)^{1/2}]$$
$$= \partial/\partial\beta \, [\mu\beta \, \Pi(\mu, \beta)/2^{1/2} \, (\mu^2 + 2\beta^2)^{1/2}]$$

It can be verified that Jeffreys prior is not a probability match in case any of the parameters μ or β is of interest.

The use of non-subjective priors has raised quite a few serious questions. These priors are usually improper and should not be used to quantify subjective belief. There are many non-subjective priors which can be used along with a given model for the data, and the choice is not obvious. However, inferences based on such priors or rather on the posteriors derived therefrom, do not change much and one can conveniently use the reference priors or the Jeffreys prior. Of course, one difficulty that persists is that different stopping rules lead to different experiments.

One important question that arises naturally in the context of Bayesian decision analysis is the robustness of the decision to possible departures of the prior distribution from the one used in deriving the posterior distribution. This is like examining the sensitivity of the posterior with respect to the prior. Fortunately, computation of summary measures of the posterior distribution for different priors can be conveniently done today through Markov chain (MC) Monte Carlo programmes. One can also approach the robustness issue by considering general non-parametric contamination classes of priors given by:

$\Pi_c = \Pi_0(1-\epsilon) + \epsilon \Pi_G$ where Π_G is some non-parametric prior.

Robustness has been discussed in detail by Carlin and Louis (1996) and Gelman et al. (1995).

7.9.2.1. Dirichlet Process Prior

A Dirichlet process is a set of probability distribution whose range is itself a set of probability distributions. Introduced by Ferguson (1973), this is quite often used to describe prior knowledge about the distribution of random variables used as the underlying model in statistical inference. The Dirichlet distribution in k dimensions and parameters α_i, $i=1, 2, \ldots, k$, has the p.d.f.

$$D(x|\alpha_1, \alpha_2, \ldots, \alpha_k) = Z \prod p_j \, \alpha_j - 1$$

Here, $Z =$ the sum $s = \Sigma \alpha_i$ is the precision or concentration parameter and $m = (\alpha_1/s, \alpha_2/s, \ldots, \alpha_k/s)$ is the centre of mass (or mean). In case each of the parameters α equals unity, we have the uniform prior.

It is easy to show that the Dirichlet distribution is the natural conjugate prior for the categorical (multinomial) distribution $M(n; x_1, x_2, \ldots, x_k)$ the posterior coming out to be multinomial with parameters $(\alpha_1 + x_1, \alpha_2 + x_2, \ldots, \alpha_k + x_k)$. In the same manner, the Dirichlet process is the conjugate prior for the infinite, nonparametric distributions. Hence, given that $X_1, X_2, \ldots, X_n$ are independent and identically distributed with unknown distribution P, the posterior mean of P, given the observations, is a convex combination of the prior mean and the empirical distribution. The posterior mean shrinks the empirical distribution towards the prior mean.

7.9.3. Use of Priors in Non-Bayesian Framework

Problems of parameter estimation in classical statistics can be viewed as problems of decision-making under risk where states of nature would correspond to possible values of the unknown parameter(s) being estimated or of parameter(s) involved in some property of the estimate (defined over the entire sample space). For example, the sampling bias of the estimate of a parameter will involve an unknown parameter, while the sampling variance of the estimate of population mean will involve the population variance, which could be unknown. Even if we are not using the bias or the sampling variance or any such property directly as the outcome or pay-off associated with a certain estimator (or rule or strategy), we may use some criterion like the efficiency of the estimate (compared to the maximum likelihood estimate) and compare different estimates (or estimators). We may introduce a prior distribution of the unknown parameter(s) involved in the criterion measure to compute the average value of this measure by which we could compare the different estimators.

To illustrate the above situation, let us consider the problem of estimating the parameters of a two-parameter Weibull distribution with p.d.f. given by:

$$f(x; \alpha, \lambda) = \alpha \lambda x^{\alpha-1} \exp(-\lambda x^\alpha) \ x, \alpha, \lambda > 0$$

We decided to estimate the parameters by using moments of order r_1 and r_2 with $r_1, r_2 > 0$, not necessarily integers, equating the sample moments S_1 and S_2 respectively to the population mean and the squared population coefficient of variation and solving the equations numerically. The decision problem here is the choice of (r_1, r_2), the states of nature are defined by unknown true values of (α, λ) and the criterion used by Mukherjee and Sasmal (1980) was the generalized asymptotic relative efficiency of the estimates based on S_1 and S_2 relative to the maximum likelihood estimates. This criterion measure is obtained as the ration between the determinant of the asymptotic variance–covariance matrix of the maximum likelihood estimates and the determinant of the asymptotic variance–covariance matrix of the estimates using fractional moments. For a given sample size n, it will be a function of the orders r_1 and r_2, besides the parameters α and λ.

Given a particular sample size n, this measure does not yield a consistent picture about the relative merits and limitations of the alternative strategies (r_1, r_2) in respect of variations in the orders of the moments selected. To decide on the orders of the two moments, we can assume a joint prior of the unknown parameters to work out the expected asymptotic relative efficiency as a function of the strategy

(r_1, r_2). In fact, numerical computations with uniform priors over the range (0, 3) favoured the choice of (0.5, 1.5) across a large segment of (α, λ) combinations. Of course, the choice based on the expected asymptotic relative efficiency would depend on the choice of the prior (taken somewhat arbitrarily for the sake of illustration), and we may not get a 'global' optimum supported by all priors which are reasonable. The computation of the expected asymptotic joint relative efficiency is rather cumbersome.

A very similar problem would be faced in estimating these parameters by using two sample quantiles. The possible alternatives would be pairs (α, β) where we equate the sample quantiles of orders α and $1-\beta$ to derive the estimates of the population parameters. This could be reduced to the choice of a single decision variable if we take $\alpha = \beta$.

7.10. Prolongation of the Bayesian Paradigm

Bayesian methods and procedures for modelling complex phenomena, especially those arising in recent scientific studies in genetics, epidemiology and biostatistics and for making inferences, have been very widely and fruitfully applied. Findings of such studies are being reported in well-known periodicals, some of them recently started. In that way, Bayesian methods have been extended beyond their initial realm of posterior-based analysis. In this section, we consider briefly two such extensions, namely hierarchical Bayes and empirical Bayes methods, with some references to their uses. These two methods are related in their goals but differ in their approaches. Hierarchical Bayes refers to a modelling strategy, while empirical Bayes (EB) relates to a methodology. Both methods specify the prior distribution, hierarchical Bayes via inference involving additional degrees of hierarchy (hyperpriors and hyperparameters) and EB using observed data more directly.

7.10.1. Hierarchical Bayes Procedure

Hierarchical Bayes analysis is based on a decomposition of the prior Π via a conditional hierarchy of the so-called hyperpriors $\Pi_1, \Pi_2, \ldots, \Pi_{n+1}$ as:

$$\Pi(\mu) = \int \Pi_1(\mu|\mu_1), \Pi_2(\mu_1|\mu_2), \ldots, \Pi_{n+1}(\mu_n)\, d\mu_1\, d\mu_2, \ldots, d\mu_n$$

In the hierarchy of data, parameters and hyperparameters, X and μ_i are independent, given μ with the implications that (a) X given $\mu, \mu_1, \ldots, \mu_n$ and X given μ have the same distribution and (b) $(\mu_i|\mu, X)$ and $(\mu_1|\mu)$ have the same distribution.

The decomposition may be justified or called for in meta-analysis wherein a hierarchy among the priors is natural or when the prior information can be separated into the structural part and the subjective part at a higher level or to take advantage of MC Monte Carlo and other techniques to work out the posterior.

Consider the simple case of just one hyperprior so that the posterior distribution can be written as:

$$\Pi(\mu|x) = \int \Pi(\mu|x, \mu_1)\, \Pi(\mu_1|x)\, \text{where}$$

$\Pi(\mu|x, \mu_1) = f(x|\mu)\, \Pi_1(\mu|\mu_1)/m_1(x|\mu_1)$ with the denominator as the marginal likelihood and $\Pi(\mu_1|x) = m_1(x|\mu_1)\, \Pi_2(\mu_1)/m(x)$ with $m(x)$ denoting the likelihood.

Now, for any function of the parameter μ:

$$E^{\mu|x}\, h(\mu) = E^{\mu_1|x}\, E^{\mu|\mu_1, x}\, h(\mu)$$

The point to be noted here is that one can obtain the unconditional prior $\Pi(\mu)$ as: $\Pi(\mu) = \Pi(\mu|\mu_1)\, \Pi_2(\mu_1)$ and use this in the classical bayes procedure to work out the posterior and estimate any function of μ directly. Of course, in many situations, it could be computationally quite difficult. The hierarchical bayes procedure offers us a convenient way to derive the estimate.

7.10.2. EB Method

Consider a sequence of independent experiments resulting in observations X_i with the distribution given by the density (mass) function $f(x_i, \mu)$, $i = 1, 2, \ldots, n$, where μ_i are unobservable parameters. We want to develop decision rules δ_i about μ_i using a loss function $L(a, \mu)$. Now, we can think of two situations. In the first, observations $X_1, X_2, \ldots, X_j$ are only available for the jth decision problem or for formulating δj. In the second, the whole vector of observations $X = (X_1, X_2, \ldots, X_n)$ can be used for inferences about all the μ_i's. In fact, the second situation corresponds to the compound decision problem studied by Robbins (1951). Robbins introduced the EB method in this context, assuming the unknown parameters to be independent random variables with a common unknown prior G, with the aim of finding decision rules which perform nearly as well as the 'ideal' Bayes rule.

The risk for this compound version, which is really a conditional risk, is the average of the n risks, each computed with expectations of (Loss × Decision Function) with both decision functions depending on the entire set of observations X and expectations with respect to the entire parameter vector μ. For separable decision rules of the form $\delta_i(X) = t(X_i)$, the compound risk has a simple expression and is equal to the Bayes risk $R(t, G)$ with the unknown prior G as the sum of indicator functions. Robbins' proposal was to seek asymptotically optimal procedures satisfying $R_n(\delta, \mu) = R^*(G) + o(1)$ where $R^*(G) = \min_t R(t, G)$, given the prior G.

Robbins constructed decision rules $\delta_i(X)$ such that this condition holds uniformly in μ in the simple problem of testing $\mu_i = 1$ against $\mu_i = -1$ based on suitable estimates of G. This shows how apparently 'non-informative' observations can be of some benefit. Confining ourselves to procedures under permutation of the decision problems, in the compound case, the two EB decision problems mentioned above are mathematically equivalent. Robbins formulated the problem of estimating the prior G based on X and described the process as an attempt 'to lift ourselves by our own bootstraps'.

Since Robbins' methodologies aim at the ideal Bayes rule with no restrictions on the prior or the choice of the decision function, they are usually referred to as general or non-parametric EB methods. A host of developments have subsequently taken place, noticeably in the area of parametric and restricted EB methods. Efron and Morris (1973) provided an EB interpretation of the James–Stein estimator and proposed a straightforward EB approach. Let $t_G^*(x) = t_G^* = \arg \min R(t, G)$

be the ideal Bayes rule where $G=G_n$ is the empirical distribution of the unknown parameters. Then Robbins' procedure can be written as:

$$\delta_i(x) = t(X_i)$$

EB methods apply quite naturally to problems with high-dimensional data. EB methods designed to 'borrow' information across genes and across experimental conditions in the hope that this will lead to better estimates or more stable inferences, to stabilize expression ratios for genes with very high or low ratios, stabilize gene variances by shrinking variances across all other genes and adjust for 'batch effects' in microarray data have been reported by Johnson et al. (2007). Efron and Tibshirani (2002) demonstrate how EB methods give results which are closely related to the false discovery rate controlling procedure suggested by Benjamini and Hochberg and can be used together to replace a whole host of Wilcoxon statistics, one for each pair of genes.

Robbins extended the EB methodology for predicting sums of the form $S_n = \Sigma Y_i u(X_i)$ based on X_i and statistical inference based on biased allocation schemes. Zhang (2003) considers the problem of predicting the number of traffic accidents next year, given a pool of motorists with a pre-specified number of accidents this year, for example, those with clean records. Assuming traffic conditions remain unchanged, the number of accidents X_i this year for the ith member in the pool and Yi the number next year are independent decision variables with common mean λ_i. The problem is to predict S_n with $u(x) = I(x=a)$ for any integer $a \geq 0$. The general EB estimator of Robbins gives the predictor $T_n = \Sigma v(X_i)$ with $v(x) = x\, u(x-1)$ T_n is unbiased and asymptotically efficient for independent and identically distributed λ_i.

EB procedures combine the Bayesian way of thinking about the data and the frequentist approach to inference, particularly the method of maximum likelihood. In a sense, it forms a bridge between the frequentist and the Bayesian approaches to statistical inference. Although it originated in the context of compound decision problems in which a set of unobservable parameters generated independent observations which were used to estimate the parameter vector with a squared error loss assuming an unknown common prior distribution, EB methods have been used for selecting values of hyperparameters in prior distributions assumed for parameters as well as for dealing with nuisance parameters. In fact, EB methods have been liberally taken to imply an approach where the prior distribution is estimated from the sample data. A huge volume of literature, including both original articles and reviews, can be accessed to gain working knowledge about the EB procedure. Reviews by Zhang (2003), Morris (1983), etc., are quite revealing, and several books devoted exclusively to EB methods and applications also help interested workers.

The EB method of smoothing the standardized mortality rate used in disease mapping to understand the locational aspects of the incidence of a disease has been considered by Clayton and Kaldor (1987) using a Gamma–Poisson model, as also by Marshall (1991). The problem of measuring the uncertainty of EB estimators has not been comprehensively studied, and Lahiri and Maiti (2002) obtained a naive measure in terms of the integrated Bayes risk, following a bootstrap model.

7.11. Multiple Decision Functions

Among the relatively recent developments in statistical decision theory, methods using multiple decision functions are finding important applications in real-life problems. Here, we have the problem of making a large number m of decisions simultaneously, based on one realization of a data matrix. Usually, non-randomized binary decisions like accept or reject are considered. Each row of the data matrix corresponds to one decision, and the size of a row may be small. In the general framework, the data matrix shows some dependence structure. For example, rows in the data matrix may be dependent on a frailty-induced Archimedean copula. In this way, even non-Gaussian dependence may also be taken into account.

In this context, an alternative is a set of actions/decisions to be taken simultaneously on the basis of some input like the matrix of observations on say N random variables. Alternatives can also be taken as the decision rules that result in the action decision vectors. The states of nature (also called states of reality in some publications) correspond to some probability distributions or to some parameters involved, about which decisions are called for. Analogues of feasibility of an alternative could be offered in terms of some property possessed by an alternative and the corresponding specification.

Loss functions could be defined as the consequences of wrong actions/decisions involving some cost or benefit parameters, and we can have different loss functions as in the case of a single decision problem. We can consider the expected loss or risk (expectation over a somewhat large and complex sample space) as in the classical statistical approach to each possible state of nature. Alternatively, we can assume some prior distribution over the state space, work out the posterior distribution and compute the posterior risk for the given sample. In the first case, we can propose the minimax criterion for finding the optimal action/decision vector, while in the second case, we adopt the Bayes' rule. In either case, the computations involved are quite cumbersome and are often handled in terms of Monte Carlo methods.

The problem of multiple hypothesis testing involving m simple hypotheses is one interesting case of multiple decision functions. Similarly, multiple classification and prediction, high-dimensional variable selection, item-response modelling, wavelet thresholding as well as structural equation modelling belong to this class of decision-making. The growing interest in multiple hypothesis testing problems owes a lot to the challenges posed by data analysis in new biology, such as proteomics, functional magnetic resonance imaging, brain mapping and genetics. It is well known that data in these applications is strongly correlated (spatially or over time or over both time and space). Starting from multiple comparison procedures, a good number of procedures based on several different principles have been developed during the last two/three decades for testing simultaneously a large number of simple hypotheses, mostly using the p-values associated with the individual hypotheses.

To compare the performances of different test procedures (decision alternatives), criteria used are appropriate extensions of Type I and Type II errors and of robustness to the multiple hypothesis testing set-up. These extensions are not all unique and are interrelated to some extent in some cases. Some new criteria have also been introduced. To

Table 7.1 Number of Errors Committed in Different Situations

	Declared Non-significant	Declared Significant	Total
Null hypotheses true	U	V	m_0
Null hypotheses not true	T	S	$m - m_0$
Total	$m - R$	R	m

comprehend these criteria conveniently in the case of a large number m of simple hypotheses, of which T (an unknown number) is true and the remaining false, we consider Table 7.1, giving the number of Type I and Type II errors that we may commit:

It may be noted that R is an observable random variable (depending on sample observations and test procedures), while S, T, U and V are unobservable random variables.

The probability of Type I error for testing each hypothesis is kept at less than or equal to α (since we are considering non-randomized tests only). In the context of multiple testing, we define the per comparison error rate (PCER) as: PCER = $E(V/m)$ or error rate per hypothesis, V/m being the proportion of hypotheses wrongly rejected by considering the entire test exercise. A second extension of the Type I error probability is the family-wise error rate (FWER) = $\Pr(V \geq 1)$. Also called the alpha-inflation rate, FWER is the probability of committing at least one Type I error. If each hypothesis is tested at level α, then PCER $\leq \alpha$, and if the former is taken as α/m, then FWER $\leq \alpha$. A third extension which has found wide acceptance in the context of experimentation in search of new results or entities relates to the ratio V/R ($R > 0$) between two random variables and is called the false discovery proportion (FDP) which is taken as zero if $R = 0$. FDP is defined as false discovery rate (FDR), which is defined as:

$$E(\text{FDP}) = E(V/R | R > 0)$$

It is equal to zero if $R = 0$. The positive false discovery rate pFDR is defined as $E(V/R, R > 0)$ As m tends to be large, the number of false positives may explode. For example, with $m=30{,}000$ and $\alpha=0.05$, R is expected to be as large as 1,500. The various numbers, proportions and rates satisfy the following relations:

$$E(V)/m < \min(\text{FDR}, \text{FDX}), \max(\text{FDR}, \text{FDX}) < \text{FWER}, E(V)$$

Similarly, power in the context of a multiple test procedure could be taken as any-pair power or probability of rejecting at least one false hypothesis, per-pair power or average probability of rejecting false hypotheses or all-pair power, defined as the probability of rejecting all false hypotheses.

If a procedure controls FDR only, it can be less stringent, and a gain in power may be expected. Any procedure that controls the FWER also controls FDR. The following procedure to control FDR was proposed by Hochberg and Benjamini and later modified by them on the basis of some related findings by Simes (1986) and Hommel (1988).

Let $p_1, p_2, \ldots, p_m$ be the p-values associated with a procedure to test the hypotheses $H_1, H_2, \ldots, H_m$ respectively. Let $p_{(1)}, p_{(2)}, \ldots, p_{(m)}$ be the ordered p-values and let $H_{(i)}$ be the hypothesis corresponding to $p_{(i)}$. Consider the following test procedure:

Let k be the largest I for which $p_{(i)} \leq i/m \; q^*$ and reject all $H_{(i)}$, $i=1, 2, \ldots, k$.

For independent test statistics for the different hypotheses and for any configuration of false null hypotheses, it can be shown that this procedure controls FDR at q^*. Simes had suggested a procedure to reject the intersection hypotheses that at least one of the null hypotheses is false if, for some I, $p_{(i)} \leq i \, \alpha/m$. Hochberg subsequently modified his procedure as:

Let k be the largest i for which $p_{(i)} \leq i \, \alpha/(m-i+1)$, then reject al $H_{(i)}$ $i=1, 2, \ldots, k$.

There have been several modifications to these test procedures and interesting and useful applications of such multiple hypothesis testing problems have been reported in the literature.

It has been generally found that positive dependency of certain types leads to conservative behaviour of classical multiple test procedures. In fact, Sarkar (1998) showed that multivariate total positivity of order two (MTP_2) is particularly useful for control of FWER. This result allows an improvement over the closed Bonferroni test.

If strict control of FWER is targeted even with an 'effective number of tests', we have low power for detecting true effects. This led Benjamini and Hochberg to relax the Type I error criterion and to control FDR. Positive dependency in the sense of MTP_2 ensures FDR control of the linear set-up (LSU) test proposed by Benjamini and Hochberg. Dickhaus and Stange (2013) mention that the question of incorporating the concept of 'effective number of tests' into the LSU test is an open problem. They also point out that the question of how to modify the 'effective number of tests' proposed by them in cases where the correlation structure has to be estimated from the data remains a research problem.

Methods for testing multiple hypotheses have been sometimes classified as follows:

- Methods based on ordered p-values
- Methods based on the first-order Bonferroni inequality
- Holm's sequentially rejecting Bonferroni methods
- Methods based on Simes inequality
- Hochberg's method for multiple hypothesis testing
- Homme's method for multiple testing
- Rom's modification of the Hochberg procedure
- Methods based on re-sampling
- Methods for testing logically related hypotheses have also been considered.

Another cryptic classification speaks of one-step, step-down and step-up procedures as the three FWER.

As remarked by Dickhaus and Stange (2012), future research on multiple hypothesis testing in the classical framework should address the question of how to modify the effective number of tests in cases where the correlation structure among the p-values itself has to be estimated from data. In this case, the two inferential problems, namely estimation of the dependence structure and testing of multiple hypotheses have to be solved in parallel.

Going by the decision-theoretic approach, three different loss functions have been proposed, involving the action/decision vector a and the state vector ð, both of which can be taken as vectors of binary numbers. Thus, $a_i = 1$ may stand for the action 'reject hypothesis H_i' and $a_i = 0$ if the hypothesis is accepted. Similarly, $ð_i = 1$ if H_i is false and 0 otherwise. The loss functions are just in terms of the error rates and linked numbers or proportions. Appropriate cost multipliers may be conveniently added. The first function, that is, $L_0(a, ð) = I\{a'(1-ð) \geq\}$ is linked to false positives, that is, $L_1(a, ð) = [a'(1-ð)/a'1] I(a'1 > 0)$ is really the proportion of false positives, and the third loss function, that is, $L_3(a, ð) = (1-a') ð$, is the number of missed discoveries.

The corresponding expectations or risk functions are essentially the important error rates discussed previously, namely R_1 is the FDR, R_2 is the missed discovery rate, while R_0 is related to the FWER.

Even with simple priors over the state space, posterior risk expressions are complicated, and their computations are really cumbersome.

A slightly different decision-theoretic approach introduces a criterion that takes into account both the costs and benefits of actions with regard to true and false hypotheses and goes by optimization of this criterion (Bickel, 2004). A desirability function is defined in terms of b_i = benefit of rejecting hypothesis I when it is false and c_i = cost of rejecting hypothesis I when it is true, so that net desirability for the entire procedure is given by:

$$d(b, c) = \Sigma[b_I(R_i - V_i) - c_i V_i] = \Sigma b_I R_i - \Sigma(b_I + c_I) V_i$$

If costs and benefits are independent of the hypotheses, then the expected net desirability is $E(d) = b [1 - (1 = c/b) \text{ Q}] E(\Sigma R_i)$ with symbols explained earlier. The rejection regions should be chosen in a manner that pFDR or FDR and the expected number of rejections maximize the approximate net desirability, given a cost-to-benefit ratio. Bickel provides a procedure for estimation of net desirability and its subsequent optimization.

A good amount of work has been reported on Bayesian multiple decision problems. In the Bayesian framework, the overall loss function associated with the entire exercise covering all the M decisions simultaneously is generally a cost-weighted linear combination of Type I and Type II loss functions, which allow the use of FDR, false non-discovery rate and missed discovery rate. Adjusted missed discovery rate has also been tried out as the overall loss function in some cases. Cost coefficients are consequences of committing Type I and Type II errors.

7.12. Sequential Decision Theory

Considerations of time and cost (of observations) motivated the development of sequential decision analysis. Introduced by Wald (1945) and quickly adopted in practice, sequential analysis replaced the existing practice of using a (pre-) fixed sample size for making a decision and required observations (or groups of observations) to be taken sequentially one at a time, till a decision following some decision rule, could be reached. A sequential decision procedure has two components, namely (a) a stopping rule that tells us after every sequence of observations x_n, on the underlying random variable X, $n = 1, 2, 3, \ldots$, whether to stop sampling and decide on some action following some rule or to continue to observe one more value of X and (b) the decision rule to tell us how to reach a decision once we stop with some (random) number of observations.

Incidentally, determination of the sample size in a non-sequential decision procedure can be taken up as a decision problem by itself, for a specified decision rule, as simply illustrated as follows:

Suppose we like to estimate the parameter μ in the probability model $N(0, 1)$ using a sample of n observations on X and the decision rule $d(X)$ is to offer the sample mean x-bar as the estimate. We introduced the loss function:

$$L(n; d, \mu) = [d - \mu]^2 + c \cdot n$$

Here, c is the unit cost of observation.

The expected loss becomes $R(n; d) = 1/n + c \cdot n$ and our problem is to find an n that this is a minimum subject to n being a positive integer. This is apparently an unconstrained non-linear integer optimization problem, in which we can introduce a constraint like $k \geq n$ with k a specified relatively small integer. However, as a simplistic approach, we can treat n as continuous and find the optimum n from the following equation:

$$dR/dn = -1/n^2 + c = 0 \text{ giving } n = 1/c^{1/2}$$

Thus, we can stop sampling after $(1/c^{1/2}) + 1$ observations and compute the sample mean as the estimate, where r denotes the greatest integer contained up to r.

If we choose a $N(\alpha, 1)$ as a prior, the Bayes risk for the Bayes estimate with the proposed squared error loss would be $1/(n+1)$, and the optimum sample size would become $n = 1/c^{1/2} - 1$.

Let H_0 and H_1 be the two alternative hypotheses regarding a sequence of random variables $(x_1, x_2, \ldots)$ not necessarily identically and independently distributed. The likelihood ratio based on the first m observations is given by:

$$R_m = \Pr(x_1, x_2, \ldots, x_m | H_1) / \Pr(x_1, x_2, \ldots, x_m | H_0)$$

Wald's sequential probability ratio test (SPRT) for deciding between the two alternatives H_0 and H_1 runs as follows:

Choose two constants A and B such that $0 < B < A < 1 <$ infinity. Observe the random variables $x_1, x_2, \ldots$ one after the other. At the mth stage, if $R_m < B$, stop sampling and accept H_0; if $R_m > A$, stop sampling and accept H_1, and if $B < R_m < A$, continue sampling and take one more observation. The following results are true.

1. The SPRT terminates with probability 1, under both H_0 and H_1.
2. If the SPRT of strength (α, β) has boundary points A and B where α and β are the usual Type I and Type II error probabilities terminates with probability 1, then:

$A<(1-\beta)/\alpha$ and $B \geq \beta/(1-\alpha)$

3. If for the choice $A=(1-\beta)/\alpha$ and $B=\beta/(1-\alpha)$ the SPRT terminated with probability 1 and is of strength (α', β'), then:

$\alpha' < \alpha(1-\beta)$, $\beta' < \beta/(1-\alpha)$ and $(\alpha'+\beta') < (\alpha+\beta)$.

Wald's SPRT was widely used during the Second World War by the US Department of Defence for sampling inspection of lots of items received and subjected to inspection by an attribute to result in a defective versus non-defective classification of each item inspected. The whole idea was to minimize the amount of inspection (usually called the average sample number as a function of the fraction of defective in a lot). It is theoretically established that the SPRT requires a smaller ASN compared to a fixed sample size inspection scheme in the long run. Further, the cumulative sum control charts developed for the purpose of detecting a change in the process as early as possible are also based on the SPRT. In fact, the cumulative sum control chart for controlling the process mean using a V-mask uses a pair of reversed SPRTs and ensures a lower average run length (ARL; under the 'in-control' state) compared to that of the Shewhart control chart for the sample mean.

7.12.1. Optimal Stopping Problem

The British mathematician Cayley (1875) first published an article on sequential stopping strategy for purchasing lottery tickets. Much later, Wald introduced the concept of statistical decision theory and sequential sampling during the Second World War. His sequential probability ratio tests broke new ground and cumulative sum techniques came to be applied in the context of change point detection. Subsequently, Bellman came up with a dynamic programming method to solve such problems. The more recent Black–Scholes formula for option pricing also illustrates this problem.

Stopping rule problems are defined by the following two sequences:

1. A sequence of random variables, $X_1, X_2, \ldots$, whose joint distribution is assumed to be known

2. A sequence of real-valued reward functions:

$$y_0, y_1(x_1), y_2(x_1, x_2), \ldots, y_n(x_1, x_2, \ldots, x_n) \, y(x_1, x_2, \ldots)$$

Given these two entities, the associated stopping rule problem may be described as follows. You may observe the sequence, $X_1, X_2, \ldots$, as long as you like. For each n, after observing $X_1 = x_1, X_2 = x_2, \ldots, X_n = x_n$, we can stop and receive the known reward $y_n(x_1, x_2, \ldots, x_n)$, (this could be negative in some cases) or we may continue to observe $X_{n=1}$. We may decide to have no observation at all and receive y_0 or we may continue indefinitely to receive y. The problem is to find the time N at which we should stop to maximize the expected reward.

Let the probability of stopping at n be denoted by $\eth(x_1, x_2, \ldots, x_n)$. A randomized stopping rule is denoted by $\eth = (\eth_0, \eth_1(x_1), \eth_2(x_1, x_2), \ldots)$ where, for all n, $1 \geq \eth_n \geq 0$. We have a non-randomized stopping strategy if $\eth$ is 0 or 1. The rule $\eth$ and the sequence of observations determine the random time N for stopping. The probability function of N is given by $\lambda_n(\eth_0, \eth_1, \ldots, \eth_n)$ where $\lambda_0 = \eth_0$, $\lambda_1(x_1) = (1 - \eth_0) \, \eth_1(x_1)$ and, generally, $\lambda n(x_1, x_2, \ldots, x_n) = (\prod_1^{n-1} [1 - \eth_j] \{x_1, x_2, \ldots, x_j\}) \, \eth_n (x_1, x_2, \ldots, x_n)$ and the probability of an infinite N can be computed therefrom.

The problem is to find a rule $\eth$ such that the expected return $V(\eth)$ is a maximum.

It is sometimes more convenient to formulate the problem in terms of a loss sequence and to find the stopping time to minimize the expected loss. We may have to deal with a sequence of random rewards. At any stage, no recall of rewards at earlier stages may be allowed or such a recall could be allowed to make the reward at stage n the maximum of the rewards up to stage n. The following example is quite interesting.

The author wanted to let his flat on rent to someone who would offer him the best rent per month. He asked the housing complex office to forward any requests from interested parties for a small service charge per request forwarded. Once an enquiry or request came with a certain rent offer, the author could ask for some time to communicate his decision. If he continues to receive enquiries and to defer a decision in the hope of getting a better offer than any received so far, the flat remains unoccupied and he has to forego the rent receivable for the flat. If he decides now and here, he may lose a better offer to come later. At any time, when he stops receiving further enquiries and takes a final call to let the flat go on rent, he can get the benefit of receiving the highest offer so far. Here, the reward function has the following structure:

$$y_0 = 0$$
$$y_n = \text{Max}(x_1, x_2, \ldots, x_n) - nc$$

Here, x_i is the rent offered by the ith party, and c is the service charge per party.

7.13. Design of Clinical Trials

The design of clinical trials with alternative treatment protocols (medicines, in particular) and analysis of data arising therefrom have occupied a reasonable space in statistical research over the last four decades or so. However, the use of statistical decision theory in this context has not been commensurate with the development of statistical decision theory. Two factors have been recognized as stumbling blocks, namely the development of a measure of utility (or welfare) and the choice of a suitable prior. Of course, attempts have been made to circumvent these problems as well as to develop models and tools to accommodate the requirements of applications in real life.

Consider the clinician as the decision-maker and different ethically allowable treatments (or medicines) as actions. A state of nature may correspond to how a patient would respond to alternative treatments, which may be completely unknown. Utility or welfare may be a health outcome, like patent lifespan or quality of life, that would be realized when a specified treatment is administered to a patient. The objective is to choose the treatment that would maximize a social welfare function that sums up treatment outcomes (like five-year survival rate or mean lifespan) across a population of patients that may have heterogeneous treatment responses (because of different observable and unobservable covariates). A statistical decision function uses the data to choose an allocation of patients to treatments, according to a decision rule.

Suppose a health planner has to assign either treatment A (conventional one or placebo depending on the situation) or B (an innovation) to each member of a patient population. Each patient gives a response y having a distribution P. The planner allocates a fraction δ of patients to treatment B and $1-\delta$ to A. The problem is to find δ such that the welfare function is a maximum, where $\beta - \alpha +$ average treatment effect (ATE):

$$U(\delta, P) = \alpha (1-\delta) + \beta \delta \text{ where } \alpha = E[y(A)] \text{ and } \beta = E[y(B)]$$

With only sample data providing incomplete knowledge about the sign of ATE, we should take recourse to a decision theoretic formulation of the problem.

In the absence of a plausible prior over the state space, the maximum regret or the minimum expected utility or some such rule has been examined for its performance. The empirical success rule chooses the treatment with the highest average outcome in the trial. Manski (2004) and others showed that this rule either exactly or approximately minimizes maximum regret when the sample size is moderate. Further, the empirical success rule is asymptotically optimal. Also applicable in such situations is Wald's maximin welfare (utility) or minimax risk criterion. Maximum regret is well-defined in general settings with multiple treatments and when patients have heterogeneous observable covariates that may be used to differentiate treatments. Of course, the concept of minimax regret is quite well received in the case of two treatments where members of the patient population are observationally identical, all having the same observable covariates. The two criteria, namely minimax regret and minimax risk, yield the same choice only in some special cases. The minimax risk criterion considers only the worst outcome in a given state of nature. The minimax regret criterion considers the worst outcome relative to what is achievable in a given state.

If reasonable priors can be developed, we can surely use the Bayes decision rule. If a credible subjective prior is difficult to obtain,

Bayesians may suggest the use of some default distribution, variously called 'reference' or conventional' or 'objective' priors, and the choice is an important aspect of decision-making.

Simes (1986) reports the application of decision theory to treatment choices (chemotherapy) in advanced ovarian cancer, involving difficult value judgements in weighting beneficial and deleterious outcomes of treatments. Assessment of treatment preferences is focused on knowing what sets of utilities favour each treatment. It may be incidentally noted that estimation of utility requires clearly defined worst and best outcomes.

Stallard (1998, 2003) discusses the problem of designing a Phase II clinical trial to maximize gain function, including the cost of drug development and the benefit of a successful therapy. He extended the study to include other potential therapies which compete for the same limited resources for their development.

Muller et al. (2007) describe the application of the Bayesian approach to designing a clinical trial to compare a gel sealant to standard care for resolving air leaks after pulmonary resection. The design involves two different decisions. After each patient cohort is treated and their outcomes observed, we decide whether to continue accrual (sequential stopping rule) or to stop early. The set of possible actions is restricted to avoid unintuitive, unreasonable or impractical decisions. Only the terminal decision, namely whether to report the new sealant as superior, is Bayes, while the stopping decision is based on group sequential boundary. A Bayesian non-parametric prior, namely a dependent Dirichlet process prior, is assumed and a utility function based on time until resolution of air leaks for a future patient to whom the finally recommended treatment is administered, to formalize the decision-maker's preferences for early resolution of air leaks under hypothetical data and assumed parameter values.

To avoid the inherent problem of fixing a suitable prior, some research workers have highlighted the use of the minimax regret rule rather than the Bayes rule to decide on the terminal action:

$$\pi(\phi|D_1, \alpha) = c(L\ [\phi|D_0])\ \pi_0(\phi)$$

7.14. Robust Decision-making

In the context of statistical decision theory, robustness essentially relates to possible deviations in the optimal decisions reached on the basis of models used in the decision analysis from the true optimal ones. The models in this case correspond to the trio, namely (a) probability model assumed for the random variable(s) as the outcome(s) of the experiment to reduce the impact of uncertainty, (b) prior distribution over the state space and (c) utility of an outcome or action based on the decision (inversely taken as the loss function). These three individually and jointly influence the decision. Quite often, we use approximate models and the robustness of the decisions results from model uncertainty, somehow overcome by using some approximations or from model misspecification. A comprehensive discussion appears in Hansen and Sargent (2008) and by Berger (1993) in the context of Bayesian analysis, as well as by several other workers, including Holmes and Watson (2014), with some advising the statistician to 'shake your model via perturbed MC sampling' before freezing the decision.

It may be pointed out that not much has been reported on the sensitivity of Bayesian or frequentist decisions to choices of loss or utility, one reason being the complexity involved in such a sensitivity study. Standard choices of models for underlying variables and for the prior often lead to a lack of robustness. Thus, probability models in the exponential family are found to be very sensitive to outliers in the given data and conjugate priors can have a pronounced effect on decisions if the data are in conflict with the specified prior information. To get over this problem, flat-tailed priors have been sometimes recommended, but the derivation of results becomes complicated. Non-informative priors based on the reference prior approach or the maximum entropy approach have also been advocated. Laplace and Savage recommended uniforms prior.

A comprehensive Bayesian approach involving multiple model setups has sometimes been adopted to deal with the problem of model uncertainty by not only considering the parameters in a chosen model as random but also expanding the horizon of choice to incorporate several models altogether. In this expanded framework, we have the opportunity to explore the extent of uncertainty in a model, given the data, and to apply different routes to the basic problem of reducing uncertainty attributable to the 'model' in data analysis and data-based inferencing.

In this approach, we proceed to start with a set of models M_i, assigning a prior probability distribution $p(\theta_k|M_k)$ to the parameters of each model, and a prior probability $p(M_i)$ to each model. The set of models should, of course, share certain common properties that reflect the feature(s) of the underlying phenomenon of enquiry or of the data available on the phenomenon. Thus, for example, when dealing with failure-time data, the set of models to start with could be members of the new better than used class if so suggested by the known behaviour of the equipment whose failure times have been observed. The priors for the parameters involved in the models initially considered may be the corresponding conjugate priors. In fact, it would be reasonable to use the same type of prior for the different models. This prior formulation induces a joint distribution $p(Y, \theta_k, M_k) = p(Y|\theta_k, M_k) \, p(\theta_k|M_k) \, p(M_k)$ over the data, parameters and models. In effect, we generate a large hierarchical mixture model.

Under this full model, the data are treated as being realized in three stages: First, the model M_k is generated from $p(M_1), \ldots, p(M_k)$; second, the parameter vector θ_k is generated from $p(\theta_k|M_k)$, and third, the data Y are generated from $p(Y|\theta_k, M_k)$. Through conditioning and marginalization, the joint distribution $p(Y, \theta_k, M_k)$ can be used to obtain posterior summaries of interest.

Integrating out the parameters θ_k and conditioning on the data Y yields the posterior model probabilities:

$$p(M_k|Y) = \frac{p(Y|M_k)p(M_k)}{\sum_k p(Y|M_k)p(M_k)}$$

Where:

$$p(Y|M_k) = \delta \int p(Y|\theta_k, M_k) p(\theta_k|M_k) d\theta_k$$

is the marginal likelihood of M_k. (When $p(\theta_k|M_k)$ is a discrete distribution, integration in the above equation is replaced by summation.) Under the full three-stage hierarchical model interpretation for the data, $p(M_k|Y)$ is the conditional probability that M_k was the actual model generated at the first stage.

We can now introduce pairwise comparison between models j and k on the basis of the posterior probabilities to eventually proceed towards choosing a model in terms of the posterior odds:

$$\frac{p(M_k|Y)}{p(M_j|Y)} = \frac{p([Y|M]_k)}{p([Y|M]_j)} \times \frac{p(M_k)}{p(M_j)}$$

This expression reveals how the data, through the Bayes factor $B[k:j] \equiv \frac{p([Y|M]_k)}{p([Y|M]_j)}$, updates the prior odds $O[k:j] = \frac{p(M_k)}{p(M_j)}$ to yield the posterior odds. The Bayes factor $B[k:j]$ summarizes the relative support for M_k versus M_j provided by the data. Note that the Bayes posterior model probabilities can be expressed entirely in terms of Bayes factors and prior odds as:

$$p(M_k|Y) = \frac{B[k:j]O[k:j]}{\sum_k B[k:j]O[k:j]}$$

In so far as the priors $p(\theta_k|M_k)$ and $p(M_k)$ provide an initial representation of model uncertainty, the model posterior $p(M_1|Y), \ldots, p(M_k|Y)$ provides a complete representation of post-data model uncertainty that can be used for a variety of inferences and decisions. By treating $p(M_k|Y)$ as a measure of the 'truth' of model M_k, given the data, a natural and simple strategy for model selection is to choose the most probable M_k, the modal model for which $p(M_k|Y)$ is the largest. Model selection may be useful for testing a theory represented by one of a set of carefully studied models, or it may simply serve to reduce attention from many speculative models to a single useful model. However, in problems where no single model stands out, it may be preferable to report a set of models, each with a high posterior probability, along with their probabilities, to convey the model uncertainty.

Bayesian model averaging is an alternative to Bayesian model selection that accepts rather than avoids model uncertainty. For example, suppose interest is focused on the distribution of Y_r, a future observation from the same process that generated Y. Under the full model for the data induced by the priors, the Bayesian predictive distribution of Y_r is obtained as:

$$p(Y_r|Y) = \sum_k p(Y_r|M_k,Y)p(M_k|Y)$$

which is virtually a posterior weighted mixture of the conditional predictive distributions:

$$p(Y_r|M_k,Y) = \int p(Y_r|\theta_k,M_k)p(\theta_k|M_k,Y)dk$$

By averaging over the unknown models, $p(Y_t|Y)$ incorporates the model uncertainty embedded in the priors in a way that only circumscribes model ur certainty within a certain domain. A natural point prediction of Y_r is obtained as the mean of $p(Y_r|Y)$, namely:

$$E(Y_r|Y) = \sum_k E(Y_r|M_k,Y)p(M_k|Y)$$

Such model averaging or mixing procedures to contain model uncertainty have been developed and advocated by Leamer (1978b), Geisser (1993), Draper (1995), Raftery et al. (1996) and Clyde et al. (1996).

A major appeal of the Bayesian approach to model uncertainty is its complete generality. In principle, it can be applied whenever data are treated as a realization of random variables, a cornerstone of model statistical practice. The past decade has seen the development of innovative implementations of Bayesian treatments of model uncertainty for a wide variety of potential model specifications. Of course, different ways of selecting one among the models with which we initially intend to represent the data based on different selection criteria will be there. Sometimes, the choice should depend on the objective of selecting a model as an intermediate step in the quest for a final answer to a not-so-simple question. Each implementation has required careful attention to prior specification and posterior calculation.

One may even look at the data part in this context. The data would yield realized values of some random variables and the choice of these variables as reflected in the data does have a significant role in the model specification and selection exercise. In fact, one wonders if the Bayesian approach does provide any assistance to the research worker in the choice of variables which can minimise the extent of model uncertainty at the next stage and can lead to robust conclusions later.

The key object provided by the Bayesian approach is the posterior quantification of post-data uncertainty. Whether to proceed by model selection or model averaging is determined by additional considerations that can be formally motivated by decision theoretic considerations (Bernardo and Smith, 1994; Gelfand et al., 1992) by introducing the concept of a quantifiable utility or a quantifiable loss. Letting $u(a, \Delta)$ be the utility or negative loss of action a given the unknown entity of interest Δ, the optimal a maximizes the posterior expected utility:

$$\int \mu(a,\Delta) p(\Delta|Y) d\Delta$$

Here, $p(\Delta|Y)$ is the predictive distribution of Δ given Y under the full three stage model specification. Thus, the best posterior model selection corresponds to maximizing $0-1$ utility for a correct selection. The model averaged point prediction $E(Y_r|Y)$ corresponds to minimizing the quadratic loss with respect to the actual future value Y_r. The predictive distribution $p(Y_r|Y)$ minimizes Kullback–Leibler loss with respect to the actual predictive distribution $p(Y_r|\theta_k, M_k)$.

CHAPTER 8

Multi-criteria Decision-making

8.1. Introduction

Real-world decision-making problems are usually too complex and quite often unstructured. These cannot be considered as just the evaluation of several options in respect of a single criterion or from a single point of view that will lead to an optimum decision. In a mono-criterion approach, the analyst builds a unique criterion that captures all the relevant aspects of the problem. In many situations, we have a set of multiple conflicting objectives. Some decision problems have to involve a group of decision-makers or a team of experts or judges requested by the only decision-maker. MCDM is one of the most widely used decision methodologies in science, business and government. Decision criteria, according to Zeleny (1982), should be relatively precise, but usually conflicting, and are rules, measures and standards that guide decision-making. One view considers different cost components, like ordering and holding costs (which are usually conflicting), as components of one criterion, namely total inventory cost. However, the cost of manufacturing, on the one hand, and the gain due to enhanced customer satisfaction (which also can go in reverse directions), on the other, should justifiably be taken as different criteria.

The complex magnitude of a decision-making process and the crucial and sustained impacts of a meta-level decision coming out of such a process are well illustrated by the multi-purpose river valley projects planned and executed by the Tennessee Valley Authority in the USA and Damodar Valley Corporation in India. The major objectives of such a project include (a) generation of hydro-electricity, (b) providing irrigation water through canals from the reservoir, (c) connecting the two sides of a river by a road bridge and (d) providing facilities for recreation and tourism at the two ends and the major decisions to be taken related to the location of the dam on the course of a flowing river and the height of the dam. A lot of input data regarding the rate of flow of water along the stretch of the river at different possible locations, precipitation in the catchment area, the need for irrigation water in the neighbouring areas under cultivation, the convenience of setting up a hydro-electricity plant, etc., is needed to reach a decision. A huge amount of computation involving actual and imputed costs and of anticipated benefits over several possible durations, as well as costs of displacing local people from the area where the reservoir was to be built, had to be carried out, besides churning out opinions of a host of expert engineers, economists and social workers. This was typically a multi-person, multi-criteria and multi-period decision problem where the fall-out of a decision taken after due analysis would continue to benefit and/or afflict people in the surrounding areas as well as in distant regions for years to come. A somewhat simplistic approach is to convert all favourable and adverse consequences to monetary terms, using appropriate weights, assuming some reasonable planning horizon and taking due advantage of methods to compute imputed costs and indirect benefits. A benefit-to-cost ratio would be calculated and a ratio exceeding or falling short of unity would justify a decision (in terms of the location and the height of the dam).

Some investigators treat multi-attribute decision-making (MADM) and MCDM interchangeably. However, a well-accepted dichotomy of MCDM into MADM and MODM has also been forwarded by some exponents of decision-making. In MADM, which may involve only one objective, the distinguishing aspect is the assignment of weights or measures of importance to the different attributes as indicative of the contribution of any attribute towards achieving the objective. Exogenously assigned weights make the problem easier, though data-based assignment of weights leads to interesting methods and techniques. MODM—as the name implies—relates to a situation where different objectives are set before the decision-maker and the different objectives could have different priorities or weights. A common approach to solving an MODM problem is goal programming, where we introduce targets or goals for each of the objectives, and the eventual criterion could be a weighted total of absolute deviations of each objective actually achieved by an alternative from the target. Problems of fixing weights or priorities are common in both MADM and MODM. Philosophically, however, MADM is essentially a selection problem, while MODM is quite often a design problem.

The wide range of MCDM problem-solving methods and corresponding algorithms make a potential user somewhat confused. Some are relatively simple, while some others involve a lot of computation, some with an immediate appeal to the decision-maker and some others look better to satisfy mathematical and/or analytical interests. A whole host of methods with fanciful acronyms have appeared in the literature and more are being developed. As expected, the different methods have a large common ground, but each has some distinctive features in handling the basic tasks, namely assessing the available options/alternatives against each of the criteria, determining criteria weights, obtaining overall ranks for the alternatives and finally selecting one. The real problem is that different methods may not yield the same solution to a particular problem. Such differences arise due to (a) use of different weights, (b) different ways of treating the different objectives, scaled differently, (c) use of additional parameters that influence the solution and (d) different ways of choosing the 'best' solution.

MCDM has rightly been the exclusive subject for discussion in text and reference books, as well as in innumerable original articles and reviews published in a wide range of periodicals. Against this backdrop, the present chapter provides brief narratives on some selected MCDM methods, including some stochastic versions, supplemented by examples in some cases. Some discussions on classifications of MCDM methods as well as the essential elements in MCDM have obviously been included.

8.2. Classification of MCDM Methods

MCDM methods may be classified in many alternative ways, as indicated by Larichev (2000) in the following:

1. **Methods based on quantitative measurements:** Methods based on multi-criteria utility theory may be referred to in this grouping. Important members of this group include the following:
   - Technique for order preference by similarity to ideal solution (TOPSIS; suggested by Hwang and Yoon in 1981)
   - Simple additive weighting (SAW; suggested by MacCrimon in 1968)
   - Linear programming technique for multidimensional analysis of preference (indicated by Srinivasan and Shocker in 1973)
   - Multi-objective optimization based on a ratio analysis (MOORA; suggested by Brauers and Zavadskas in 2006)
   - Complex proportional assessment of alternatives (suggested by Zavadskas and Kaklauskas in 1996)
   - Complex proportional assessment with grey interval numbers (suggested by Zavadskas et al. in 2008)
   - Others in the group are multiplicative exponential weighting and elimination and choice translating reality (ELECTRE)

   The choice of the utility function and the parameters therein which have to be assigned numerical values cause differences in solutions to the same problem.
2. **Methods based on qualitative initial measurements:** Two widely used methods in this group are the analytic hierarchy process (AHP; suggested by Saaty in 1977) and fuzzy set theory methods (suggested by Zimmerman in 2000).
3. **Comparative preference methods based on pairwise comparison of alternatives:** Modified ELECTRE (given by Roy in 1990), preference ranking organization method for enrichment evaluation (PROMETHEE; suggested by Brans et al. in 1994), TACTIC

Not an abbreviation. (proposed by Vansnick in 1986), ORESTE (Organization, Rangement et Synthese de donnes relationelles, proposed by Roubens in 1982) and a few other methods belong to this group.
4. **Methods based on qualitative variables not converted to quantitative ones:** These include methods of verbal decision-making analysis based on qualitative data in decision environments marked by high levels of uncertainty (Berkeley et al., 1991; Flanders et al., 1998; Larichev, 2000).

The above classification is not exhaustive, since the literature on MCDM is growing fast and in many directions. Some of the methods have found wide applications, while there are others which are not so widely used. Some methods are oriented towards certain specific types of decision problems, like facility location. Some methods attract attention to some deficiencies in the theoretical background. In fact, MCDM methods have been categorized in the following manner by some researchers:

1. Value measurement methods such as SAW and weighted aggregated sum product assessment
2. Goal or reference level models such as TOPSIS and VIKOR
3. Outranking methods such as PROMETHEE, ELECTRE, ORESTE and gained and lost dominance score

8.3. Essentials in MCDM

Steps involved in different MCDM methods and procedures differ, depending on the initial information, the involvement of the decision-maker with their preferences and perceptions, the level of sophistication in analysis desired and related issues. Some essential tasks have to be carried out in the context of MCDM. These are as follows:

- Establish a system of objectives (criteria or functions thereof) by which alternatives are to be assessed and compared
- Identify or generate (depending on the situation) a set (usually finite) of feasible alternatives or options which can be implemented

(may be at the cost of some constraint violation, attracting penalty) to achieve the goals
- Evaluate each criterion in terms of its impact on the decision-making function to derive criteria weights
- Develop a set of performance evaluation of alternatives or options for each criterion
- Choose a method of ranking the alternatives based on how well they satisfy the criteria
- Aggregate alternative evaluations or preferences
- Accept one alternative as the best (the most preferable) or some alternatives as the few best
- Gather more information and go to the next iteration of MCDM if the initial solution is not accepted (may be, as being not implementable)
- Make the final recommendation for decision-making (as a task of the executive)

8.4. VIKOR

VIKOR as an MCDM method was developed by Opricovic in 1979 to solve decision problems with conflicting and non-commensurable (expressed in different units) criteria. Assuming that compromise is acceptable for conflict resolution, the decision-maker likes to have a solution that is closest to the ideal. VIKOR works on the idea of a compromise solution proposed initially by Po-Lung Yu in 1973 and by Milan Zeleny later. (VIKOR is a Serbian acronym for VIseKriterjumska Optimizacija I Kompromisno Resolve.)

As usual, we start with the decision matrix with alternatives A_j, where $j = 1, 2, ..., m$, along the rows and criteria C_k, where $k = 1, 2, ..., n$, along the columns. The cell entry a_{jk} indicates the extent to which alternative j satisfies or performs on the kth criterion. The steps in VIKOR can then be stated as follows:

Step 1: Determine the best and the worst values for each criterion function (defined over the space of alternatives). With a benefit criterion, the best corresponds to the maximum value $\max_j a_{jk}$, and for a cost criterion, it is the minimum value.

Step 2: Compute values of $S_k = \Sigma_k(w_k [\max_k a_{jk} - a_{jk}]/[\max_k a_{kj} - \min_k a_{kj}])$

Step 3: Compute values of $Q_j = v(S_j - S^*)/(S^\wedge - S^*) + (1-v)(R_j - R^*)/(R^\wedge - R^*)$ where v is introduced as a weight for the strategy of maximum group utility, whereas $1-v$ is the weight of the individual regret. These strategies could be compromised by the choice $v = 0.5$, and here, v is modified to be taken as $v = (n+1)/2n$ derived from the relation $v + 0.5(n-1)/n = 1$, since the criterion related to R is included in S too.

Step 4: Rank the alternatives, sorting them by the values of S, R and Q from the minimum to the maximum value to yield three rank vectors.

Step 5: Propose a compromise solution: The alternative $A(1)$, which is ranked the best according to the measure Q (minimum) if the following two conditions are satisfied: (a) acceptable advantage $Q(A(2)) - Q(A(1)) \geq 1/(m-1)$ where $A(2)$ is the alternative ranked second according to the measure Q and (b) acceptable stability in decision-making, implying that the alternative $A(1)$ must also be ranked the best according to R and/or S. This compromise solution is stable within a decision-making process, which could be the strategy of maximum group utility when $v = 0.5$ is needed or by consensus if v is about 0.5 or with veto (if $v < 0.5$). If one of the conditions is not satisfied, then a set of compromise solutions is proposed which consists of alternatives $A(1)$ and $A(2)$ only if the second condition is not satisfied or of alternatives $A(1)$, $A(2)$, ..., $A(m)$ if the first condition is not satisfied, where $A(m)$ is determined by the relation $Q(A(m)) - Q(A(1)) < DQ$ for maximum m (the positions of these alternatives are 'in closeness').

The compromise solution obtained above should be acceptable to the decision-maker because it provides the maximum utility of the majority (reflected in min S) and a minimum individual regret of the opponent (represented by min R). The measures S and R are integrated into Q for a compromise, the basis for an agreement established by mutual concessions. The VIKOR method has been extended to decision-making with interval data as well as to solving problems in a fuzzy environment, where both criteria and their weights could belong to fuzzy sets. The usual triangular membership function is used.

8.5. Analytic Hierarchy Process (AHP)

AHP generates a weight for each evaluation criterion based on the decision-maker's pairwise comparison among the criteria to get over the problem that no alternative may be found to be the 'best' according to all the criteria. A higher weight implies a greater importance for the criterion in making overall prioritization. Next, for a fixed criterion, AHP assigns a score to each alternative according to the decision-maker's pairwise comparison among the alternatives based on that criterion. Finally, AHP combines the scores for the alternatives and the criteria weights. A final prioritization of the alternatives is in terms of the weighted total score for each. The pairwise comparisons which form the bedrock of AHP are somewhat analogous to Thurstone's product scaling, though the latter does involve several judges or decision-makers stating their preferences for one product or alternative compared to the second when the two are presented as a pair. Moreover, Thurstone's method does not involve multiple criteria.

AHP can be implemented in the following three simple computational steps:

1. Computing the weight of each criterion, yielding a vector
2. Computing the matrix of scores for each alternative in respect of each criterion
3. Ranking the alternatives based on the weighted total scores

With k criteria, pairwise comparison by the decision-maker yields the $k \times k$ matrix A with elements a_{ij} where $a_{ij} > 1$ if criterion i is regarded as more important than criterion j, $a_{ij} < 1$ otherwise. Obviously, $a_{ii} = 1$ for all i. If both the criteria are equally important, then also $a_{ij} = 1$. The entries a_{kj} and a_{jk} satisfy the constraint $a_{jk} \cdot a_{kj} = 1$.

The relative importance of one criterion relative to the other, when presented in a pair, is measured on a scale from 1 to 9 as follows:

Value of a_{jk}	Interpretation
1	Criteria j and k are equally important
3	Criterion j is slightly more important than k
5	Criterion j is more important than criterion k
7	Criterion j is strongly more important than k
9	Criterion j is absolutely more important than k

It may be incidentally mentioned that the strength of the relation between a product feature and a technical parameter is generally expressed on a scale of 1, 3, 6 and 9 in constructing the house of quality in quality function deployment.

We now normalize the entries in this matrix to make the column sums equal to one, and we get elements $b_{ij} = a_{ij}/\Sigma_i b_{ij}$. Finally, these normalized entries are averaged over rows to yield the criterion weights as:

$$w_i = \Sigma_j b_{ij}/k \text{ for } i = 1, 2, \ldots, k$$

Example 8.1. Consider an example where the quality of water in a river in three different ecological regions is to be arranged in a hierarchy based on four important quality parameters, namely dissolved oxygen, total dissolved solids, total coliform count and the ratio between biochemical oxygen demand and chemical demand. While the first parameter corresponds to a positive attribute of water quality, the other three are related directly to water pollution. The decision problem here is to choose the region with the most polluted water quality so that an improvement exercise can be first taken up there.

First, we present to an expert or the decision-maker these quality criteria in pairs and suppose we obtain the following matrix of scores:

$$A = \begin{matrix} 1 & 3 & 5 & 1/3 \\ 1/3 & 1 & 1/7 & 1/5 \\ 1/5 & 7 & 1 & 1/3 \\ 3 & 5 & 3 & 1 \end{matrix}$$

It can be seen that $a_{jk} \cdot a_{kj} = 1$ for all pairs (j, k). Criterion 4 has been regarded as the most important while Criterion 2 as the least important.

The corresponding normalized matrix with column sums equalling unity works out as follows

0.2205	0.1875	0.5469	0.1786
0.0735	0.0625	0.0156	0.0710
0.0441	0.4375	0.1094	0.1786
0.6617	0.3125	0.3281	0.5357

The row averages yield the vector of criteria weights as $w' = (0.2834, 0.0647, 0.1924, 0.4595)$. Thus, based on the preferences expressed by the experts, parameter (criterion) 4 is the most important criterion. To check the consistency of paired comparisons yielding the criterion weights, we calculate the ratio of elements in the vector Aw to the corresponding elements in the weight vector w, and these come out as 5.61, 4.22, 4.37 and 4.78. The consistency index (CI) is obtained as $CI = (x-m)/(m-1)$ where x is the average of the ratios just obtained. Thus, CI works out as 0.25. To interpret this value, we note that the value of the random index (RI), that is, the consistency index when the entries in A are completely random. The value of this RI for $m=4$ is given as 0.90 so that $CI/RI = 0.28$, which indicates slight inconsistency.

Given the decision matrix (data matrix indicating the level or value of each of the four parameters for each of the three regions after some appropriate transformation) with criteria appearing in the columns and rows representing the regions, indicated as follows, we find out the weighted score for each of the three regions.

Region	DO_2 (%)	TDS	TCC	BOD/COD
1	1.8	14	21	2.0
2	2.2	16	20	1.8
3	2.0	15	17	2.1

These came out as 1.9237, 1.9389, 1.9559 respectively. Since these figures relate to aspects of water pollution, the best region should be Region 1—a fact not apparent from values in Row 1 compared to values in the other two rows. One may argue that dissolved oxygen is really not an aspect of pollution. One could consider values in Column 1 with a negative sign, to yield weighted totals 0.9035, 0.6919 and 0.8223 respectively, and this implies Region 2 to be the best. In any case, what must be remembered is that the weights were obtained without taking account of the decision matrix.

8.6. Analytic Network Process (ANP)

The ANP can be regarded as a generalization of AHP, both suggested by Saaty (2004), with Saaty and Takizawa (1986) developing ANP. While AHP uses a linear hierarchy among the elements, from the goal at the top to the alternatives at the bottom, a non-linear network connects clusters of elements in ANP. ANP takes care of dependencies and feedback between and within clusters of elements. As in a network, there are nodes representing clusters and arcs indicating dependencies. The level of each may both dominate and be dominated in pairwise comparisons.

Let $C_1, C_2, ..., C_m$ be m clusters, with Cluster k having n_k elements. We built a super-matrix W_{11} of order $n_1 \times n_1$ representing pairwise comparisons among the elements in C_1. Similarly, we have the sub-matrix W_{12} corresponding to Cluster 2 and so on and the sub-matrix W_{1m} for pairwise comparison among elements in cluster m. These sub-matrices appear along the rows of the super-matrix W, in which the sub-matrix W_{21} of order $n_1 \times n_2$ is for pairwise comparison between elements of Cluster 1 and those of Cluster 2. The last sub-matric $W_{m \times m}$ corresponds to elements in Cluster m. In fact, sub-matrices along the diagonal represent comparisons among elements within a cluster, while an off-diagonal sub-matrix is meant to take care of relations or dependences between elements in one cluster and those in another. A comparison to reveal possible dependences is made using the Saaty scale. Thus, we may have a cluster of criteria which could be interdependent, a fact revealed through elements in a sub-matrix for the criteria. Similarly, alternatives could be inter-related among themselves as well as with each of the criteria. In that way, AHP ignores these dependences. W is raised to an arbitrary large power to obtain the cumulative effects of the elements on each other. It may be incidentally added that, in some contexts, some of the interrelations may not really mean anything.

8.7. Data Envelopment Analysis

Data envelopment analysis (DEA) is a relatively simple, non-parametric method of comparing the efficiencies of multi-input, multi-output DMUs based on observed data. Such units are engaged in producing similar outputs using similar inputs, most often working within the same corporate organization, but each enjoying some authority to decide on the deployment of the resource inputs. Examples could be branches of a bank, schools working under the same board or council, hospitals under the same health department, service units of a municipal corporation and the like. Sometimes, the DMUs could be different organizations engaged in the same type of business. Efficiency (sometimes referred to as technical efficiency) is defined as the ratio between the weighted total of outputs produced and the weighted total of inputs used, where weights are endogenously generated from the data and not exogenously assigned by experts. In fact, these weights are determined by repeated application of LP in DEA. DEA is preferred to other comparable forms of econometric analysis which assume some parametric model linking outputs as functions of inputs.

With n DMUs consuming varying amounts of m different inputs to turn out s different outputs, let DMU j consume an amount x_{ij} of inputs $i = 1, 2, \ldots, m$ to produce an amount y_{rj} of output $r = 1, 2, \ldots, s$. Let u and v be the vectors of weights to be associated with the input vector X_j and the output vector Y_j for any DMU j. Then the original input-oriented DEA model to find the weights u and v and therefrom the efficiency for each DMU as proposed by Charnes, Cooper and Rhodes (as the CCR model) can be stated as:

Maximize $w_0 = v' Y_0$ subject to $u' X_0 = 1$, $v'Y_0 - u'X_0 \leq 0$, $u, v \geq \varepsilon$

The problem is solved n times with $(X_0, Y_0) = (X_j, Y_j)$ where $j = 1, 2, \ldots, n$. Values of w partition the set of DMUs into efficient DMUs with $w = 1$ and inefficient ones with $w < 1$ with the efficiency frontier corresponding to $w=1$. The output-oriented model, which is just the dual of the LP problem stated earlier, was proposed by Banker, Charnes and Cooper as the BCC model.

Other DEA models include multiplicative models that allow a piecewise log-linear or piecewise Cobb–Douglas envelopment. If we omit the contraction factor ϕ and focus on maximizing the sum of the slacks in the BCC model, we get another variant of DEA. If we have some prior knowledge about the weights or factors, we can incorporate such knowledge into the model by, for example, putting lower and/or upper bounds on their values, resulting in less flexible models compared to the original CCR or BCC models where no restrictions on the factors or weights are introduced (Thanassoulis et al., 1987). Banker and Morey (1986) showed how to incorporate categorical variables into DEA. Sahoo (2007) considered a model with variable returns to scale as opposed to the constant returns assumed in classical models. There has been some contributions to the dynamic DEA model. Johnson (1996) considers the use of infinitely many DMUs. Tone (2000) used a limited number of additional LP problems to be solved in respect of inefficient DMUs to work out possible improvements in their efficiency by significantly reducing their consumption of inputs or production of outputs. Applications of DEA models have been wide ranging, from banking to school education, from healthcare to transportation, from corporate failure analysis to bankruptcy prediction problems and many others.

One limitation of DEA is that it does not provide a basis for comparing efficient DMUs among themselves. It is quite possible for several DMUs to have a unit efficiency score in the classical DEA models. For this purpose, super-efficiency models based on slacks have been proposed. Also, a cross-efficiency matrix can be constructed and the column averages can distinguish among the efficient units.

If we recognize random variations in inputs and/or outputs because of errors in measurement or of sampling or other chance factors, we have to formulate and solve a stochastic DEA problem. One approach will be to look upon DEA as a problem in a chance-constrained programming problem (Olesen & Petersen, 2016) with both constraints and the objective function as random and to come up with a chance-constrained efficiency index. The problem thus formulated is a non-convex programming problem, and to avoid computational complexity, upper and lower bounds for the efficiency measures were suggested. Sengupta (1998) also studied the chance-constrained case for single-output units. Statistical analysis done by Banker showed that DEA provides the maximum likelihood estimate of the efficiency frontier. A bootstrapping method is proposed to estimate the frontier. Morita and Seiford (1999) considered efficiency as a random variable and discussed the expected efficiency score, quantiles of the efficiency score and the probability of the score exceeding a threshold value as possible efficiency measures and introduced the concepts of reliability and robustness of the efficiency result. If an efficient DMU remains efficient for large deviations in inputs and outputs from their assumed values, such a DMU has high reliability. Otherwise, if an efficient DMU turns out to be inefficient for small changes in data, such a DMU is not reliable.

I-DEA (DEA with incomplete data), often incorporating benefit-of-doubt modes, has been sometimes applied to work out weights for different indicators of national development. Seiford and Zhu (2002) showed that both input-oriented and output-oriented BCC models can be used to characterize the efficiency of DMUs when either negative input or negative output values occur. They refer to the translation invariance and the resulting classification invariance to data transformation as desirable properties of DEA.

8.7.1. Ranking of DMUs

An important limitation of DEA that has attracted the attention of investigators recently is its inability to rank the DMUs, particularly the efficient one with 100 per cent efficiency, when dealing with a large number of DMUs converting several outputs to more than one output. In fact, quite a few DMUs are found to be (fully) efficient in traditional DEA, though all of them may not have the same performance level. Among approaches to remove or reduce this deficiency, some consider restrictions on weights for inputs and outputs, other make use of additional DEA efficiency computation for each DMU or use virtual weights or even consider merger of DMUs by adding their inputs and outputs linearly. In some of these approaches, the number of efficient DMUs decreases, and in some others, a near complete ranking of efficient DMUs could be achieved. However, ranking of the DMUs differ from one approach to another and the researcher has to remain careful about the procedure and the assumptions in each approach.

In DEA models with assurance regions introduced by Thompson et al. (1986), additional constraints on weights are incorporated to integrate decision-maker's preferences for certain inputs and outputs. In cone ratio method, these constraints appear as linear inequalities, while in the linked cone method interrelationships among input and output weights are used. Thanassoulis et al. (1987) adopted a method of distribution of virtual input and output values which convey information about the importance a unit attaches to particular inputs and outputs to attain its maximum efficiency rating., focusing attention on good operating practices. Some authors put lower bounds on the weights and others used both lower and upper bounds on the weights. These methods which tend to modify weights in the classical DEA cannot achieve a complete ranking of the DMUs, though the number of efficient DMUs may come down.

A common exercise in this connection is to build up the cross-efficiency matrix, in which efficiency for each DMU (presented in a row) is computed by using its optimal weights and also by using optimal weights for all the other DMUs (presented along the columns). For n DMUs under consideration, we get an $n \times n$ cross-efficiency matrix, and we rank the DMUs on the basis of the row averages. A problem arises when alternative optimal weights are obtained for any DMU/DMUs.

The super-efficiency ranking model proposed by Andersen and Petersen (1993) eliminates the constraint that the efficiency of a DMU cannot exceed unity. These super-efficiency scores can provide a basis for ranking but can sometimes yield very high values and the model may not yield any feasible solution in some cases. Talluri et al. (2002) proposed the discriminatory BCC model, in which they defined a composite DMU as a hypothetical DMU composed as an aggregate of efficient DMUs that are in the reference set of an inefficient DMU. Each DMU is assessed against its own composite DMUs as well as against the composite DMU of the other DMUs. A DMU that performs well when matched against several composite DMUs has a good overall performance. The average efficiency score of a DMU is assessed by the composite DMU of aa the DMUs. is taken as the discriminatory score to provide a basis for ranking of DMUs.

Among occasionally used methods to tackle the problem, mention may be made of the contributions by Doyle and Green (1994), Sinuany-Stern (1994), Bardhan et al. (1996) and Srinivas and Baker (2002). Singh and Chand (2007) introduced a different approach to overcome the limitations of DEA through the merger approach. They argue that if an efficient DMU A when merged with an inefficient DMU C remains efficient, while another efficient DMU B becomes inefficient when merged with C, then DMU A is comparatively better than DMU B, though both are efficient. The total number of efficiency scores to be obtained for each DMU will be $n(n-1)/2$ to be obtained through solving revised formulations of the LP problem for merging of inputs and outputs of two DMUs. The authors provide an example to show differences in ranking between some of the other methods (which fail to provide complete ranking) and this method, and the results show a lot of variation.

8.8. TOPSIS

Among all the MADM methods, TOPSIS is quite an effective one in terms of its intuitive appeal, nice construction and computational simplicity. TOPSIS uses the intuitive principle that the selected alternative should have the shortest distance (Euclidean) from the best solution and the farthest distance from the worst solution. A solution is a point with co-ordinates as the attribute values/levels. In a higher the better situation (originally or after an inverse transformation of an attribute), the best solution contains the maximum attainable values of the attributes, and the minimum values constitute the worst solution.

In one MADM approach, the alternative which has the shortest Euclidean distance from the best solution is selected. However, a solution that is the shortest distance from the best may not be the farthest from the worst. TOPSIS considers both these distances simultaneously. This distance may be denoted by $d(B, W)$. The decision criterion in TOPSIS is that the smaller the value of $d(B, W)$, the more the alternative is preferred.

TOPSIS has been applied in various contexts. One important application has been in the area of quality function deployment. A slightly modified version called A-TOPSIS has been developed for comparing alternative algorithms.

Unlike in AHP, where weights for the different decision criteria are determined by preferences indicated by the expert or the decision-maker and using some arbitrary scoring system, in TOPSIS, these are derived from observed data. In fact, the weight for a given criterion in TOPSIS is obtained using the entropy measure of the observed values corresponding to this category or using the coefficient of variation or some other measure of scatter or variability among the alternatives in respect of their performance on a given criterion.

To bring out the differences between AHP and TOPSIS, in terms of procedure and results, we will apply the entropy principle to determining the criteria weights, and for the sake of illustration, we will consider the previous example. Let x_{ij} be the element in the (i, j) th cell of the decision matrix.

Step 1: Elements of the decision matrix are normalized to obtain probabilities estimated in terms of proportions a $p_{ij} = x_{ij}/\Sigma_i x_{ij}$ for $j = 1, 2, ..., n$

Step 2: Compute the entropy measure for each criterion j as:

$$E_j = -\alpha \, \Sigma_I p_{ij} \ln p_{ij} \text{ for } j = 1, 2, ..., n$$

Quite often, the value of α is taken as 1.

These measures, for example, considered in Sub-section 8.10.2, work out as:

$$-E_1 = 0.4623, \; -E_2 = 1.0993, \; -E_3 = 1.0335 \text{ and } -E_4 = 0.4578$$

The degree of diversity is then calculated as $D_j = 1 - E_j$. The entropy weights W are then obtained as $W_j = D_j/\Sigma D_I$ for $j = 1, 2, \ldots, n$. Let us compute these weights for the example to get:

$$W_1 = 0.2073 \quad W_2 = 0.2977 \quad W_3 = 0.2883 \quad W_4 = 0.2067$$

Step 3: Transform the decision matrix X to a normalized matrix $R = (r_{ij})$ where:

$$R_{ij} = X_{ij}/\sqrt{\Sigma x_{ij}^2} \text{ so that } \Sigma_{ij}^2 = 1$$

Step 4: Elements in the above matrix are weighted by the appropriate criteria weights to yield the following matrix $V = (v_{ij})$ where $v_{ij} = W_j r_{ij}$

Step 5: Define the 'ideal positive' and 'ideal negative' solutions indicated by:

$$V_j^+ = \min v_{ij}, \text{ minimum over } i \text{ and } V_j^- = \max v_{ij} \text{ maximum over } i \text{ for } j = 1, 2, \ldots, n$$

Step 6: Compute the distance of entity i from the positive ideal and negative ideal as:

$$D_i^+ = (\Sigma[v_{ij} - V_j])^2)^{1/2} \text{ and } d_{i-} = (\Sigma[v_{ij} - V_{j-}]^2)^{1/2} \text{ the sums being over } j.$$

Step 7: Compute the composite index for each entity to determine the closeness of an entity to the ideal solution in terms of $CI_I = d_i^+/(d_i^+ - d_{i-})$, $i = 1, 2, \ldots, m$. The final rank for entity k is obtained this way, and the higher the rank, the closer the entity is to the ideal solution.

8.9. Combinations of DEA, AHP and TOPSIS

In dealing with different situations where several alternatives (could be DMUs or other entities) have to be ranked on the basis of observed data on multiple criteria that carry different weights to different decision-makers, researchers have sometimes used AHP and TOPSIS together or AHP and DEA, one for developing the criteria weights and the other for ranking the alternatives.

Recently, a new performance measurement procedure called operational competitiveness rating (OCRA) has been proposed (Parkan, 1994), essentially as a benchmarking tool to measure the performance efficiency of a production unit (PU) within a set of such units. Based on a non-parametric model, the OCRA procedure involves the solution of a LP problem to obtain an inefficiency index for each PU relative to other units within the set considered. The index is computed on the basis of inputs consumed and outputs yielded by each unit. This non-parametric procedure is somewhat akin to DEA. The procedure has been applied to banks and other service-producing units, besides manufacturing and processing units. OCRA has been criticized for the subjectively determined calibration points used as weights for inputs and outputs to come up with a simple ratio to be optimized. The complementary perspective of deriving an index of relative inefficiency has also been applied in practice to the cost of input resources and the value of output goods and services.

Resources consumed by each of k PUs are put into m cost categories and values generated by output goods and services into N revenue categories. Then the resource consumption performance rating and the revenue generation performance rating for PU_I are obtained to subsequently yield the overall performance rating. Critics of OCRA point to the subjectivity of the calibration constants expected to reflect management's perceived priorities. (A direct and possibly elaborate method for this purpose could be AHP.)

Wang (2006) points out that, in OCRA, a cost category with large cost/revenue ratio is more important than a cost category with a small ratio, creating an illusion to management.

8.10. The Combined Compromise Solution (CoCoSo) Model

Based on the idea of compromise solution to a multi-objective programming problem, the CoCoSo method has been tried out as an alternative MCDM procedure. Starting with the input or data matrix (x_{ij}) for m alternatives and n criteria, we first normalize the data by taking:

$$r_{ij} = (x_{ij} - \min x_{ij})/(\max x_{ij} - \min x_{ij}) \text{ for a benefit criterion}$$
$$= (\max x_{ij} - x_{ij})/(\max x_{ij} - \min x_{ij}) \text{ for a cost criterion}$$
$$(\text{max and min over alternatives})$$

We now assign a score S_i to the ith alternative as $S_i = \Sigma w_j r_{ij}$ summed over criteria j where criterion j carries a weight w_j determined as in AHP or otherwise. We also associate another value to alternative i as $P_i = \Sigma r_{ij} w_j$ obtained from grey relational number generation approach. We now develop three versions of relative weights of the alternatives which are as follows:

$$k_{ia} = (P_i + S_i)/\Sigma(P_j + S_j) \qquad k_{ib} = S_i/\min S + P_i/\min P_j$$

and

$$k_{ic} = (\lambda S_i + [1-\lambda] P_i)/(\lambda \max S_j + [1-\lambda] \max Pj)$$

The final selection among the alternatives is based on:

$$k_I = (k_{ia} \cdot k_{ib} \cdot k_{ic})^{1/3} + 1/3(k_{ia} + k_{ib} + k_{ic})$$
$$B_i^r = \int_X f(x) \int_{W_i^{r(x)}} f(w) \, dw \, dx$$

8.11. OCRA

Recently, a new performance measurement procedure called OCRA has been proposed (Parkan, 1994) essentially as a benchmarking tool to measure the performance efficiency of a PU within a set of such units. Based on a nonparametric model, the OCRA procedure involves the solution of a LP problem to obtain an inefficiency index for each PU relative to other units within the set considered. The index is computed on the basis of inputs consumed and outputs yielded by each unit. This non-parametric procedure is somewhat akin to DEA. The procedure has been applied to banks and other service-producing units, besides manufacturing and processing units. OCRA has been criticized for the subjectively determined calibration points used as weights for inputs and outputs to come up with a simple ratio to be optimized. The complementary perspective of deriving an index of relative inefficiency has also been applied in practice to the cost of input resources and the value of output goods and services.

Resources consumed by each of k PUs are put into m cost categories and values generated by output goods and services into N revenue categories. Then the resource consumption performance rating and the revenue generation performance rating for PU_i are obtained to subsequently yield the overall performance rating. Critics of OCRA point to the subjectivity of the calibration constants expected to reflect management's perceived priorities. A direct and possibly elaborate method for this purpose could be AHP.

8.12. PROMETHEE and GAIA

PROMETHEE and geometric analytic interactive aid (GAIA) are multi-criteria decision aids which were introduced by Brans (1962) and Bernard Ray in the late 1960s, followed by Mraeschal and Brans (1988). Claimed rightly as aids rather than methods for MCDM, these have found useful applications in (a) choice of one alternative from a given set, based on pairwise comparative evaluations in respect of multiple criteria, (b) prioritization determining the merits of the members in a set of actions, (c) resource allocation among a set of actions, (d) ranking of alternatives and (e) conflict resolution. The prescriptive part PROMETHEE provides both a complete as well as a partial ranking of the alternative actions, while the descriptive complement GAIA (a) allows the decision-maker to visualize the main features of the decision problem and (b) enables the decision-maker to identify conflicts and synergies among criteria, as well as to identify clusters of actions and to highlight remarkable performance.

Six versions of PROMETHEE have been developed over the years: Version I provides a partial ranking of the alternatives; Version II yields a complete ranking; a ranking based on intervals is provided in Version III; Version IV relates to the continuous case; Version V deals with MCDM, including segmentation constraints, and the last version attempts to represent the human brain.

The method starts with a matrix in which rows correspond to n actions (decisions) a and columns correspond to q criteria k, an element $f(a, q)$ giving the evaluation of action a in respect of criterion k. The evaluations may be subjective assessments or objective ones, based on quantitative information about the actions. Based on this matrix alone, we may not be able to rank the alternatives. In fact, one action is preferred to a second if the evaluation of the first is at least as great as that of the second in respect of each criterion, with at least one strict inequality. If the evaluations are identical for all criteria, the decision-maker becomes indifferent between the two actions. In the case of one action having a higher evaluation than another in respect of some criteria and lower in respect of others, the two actions are incomparable. A preferred action dominates another. An undominated action or alternative is called an efficient solution, and in most cases, the alternatives are efficient. Thus, a choice among such efficient solutions must be based on some additional information reflecting weights of the criteria and the decision-maker's perceptions. To this end, we next consider pairwise differences:

$$d_k(a_I, a_j) = f_k(a_I) - f_k(a_j)$$

We now develop a preference degree:

$$\prod k(a_i, a_j) = P_k[d_k(a_I, a_j)]$$

Here, P_k is a positive preference function lying between 0 and 1 such that $P_k(a_i, a_j) > 0$ implies $P_k(a_j, a_i) = 0$. The greater the value of the deviation d, the larger the preference P. For a criterion to be maximized, P_k should be a sigmoid function of d_k. The V-shaped function with indifference is defined as:

$$P_k(x) = 0 \quad \text{for } x < q_k$$
$$= (x - q_k)/(p_k - q_k) \quad \text{for } p_k \geq x \geq q_k$$
$$= 1 \quad \text{for } x > p_k$$

Here, q_j and p_j being the indifference and preference thresholds respectively. The simple V-shaped function is defined as:

$$P = 0 \quad \text{for } d < 0$$
$$= d/p \quad \text{for } 0 < d < p$$
$$= 1 \quad \text{for } d > p$$

Besides this linear preference function, U-shaped, level and Gaussian functions have also been used. The Gaussian function has the following form:

$$P = 0 \text{ for } d < 0 \text{ and } P = 1 - \exp(d^2/2s^2) \text{ for } d > 0$$

where s is a parameter (like p and q) representing some intermediate value between p and q.

Next, we define aggregated preference indices $\prod(a_I, a_j) = \Sigma_k w_k \prod(a_I, a_j)$.

As the degree to which action a_I is preferred to action a_j over all the criteria, and $\prod(a_j, a_i) = \Sigma_k w_k \prod(a_j, a_I)$ with the requisite that $0 < \prod(a_I, a_j) + \prod(a_j, a_I) < 1$,

$\prod(a_I, a_j) \sim 0$ implies a weak global preference for a_I over a_j; $\prod(a_I, a_j) \sim 1$ implies a strong global preference for a_I over a_j. Six other requisites are also taken for granted, including one that states 'an appropriate method should provide information on the conflicting nature of the criteria.' Now, each action a faces $(n-1)$ other actions, and we define two outranking flows for each action a as:

- Positive outranking flow $ð^+(a) = \Sigma_{x \in A} \prod(a, x)$
- Negative outranking flow $Đ^-(a) = \Sigma \prod(x, a)$

These flows indicate how an action is outranking (being outranked) by all others. Ranking the alternatives/actions based on the two flows will usually yield two different rankings and their intersection provides a partial ranking in PROMETHEE I in terms of (preference, indifference, incomparability). In PROMETHEE II, all the alternatives are made comparable by considering the net outranking flow defined as: $ð(a) = ð^+(a) - ð^-(a)$.

8.12.1. GAIA

As remarked earlier, GAIA helps in visualizing the PROMETHEE exercise in terms of possible conflicts among the criteria and in coming up with a complete set of rankings for the alternatives/actions. It takes off from the $n \times k$ matrix of single-criterion net flow for each action against each criterion and proceeds to determine the GAIA plane in terms of the first two principal components.

8.13. MACBETH

Developed by a group of European research workers Bana e Costa, Vapnik and De Korte towards the end of the last century, measuring attractiveness by a categorical-based evaluation technique (MACBETH) as a method for MCDM is somewhat distinct from other methods in the sense that it draws upon semantic differences judgements to evaluate the alternatives in respect of each of the criteria under consideration as well as to determine the criteria weights. It has found a wide range of applications, from agriculture and manufacturing, through energy and defence, to public policy analysis, either singly or in combination with AHP, evaluation based on distance from the average solution and even Multi-MOORA (discussed in the next section). The basic principle is to build a quantitative model of values based on verbal difference judgements revealed in answers to some questions pertaining to 'attractiveness' of the alternatives or their impacts. However, some cases where this method does not provide correct decisions in terms of final choice of an alternative considering the different criteria have also been noted (Solomon, 2008).

The method has been characterized by its proponents as being:

Humanistic: Helping decision-makers to ponder, communicate and discuss their value systems and preferences (without being inclined to accept pre-decided choices).
Interactive: Through the question–answer protocols, through which differences in attractiveness between alternatives in each possible pair are revealed.

Constructive: By building up robust convictions among the decision-makers to pre-empt final decisions to pre-exist. A good account of the method, including its historical development, can be found in Costa, De Corte and Vansnick (2008).

The decision matrix which is the starting point in any MCDM method provides a value assessment (by way of a cardinal measure) of each of the alternatives for each of the criteria is replaced here by a matrix where a pair of alternatives (x, y) the perceived difference in attractiveness is noted in one of seven possible categories: no difference, very weak difference, weak difference, moderate difference, strong difference, very strong difference and extreme difference. A number of judges or experts are involved. We eventually want some interval scales for the differences beyond ranking.

The steps usually involved in applying this method are the following:

1. Decide on the criteria to be adopted and form the value tree.
2. Alternatives are identified and the ordinal performance level of each alternative against each criterion is defined. At least the upper (good) and the lowest (neutral) levels are required to be chosen. The upper level has a score of 100, and the lower level has a score of 0. These do not necessarily reflect the best and the worst performance of an alternative respectively.
3. A matrix is set up for the alternatives where, for each criterion, the alternatives are arranged according to their relative importance from left to right. This is done to quantify the qualitative performance levels and convert the quantitative performance levels to the MACBETH scale. The same procedure is applied to the criteria also.
4. Pairwise comparisons are made between the criteria and alternatives based on differences in attractiveness. These are mapped onto a seven-point semantic scale to arrange the alternatives in descending order of their importance. The equivalent numerical scale values are shown in Table 8.1.

Table 8.1 Semantic Scale of MACBETH

Semantic Scale	Significance	Equivalent Numerical Scale
Null	Indifference between alternatives	0
Very weak	An alternative is very weakly attractive	1
Over another		
Weak	One alternative is weakly attractive over another	2
Moderate	One is moderately attractive over the other	3
Strong	One is strongly attractive over another	3
Very strong	One is very strongly attractive over the other	5
Extreme	One is extremely attractive over the other	6

5. Judgements provided by the decision-maker are checked for consistency. In the case of any inconsistency, M-MACBETH software is used to suggest possible alterations to make the judgements consistent.
6. The consistent judgements are converted into a suitable numerical scale by using the LP model.
7. Finally, the weighted global scores representing the overall effectiveness of the alternatives considered are computed with the help of some additive aggregation model to rank the alternatives. The overall score $V(A_i)$ for an alternative A_i is simply taken as $V(A_i) = \Sigma w_j \, v_j(A_i)$ where w_j is the weight for criterion j and $v_j(A_i)$ is the MACBETH score of alternative i on criterion j.

The following example illustrates the computation of the scores v's.

Example 8.2. Let A_1, A_2 and A_3 be three alternatives preferred by the decision-maker in the perceived order (of importance) $A_2 > A_3 > A_1$ and let the strength of preferences be indicated as follows:

Alternative	A_2	A_3	A_1
A_2		No	Weak	Strong
A_3			No	Weak
A_1				No

Denoting by $v(A_1)$, $v(A_2)$ and $v(A_3)$, the MACBETH scores of the corresponding alternatives and noting that $v(A_2)=100$ and $v(A_1)=0$, we get the equations:

$$V(A_2)-v(A_3)=2\alpha, \ v(A_3)-v(A_1)=3\alpha, \ v(A_2)-v(A_1)=4\alpha \text{ or}$$

$$100-v(A_3)=2\alpha, \ v(A_3)-0=2\alpha \text{ and } 100-0=4\alpha$$

yielding the solution $\alpha=25$ and the score for $A_3=50$.

8.14. Multi-MOORA

MOORA was developed by Brauers and Zavadskas in 2004 and was supplemented and extended in 2010 in the form of multi-objective optimization on the basis of ratio analysis plus the full multiplicative form (multi-MOORA). Multi-MOORA takes advantage of several MCDM methods developed earlier. Thus, it combines three subordinate rankings obtained by the fully compensatory, incompletely compensatory and non-compensatory models entitled ratio system, full multiplication form and reference point approach. Also, preferences in this general method are combined by different aggregation methods, such as dominance theory, arithmetic mean and geometric mean ratio, Borda rule, improved Borda rule, dominance-directed graph, ORESTE method and rank position method. Each of these methods suffers from some limitations or the other, and this is one reason why multi-MOORA combines all these methods. An interested reader should go through the comprehensive review by Hafezalkotob et al. (2019). The method has been used for a variety of purposes, including testing the economy of the Belgian region, deciding on a bank loan for buying a property, ranking European Union states according to their performance, personnel selection, etc.

Kundakci (2016) discusses the combined use of MACBETH and multi-MOORA, and the application is briefly taken up in the following example.

Example 8.3. The problem is to select a diesel automobile based on nine criteria, namely price, fuel consumption (litre/100 km), safety, brand image, after-sales service, comfort, design and engine power (HP) and carbon dioxide emission (gm/km) mentioned respectively as $C_1, C_2, ..., C_9$, considering nine different automobile models indicated as A_1 to A_9. To convert the performance level for all the criteria into proportionate quantitative MACBETH scores, they are compared pairwise on a seven-point scale. The M-MACBETH software was applied to check the consistency of these judgements and the latter were found to be consistent. The M-MACBETH software converts the ordinance performance levels into proportionate cardinal scores using LP models. The following values indicate the weights of the criteria.

Criterion	C_1	C_2	C_3	C_4	C_5	C_6	C_7	C_8	C_9
Weight	0.0200	0.1684	0.1579	0.1474	0.1158	0.0842	0.0737	0.0421	0.0105

After the MACBETH method was used to find the criteria weights, the multi-MOORA method was applied to work out the rankings of the competing automobile models. Some of the data used to develop the decision matrix are qualitative, while others are quantitative. Information about the models on each of the criteria was obtained from different credible data sources to build up the normalized decision matrix as given in the following table:

Optimization Direction	Min	Min	Max	Max	Max	Max	Max	Max	Min
Alternatives	C_1	C_2	C_3	C_4	C_5	C_6	C_7	C_8	C_9
A_1	168,000	4.2	35.0	5	5	5	5	136	109
A_2	179,697	4.1	34.5	5	4	4	5	190	107
A_3	140,600	4.5	33.0	3	3	3	3	150	119
A_4	134,950	4.3	28.0	3	2	4	4	190	112

Optimization Direction	Min	Min	Max	Max	Max	Max	Max	Max	Min
Alternatives	C_1	C_2	C_3	C_4	C_5	C_6	C_7	C_8	C_9
A_5	151,980	5.6	35.0	3	4	4	3	179	147
A_6	181,632	4.0	35.0	5	3	4	5	190	106
A_7	160,629	4.8	33.0	2	3	3	2	189	125
A_8	162,900	4.5	35.4	3	4	3	2	143	119
A_9	178,000	4.2	32.0	2	3	2	3	180	110

Thereafter, the normalized decision matrix and the weighted normalized decision matrix are computed. Alternatives are then ranked with the ratio system of MOORA, based on $y_i^* = \Sigma v_{ij}$ (for criteria to be maximized) $- \Sigma v_{ij}$ (for criteria to be minimized) and $v_{ij} = w_j x_{ij}^*$, where x_{ij}^* is the normalized measure, presented as follows:

Alternative	A_1	A_2	A_3	A_4	A_5	A_6	A_7	A_8	A_9
y^* value	0.135	0.116	0.107	0.067	0.067	0.063	0.061	0.033	0.031

For the reference point approach of MOORA, distances between the alternatives and the reference points in respect of each criterion were calculated. The highest values are chosen for maximization criteria, such as safety, brand image and comfort, and the lowest values are chosen for minimization criteria, like price or fuel consumption. The best alternative is chosen by the Chebyshev min–max metric. Ranks for the alternatives are found from the maximum distance values, which came out as: 0.014, 0.018, 0.027, 0.033, 0.027, 0.022, 0.041, 0.027 and 0.041 respectively, for the alternatives A_1 to A_9. The ranking obtained in the full multiplicative form of MOORA was based on the following U_i values (in descending order) where $U_i = A_i/B_i$, $A_i = \prod x_{ij} w_{ij}$ (weighted product of the elements in the decision matrix giving performance measures of the alternative i in respect of the criteria) for the criteria to be maximized and B_i is the same quantity for the criteria to be minimized.

Alternative	A_1	A_2	A_3	A_4	A_5	A_6	A_7	A_8	A_9
U value	0.286	0.274	0.267	0.239	0.235	0.235	0231	0.208	0.207

The final ranking is obtained using dominance theory from the above three rankings. It comes out that the final ranking is $A_1 > A_2 > A_6 > A_5 > A_3 > A_4 > A_8 > A_7 > A_9$.

The combination of MACBETH and multi-MOORA methods draws its strength from the advantages of these two MCDM methods. MACBETH requires only qualitative judgements to determine criteria weights and to score the alternatives, while multi-MOORA has the advantage of being robust by combining the three rankings. In future studies on combining MCDM methods, one can try AHP for determining criteria eights and club AHP with multi-MOORA.

8.15. Stochastic Multi-criteria Acceptability Analysis

In the above-mentioned procedures, we have not considered the possibilities of uncertainty or imprecision in measurements of the different criteria, as well as preferences of the decision-makers about the criteria as revealed in the weights associated with those, and we could envisage more than one decision-maker trying to rank several alternatives before eventually choosing one. It is also the situation in some cases that the uncertainties in measurements arise from some common sources, like some environmental factors, thus making the uncertainties interdependent. In fact, the general treatment of such situations has been attempted in a series of articles by Lahdelma et al. (2003). By considering both weights and criterion measurements as random variables with appropriate joint distributions, there have been several versions of Stochastic multi-criteria acceptability analysis (SMAA) as proposed and studied by them.

The decision problem considered can be stated as follows:

There are m alternatives to be judged in terms of n criteria. The preference structure of the decision-makers is represented by a real-valued utility or value function derived from the weights applied to the measurements of the criteria. Alternative I is characterized by the vector of measurements $X_I=(x_{i1}, x_{i2}, ..., x_{in})$ and the value function is taken as $u(X_i, w)$ where the weights are duly normalized to ensure that $w_j \geq 0$ and $\Sigma w_j = 1$. We assume a joint distribution of the random vectors X_I forming a matrix X of stochastic variables with a density $f(x)$ defined over the space S in the real $m \times n$ dimensional Euclidean space. The value function is used to map the stochastic criteria and the weight distribution to the value distribution of the random quantities $u(X_j, w)$. Based on the value distributions, the rank of each alternative is defined as an integer:

$$\text{Rank}(i, w) = 1 + \Sigma_k \eth(u[k, w] > u[i, w])$$

Here, ð (statement true)=1 and ð (statement false)=0. As usual, a higher rank implies a worse alternative. SMAA is based on the analysis of stochastic sets of favourable rank weights $W_i^r(X) = (w \in W | \text{rank}[i, w] = r)$. W represents the space of vector w.

The rank acceptability index b_i^r measures the variety of different preferences that grant r to alternative i. It is, in some sense, the share of all feasible weights that makes the alternative I for a particular rank r. It is computed numerically as a multidimensional integral over the criteria distributions and the favourable rank weights using the formula:

$$B_i^r = \int_X f(x) \int W_i^r(x) f(w) \, dw \, dx$$

The most acceptable alternatives are those with high acceptability and high ranks (1 or close to 1). These alternatives are taken as candidates for the most acceptable solutions. The first rank acceptability index is called the acceptability index a_I. The acceptability index is useful in classifying alternatives as stochastically efficient ones with $a_I > 0$ and weakly efficient or inefficient ones with a_I zero or near zero.

The holistic acceptability index a_i^h can be computed for each alternative as a weighted total of rank acceptability, emphasizing the best ranks. This index is expected to provide a rough measure of the overall acceptability of each alternative.

The central weight vector w_i^c is the expected centre of gravity of the favourable first rank weights of an alternative. This stands for the preferences of a hypothetical decision-maker supporting this alternative. The central weights of different alternatives may help us understand how different weights correspond to different choices with the assumed preference model. The central weight is obtained numerically as a multidimensional integral. We also calculate a confidence factor as the probability of an alternative to obtaining the first run when the central weight vector is chosen. The confidence factor, also numerically obtained as a multidimensional integral, indicates whether the criteria data are precise enough to discern the efficient alternatives.

Lahdelma et al. (2007) discuss the strategic decision-making problem of an electricity retailer choosing one among nine alternatives in terms of the following four criteria:

1. Long-term profit from the entire planning horizon
2. Short-term profit for the first year
3. Market share of the sales volume at the end of the planning horizon
4. Green electricity market share of the sales volume at the end of the planning horizon

They analyse the sample results and also make use of a multivariate normal distribution to get more or less similar results.

8.16. Fuzzy MCDM

Uncertainty that is usually taken care of by fuzziness is quite a reality in applications of MCDM methods, singly or in combination. Here, fuzziness may creep in three different ways: the alternatives could be crisp sets, while the criteria (qualitative in nature) could be fuzzy; the criteria could be crisp, while the alternatives with linguistic expressions may be fuzzy, or both alternatives and criteria could be fuzzy. Depending on the situation, fuzzy sets and fuzzy algebra are brought in, with an appropriate choice of membership functions. Eventually, a crisp solution has to be obtained. In many applications reported in the literature, two or more MCDM methods have been combined when dealing with fuzzy data.

Eventually, we come to deal with fuzzy evaluation numbers for the alternatives and several methods have been proposed to rank fuzzy numbers. None of these can satisfactorily rank the fuzzy numbers in all cases, and problem-specific solutions have been suggested by some researchers. We will just consider the problem discussed by Chu and Lin (2009) in which there are subjective criteria with qualitative definitions and expressed in linguistic terms, besides objective ones expressed in numerical terms, and importance measures or weights of all the criteria are expressed in linguistic terms. Ratings of alternatives under the subjective criteria and the criteria weights are represented by triangular fuzzy numbers (TFNs). Values of alternatives under objective criteria are normalized in such a way that ranges of triangular numbers belong to the closed interval (0, 1). The membership function of the final fuzzy evaluation score for each alternative is developed through interval arithmetic and α-cuts of fuzzy numbers. The Riemann integral based mean of removals is applied to defuzzify all the final fuzzy evaluation numbers. The authors illustrate their procedure in terms of an example in which a company wants to find the best of three possible locations to serve its customers by engaging a group of four decision-makers who use four subjective criteria, namely (a) transportation availability, (b) human resources, (c) market potential and (d) climatic conditions, besides one objective criterion, namely the cost of investment. For each subjective criterion, they have a set of ratings for the alternatives, namely very poor, poor, fair, good, very good, and for the weights of the subjective criteria, they use the linguistic set (very low, low, medium, high, very high). These linguistic sets are then converted to sets of TFN, namely:

Rating of alternatives: Very poor (0, 0, 0.2), poor (0, 0.2, 0.4), fair (0.3, 0.5, 0.7), good (0.6, 0.8, 1.0) and very good (0.8, 1.0, 1.0)

Criteria weights: Very low (0.0.0.3), low (0, 0.3, 0.5), medium (0.2, 0.5, 0.8), high (0.5, 0.7, 1.0) and very high (0.7, 1.0, 1.0)

Van Laarhoven and Pedrycz (1983) extended AHP to the fuzzy environment using TFNs as fuzzy ratios and the logarithmic least squares method to determine fuzzy priority vectors. Buckley (1985) used trapezoidal fuzzy numbers for fuzzy ratios and the geometric mean method to find out fuzzy weights. The extent analysis method proposed by Chang (1996) uses TFNs as fuzzy ratios generating fuzzy preference relations, and the degree of possibility for comparing TFNs results in crisp priority vectors which are synthesized to yield final ranking of the alternatives. This relatively simple method of Chang has been modified by Biswas and Kumar (2019) by using intuitionistic TFNs and a special intuitionistic triangular fuzzy degree of possibility.

8.17. Challenges Ahead

MCDM has to grapple with many problems imposed by uncertainty in data and in the environment and even in methods of evaluation of alternatives. Uncertainty in inputs includes their stochastic nature, inherent imprecision and fuzziness in preferences. Another emerging area of research on MCDM concerns evolutionary multi-objective optimization. MCDM has also drawn upon concepts and measures of multi-attribute utility and developments in the field of soft system analysis. Bonissone (2008), Kou et al. (2011), Stewart (1997) and several others have brought out some challenging problems in connection with MCDM methods which need further study.

A few of the problem areas identified are the following, among others:

- High dimensional objective space, with objectives and criteria often interdependent and interacting, complicates the search for solutions and their evaluation.
- Uncertainty, imprecision and fuzziness in inputs (including the initial data as well as the preferences) and in the solution evaluation methods.
- Context-dependent eliciting, representing and aggregating preferences.

- Leveraging of domain knowledge in the decision-making process. Currently, MCDM methods do not provide a scope to decision-makers and/or agents with knowledge about the underlying problem and rationality, implementability or utility of different possible solutions.
- Deployment and maintenance of adaptive, distributed decision-making systems.

Some point out that behavioural aspects of decision-making are largely ignored in the currently available MCDM methods, while these aspects are gaining wider acceptance within the broad framework of decision analysis and definitely in decision-making. The need to offer alternative methods for treating risk, like the prospect theory, to develop methods for effective visualization of the decision space and to come up with standards for validation of MCDM procedures are issues harped on by some researchers. In this connection, it may be useful to bear in mind that trade-offs (in Pareto-optimal, non-dominated or efficient sets) are not properties of criteria or objectives but of sets of feasible solutions. The proper task of decision-making is to work on designing proper sets of alternatives, rather than considering them to be fixed and given a priori. Speaking of the behavioural aspects, it is important to involve the decision-maker—who could be a single person or a small homogeneous group or even a large group operating on behalf of a still larger group—in the process of solution refinement and solution selection explicitly. How do we achieve this remains a big question for the time being.

CHAPTER 9

Social Choice Problems

9.1. Introduction

Complex problems in allocating natural resources among public and private enterprises to enrich these resources as well as to make proper use of them in generating goods and services for meeting the needs of people are now being formulated as problems in operational research, admitting that gaps and doubts will characterize such formulations. We can only expect some reasonable solutions to such problems, without venturing into the field of optimization. Problems of balancing costs and benefits associated with different power-generating mechanisms (where costs include opportunity costs as well as costs of adverse impact on the environment), those associated with different alternative uses (civil as well as military) of scarce raw materials, those linked to alternative tax structures and direct tax slabs or those resulting from the allocation of a fixed proportion of national income among primary, secondary and tertiary levels of education as well as with research and development, etc.

Going beyond concerns about national development, methods and techniques for making satisficing choices among alternatives in the socio-economic or political system of a nation or a country now find applications in international negotiations and initiatives concerning globalization, climate change, etc. In fact, the international dimensions of applicability of decision-making have been gradually expanding, and we should, in turn, accommodate these dimensions in the activities of our academic and professional bodies concerned with the discipline.

The theory of social choice is essentially a bundle of models and results concerning the aggregation (not just totalling) of individual inputs (votes, preferences, judgements, welfare assessments, etc.) into collective outputs (collective preferences, judgements, decisions, welfare programmes and the like). The goal is to choose a winning outcome (policy, candidate in an election, gain in welfare) from a given set of options. Questions that are raised and resolved in this theory are: What are the merits and limitations of a particular voting system? When is a voting system justified to be called democratic? When can it be called 'fair'? How to rank different social alternatives in order of social welfare? Answers to such questions have to be provided not from examples or experiences but from general models to be developed and on the basis of theorems to be proved. In a somewhat cryptic way, social choice theory is preoccupied with aggregation—aggregation of preferences, judgements and gains in welfare. Individual preferences for some alternatives over certain others, along with individual indifferences between two or more alternatives, behave somewhat uncomfortably to being treated in terms of established models and methods. Rooted in the pioneering investigations by Condorcet and Borda in the 18th century and dished out to many by Dodgson (better known as Lewis Carroll) in the 19th century, social choice theory owes a lot to the contributions by Arrow, Sen and Black during the last century.

Social choice theory, in some sense, deals with multi-person, MCDM, in the face of uncertainty and, in some cases, under competition. In fact, it involves participatory research and collaborative decision-making by a group displaying a wide variety of knowledge, values and perspectives that make a collective decision quite difficult to achieve. There are many social issues, such as planning and management of surface water, urban transportation or collection and utilization of urban waste, which have to reckon with the consequences of different available options in current times as well as in the future. In this and similar situations, we have to deal with multiple stakeholders as well as implementing agencies who do not share the same perspective or the same value system or the same concern.

Social choice theory has thrown up many controversies and counter-examples. Arrow's impossibility theorem is an oft-quoted recourse in uncomfortable situations. It has enriched discussions not merely in economics, political science or philosophy but also found important references in mathematics and even in computer science. Its influence extends across economics, political science, philosophy, mathematics and, recently, computer science and biology. Apart from contributing to our understanding of collective decision procedures, social choice theory has applications in the areas of institutional design, welfare economics and social epistemology. Some exponents treat the Arrow's theorem as a starting point for discussing major developments in social choice theory. While the Nudge theory propounded by behavioural economists is applicable to decision-making by individuals and groups in general, it has a special appeal in the context of social and administrative choices. It overlaps with several other branches of knowledge and justifies its inclusion in any discussion of macro- or meta-level decision-making. Several such problems belong to the domain of social choice.

Needless to say, this chapter does not intend to go into the details of social choice theory and is limited to its exposition as a group decision-making process. Some useful and interesting materials can be found in Walsh (2020), Moulin (1994), Regenwetter et al. (2006), Regenwetter et al. (2007), Regenwetter et al. (2009) and Sen (1971) among some others. Some space has been provided to a few selected topics, such as probabilistic social choice functions (PSCFs), social network and computational social choice. A relatively less discussed topic, namely Nudge theory, has been briefly discussed, though the topic is not directly aligned with social choice problems. There are interesting and useful applications of nudges to help individual as well as collective decisions in the socio-political context.

9.2. Distinctive Features of Social Choice

The Stanford Encyclopedia of Philosophy clearly spells out the core of social choice theory. According to this volume,

> Social choice theory is the study of collective decision processes and procedures. It is not a single theory, but a cluster of models and results concerning the aggregation of individual inputs (e.g., votes, preferences, judgements, welfare) into collective outputs (e.g., collective decisions, preferences, judgements, welfare). Central questions are: How can a group of individuals choose a winning outcome (e.g., policy, electoral candidate) from a given set of options? What are the properties of different voting systems? When is a voting system democratic? How can a collective (e.g., electorate, legislature, collegial court, expert panel, or committee) arrive at coherent collective preferences or judgements on some issues, on the basis of its members' individual preferences or judgements? How can we rank different social alternatives in an order of social welfare? Social choice theorists study these questions not just by looking at examples, but by developing general models and proving theorems.

Certain features of social choice theory make it somewhat distinct from the usual decision theory framework. Here, the alternative could be concrete (like candidates in an election or locations for establishing a facility for public service) or abstract (like a trade policy or a policy for professional education): These could be nominal (like candidates in an election or countries to which some services are exported) or categorical (like types of jobs or positions where reservations may be justified for some disadvantaged groups of people) or numerical (like amounts of pension or some social relief to be paid to a given class of people). Discussions have generally been confined to a finite number of alternatives. A choice among the alternatives is made collectively by a group of decision-makers or agents and not by a single person. Inputs for the choice is the set of preferences (usually binary) for each alternative by each decision-maker. Preferences could be indicated in terms of a complete ranking of all the alternatives or an incomplete ranking of some selected alternatives or a partial ranking, to give out the best and the worst. Preference relations are often assumed to be strict in the sense that indifference between any two may be ruled out. Such preferences may be obvious in the familiar framework where outcomes or pay-offs or even their utility equivalents provide the inputs, not ruling out the possibility of any of the measures being identical to the alternatives. In social choice theory, a major task is the aggregation of preferences that would yield a group preference pattern and lead to a choice of the 'best' alternative. While preferences are individualistic and subjective, the rules for aggregation are objective. In fact, these rules play the role of real alternatives in a decision problem involving aggregation of preferences. Once collective preferences have been obtained through a chosen rule, alternatives are ranked (rank being considered as the criterion) to find the optimal choice of an alternative.

9.3. Preference Aggregation

At the heart of social choice theory is the analysis of preference aggregation, understood as the aggregation of several individuals' preference rankings of two or more social alternatives into a single, collective preference ranking (or choice) over these alternatives. Judgement aggregation and belief merging (dealing with alternatives which are propositional variables or propositional formulae) are more recent tasks that pose some interesting problems in computational social choice.

The basic model is as follows. Consider a set $N=(1, 2, ..., n)$ of individuals ($n \geq 2$). Let $X=(x, y, z, ...)$ be a set of social alternatives, for example, possible amounts of (voluntary) labour to be given by members of a society, ecosystems to be enriched, policy platforms, election candidates, or allocations of goods, etc. Each individual $i \in N$ has a *preference ordering* R_i over these alternatives: a complete and transitive binary relation on X. For any $x, y \in X$, $x R_i y$ means that an individual i weakly prefers x to y. We write $x P_i y$ if $x R_i y$ and not $y R_i x$ (individual i strictly prefers x to y) is true, and $x I_i y$ if $x R_i y$ and $y R_i x$ (individual i is indifferent between x and y) are both true.

A combination of preference orderings across the individuals, $(R_1, R_2, ..., R_n)$, is called a *profile*. A preference aggregation rule, F, is a function that assigns to each profile $(R_1, R_2, ..., R_n)$, in some domain of admissible profiles, a social preference relation $R = F(R_1, R_2, \ldots, R_n)$ on X. When F is clear from the context, we simply write R for the social preference relation corresponding to $(R_1, R_2, \ldots, R_n)$.

For any $x, y \in X$, $x\,R\,y$ means that x is socially weakly preferred to y. We also write $x\,P\,y$ if $x\,R\,y$ is true and not $y\,R\,x$ (x is strictly socially preferred to y), and $x\,I\,y$ if $x\,R\,y$ and $y\,R\,x$ (x and y are socially tied). For generality, the requirement that R be complete and transitive is not built into the definition of a preference aggregation rule. However, we want any aggregation rule to eventually come up with a social ordering or ranking of the alternatives, possibly with ties.

The paradigmatic example of a preference aggregation rule referred to as the voting paradox is *pairwise majority voting*, as discussed by Condorcet (1785). Here, for any profile $(R_1, R_2, \ldots, R_n)$ and any $x, y \in X$, $x\,R\,y$ if and only if at least as many individuals have $x\,R_i\,y$ as have $y\,R_i\,x$, formally implying $|\{i \in N : x\,R_i\,y\}| \geq |\{i \in N : y\,R_i\,x\}|$. As can be easily seen, this does not guarantee transitive social preferences.

Consider the case of three agents assessing three social alternatives, A, B and C, and let the preference profiles of the three agents be ABC, BCA and CAB (where, by the profile ABC, we really mean A>B>C). Suppose we decide to use pairwise comparison and to prefer any alternative to another based on the number of agents preferring the first to the second. We find two voters preferring A to B, and two voters prefer B to C, implying an order like A then B then C. But again, two voters prefer C to A. Thus, we do not get a social order, but a cycle occurs. In fact, Agent 1 can satisfy their maximum by choosing A as the top, similarly to Agent 2 or Agent 3. But no social maxima can be reached. This is the voting paradox. To overcome this problem, other aggregation procedures were suggested initially by Borda (1781), Dodgson (1844) and Duncan Black (1948).

How frequent are intransitive majority preferences? It can be shown that the proportion of preference profiles (among all possible ones) that lead to cyclical majority preferences increases with the number of individuals (n) and the number of alternatives ($|X|$). If all possible preference profiles are equally likely to occur (the so-called 'impartial culture' scenario), majority cycles should therefore be probable in large electorates (Gehrlein, 1983). (Technical work further distinguishes between 'top-cycles' and cycles below a possible Condorcet-winning alternative.) However, the probability of cycles can be significantly lower under certain systematic, even small, deviations from an impartial culture (List & Goodin, 2001; Regenwetter et al., 2006; Tsetlin et al., 2003).

N.B. For the sake of convenience, we will use the symbolic representation $x>y$ to indicate 'x is preferred to y'—weakly (including indifference) or strongly—by adding the appropriate word separately.

9.4. Axioms and Arrow's Impossibility Theorem

Arrow's theorem focuses on preference aggregation rules. These are simply functions that take the preference profile ρ as an input and produce a collective preference relation that compares the alternatives. An arbitrary preference aggregation rule is denoted by f, so that $f(\rho)$ describes the group's preferences over the alternatives when the individual preferences are as described by ρ. We denote the preference relation returned by f at ρ by $f(\rho)$, so that $x\,f(\rho)\,y$ implies that xy by the social preference relation returned when the profile of individual preferences is $\rho \in R\,n$. Finally, Arrow requires that f return a social preference relation for all possible preference orderings ρ—this requirement is referred to as the unrestricted domain.

Arrow lays out four simple axioms that he argues any reasonable aggregation rule should satisfy. He then proves that these axioms are incompatible with each other; that no rule can simultaneously satisfy all four. In so doing, his result implies that any aggregation rule—regardless of what is being aggregated or for what purpose—must violate at least one of these axioms. Put differently, every democratic institution, be it electoral, legislative, administrative or judicial in character, violates at least one of these axioms. We now define each of these four axioms in turn:

1. **Pareto optimality:** Arrow's first axiom requires that the aggregation rule be minimally responsive to the preferences of the individuals, in that it respects a unanimity condition. More formally,

an aggregation rule f satisfies Pareto if, whenever every individual I strictly prefers x to y, the aggregation rule franks x strictly higher than y.

2. **Independence of irrelevant alternatives:** Arrow's second axiom requires that the aggregation method should not consider irrelevant alternatives when comparing any pair of alter, $(R_1, R_2, ..., R_n)$ and $(S_1, S_2, ..., S_n)$ natives. Specifically, the independence of irrelevant alternatives axiom requires that the group members' preferences about some alternative c not affect how the aggregation rule f ranks two different alternatives, $a=c$ and $b=c$. Thus, for two preference profiles $(R_1, R_2, ..., R_n)$ and $(S_1, S_2, ..., S_n)$ such that for every individual alternatives, a and b have the rank orders in both, then the rank orders of a and b will remain the same under the aggregation rule.

3. **Transitivity:** Arrow's third condition focuses on the ability of a preference aggregation rule to generate an unambiguous winner (or a collection of unambiguous winners, if there is a tie). An aggregation rule that generates the social ranking $x>y$, $y>z$ and $z>x$ (referred to as a cycle) does not provide an unambiguously 'best' alternative when comparing alternatives x, y and z. Arrow's transitivity axiom, requiring that f produce a transitive social order, rules out this possibility and more: If f produces an order in which $x>y$ and $y>z$, then it must also be the case that $x>z$. It may be added that the assumption of unrestricted domain and of transitivity together rule out pairwise majority decision if at least three alternatives and three agents (voters) are to be taken into account.

4. **No dictator:** Arrow's final axiom requires that the preference aggregation rule be responsive to the preferences of more than one person. An aggregation rule f is 'dictatorial' if there is one particular voter whose individual strict preferences always determine the social preference ordering, irrespective of the preferences of the other voters. Formally, if a person d is a dictator, for any alternatives x and y and for any profile in the domain of the choice function, and if $x P_d y$, then $x P y$. Other people's preferences can still influence social preferences, but only when the dictator is indifferent between two alternatives.

Arrow's impossibility theorem (general possibility theorem as Arrow called it) or Arrow's paradox can be formally stated as follows: Whenever the set of alternatives contains three or more elements, the following three conditions become incompatible with one another.

- Unanimity or weak Pareto efficiency (implying no imposition)
- Non-dictatorship
- Independence of irrelevant alternatives

Arrow's theorem has become crucial to later developments in social choice theory and has greatly influenced the arena of welfare economics as a whole. Some political philosophers have even interpreted the theorem to state that 'democracy as a government by the will of the people' is ab initio an illusion.

Two ways of overcoming the impossibility pointed out by Arrow, as suggested by Mulin (1994), are (a) preferences restricted to being single-peaked, which, in some sense, implies that majority voting yields a satisfactory aggregation and (b) social welfare relations are acyclic. In this connection, one may note that Nakamura's theorem (1979) sets narrow limits to the decisiveness of society's preferences.

9.5. Consistency of Social Choice Functions

Social choice functions or rules for preference aggregation operate on preference profiles to produce a choice of an alternative acceptable as the most preferred by a group of voters, agents or decision-makers or as a social choice. Towards this, choice functions are required to satisfy several consistency conditions, namely agenda consistency, population consistency, Condorcet consistency, cloning consistency and composition consistency. Among these, population consistency, that is, consistency with respect to a variable electorate and composition consistency, that is, consistency with respect to components of similar alternatives, are common among non-PSCFs and PSCFs, though their definitions and implications vary in the two cases. In fact, the axioms requiring these two consistency conditions for PSCFs characterize a choice function by Fishburn (1972) which returns the so-called maximal lotteries, which are sure to exist, computable by applying LP and generally unique.

Population consistency of a PSCF demands that any two lotteries, say a and b, are chosen in both preference profiles R and S. A combination of these two, say $1/2a + 1/2$, also has to be chosen when both preference profiles are merged. Formally, a PSCF satisfies population consistency for all $A \in F(U)$, R and R' and any convex combination.

Population consistency is arguably one of the most natural axioms for variable electorates and is usually considered in a slightly stronger version, known as reinforcement or simply consistency, where the inclusion in the equation above is replaced with equality whenever the left-hand side is non-empty. Note that population consistency is merely a statement about abstract sets of outcomes, which makes no reference to lotteries.

9.6. Probabilistic Social Choice Functions

The aggregation rules offered by Borda or Copeland are deterministic except when there are ties, in which case ties are broken by lotteries. Probabilistic choice functions for this task have been a post-Arrow development. Consistent with respect to a variable electorate and components of similar alternatives are two important axioms in the context of traditional non-PSCFs. In the context of probabilistic choice functions, these axioms uniquely characterize a choice proposed by Fishburn (1973), which returns the so-called maximal lotteries (a maximal lottery is a randomized weak Condorcet winner—a lottery preferred weakly to every other lottery by an expected majority of decision-makers or agents) and lotteries correspond to alternatives. Maximal lotteries are sure to exist in view of Neumann's minimax theorem in game theory. These are generally unique and can be computed conveniently as solutions to primal and dual LP problems.

We consider a set $N = (1, 2, \ldots, n)$ of agents or members of a decision-making group and a finite set of alternatives, A. Each agent offers a complete and transitive preference relations in $A \times A$ which are asymmetric and anti-symmetric (for strict preference relations, disregarding indifference). A preference profile maps each agent $i \in N$ to a preference relation. Let the set of all lotteries for probability distributions over A be given by $\wedge(A) = \{p(x) > 0, \text{ for all } x \in A \text{ and } \Sigma p(x) = 1\}$.

Formally, a PSCF is a continuous function f that maps a preference profile to a non-empty subset of possible (two-option) lotteries. In fact, a PSCF gives, for each alternative, the probability that the alternative will yield the outcome (pay-off) or the corresponding utility, so that the expected utility of the alternative can be worked out.

Two important properties of a PSCF are (a) unanimity and (b) decisiveness. The first implies that in a two-agent (voter), two-alternative situation if both the voters prefer one alternative, say x, over the other, say y, then alternative x corresponds to a lottery with probability one for the associated utility and will be selected. The second property implies that if for every preference profile where f is a multi-valued function (with multiple lotteries), there is an arbitrarily close profile that only yields a single lottery for selection.

A PSCF is anonymous if its outcome is invariant under permutations of the agent. Thus, the collective choice here is independent of the decision-makers' identities. The function is called neutral if permutation of alternatives in the preference profile leads to lotteries in which alternatives are permuted accordingly. This implies impartiality towards the alternatives.

Let us define the majority margin matrix M of order $m \times m$ with elements:

M_{xy} = Number of times (agents) alternative x is preferred to alternative y – number of times alternative y is preferred to alternative x

If the output of a neutral PSCF f depends only on the matrix M, it is called a pairwise PSCF. Such a function can apply in situations where preferences are incomplete or even intransitive.

In Copeland's rule, alternatives are ordered by using (number of pairwise victories) – (number of pairwise defeats), as is used in many round-Robbin tournaments. (This provides a Smith-efficient Condorcet method.) If there is no Condorcet winner, this method often leads to ties. For example, when a three-alternative majority rule cycle occurs, the second-order Copeland method uses the sum of the Copeland scores of the defeated opponents to find out the winner.

Three important PSCF correspond to (a) random dictatorship, (b) Borda's rule and (c) maximal lotteries. Two probability allocations may arise from Borda's rule, by taking the probabilities as proportional to the maximum Borda score and by taking them as proportional to Borda's score. The last three, excluding the random lottery, are pair-wise choice functions.

In a random dictatorship, one of the decision-makers/agents is picked up at random and their most preferred alternative is implemented as the social choice. This is well-defined only for strict preferences. Of course, it has been extended to random serial dictatorship when references are not strict. In a random dictatorship, the probabilities assigned to different alternatives are directly proportional to the number of agents who give the highest rank to a given alternative. Borde's rule is a randomized weak Condorcet winner—a lottery weakly preferred to every other lottery by an expected majority of decision-makers (analogous to mixed maximin strategy in Nash equilibrium in the context of games). Borda score for alternative $x = \Sigma_{y \in A} M_{xy}/2 + n(m-1)/2$. A maximal lottery is one with max $\Sigma_i (m-1) n(i)$. In Borda's rule or in maximal lotteries, probabilities assigned to the alternatives are directly proportional to their scores under these rules or schemes.

Example 9.1. Let us consider the following preference profile relating to five agents and three alternatives, a, b and c, in which the preference order for two agents is (a, b, c); for two others, it is (b, c, a), while for the remaining agent, it is (c, a, b). The M-matrix comes out as

$$M = \begin{array}{c|ccc} & a & b & c \\ \hline a & 0 & 1 & -1 \\ b & -1 & 0 & 3 \\ c & 1 & -3 & 0 \end{array}$$

Note: b was preferred to c by 2+2=4 agents while c was preferred to b by only one agent, giving the entry 4−1=3. Similarly, the other off-diagonal elements were obtained, diagonals being zero by definition.

Random dictatorship yields the probability allocation 2/5, 2/5 and 1/5 to the alternatives *a*, *b*, and *c*. Borda scores being 5, 6 and 3 respectively, the probabilities assigned to the alternatives are 5/14, 6/14 and 3/14. Borda maximum score returns b pairwise.

PSCFs have been characterized in terms of three important properties, namely efficiency, strategy-proofness or non-manipulability and participation. Efficiency (in its various forms) is related to optimality, strategy-proofness bears on robustness and participation is concerned with the consequences of absenteeism from voting. Avoiding formal definitions, a PSCF is efficient if it never returns to dominated lotteries. Deterministic, bilinear and SD are different variants of dominance, and for PSFC, SD is spoken of. In fact, if p and q are two different choice functions or aggregation rules, p stochastically dominates q if and only if, for every von-Neumann utility function compatible with the dominance relation, the expected utility under p is at least as great as that for q. Stated somewhat differently, we can say p stochastically dominates q if and only if for each alternative (lottery) probability that p selects an alternative that is at least as good as x is not smaller than the probability that q selects such an alternative. The implication is that no agent (voter) can be better off without making another one worse off. A PSFC is strategy-proof if it cannot be manipulated by misrepresentation of the preference profile. This implies that no agent can get a more preferred outcome by misrepresenting their preferences. It also relates to insincere reporting by a voter being influenced by preference profiles already known by other voters. Participation takes care of the fact that if an agent abstains from voting, they cannot be better off, and that a participating voter is always strictly better-off (unless they have already obtained their most preferred outcome).

There exists an interesting trade-off between these properties, and this has given rise to many impossible results. For example, population consistency and the Condorcet rule are not mutually consistent, participation and the Condorcet rule do not go together, etc. Brandt et al. (2016) prove that no anonymous, neutral, SD-efficient and SD-strategy-proof probabilistic choice function exists. Gibbard's theorem states that random dictatorship is the only anonymous, strongly strategy-proof, ex-post efficient PSCF when preferences are strict (no indifferences revealed by the agents).

A random dictatorship that yields a single lottery satisfies population consistency, though it does not satisfy the composition consistency axiom. However, the maximal lottery has strong Condorcet property and Pareto optimality. The first property implies that if X is partitioned into non-empty subsets A and B such that for all a in A and all b in B, more voters reveal preference for a over b, than for b over a, then an alternative in A is certain to be selected. The implication of the second property is that if it is possible to assign weak orders on X to the voters in such a way that the paired comparison voting data are consistent with these orders, and if an alternative x Pareto dominates another alternative y but none prefers y to x, then y is certain to be selected.

The use of PSCFs has been criticized by some social scientists. However, such criticisms have not dampened the applications of PSCFs.

9.7. Social Choice and Social Network

Individuals, as members of a group (an organization, a society or an electorate), do not reason or act in isolation. They know whom to trust, whom to count upon, who can influence whom or with whom pertinent information can or should be exchanged. They tend to consult others before forming and stating their preferences and persuade and influence others in a bid to muster support for their choices. Thus, preferences as revealed by individuals in an exercise to reach a collective decision may not represent their positions, just by themselves alone. Interactions among members may well be represented by networks of different configurations, and the contribution of social networks (Easley & Kleinberg, 2010; Jackson, 2008) to providing a better understanding of social choice has been recognized rather late in the day.

Grandi (2017) gives a good account of the subject, starting with an exposition of two complementary views on social choice. In the first view, individuals express their tastes over a set of alternatives, without there being any objective or true judgement on which alternative is best for the group as a whole. The idea behind this is to ensure representativeness of the collective choice with respect to the preference profile of individual ballots. In the second view, the social choice mechanism addresses the problem of reconstructing an underlying correct ordering of the alternatives from the 'noisy' estimates received from individual voters. A social choice mechanism or procedure is evaluated, in this view, by (a) devising a suitable noise distribution and (b) proving that the mechanism maximizes the probability of recovering the correct order under the given noise distribution. (A point to illustrate this view is forwarded by Condorcet's jury theorem in binary voting, where the majority rule is the maximum likelihood estimate for an assumed noise distribution where each voter is correct with a probability exceeding 0.5.)

Following up the 'noise' involvement, social networks, which essentially represent an asymmetric information situation, tend to transform an underlying and unknown 'global view' of the alternatives in relation to the collective interest and needs of society or the group is transformed into a multiplicity of local realities, each being observed by a voter in their 'neighbourhood' as depicted by a network. This transformation creates 'noises' and results in preferences and their aggregation yielding choices that differ from those in standard situations with individuals acting in isolation to a remarkable extent.

Different types of networks connecting voters as nodes with arcs representing different types of information exchange and/or interaction produce different types of local realities. Influence or trust or delegation networks are directed graphs, while general social networks and information exchange networks correspond to undirected graphs. There is a large volume of work done on opinion diffusion models through networks, and one wonders whether such models can be taken as noise distribution models. Beyond sharing information and interacting before revealing preferences, voters' utilities on collectively decided alternatives may also depend positively on the utilities of their neighbours in the network to reflect voters' desire to see that others 'are satisfied with the chosen alternatives. This situation has been referred to as one of the empathetic alternatives'.

9.8. The Nudge Theory

Decisions by individuals and groups are generally assumed to be made by the concerned individuals or groups themselves as responses to certain environments. However, such decisions are and can be indirectly influenced—though not directly controlled or modified—by the choices and behaviour of others. One step beyond this is a situation where some individuals or groups target some decision-makers and try to influence the latter's decisions, ostensibly for their own advantage. Thaler (2008)—regarded as the father of behavioural economics—formally introduced the nudge theory to explain how the behaviours and choices of some decision-makers influence others' decisions bearing on health, wealth and welfare. In fact, Thaler and Sunstein showed how nudges can lead to improvements in such decisions by way of positive reinforcement and indirect suggestions to influence the behaviour and decision-making of groups and individuals.

Nudge theory is a flexible, modern concept for understanding how people think, make decisions and behave. It helps people improve their thinking and decisions, manage changes of all sorts and identify and modify existing unhelpful influences on people. In fact, the positive and behind-the-scenes contribution of this theory is to explore, understand and explain existing influences on how people behave, especially influences which are unhelpful and even harmful, with a view to removing or altering such influences. Incidentally, we find lots of nudges everywhere in advertisements and campaigns, as well as in government and civil societies—some deliberate and some accidental. And not too often, nudges can be misleading or confusing.

Nudges are small, inexpensive changes in the environment that are easy to implement. This 'environment' is characterized by the quality and amount of information available to the decision-maker with regard to the problem at hand. A nudge is any aspect of the choice architecture that alters people's behaviour in a predictable way without forbidding any options or significantly changing their economic behaviour. Looked upon as an intervention, a nudge is not a mandate. Nudges play a role in decision-making even without decision-makers' recognition. In fact, of the several types of nudges, a common type corresponds to default, implying that in a situation where the decision-maker remains undecided about making a choice, the visible presence or the ready reckoning of some decision taken by someone else is conveniently picked up by the faltering decision-maker as a 'default' choice. This is a common practice which offers a hesitant decision-maker the option to observe choices made by others and, using one's own way of assessing economic or social values of different choices, to choose one that appeals to be the best. Another important case for using a nudge is to increase the salient features of the choice initially thought of by the decision-maker in the hope of an improvement over the initial choice. A third type of nudge, referred to as the social proof heuristic, speaks of the influence of a choice that has stood up to social welfare or acceptability, also finds applications in social choice problems.

Dealing with management of change, conventional management and leadership involves instructions or actions which direct or induce people to change the way that the authority requires. Nudge theory, on the other hand, is typically an indirect approach which alters situations or environments for people, such that choices are designed to produce options for helpful voluntary change in people. While the former involves forceful intervention or is directed at the person or group whose change is sought, the latter promotes voluntary choices and is directed at the situation or environment in which people exist and operate.

Some useful applications of nudges by administration to improve people's behaviour in certain areas have been documented in the literature, and a few such are mentioned as follows:

- In the UK, people in arrears with their taxes were sent reminders worded to convey normative social messages like '9 out of 10 people in your area are up to date with their tax payments'. By making them seem like outliers, tax payments from people to whom such reminders were sent went up by 15 per cent compared to the norm.

- An experiment in the Philippines provided smokers with a savings bank account for six months. At the end of this period, a urine test for nicotine was carried out on them. If they passed, they got back all their money. If they failed, the money would be given out to charity.
- When eating out, one may often find a very expensive item on the menu. The restaurant does not really expect customers to buy that item, but rather expects some people to go in for the next less expensive item. When relative prices are compared, the second most expensive item can seem like a good bargain.

While the nudge theory has found useful applications in social choices, political problem resolution and economic decisions, its limitations have been pointed out by several critics on the ground of inadequate empirical evidence to establish improvements through the impact of nudges. Some enthusiasts may even argue that the results of nudge theory applications may not stand the test of 'falsifiability'.

9.9. Computational Social Choice

Computational social choice has become an intellectually attractive interdisciplinary field of research, involving primarily economics, computer science and artificial intelligence to solve collective decision problems, as have been treated within the ambit of social choice theory, essentially from a computational perspective. One major input into this rapidly growing field of research came from an interest in concepts and procedures from social choice theory for solving certain tricky questions which arise in computer science and artificial intelligence application domains. In turn, advances in theoretical computer science have contributed significantly in handling some knotty problems in social choice theory, like designing a voting protocol that makes it possible for a voter to cheat in some way or the other (it may well be the case that cheating successfully turns out to be a computationally intractable problem, which may therefore be taken as an acceptable risk) or specifying and verifying social procedures like fair division algorithms in the case of resource allocation, proving certain desirable properties of a preference aggregation procedure—all of which are computationally complex (NP-hard; Brandt et al., 2012). There exist problems in computer science which resemble those studied in social choice theory. For example, ranking systems in the social choice context are analogous to page ranking systems in the context of search engines (more generally in reputation systems). The Sydney Coordinated Adaptive Traffic System for controlling traffic lights has the controllers at different intersections vote for what should be the common cycle time for the lights. Similarly, the space shuttle had five controllers voting on whose actions to follow. Chevaleyre et al. (2005) and Walsh (2020), among a few others, provide useful reading materials on the subject.

Computational social choice theory has been used to address the following, among some other, issues which were either treated inefficiently or ignored earlier:

- Computationally hard rules for aggregation of preferences
- Social choice in combinatorial domains
- Computational aspects of strategy-proofness and manipulation
- Distributed resource allocation and negotiation
- Communication requirements in social choice
- Logic-based analysis of social procedures

CHAPTER 10

Decision-making Models

10.1. Preliminaries

Over the years, several different approaches to decision-making have been discussed by cognitive scientists who study 'how people decide?' as well as by those who prefer to use mathematical models and methods to study 'how people should decide?' Of course, there are others who take intermediate positions and blend the methods and techniques used by these two groups. These approaches have to be recognized as distinct from decision-making tools which may be used for other purposes also. Some of these approaches apply to the bigger context in which the decision-making problem arises, while others look at the latter only. Exercises in the first category lay due emphasis on identification and concrete formulation of the problem in a wider context in which decision-making occupies a role. Problems are taken to have been already identified in the second category, where decision-making is the dominant issue.

Planners and executives are sometimes faced with problems which they have not come across earlier, nor have such problems been studied by others within their knowledge. Decisions have to be taken instantly in some cases and after due deliberations in certain others. Even in the latter situation, relevant and adequate data may or may not exist.

Exigencies and constraints may not always permit collection and processing of such data in some cases. Out-of-the-box thinking coupled with innovative ideas may help in generating some alternative solutions. However, feasibility cannot be tested or verified analytically and may have to be taken for granted on the basis of a consensus among stakeholders. Risk of failure during or after implementation has to be accepted and something like a leap into the dark may have to be undertaken only in the belief that action delayed or avoided may be worse than the outcome of a 'blind' decision put into action right now.

One can distinguish between two sets of frameworks for decision-making, namely one using mathematical models and methods to focus on 'what should we do?' and a second based on cognitive sciences to answer 'what do we do?'.

Frameworks of the first type assume an ideal decision-maker who seeks to make the best decision by becoming fully informed and able to compute with perfect accuracy with full alignment to a pre-defined set of goals.

We bring in probabilities to take account of uncertainties in the criteria (properties of alternatives or impacts of outcomes) to calculate risks, as we do in failure modes, effects and criticality analysis.

Beyond these two frameworks, there are decision-making theories that seek to address issues like the following:

- People may have uncertain aspirations that vary from one context to another.
- Existing frameworks do not adequately deal with outcomes that are spread over time, instead of relating to one point (or period) of time.
- Decision complexity is too much to determine an optimality principle.
- Probability theory may not be sufficiently robust to errors in assumptions.
- Current theory places focus on the belief that 'what we know we don't know' and on attempts to use this tacit knowledge, instead of 'what we don't know, we don't know' (ludic fallacy; Taleb, 2007).

We may argue that decisions made by individuals differ markedly in their formulation and implementation from decisions taken by organizations. True, the nature and magnitude of consequences differ in these two cases; although in both situations, decisions are eventually made by individuals or groups of individuals. A noticeable difference is in terms of individual emotions and instincts versus collective wisdom and behaviour. In what follows, we focus on organizational decision-making, especially those based on logical models and analytical reasoning, taking due account of any previous experience or information relevant to the situation. To be noted is the fact that stress will not be laid on quantitative models, methods and techniques, though due advantage has been taken of relatively simple quantitative analysis in the different perspectives and procedures for decision-making discussed in this chapter.

In the professional arena, nomenclature and form matter, besides—of course—substance. Thus, some constructs are known as 'approaches', some as 'frameworks', some others as 'methodologies' as distinct from 'models' or 'methods' or even 'techniques. While the aim remains the same, namely to solve a problem (as an umbrella concept to cover not just business problems or problems of social or administrative choice, but even the problem of removing some deficiencies or limitations in an existing method or model) and to effect improvement in the area(s) of concern, some of these constructs are used to satisfy this aim in its entirety, while some others apply to certain facets of the aim only. By tracing the development of such constructs and their uses in the context of decision-making, the distinctions among the various constructs will appear to be blurred. However, it will be better to keep the distinctions in mind, sometimes at the cost of de-emphasizing the nomenclature associated with a give construct.

An approach is somewhat indicative, broadly identifying the issues to be taken into consideration, hinting at the nature of the procedure or tasks involved, highlighting the priorities and also suggesting the areas of application. A framework provides the boundaries within which attempts will be made to achieve the aim and a broad outline of the steps involved. A methodology is an inclusive and comprehensive account of the steps or sequence of tasks or processes to be planned and executed. A method is specific to a class of tasks like collection of primary data, analysis of longitudinal data, testing of multiple hypotheses, predicting the outcome of a decision or calculating the risk associated with a possible action when implemented. A model is a representation of a process (like the entire decision-making process) or of a component therein (like developing a consensus ranking of a set of individuals), in its generality, and not related to a given problem or a given context or a given set of actions or outcomes thereof. Different techniques and tools (mostly quantitative) may be involved in a method, and the same technique or tool may be involved in more than one method. The use of models, methods and techniques is greatly facilitated and sometimes badly needs algorithms and software. In this context, we may just mention that a theory should—to justify its position—include concepts, models, methods, techniques, results and applications.

It is neither possible nor desirable to maintain a studied distinction consistently among the different approaches or between an approach and a framework or between an approach and a methodology. However, distinctions among methodologies, methods and techniques can be conveniently made in most cases.

We attempt to cover briefly a few oft-used perspectives and procedures for decision-making, essentially as the most important component of the problem-solving exercise carried out by individuals. These could be known variously as frameworks, methodologies, models, methods or even as tools, with the scope of application and coverage of tools and techniques varying from one construct to another. In fact, one exercise in this realm has come to occupy the elevated status of a theory that goes beyond decision-making in its content. These have been tried out in various organizations, mostly with a lot of success. Since this book accords due recognition to decision-making as distinct from decision analysis, the discussions contained in this chapter should appeal to those who are interested and/or engaged in decision-making, even though the content may not fall in line with the tenor of discussions in several other chapters.

Some of these constructs (combining perspectives and procedures) were developed to resolve some complex, high-value problems. Some others came up as deciding components of exercises to solve business problems and to improve process performance, while a few others were propounded by professionals and research workers looking critically at decisions being taken in diverse organizations and distinctive contexts. All these have been named as 'models' here. In the sense that a model is a representation of a real-life entity like a decision-making process, these can be justifiably branded as 'models'. representing the processes spelt out in them.

10.2. Approaches in Managerial Decision-making

A few widely known and practised approaches or methodologies (some are known as models), which invoke creative ideas and involve more qualitative analysis than quantitative tools, constitute the first category of models treated in this chapter. In another category of models, advantage is taken of mathematical models and quantitative tools. Some models came up in the context of problem-solving and process improvement exercises. As expected, some of the steps run through all these models, while each model offers some distinctive features. Not all these models apply in all situations, some cover the implementation exercise also. A few of these have been elaborated in a later section. A large communality—conceptual and operational—is one justification for avoiding discussions of a whole lot of models.

We first mention some models that belong to the first category. There are others, which are as follows:

1. Vroom–Yetton (1973) and Vroom–Jago (1988) normative models for deciding how to decide (situational leadership theory), also known as constructive controversy models.
2. BRAIN, BRAN and brand—balancing intuition with logic.
3. Control, influence and accept model (giving the greatest attention and putting in the best effort right when problems arise).
4. Soft systems methodology (understanding very complex issues).
5. Observe, orient, decide, act (OODA) loop—understanding the decision cycle.

6. Cynefin framework (using the appropriate problem-solving process).
7. Appreciative inquiry (solving problems by looking at what's going right).
8. The simplex process (a robust, creative problem-solving tool).
9. Four-step innovative process.
10. Strawman concept (build an initial may-be-crude-and-ready solution, knock it down and create a solid final solution).
11. Hurson's productive thinking model (focusing on creative thinking).
12. Action learning sets (by doing and discussing).
13. Time, diagnosis, options, decide, assign and review (TDODAR) decision model—considering your options under pressure.

A few models which can be put in the second category are the following:

14. Kepner–Tregoe four-step matrix model—making unbiased risk-assessed decisions.
15. Business question, analysis plan, data collection, insights, and recommendations (BADIR) framework.
16. Recognition-primed decision process.

The following illustrates models belonging to the third category:

17. The plan-do-check-act (PDCA) model of Deming is more appropriate for operational management and extends to the task of setting objectives and targets. Here, 'planning' takes care of decision-making, and the remaining three phases are concerned with evaluating and maintaining conformity with the decisions defining the process plan.
18. Six Sigma methodology is a highly disciplined, top-down, quantitatively oriented, project-based approach to solving business problems involving six steps: define, measure, analyse, improve and control (slightly changed to define, measure, analyse, develop and verify in the case of new product development).
19. The 8D methodology adds one more step to the six Sigma methodology.
20. Model 20 is an elevated exercise contained in the theory of constraints (TOC).

The aforesaid models were developed in different contexts with varying focus on problem identification, situation analysis, compilation and processing of data, use of previous decision situations and actions taken therein, use of quantitative techniques and stress on implementation. While some of the models have a somewhat general applicability, others are oriented to meet the demands of some specific situations. As can be expected, more and more such models are being and will be developed and documented in management science literature. The models mentioned above have been advocated by many research workers and professionals as the more useful ones. However, some exponents of decision models refer to the following five models as the more important ones:

- Vroom–Yetto–Jago decision model
- OODA loop
- Recognition-primed decision model
- Paired comparison analysis
- The ladder of inference

Paired comparison analysis, as the very name implies, is really a method for choosing an alternative and does not—by itself—constitute a model for the entire decision-making activity. In fact, this analysis can be and is involved in a wide range of DMPs for ranking of alternatives. Thurstone's method of paired comparison has been a widely applied tool for this purpose and has been discussed in an earlier chapter. Aggregation of paired-comparison results over several experts or judges is an interesting exercise in decision theory. The possible results of such a comparison according to one criterion may differ from the results for another criterion. It may be somewhat problematic to deal with the 'indifference' of the expert between the elements within a pair. Other problems associated with paired comparisons include the lack of transitivity across alternatives. A more detailed discussion of this method appears in Section 10.6.

The last model starts with reality and facts as revealed by available data, selects the part of reality that seems to be relevant and credible and interprets reality as the premises for reaching some conclusion. It should be noted that axioms and model assumptions (which may be warranted by reality) are part of the premises in usual inferencing procedures. Of course, to reach some useful and valid conclusions starting from the premises, we need to process the premises and we generally invite some assumptions during the course of such processing.

10.3. Qualitative Decision-making Models

The following sub-sections are devoted to some elaborations for models belonging to the three different categories of models enumerated above.

10.3.1. Vroom–Yetton and Vroom–Jago Models

In the first model, as explained in *The New Leadership: Managing Participation in Organizations* (1988), emphasis is placed on identifying and operationalizing criteria for deciding on the 'best' option or alternative, even prior to generating the options, since some options may not be worth any consideration at all if certain rules are adopted in the beginning to evaluate or judge the feasibility or acceptability of any option. In that way, this model differs typically from a model where options or alternatives are first identified (though not necessarily enumerated), some evaluation criteria are developed independently of this task, and then the alternatives are evaluated to choose the 'best'. In fact, this model involves a decision about the 'quality' of the decision to be reached on a particular problem, on the argument that different problems with differences in their anticipated impacts on the system may demand decisions of commensurate quality in terms of attention to details about data, methods and tools for analysis and the level of integration of analysis results with pragmatism. This model also enhances the commitment of subordinates to implementing the decision. It also takes due cognizance of time constraints.

This is indeed a decision tree (in some sense) model for determining the level of group involvement in the decision-making process in an organization, in which the leader is required to diagnose a problem situation and assess the effect participation of subordinates will have on the quality of decisions, the level of staff member acceptance of the decision and the time available for making the decision. Organizational decisions may be broadly recognized as autocratic (by the leader alone) or consultative (leader deciding whom to consult on what and how to make use of the results of consultation) and democratic (involving all concerned with making and implementing the decision). It can also be collaborative in some situations. Autocratic decision-making may face problems of inadequate commitment of support staff in implementation. Decision-making will be fast, as may be demanded in some situations. Consultative and democratic procedures are definitely better and more effective, provided time constraint is not a roadblock.

10.3.2. BRAN, BRAIN and Brand Analysis

BRAN analysis is usually restricted to identification and assessment of one alternative or simply to assessment of a single alternative already identified and presented to the decision-maker. Before any other alternative is considered, the current alternative is evaluated in terms of its (reported or potential) benefits or positive outcomes, along with possible risks associated with its implementation in terms of negative impacts on some aspect(s) of the system under consideration. This is followed by a search for other alternatives or options. Finally, an assessment is made of the possible outcome if nothing is done by the decision-maker. The last step may mean that the decision-maker goes back to the initial option, without accepting any of the other alternatives or even staying away completely from choosing any of the alternatives (only when this is allowed).

This model to balance intuition against logic, required to establish a trade-off between speed and effectiveness in decision-making, has been known by the acronym BRAN or BRAIN. If before the decision to do nothing is taken, the decision-maker makes use of their intuition or, according to some exponents, intelligence to take a final stand. It has been represented by some users as a simplified and implicit version of SWOT analysis, focusing on strength, weakness, opportunity and threat. Several applications of this analysis have been reported from the mother and child care sector faced with decision-making problems.

10.3.3. Control, Influence and Adapt Model

The first model proposed by Thompson and Thompson (2008) in their book entitled *The Critically Reflective Practitioner*, is to be adopted for a personal perspective in a volatile, modern world where one has to be flexible, pro-active and tenacious. This is a versatile problem-solving and stress-management tool that identifies ways to respond to changes and challenges. The focus is to identify elements and issues in the decision problem and to put them into three categories, namely those which you can control, those which you cannot control but can influence and modify and those which can neither be controlled nor influenced and have to be accommodated or adapted. In the first category, there are your own emotions, attitudes and behaviour, which play an important role in the decisions you make. It is also possible to delegate some tasks to members of your team with, of course, clear instructions. There are issues (in the second category) where you can override others or enter into a win–win situation or even—being in a minority or subordinate position—influence the way your stakeholders or seniors or superiors think and act. Finally, one should be able to identify issues or situations which cannot be changed or modified by the decision-maker, and the latter has to adapt themselves to the changes or challenges or problems by honing one's skills for adaptation. Imagine a sudden and substantial increase in the price of a raw material for the best-selling product of an organization. To face the problem, decision alternatives are thrown up—in some sense—by this approach. We may increase the selling price of the product to pass on the cost increase to the customers. There lies the risk of a fall in demand. It may be better to find a different raw material to serve the purpose without enhancing the selling price. But customers' acceptance or preference may change. We may try to identify a supplier and negotiate for a cheaper price. This is somewhat uncertain. However, we can try to influence the supplier with some inducement to supply some other material(s) also. The last option—not so desirable—will be to withdraw the product from the market.

10.3.4. Soft Systems Methodology

The soft systems methodology derived from systems thinking and systems engineering by Checkland and his associates in the Lancaster University Systems Department has been very successfully applied in solving semi-structured and unstructured decision problems faced in complex situations to deal with 'soft problems': How to improve healthcare delivery? How to manage disaster planning? When should mentally deranged criminal offenders be taken away from custody to a special home? What to do about begging and begging on the main roads by hired agents posing as physically handicapped poor people? How to reduce the prevalence of cybercrimes related to credit/debit cards? The model is represented by the following seven steps:

- Enter a situation considered problematic
- Express the problem situation
- Formulate root definitions of relevant systems of purposeful activity
- Build conceptual models of the systems named in the root definitions
- Compare models with real world situations
- Define possible changes which are feasible for implementation
- Take action to improve the problem situation
  Elements in the root definitions were identified by David Smyth in 1975 as people, processes and the environment that contribute to a situation or issue or problem that needs analysing. These are spelt out in the mnemonic CATWOE for six elements:
- Customers who are affected by the issue
- Actors involved in the situation, also involved in implementing solutions
- Transformation process
- Weltanschauung or worldview of the big picture and of the wider impacts of the issue of bonds
- Owners who have a role to play in the solution
- Environment in terms of the constraints and limitations affecting the solution and its success in terms of impacts

10.3.5. OODA Loop

The OODA loop, initially proposed by the US military strategist J. Boyd in the context of warfare and subsequently presented as a strategy for making complex decisions under uncertainty and involving stiff contest and/or competition, has since emerged as a model for organizational decision-making for improving operational efficiency. This model is not meant for a one-shot decision but is applied to a learning process to ensure faster and better decisions in successive cycles. In this sense, it bears a semblance to the PDCA cycle (proposed by Deming in the context of quality management) and its variants.

Boyd referred to uncertainty—due primarily to ambiguity—in the environment within which the organization operates and the manner in which the environment changes, in the validity of actions taken in the past in responding to similar decision problems, the likely changes in outcomes of possible actions that can be contemplated in the present decision-making situation and the like. The model makes use of data as well as mental models, rather than the traditional quantitative models used in decision-making. Some exponents of the OODA loop refer to possible links between uncertainty as comprehended by Boyd and incorporated into OODA and a set of well-known scientific principles and results, namely Gödel's incompleteness theorem, Heisenberg's uncertainty principle and the second law of thermodynamics (dealing with entropy). Boyd argues that any logical model is incomplete and possibly inconsistent and needs to be continuously refined and updated in the light of new observations. Further, our ability to observe reality with due precision is limited; if we like to have more precise information in respect of some aspects or entities, we will lose precision on some other related aspects or entities. Entropy or disorder increases as a system becomes closed and inward-looking to justify and adopt earlier perspectives, models and procedures.

Boyd emphasized the 'destruction' of models constructed earlier and the 'creation' of new models to fit into the changing environment at present. Towards this, he encourages an organization to be outward-looking, agile and capable of developing new mental models to respond adequately to changes in demand or to disruptions in the supply chain or the emergence of new and strong competitors and similar other contingencies, more quickly than competitors. To quote Boyd, 'if we cannot communicate with the outside world—to gain information and understanding—we die out to become a non-discerning and non-interesting part of that world.'

The loop consists of the following four steps:

Observe: This is an information-gathering exercise that may involve generation of data beyond compilation of already available data as well as information that are and can be made available. In this phase, we do not prioritize the information. From this phase, we get a broad range of inputs, such as circumstances as they unfold themselves, outside information, interaction with the environment, feedback from all the other stages during the preceding cycle and the like.

Orient: Boyd noted two problems in the first phase. We may often observe imperfect or incomplete information, and we may be inundated by so much information that it will be difficult to disentangle signal from noise. It must be pointed out that what ultimately counts is not more information but better judgement derived from information. In fact, information gathered in the previous phase has to be oriented to yield a roper understanding and knowledge about the environment and about the possible options or alternatives that we have along with their anticipated outcomes. During this phase, in fact, we require to shed off past perspectives and viewpoints and to develop new ones. In the words of Boyd, we need destructive deduction and creative induction to throw up possible alternatives or options.

Decide: Based on the options informed by the foothold gained in the previous phase, the decision-maker predicts what the best course of action will be, based on the understanding of the situation. Thus, the third phase really throws up what may be called a hypothesis, partly based on creative induction from the 'oriented' observations.

Act: This phase is devoted to verification of the hypothesis contained in the decision reached in the previous phase, based on data arising from the implementation of the said decision. In a slightly different elucidation of this step, some would first verify if the hypothesis is right and, if so, implement the decision. Such a verification will be in terms of the validity of the prediction about the outcome in the current environment rather than on the realized outcome (which will be available only after the decision has been implemented). Findings from the verification exercise should be fed forward to the first phase of the next cycle of operations have been implemented. Findings from the verification exercise should be fed forward to the first phase of the next cycle of operation.

Applications of the OODA loop have been reported by many businesses and commercial organizations outside the defence system. Of course, it has found wide acceptance in the field of cybersecurity and related fields. Management scientists and executives feel that the OODA loop has a bright and expanding future, particularly in the context of big data and predictive analytics emerging to provide a real boost to tasks involved in the first three phases of the loop.

10.3.6. The Simplex Process

This is a robust, creative problem-solving process proposed by Min Basadur (1995) that starts with finding the problem and goes up to 'action' or implementation of the solution decided upon. It proceeds in the following eight steps:

- Problem-finding by raising questions: What would our customers want us to improve? What could clients do better if we could help them? What is failing in the process?
- Fact finding—what are the issues to be resolved? Relevant data is collected and processed.
- Problem definition in terms of a concrete and clear statement of 'why?' and 'what is stopping now?'
- Finding ideas through brainstorming or creative thinking or out-of-the-box thinking (going beyond the boundaries of the given context or environment, if needed) to solve the problem.
- Evaluation of ideas as inputs for potential solutions and selection of one or more.

- Action planning to implement the selected idea or potential solution by procuring and deploying the necessary resources.
- Gaining acceptance of stakeholders and of people to be involved in implementation.
- Action to put the solution to practice.

The first three steps constitute the first phase, namely problem formulation. The next two steps delineate the second phase of solution formulation and the remaining three steps correspond to the third phase of implementing the solution.

Some exponents have canvassed the process in six or seven steps. The core lies in generating ideas and, in that way, in innovative thinking. Potential solutions are the alternatives, selecting one or more is the decision problem.

10.3.7. Strawman Framework

In the Strawman framework used by Mckinsey, no attempt is initially made to identify all possible or even a handful of (feasible) alternatives, often because this task is pretty problematic and time-consuming and may not be found essential. Instead, a draft version of the solution that is easily identifiable through brainstorming could be just a rough or crude one on which a team can debate and argue to reject the solution outright (without investing time and effort into implementing it and noting the outcomes thereof, obviously avoiding pride of ownership) or to find out the limitations of the starting solution which can be removed to improve upon it before implementing the latter on a trial basis. Common in the context of software development, this approach is like a sequential attempt to provoke the generation of a new and better proposal through constructive criticism. This approach has some similarity with the simplex method for solving LP problems.

10.3.8. Hurson's Model

T. Hurson (2007) proposed a framework rather than a technique involving brainstorming and lateral thinking, based on CPS and

NASA's IDEF0 for function modelling to IDEF14 (for network design). He suggested the following six steps to develop good ideas which can provide reasonable alternatives to consider or reasonable criteria for comparison across alternatives:

1. What is going on? To understand what the problem is that we are going to solve.
2. What is success? To tell us about the targeted future state.
3. What is the question? It is really a whole set of catalytic and interrelated questions which have to be addressed and answered to solve the problem.
4. Generate answers to the questions. Focus on creative and critical thinking skills.
5. Forge the solution from the ideas developed as answers to the questions. This step is also known as 'Think x'.
6. Align resources to put the solution into practice and observe the outcome(s).

Once the outcome(s) is (are) known, the steps should be repeated if deviations from the outcome(s) from the targeted future states are found to be non-trivial.

10.3.9. TDODAR Model

The TDODAR model is a simple and intuitive model for decision-making predominantly used in aviation. It is particularly useful for making considered decisions in emergencies and pressured situations when there is a real element of uncertainty about what to do. Fully expanded, it stands for: time, diagnostics, options, decide, act and review. This model is more useful in situations where time is an important factor, such as in patient management in a healthcare system, when an IT system crashes just before a report is to be churned out and when some product or service defects surface just before the market launch of the product or service.

Taking due notice of the time at our disposal, diagnosis of the problem to comprehend what exactly the problem is, what are the possible causes right from the obvious to the least apparent, how do the potential causes contribute to the problem and related issues is an essential task. This can be aided by the five why's or root-cause analysis. Diagnosis findings are important to avoid confirmation bias, leading to situations where one may be tempted to decide and act on pre-conceived ideas. Unless options are quickly identified—may be through experience or intuition—time constraint will hinder decision-making. Usually, option generation is a team process, and we can take recourse to Delphi or brainstorming for this purpose. We need to analyse logically the options available to choose one. In the act step, we have to allocate responsibilities among members of the team as to who should do what. We cannot withdraw from the scene right at this stage. In fact, we should wait to review implementation and the outcome to find out if the problem situation has been resolved.

10.4. Models Using Quantitative Methods

We now present outlines of three models which can be put in the second category, without providing details of the quantitative tools involved therein.

10.4.1. Kepner–Tregoe Model

In the Kepner–Tregoe approach (proposed by C. H. Kepner and B. Tregoe in the 1960s), the steps involved are (a) situation appraisal, (b) problem analysis—problem defined and its root causes determined, (c) decision analysis—alternatives identified and the risk associated with each is assessed in terms of probabilities of undesired impacts and (d) potential problem analysis, where the 'best' alternative is further scrutinized against potential problems and negative consequences and actions proposed to minimize the risk associated with this 'best' alternative. In this approach, emphasis is laid on assessment and prioritization of risks (considering the outcome and the way to achieve it). This may not yield a perfect solution, but we can expect to get the best possible choice.

The steps involved in the Kepner–Tregoe model (often referred to as the gold standard in creative thinking skills) can be further elaborated as follows:

- Establish strategic and mandatory requirements (must indicate what all we must have), operational objectives (want to tell what all we want to have) and restraints (limit in the system). In some sense, must and limit define what are called 'feasibility' criteria for any alternative.
- List as many alternatives or courses of action as may be possible—whether immediately feasible or not. In most business problems, we can reasonably assume a countably few alternatives, at least initially. This initial set may have to be enlarged only if a desirable solution does not emerge from this set.
- Rate each alternative as GO or NOT GO on the basis of each MUST and each LIMIT.
- Rank objectives and assign a priority weight w_j in the range of 1–10 to the jth objective.
- Assign a relative score x_i in the range of 1–10 to each feasible alternative to indicate how well the alternative satisfies a given objective. For each alternative i, calculate $\Sigma w_j x_j$.
- Identify the top two or three alternatives based on this sum.
- List the adverse consequences of the selected alternatives and calculate the risk = (Probability that the effect takes place × seriousness of the impact if the effect occurs) for each of the top alternatives and for each anticipated adverse consequence and then sum up the possible consequences. Calculate the overall risk and analyse the weighted score for each of the top alternatives against the adversity rating and then make a final choice of a single alternative, as the one that best balances the score with the risk. The probability of occurrence and the seriousness or severity of impact may not admit direct computation and can be simply taken as either high or medium or low to be taken as 10, 5 and 1 somewhat arbitrarily.

It thus comes out that the Kepner–Tregoe approach bears a lot of similarity to several MCDM methods, as one should expect. The Kepner-Tregoe problem-solving approach goes beyond selecting an alternative to considering the winning alternative against each adverse consequence and suggesting a plan of action to minimize the adverse effects. An explicit consideration of risk makes the approach somewhat different from the usual MCDM models for decision-making. The Kepner–Tregoe model combines decision and action. However, one may point out the fact that troubleshooting in the context of big data and predictive analytics is emerging to provide a real boost to tasks involved in the first three phases of the loop.

10.4.2. Recognition-primed Decision Process

The recognition-primed decision process—propounded by psychologists Klein, Calderwood and Clinton-Cirocco and published in *Sources of Power: How People Make Decisions* (1999)—is based on mental simulation of future consequences of a decision and recognition of patterns of happenings in the past. Applicable mostly in emergency service situations, like fire-fighting, this model stresses experience and intuition, does not attempt identification of possible alternatives but takes up only one and decides to choose another only when the mental simulation exercise hints at possible risks and adverse impacts. The three steps involved are (a) experiencing the situation through listening and looking at the situation as it unfolds, (b) analysing the situation in terms of recognizing similar situations experienced earlier and decisions taken there along with the consequences and (c) acting and implementing the decision.

This model works in operational settings, and it fuses two processes, namely situation assessment to generate a plausible course of action (essentially a decision alternative) and mental simulation to evaluate the course of action suggested. Alternatives are not identified through a semi-random process of deliberations nor are those to be compared one with the other. Rather, the alternative is first proposed on the basis of experience and duly recognized in terms of (a) understanding the goals that the situation allows to be achieved, (b) increasing the salience of the cues within the context of the situation, (c) framing expectations to serve as a check on the accuracy of the assessment and (d) identifying the typical action to take. It is quite possible that recognition reveals flaws in previous actions, needing modification of the action taken previously or even rejecting that action in favour of some other option recognized as the obvious reaction or response to the current situation. This is why the model is characterized as 'primed' and not 'completely determined' by recognition of the present situation as one experienced earlier.

This model differs from the classical decision-making models in that it is focused on satisficing rather than on optimizing and finding the first option that does work rather than the best option. It involves the experience of the decision-maker explicitly and, in that way, finds some place in the case-based decision theory. It also recognizes human intuition, imagination and logical thinking. It may be noted that some explain mental simulation as analogous to a Bayesian network model that works on subjective probabilities.

10.4.3. BADIR Framework

The BADIR framework—sometimes called the data-to-decision framework—suggested by Jain and Sharma (2015) in their book entitled *Behind Every Good Decision*, duly expanded, stands for business questions (with a generic understanding of business as a goal-oriented system or organization), analysis plan (to consider the tools to be used for examining the hypotheses of interest and for extracting useful and intelligent information from data for this purpose), data collection (covering relevant data of different types to be collected from different sources through different mechanisms), insights into what all is happening and how, to be derived from information extracted from data through the use of analytics and to give recipes or alternatives for solving the problem and recommendations to be made about the way impacts of the proposed solution on the system under consideration can be realized.

This five-step process combines data science to proceed from an inquiry to gain insights about an underlying problem and decision science to proceed from the inputs provided by the insights to arrive at the impacts of alternative solutions for eventually choosing one. It applies big data to formulate decisions. It starts with the proposition that data exist everywhere, but big data constitute a situation where it is well-nigh impossible to parse what information is relevant and actionable for our business. This is because information thrown up by data analysis may be interesting by itself or may even be worth knowing but ultimately irrelevant to decision-making. This led the proponents to use machine learning and statistics as relevant tolls.

The five steps involved in the framework are as follows:

1. Find related and actionable business questions. A well-defined and well-thought-out question that pinpoints some business pain is the critical starting point. This entails an understanding of the context, the segment of business currently affected or likely to be affected (adversely), the potential reasons that have been realized and similar other issues that can sharpen the question and also realize if the question can be resolved.
2. Formulate a hypothesis-driven plan for analysis of data to be collected (in the next step). We should note that we are not in an open inquiry where we first collect data and then decide on the type of analysis. We did come up with some findings that may or may not shed light on the question we started to resolve. In this step, we should fix up: (a) Analysis goals, which should be broken down narrowly into verifiable objectives for better understanding and more effective control. The goals/objectives should be SMART, that is, specific (not diffused), measurable (not just identifiable), attainable (not simply visualized), relevant (in the particular context and not generic) and time-bound (not left to any time schedule). (b) Hypothesis linked to the business question that can be verified empirically and can provide an understanding of the cause-and-effect relations bearing on the problem at hand. A hypothesis is an informed guess about such a relation in the entire domain of inquiry or within a sub-domain that may have to be anticipated, like a clustering of customers based on some demographic or psychographic features. These two entities may emerge from a brainstorming session in some cases. (c) Methodology for analysis, including data gap analysis, models to be adopted (like the popular SWOT model) analytics to be used and other related

matters should be chalked out during this step. (d) Data specification, including the level at which and the frequency with which data should be collected. (e) Project plan to be developed for the hypothesis-driven inquiry.
3. Collect relevant and adequate data, as envisaged in the analysis plan. Data cleaning and validation exercises should be properly carried out to ensure quality and credibility of data and to avoid a garbage-in, garbage-out situation. Checking relevance and quality of data are vital steps to validate any insight that we are going to derive.
4. Derive insight into the problem and its root causes as well as its dimensions and differentials, by using appropriate statistical methods and machine learning tools. The insight gained should enable identification of possible options or alternative ways to fix the problem as well as some idea about their potential or predicted effectiveness.
5. BADIR stops at examining the data patterns, proving or disproving the hypothesis (or hypotheses) and presenting findings thereon to make recommendations about the option or alternative to be chosen for implementation. By itself, the framework does not directly provide a choice among the alternatives, which should be implemented.

BADIR has some similarity with the six Sigma methodology involving the define, measure, analyse, improve and control steps. Both these approaches to problem-solving focus on data and on analysis. In fact, six Sigma is more explicit in its demand for quantitative methods for analysis and is more focused on actions (to improve the current state of the system), including both implementation of the decision and stabilization of the system at the improved level. BADIR's focus on these latter tasks is not prominent. Like six Sigma, BADIR has been finding applications in newer areas.

10.5. Models for Problem-solving

In Section 10.3, we discussed problems and procedures for decision-making which surely belong to the domain of 'organizational decision-making', though the models in that section generally avoid mathematical models and methods. The use of appropriate analytics to process data and information are involved in models dealt with in Section 10.4.

We now take up a few widely known and practised approaches or methodologies (some are known as models) adopted by organizations to solve some of their 'business' problems, which include decision-making as an important step. In fact, some of these models are more concerned with 'actions' rather than 'decisions' to solve their problems. Some of the composite problem-solving approaches or methodologies (as distinct from methods) which integrate decision-making with pertinent technical components to solve a business problem have grown not merely in their methodological content but also in their applicability. We will emphasize more the decision-making element in such approaches. In that connection, we remember that these approaches focus on the types of decisions that we have to take initially or as we go along to solve a problem, rather than the methods of making those decisions.

Beyond problem-solving and coming up with situations or occasions which do not throw up 'problems', organizations are and should be involved in designing and executing 'improvement' processes. In fact, a good volume of literature has grown around 'continuous process improvement' and this very important 'improvement' exercise comes up with many strategic decision problems. Thus, we must decide which process or which entity (abstract or concrete) should be improved first. What are the feasible improvement strategies? How to evaluate the outcome of a strategy being implemented? How to choose a satisfactory if not optimal strategy? These questions are not directly addressed in some of the improvement methodologies but are in-built into them. In what follows, we just provide a sketchy account of some of the so-called 'models' for organizational decision-making, including approaches for problem-solving and continuous improvement.

In an earlier section, we mentioned three such methodologies, namely the PDCA cycle proposed by Deming, the six Sigma approach to solving business problems linked to the quality of products and services and the 8D methodology which adds some additional steps to the six Sigma approach. As expected, each of these models involves decision-making in different steps or stages, based essentially on appropriate statistical analysis of relevant data collected with due care. The first phase 'plan' in the PDCA cycle embraces a number of decisions. Similar is the case with phases 'define' and 'analyse' in the context of the six Sigma methodology and its extension, namely the 8D methodology.

10.6. Paired Comparison Analysis

The method of paired comparisons has been found useful for working out the relative importance of several different alternatives and thereby comparing them among the alternatives, especially when the alternatives are not too few and are quite different one from the other (not in terms of some numerical outcomes) or when the priorities are not that clear or when evaluation criteria are subjective. Applications of this method have been made for purposes such as site selection, possible policies of an organization in respect of recruitment or compensation, policies relating to market competition and similar other choice problems. It is a simple method that can provide reasonable solutions to choice problems in situations where we do not have adequate and unambiguous data or we are unable to directly compare the alternatives with respect to a chosen criterion. The method can be practised routinely by following the steps:

1. Enumerate the alternatives (say m in number) and identify those by assigning letters A, B, C, etc.,
2. Enter the alternatives in an $m \times m$ table with rows and columns marked successively by the letters A, B, C, etc. A cell corresponds to a combination of alternatives.
3. Cross out diagonals (no need to compare an alternative with itself) as well as cells with the same alternative combination included previously. This is to ensure that a pair of alternatives is considered only once.
4. In each open cell, compare the row alternative with the column alternative and put the letter corresponding to the alternative in the pair that is perceived as more important.

5. Rate each relative importance within a pair by a number from 0 indicating no difference in importance to 3 a marked difference in importance.
6. Add numbers for each alternative (say columns) or express those as percentages of the total to indicate the relative positions of the alternatives.

The logic behind this method being preferred over the method of ranking the alternatives in terms of perceived importance is that usually ranking can be done conveniently in the case of only a few alternatives and that ranks do not reveal differences in importance among the alternatives with consecutive ranks.

An example could be a choice problem faced by a person willing to donate some amount to some socially useful work. Several suggestions under consideration are as follows:

A: Donation to a local charitable trust or orphanage
B: Grant of scholarship to needy and meritorious students of alma mater.
C: Donation to an international agency like UNICEF
D: Donation to the National Disaster Relief Fund

The potential donor is not clear about their objective and hence cannot spell out criteria for finding the ranks or measures of importance of these four somewhat disparate alternatives. Maybe multiple criteria can be brought in, but that would create complications. Instead, we follow the steps involved in paired comparison to yield the following:

	A	B	C	D
A	X	B(2)	C(3)	A(1)
B	X	X	B(2)	B(3)
C	X	X	X	D(2)
D	X	X	X	X

Figures within parentheses indicate the perceived difference in importance of the row alternative over the column alternative, 9 indicating no difference, 1 a minor difference, 2 a perceptible one and 3 a marked difference. The total rating received by the alternatives are respectively 1, 7, 3 and 2. Hence, the second alternative is perceived to be the most important to the potential donor as the decision-maker.

10.7. Theory of Constraints

Problem-solving methodologies, developed and tried out in forward-looking manufacturing and service organizations, have to emphasize both decision-making and decision implementation (followed by mid-term evaluation and course correction). One of the wholesome approaches to problem-solving that avoids complex quantitative analysis but stresses on logical arguments, has been elevated to the status of a 'theory'. This is the TOC propounded by Goldratt (1990). The basic philosophy behind TOC lies in the propositions that:

1. Every system (a profit-making organization or a comprehensive process carried out by any goal-seeking organization) must have at least one constraint
2. Existence of constraints represents an opportunity for improvement

A constraint is anything that limits the system from achieving higher performance than its goal(s). It could be something concrete, like a material or a machine, or it could be abstract, like a policy or a mindset among workers. In TOC, constraints are not 'resource bottlenecks'. These are 'positive' entities in that a gradual 'elevation' of the system's constraints will improve its performance. TOC came up as an extension of optimized production scheduling (OPS) in the context of manufacturing. The OPS involved nine rules.

The basic principle, along with the five focusing steps mentioned in the drum, buffer and rope (DBR) scheduling guided by it and the buffer management information system, constituted the broad framework of TOC. In the DBR scheduling,

- Drum represents the system schedule or the pace at which the constraint works (since the constraint as the weakest link determines the pace of the system as a whole).
- Rope stands for communication between critical control points to ensure their synchronization.
- Buffer is the strategically placed inventory that protects system output from variations or deviations that occur in the system. Among buffers, time buffers are quite important, though there are also constraint buffers, assembly buffers and shipping buffers also.

In fact, the theory has subsequently been modified to provide solutions to complex decision problems based on common knowledge, intuition and logic, assisted by a proper information system and using simple tools like decision trees. The methods involved in it focus on the following three serious management questions:

1. What to change?
2. What to change?
3. How to bring about the change?

The first two relate to decision-making and are directed at identification of alternatives as well as to generation and deployment of criteria, keeping in mind the goals and objectives of the organization. The second is also concerned with the development of implementable solutions. Quite expectably, the solution will imply certain changes in the current way of carrying out different interrelated activities. The third question also relates to a choice among alternative mechanisms for effective implementation of the changes proposed in the solution.

TOC measures system performance not in terms of traditional accounting norms but through three entities derived appropriately from an adequate information system, namely (a) throughput relating to the rate at which the system generates money through sales, (b) inventory covering the in-things the system intends to sell and (c) operating expenses representing the money involved in turning inventory into throughput.

Primarily concerned with managing changes for the better by removing bottlenecks to organizational performance, TOC looks upon an organization as a system with interconnected elements or links, and the entity to be changed first is the weakest link that has the largest negative impact on organizational performance. The latter admits many dimensions and identifying the 'weakest link' is not an easy task. More than the problem of dimensionality, this link or the entity to be changed could be something like a policy for personnel assignment to different jobs or for procurement of supplies from vendors or for interaction with the outside environment, or some such issue and inertia sets in everywhere, causing bottlenecks. Existing policies have to be somehow compared among themselves across areas of operation to find out the weakest link. Thereafter, for the selected policy arena, policy alternatives may not be obvious and may have to be generated through securing and processing relevant information. It may be difficult to identify some suitable criterion (criteria) to evaluate these alternatives. Similar problems arise with attempts to answer the third and most important question.

A somewhat similar spirit works through the famous 'squeaking wheel approach', also known as 'muddling through' advocated for management of change by Lindblom. Here also, introducing and managing changes in small doses in areas (operations or policies guiding those) where changes can be wrought out most conveniently has been suggested in preference to changing lock, stock and barrel.

TOC has been very widely adopted in many organizations in both the manufacturing and service sectors. However, applications for services are not that many. It is worthwhile to mention that applications of TOC have been so popular that an international certification organization, the Theory of Constraints International Certification Organization, known by the acronym TOCICO has come to stay to guide and promote TOC on proper lines. Mabin and Balderstone (1999) provide a good account of TOC along with its development and applications.

TOC is to be comprehended in terms of the following few basic principles:

- Systems thinking is quite important in managing change and solving problems.
- An optimal system solution deteriorates over time as the system's environment changes. A process of ongoing improvement is required to update and maintain the effectiveness of a solution. This was pointed out by Box (1997) who spoke of evolutionary operations to adjust the optimal treatment combination obtained from a response surface study in an industrial optimization experiment.
- Even if all components or parts of a system perform as well as they can, the system as a whole may not perform as well as it can. This is somewhat like the fact that the system reliability of a parallel system is at best equal to the reliability of its weakest link.
- Systems are analogous to chains. Each system has a 'weakest link', recognized as a constraint that ultimately limits the success of the entire system.
- Strengthening any link other than the weakest one does nothing to improve the strength of the whole system to perform.
- Knowing what to change requires a thorough understanding of the system's current reality, its goal and the magnitude and direction of the difference between the two.
- Most of the undesirable effects (UDEs) within a system are due to a few core problems.
- Core problems are never superficially apparent. They manifest themselves through a number of UDEs linked by a network of cause and effect.
- Elimination of individual UDEs gives a false sense of security, while ignoring the underlying core problems. Solutions which proceed on this line will be short-lived. On the other hand, the solution to the core problem simultaneously eliminates all the resulting UDEs.
- Core problems are usually perpetuated by a hidden or underlying conflict. A solution to a core problem requires challenging the assumptions underlying the conflict and invalidating at least one such assumption.
- System constraints could be physical or policy issues. Physical constraints are relatively easy to identify and simple to eliminate. Policy constraints are usually more difficult to identify and eliminate, but

removing them usually results in a larger degree of system improvement than the removal of a physical constraint.
- Inertia is the worst enemy of a process of ongoing improvement. Solutions tend to assume a mass of their own that resists further change. It must be remembered that once a solution has been implemented to pull up a weak link, we should once again look at the new system and identify the weakest link there. Thus, after implementing a solution, the modified system has to be examined further to identify weak links in the system that should be taken up for possible elimination.
- Ideas are not solutions. Ideas focused on the problems and transformed through enterprise into concrete entities do provide solutions.

Taken liberally, these principles are neither new nor novel. In fact, some management experts see a lot of communality between TOC and methods like just-in-time or materials resource planning or lean manufacturing. It should be noted that TOC is a theory, while the others are methods or techniques imbedded in improvement methodologies. TOC differs from improvement methodologies like six Sigma and its variants or 8D, which has a provision for a bandage solution before attempting to find a fully effective solution or similar other methodologies in the sense that improvements to some selected business problems woven around some processes may not result in expected improvement in system performance. System performance improvement is what is targeted in TOC. The focus of TOC is on constraints on system performance or weak links in the system, regarded as a chain of links.

Like other problem-solving approaches, TOC also follows a sequence of steps. These are as follows:

1. **Identify the system constraint:** Which part or component of the system constitutes the weakest link? Is it a physical (resource) constraint or is it a policy constraint? This requires an assessment of the performance of each identified part or component in terms of some suitable performance parameters, followed by delineation

of the weakest link and a cause-and-effect analysis of such a link. The underlying cause or cause system is the constraint. It is possible to consider the UDE to indicate the weakest link. An UDE is like a defect or non-compliance with customer (internal or external) customer(s) or some avoidable waste and the like. If a set of objectives has been set for each component, the gap between the current performance and the corresponding objectives can help in identifying the weakest link. As already remarked, system constraint is not generally obvious and has to be found out through a process of evaluation and search.

2. **Decide how to exploit the constraint:** By the word 'exploit', Goldratt meant that we should wring every bit of capability out of the constraining component as it currently exists. In other words, 'what can we do to get the most out of this constraint without committing to potentially expensive changes or upgrades?' The important point is to first focus on the constraint which corresponds to a component or part that is currently yielding several UDEs by making incremental, easy-to-manage changes or modifications to reduce the nature and frequency of UDEs.

   This step is somewhat similar to the bandage solution in the language of the 8D methodology.

3. **Subordinate everything else:** Once the weakest link has been identified (Step 1) and we have decided what to do about it (Step 2), we adjust the rest of the system to a setting that will allow the weakest link to operate at maximum effectiveness. We may have to 'de-tune' some parts of the system, while 'revving up' others. Once we have done this, we must evaluate the results of our actions. Is the constraint still constraining the system's performance? If not, we have eliminated the constraint and we proceed to Step 5. If it is, we still have a constraint, and we continue with Step 4.

   Step 3 involves both implementation of some actions as well as evaluation of the appropriateness of such actions.

4. **Elevate the constraint:** If in Steps 2 or 3, we fail to eliminate the constraint, then we come to this step to do something more about the constraint. It was not until this step that we decided to introduce some major changes to the system as it exists now. Such

major changes may be by way of disinvestment, capital improvements or other substantial system modifications. In fact, this step involves considerable investment in terms of money, time, energy or other resources. Therefore, it is crucial to be sure that we were not able to break the constraint in the first three steps. 'Elevate' the constraint means that we take whatever action is needed to remove the constraint. When this step is completed or the corresponding actions have been implemented, the constraint is eliminated.

5. **Go back to Step 1, beware of 'inertia':** If in Step 3 or 4, depending on the situation, we have been able to eliminate a constraint, we must go back to Step 1 and repeat the cycle again, looking out for the next thing constraining the system performance. The caution about inertia reminds us that we must not become complacent; the cycle never ends. Further, we should always remember that, because of independency among components or parts and because of natural variation due to chance causes, each subsequent change we make in the system will have new effects on those constraints which we have already eliminated. We may have to revisit and update them also.

The five steps dealt with earlier have a direct relationship with the following three crucial management questions pertaining to change in the system:

1. What to change?
2. What to change?
3. How to bring about change?

Step 1 answers the first question, where we look for the constraint and even the second one partly. The answer to the second question is implicitly given in Steps 2 and 3 to reach a decision. Steps to elevate and subordinate are meant to answer the last question.

The tools used by Goldratt include five distinct logic trees and the rules of logic that govern their construction. The trees are the current reality tree, the evaporating cloud, the future reality tree, the prerequisite tree and the transition tree. The rules are called the categories of legitimate reservations. Unlike six Sigma and some other approaches to continuous improvement, TOC does not involve the application of sophisticated quantitative analysis. Measurements are implicitly involved, while opinions are more explicitly required. Of course, available data bearing on performance parameters of different components or parts of the system do call for compilation and summarization—if not more elaborate analysis. Additional data for this purpose have to be identified and collected.

CHAPTER 11

Alternatives and Constraints

11.1. Introduction

In quite a few search problems, alternatives or options available to a decision-maker may not be obvious at the beginning of the decision-making process and may have to be generated by following certain logical procedures. It may not be possible even to know beforehand the number (finite or infinite) of such alternatives, nor be required necessarily. It may be desirable in some situations to start with just one alternative or a few alternatives and to search sequentially for better alternatives, in the sense of satisfying the objective or goal behind the decision-making process. Thus, we do need to search the entire space of alternatives and then proceed through local searches to eventually arrive at the best solution within the space of alternatives.

As is easily understood, an alternative need not be a single entity or a scalar. It could be a portfolio, a set of probabilities, a package of benefits or rewards, a strategy or, in general, a vector. And in the latter case, the size of the group or set could be given a priori or could itself be a decision variable. It is also possible to have groups of entities having varying numbers of components as the alternatives.

We may face real-life situations where alternatives (which imply some actions to be taken) have to be developed through consultations or discussions among some experts or consultants, from within or outside the system, followed by some procedures to reach a consensus about alternatives to be considered for further assessment.

It should be appreciated that in a large variety of decision-making situations, particularly those involving multiple decision-makers and dynamic search procedures and those where the focus is on satisficing solutions, generating more and more improved solutions/alternatives based on cumulative experience plays a vital role in solving the problem. In fact, the algorithms make good use of probability and local search to sequentially build up the final solution.

Before we proceed further, we may note that in some decision-problems, the most important and, may be, difficult task is to visualize alternatives that can be tested within available resources for feasibility and to formulate those concretely for testing feasibility as well as for evaluating in relation to the objective(s) to be achieved by solving the decision problem. It may be easier to compare the alternatives in terms of evaluation of their outcome(s) against some criterion (criteria). A search for alternatives, keeping an eye on the objective(s) and the criterion (criteria), including the process of 'designing' such alternatives, dominates many real-life decision problems.

All decision problems involve discreetly or explicitly some constraints, primarily in the choice of alternatives. Sometimes, decision variables in the alternative(s) chosen as optimal or as 'satisficing' are constrained to lie in some ranges. While the former reflects limitations on resources required to implement any alternative into action, the latter may call for special efforts to process the alternatives unless these limitations are met. In any case, it has to be remembered that constraints are always present, not as bottlenecks to complicate or even rule out solutions to decision problems. In fact, constraints sometimes help us to narrow down our search for the 'best' alternative, and in most cases, their presence has motivated decision theorists to investigate ways and means to tackle the issues posed by constraints or even to turn constraints into advantages.

In this chapter, we will briefly consider several approaches to building up alternatives, not to identify all possible alternatives or to completely sweep the search space but to come up sequentially with improved alternatives to reach the optimal or even a satisficing solution as quickly as possible. We will also deal with constraints and feasibility of alternatives, as well as methods to make good use of infeasible solutions.

11.2. Issues in Optimization

In classical optimization problems, alternatives are all identified right at the beginning, though those need not be and are not generally enumerated or considered in the steps involved in the search for the optimal solution. In fact, at each step, we consider only one alternative and assess it before proceeding to the next step or deciding to stop the search with the current alternative taken as the optimal. However, when dealing with discrete optimization problems as well as with combinatorial optimization problems with a very large space of alternatives, search algorithms focus on the generation of alternatives in a manner that helps in reaching the desired solution early.

Identifying initial alternatives or solutions to complex optimization problems, like the travelling salesman problem or job-shop scheduling problem, has given rise to interesting developments in the area of heuristics to solve such problems. Particular mention may be made of genetic algorithms in which the initial solutions are strings of parameter values, usually taken as 0 and 1, which are referred to as chromosomes. In fact, genetic algorithms are instances of evolutionary algorithms in which we proceed to generate improved solutions through local search guided by some numerical measure linked directly or otherwise with the final goal and moving probabilistically within the neighbourhood.

In problems of optimization, we generally come across some constraints on the possible alternatives by way of some relations (equations or inequalities) connecting the decision variables and the states of nature, along with some externalities like available resources or prevailing regulations restricting the choices or alternatives. In fact, the optimal solution has to be found among the alternatives which satisfy the constraints and are called 'feasible'. The concept of partial satisfaction with some specified probability of a constraint has sometimes been introduced in probabilistic programming. In some cases, we do not regard all the constraints as inviolate. In fact, a constraint may relate to a scarce material or energy resource not normally available beyond a specified limit or some restriction that should not be normally ignored or bypassed. In a manufacturing set-up, engaging the workforce for more than the stipulated time per day, a violation to meet exigency, may attract some penalty imposed by the competent authority; there could be market and the consequence of procuring more could invite some penalty.

In some problems, the constraints are such that determining the feasibility or otherwise of an alternative is an extremely difficult task and may call for appropriate algorithms. Thus, in a sequencing problem, involving five jobs each to be processed through each of five machines according to prescribed machine sequences for the five jobs (which may not be all identical), there are $(5!)^5$ or approximately 25×10^7 possible job sequences on the five machines (which are the alternatives), and to find out which of these satisfy the given technological orderings of machines for each of the jobs, we badly need algorithms which are still to be developed in cases of medium numbers of machines and jobs. In this case, for an alternative job sequence for each of the machines to be feasible, we have to check whether at any stage the job is free (waiting for processing on the next machine as prescribed by the technology), the machine is free (it is not currently processing any jobs), the job is next to the machine and (according to the alternative) the machine is next to the job. When technology prescribes different machine sequences for different jobs, checking the feasibility of an alternative is really a complex job. In the design of truss structures, one possible definition of this problem is to find the cross-section area of the bars that minimizes the structure's weight subject to limitations on the nodal displacements and on the stress of each bar. While the structure's weight can be conveniently calculated, from the design variables, the values of nodal displacement and of the stress in each bar are to be determined by solving the equilibrium equations defined by the finite element model.

11.3. Desiderata for Alternatives

In general, decision theory, identifying or developing alternatives—quite often actions or even groups of actions to be taken to achieve some goals or objectives behind the decision-making problem—may not be a routine task, may require a comprehension of the goals and objectives prompting the decision problem and the criteria to be introduced in assessing the alternatives, may involve search for requisite information, may require a revisit of the same decision problem or similar decision problems solved earlier, along with the alternatives considered and the alternatives eventually analysed or those found optimal, may call for out-of-the-box thinking to yield some innovative alternatives, may justify a look at available resources and their deployment to carry out any suggested alternative, may not be distinct one from the other in terms of consequences and may not be too many to complicate further processing.

An important point that is sometimes overlooked is the requirement that alternatives must be comparable, in the sense of being more or less similar in respect of features or aspects which are not directly involved in the comparison of 'expected utility' or any other criterion measure but are likely to influence the latter. This comparability is crucial to justifying comparisons among the alternatives. For example, a marketing department may like to choose one among several publicity materials to be put on some electronic media to attract the attention of potential customers. If some material is better designed to have a long-lasting impression on the viewers, it may take a longer time to display, and some other material can only create a short-term impression, it may take a shorter display time. A choice between the two is not a logical proposition. To be comparable, the different materials (the alternatives in this case) should have more or less equal time for viewing and should be more or less similarly designed. Cost could vary, conversations could vary, portrayal of the product or the service under consideration could vary, but not the time ranges when the materials get displayed. All this is just to remind us of the fundamental principle that only comparables can and should be compared.

Some researchers have listed the following as some desiderata for alternatives. Decision alternatives should be:

- Value-focused, implying that they are explicitly designed to address the decision goals and objectives as well as the evaluation criteria in terms of which the alternatives will be linked to the goals and objectives.
- Technically sound, meaning that in developing alternatives for achieving the objectives, the project team has drawn on the best available information about cause and effect relationships and has designed diverse alternatives based on sound logical analysis to facilitate a choice among the alternatives.
- Clearly and consistently defined, meaning that all alternatives are defined to a sufficient and consistent level of detail using logically consistent assumptions, and that a base case against which all alternatives can be compared has been clearly established.
- Manageable in number and high in quality, meaning that poor alternatives which are likely to be dominated by others are weeded out or have been appropriately refined to become viable choices.
- Comprehensive and mutually exclusive, implying that individual elements or components of a strategy are combined into complete packages, and that the packages are directly comparable. It may not be feasible to exhaust all possibilities but care must be taken to ensure that any potentially useful alternative is not left out.
- Able to expose fundamental trade-offs, meaning that they emphasize rather than hide difficult but unavoidable value-based trade-offs and present real choices for decision-makers.
- Developed collaboratively with the people most affected, because difficult trade-offs are easier to make and to accept when people believe that a thorough search for good alternatives has been conducted and that the alternatives which have the promise of being the best or close to the best are on the table.

11.4. Development of Alternatives

Decision alternatives have to be considered in two different contexts, both within the framework of general decision theory, namely decisions being taken for the first time (at least by the individual or group decision-maker in the present problem) and decisions taken earlier on the same problem or similar problems (may be by other decision-makers). Such a question may not be relevant in the context of general optimization problems. Thus, we need to address three different problems, namely (a) generating alternatives for decision problems with no previous analogues, (b) developing alternatives for decision problems with some previous analogues and (c) selecting alternatives from an identifiable set for further and/or sequential consideration. One common task is to start with a few or even just one alternative and take it further to generate branches or to effect possible improvements or to generate some more alternatives.

Let us take the second case first. We look back at alternatives that were considered earlier, including those which were discarded and those which were further processed as well as those finally chosen. It is possible to think of some more alternatives. In respect of those which were discarded, we may note whether they can now be improved to become viable alternatives. In fact, it is worthwhile to examine each alternative considered earlier for such enrichment, wherever possible. Once we come to a set of alternatives, we can conduct a brainstorming exercise to (a) find out if we have overlap over the alternatives, may be in terms of identical consequences and resource requirements or if some alternatives are dominated by some other(s) or some alternatives may turn out to be infeasible, (b) to develop hybrids by considering reasonable mixtures or combinations of two or more of the alternatives, (c) to fill in a gap between, say, two close alternatives, by identifying another distinct alternative left out of the initial exercise and (d) to carry out a SWOT analysis of the alternatives in the initial set in order to remove weaknesses and to increase strengths, to reduce chances of domination (threats) by others and to enhance the opportunity to be considered favourable for the final choice.

The first case often throws up the challenge of innovation. Creative thinking capabilities to recognize the potential of alternatives selected or finally chosen for other types of decision problems need not be neglected from the purview. Advantage can be taken of ideas and techniques of the theory of inventive problem-solving, algorithms of inventive problem-solving and related tools. Even small trials can be carried out to identify some options in terms of experimental set-ups as alternatives, provided the decision to be taken has a high-value impact to justify spending time and money on coming up with promising alternatives. A decision tree also helps as a support tool to gradually develop an alternative in detail, starting from some basic elements.

11.5. Pooling Expert Opinions

In several research investigations, one has to make a choice among alternative decisions, courses of action or even some objects or subjects judged by some criterion or criteria used by a group of experts. These experts have to be chosen in a manner that suits the context, may be allowed to interact among themselves fully or partly or may not be allowed to interact at all, may be required to provide estimates in one go or allowed to revise on the basis of some feedback provided from the previous round of exercise till there is sufficient convergence. Estimates spoken above may mean ranks assigned to the different entities considered or paired comparisons leading to one of the two entities being preferred to the other or some distance measure between the two members or even probabilities of an event likely to occur in the future.

There are different situations in which experts act and different procedures for choice between any two or among all the candidates may be followed. Accordingly, there are different ways of making use of expert opinions (including an assessment of the extent to which experts agree among themselves) and arriving at some numerical basis for making a choice among the candidates. In this context, we will consider only one or two situation procedure combinations, just to illustrate the overall problem.

Three different types of interactions among experts have been usually considered to generate an initial set of alternative solutions to a decision problem. These are as follows:

1. Experts exchange information freely among them
2. Experts can exchange information to a limited extent only

3. Experts remain isolated and express themselves independently of others

In the round table scheme, the whole group of experts tries to work out a common opinion or estimate (of an unknown parameter). The environment may help build a creative atmosphere with experts enriching ideas of one another. On the negative side, the method makes rigid demands on each expert to speak out one's opinion even if it does not agree with that of the majority and to reject one's own opinion if it realized to be not true in the light of opinions expressed by others.

A modified version of the situation where experts can have restricted interaction is called brainstorming. During any round of a brainstorming session, any idea thrown up is neither discussed nor rejected. Each expert thinks over the opinions or ideas or estimates offered by the other participants, and in a subsequent round, some ideas are accepted and some others are rejected on the basis of afterthoughts. Any decision-making situation where we should take advantage of collective wisdom at least to generate alternate decisions—if not along with their respective merits and limitations—can involve a suitable brainstorming exercise, preceded by a well-prepared presentation on the decision problem, its origin, nature and consequences. Earlier attempts to solve the problem and the need to take a fresh look may also be touched upon.

If experts do not interact with one another and provide independent ideas or estimates, these are subsequently processed by using appropriate algebraic or statistical tools to form the initial set of alternatives.

11.5.1. Delphi Method

The Delphi method is the best known procedure for feedback. Experts are asked for their answers to several questions, usually along with the arguments in their favour. The analyst studies the answers of experts and finds their points of agreement. If the expert opinions are not in sufficient agreement, the analyst gives each expert more data about the system as well as answers and supporting arguments given by the other experts. The experts give their revised opinions on the basis of the additional data provided. An important drawback is the excessive time that may be required to ensure convergence or sufficient agreement among the expert opinions to allow averaging.

Take the example (Makarov et al., 1987) where 10 experts are required to estimate an unknown parameter and the following estimates are obtained: 35, 35, 32.2, 34, 38, 34, 37, 40, 36 and 35.5, yielding an average of 35.5 and a standard deviation $\sigma = 2.2136$. Thus, we can claim that the interval (33.917, 37.083) contains the true parameter value with a probability of 0.95. Now, think of a Delphi exercise where the experts are provided with the median value of the estimates and the interquartile range, along with justifications for some estimates falling outside this range. The interval of feasible values for the estimated parameter is divided into k sub-intervals, and each expert is to estimate the probability that the parameter will lie in each of the sub-intervals. Assume that p_{ij} is an estimate of the probability that the parameter will lie in the jth sub-interval in the opinion of the ith expert. We can then take the probability of the parameter lying in the jth sub-interval as $\Sigma \alpha_i p_{ij} / \Sigma \alpha_i$ where α_i represents the weight assigned to expert i. Most often, these weights are taken to be equal.

It is quite imaginable that the experts were isolated one from the other, and at the end of one round in which their estimates were noted, feedback in terms of the median value and the interquartile range could be provided. This procedure can be repeated until the range of estimates/opinions comes down to a pretty low level and the number of estimates/opinions outside this narrow range becomes small.

Let us now enter a path less trodden by decision-makers. A national statistical agency in a large country wants to plan and conduct a survey on migrant labour to comprehend problems arising in the context of interstate as well as intrastate migration of labour from the point of view of social and economic security. The agency sets up an expert group to work out the survey methodology in all relevant details, given some broad objectives by the concerned ministry, which is interested in getting some policy inputs for developing a national labour policy that is conducive to national development combining both economic growth and distributive justice. The first and most complicated task for the expert group is to discuss and decide on standard operational definitions of the terms 'labour' and 'migration'. The decision problem is, first, to come up with a definition of 'labour'. Alternatives are 'anyone in the age group of 15+ (or 18+) who is in the labour force, that is, either available for and seeking a job or already placed in a job', 'anyone in the relevant age group who is in the workforce', 'anyone in the workforce who has volunteered to join a suitable job in a different state or in a place within the same state but with a different 'usual place of residence' or 'only those in the workforce who are currently working in some manual jobs or are working in some small or medium establishments in the service sector which has no stability in operations'. The group can also look out for some definitions offered by international organizations, like the International Labour Organization or Organisation for Economic Co-operation and Development or similar other bodies. It is also possible to consider definitions adopted by some non-official surveys conducted by some reputed research organizations or some civil society groups. If the group tends to examine only some readily available definitions and selects one out of those few, the findings of the survey may not be comparable with the so-called 'benchmark' survey adopting a different definition. The selection of one definition out of several alternatives would depend on the relevance and the effectiveness of a definition to meet the objectives behind the survey, and the latter may not always be crisply stated completely. The point to remember in this connection is that it is better to spend more resources on identifying as many useful alternatives as possible than to evaluate a few alternatives elaborately in relation to the objectives. Not too often, this point is glossed over by the 'expert groups'.

11.6. Domain Knowledge in Designing Alternatives

In planning a scientific or engineering experiment or even an agricultural field experiment, several decisions have to be taken in consonance with the objectives of the experiment as formulated ahead of the experiment. Details could vary from an exploratory experiment to a comparative experiment or to an optimization experiment. In dealing with a comparative or an optimization experiment, the first entity to be decided upon is the 'response' or 'yield' to be noted in respect of each experimental unit. The response or yield variable has to be the variable of interest to the experimenter, should be determinable with reasonable accuracy with available measuring equipment, should reflect variations across experimental units between and within various treatments or treatment combinations and should remain more or less stable during the course of measurement. In fact, the choice of the experimental material as well as that of an experimental unit are also decision problems that are not that easy to resolve. The shape and size or other characteristics of an experimental unit, each giving rise to a value of the response variable, definitely call for domain knowledge to a great extent. Knowledge of appropriate statistical tools may help consolidate the use of domain knowledge. In the case of multi-response experiments, some more complex decision problems have to be faced.

Then comes the question of deciding on factors on which the chosen response variable depends. Herein comes the role of domain knowledge to guide the experimenter in deciding on the more important factors which affect the response significantly. Factors to be allowed to vary within the framework of the experiment should not be too many to complicate analysis and inferencing and should not be too few to miss out some factors that do explain a non-trivial part of the random variations observed in the responses. For each factor selected, one must identify the levels at which the factor will be controlled during the experiment. The number and the location of levels or values of a factor over its permissible range (again dictated by subject knowledge) are decision problems in which data inputs may be sparse and a good understanding of the objective(s) and sound knowledge of the subject under investigation have to be our guides. Thus, given the knowledge of possible non-linearity of the response variable over factor levels, at least three levels must be chosen to take care of suspected non-linearity. Levels chosen must adequately cover the known range of variation of the factor.

Speaking of combinations of factor levels, care must be taken about possible technical or technological contradictions and complexities. For example, dealing with a very simple three-factor experiment with factors such as A, B and C, each with two levels, it is quite possible that a high level of A is incompatible with a low level of B. Decisions regarding choice of factor levels, keeping an eye on the eventual requirement for convenience in estimation of treatment contrasts and factorial effects, still await satisfactory resolution.

11.7. Probabilities as Alternatives

Just as randomized decision rules in testing statistical hypotheses are required to assign probabilities to two alternative partitions of the sample space, we can think of allowing the decision variable(s) in many applications of optimization methods to be random and can reformulate the original problems as problems of optimally determining probabilities with which different (non-random) values of a decision variable can be accepted. Stochastic programming problems with random decision variables are quite intractable, though they appear to be quite interesting, at least in theory. Let us illustrate the point by considering the classical newspaper boy problem, in which we assume that the newspaper vendor orders a fixed quantity q to be determined optimally in the sense that the expected total cost of shortage and excess, given that demand is random with a specified distribution, is minimized. As is well-known, the optimal order quantity q_0 is the quantile of order $(c_2/[c_1+c_2])$ in the demand distribution, where c_2 is the shortage cost per unit, and c_1 is the cost of excess per unit. This is a decision problem which is generally repetitive, and it is quite possible to order a random quantity on any occasion. In fact, we can work out a 'most favourable' distribution of order quantities (instead of determining an optimal order quantity to be ordered every time, as in traditional inventory analysis) and, on a given occasion, draw a random observation from this distribution to become the order quantity. We can think of quantities, say $q_1, q_2, \ldots, q_k$, spread around the usual optimal order quantity and assign probabilities $\prod_i = $ Prob (order quantity $= q_i$) where these probabilities have to be determined to satisfy constraints like $\Sigma\prod_i = 1$ and $\Sigma\prod_i q_i = $ mean demand, besides the non-negativity constraints, so that the overall expected cost is a minimum. It can be proved from Jensen's inequality that the minimized overall expected cost is smaller than the usual minimum expected total cost with a fixed optimal order quantity. The number k and the values $q_1, q_2, \ldots, q_k$

have to be decided on the basis of experience or some other criteria. Techniques mentioned earlier, like Delphi or other forms of pooling expert opinions, may be tried out. In this formulation of the problem, the decision variables or alternatives are the sets of probabilities (Π_j, $j=1, 2, \ldots, k$).

It must be noted here that, since determining these probabilities optimally becomes a LP problem, the number of q values and the associated probabilities can only be as many as the number of constraints in the problem. In this way, only two or three non-zero values may eventually arise.

This procedure can be thought of in other one-shot decision problems also.

11.8. Alternatives in Evolutionary Algorithms

Evolutionary algorithms have been developed to solve complex optimization problems, especially those involving non-linear and even non-regular objective functions, integer decision variables and extremely large search spaces that arise in the design and control of many complex real-life systems, like the problem of determining optimal redundancy in a large system with the distributed (series parallel) configuration. These algorithms differ from classical optimization algorithms in several ways. Let us look at the way alternatives are generated and selected in each iteration of an algorithm. To make the point of difference simple, we consider the simplex algorithm or an interior point algorithm to solve a LP problem in continuous variables. Generally, given the constraints, we can identify the search space and any point within it (any possible solution to the problem). We start with a single point (individual) and, on the basis of some evaluation relative to the objective function, move to another point in the search space, proceeding in a manner specified by the algorithm. In an evolutionary algorithm, we usually start with a set of initial alternatives (individuals or possible solutions) coded in some manner, if needed. This set is called a population, and its size or the number of points in the search space it includes is specified. For each individual, a fitness function value is computed to assess the probability of whether the solution should be retained or replaced in the next iteration. Those to be retained will undergo some variation to generate what is called the offspring generation of individuals who are at least as good as those in the parent population. Thus, three distinguishing features of alternatives in an evolutionary algorithm are that they (a) form populations in different generations, (b) are fitness-oriented for comparison among alternatives within a generation and (c) are generated—except for the parent population—through a number of variations to generate new and better solutions.

It may be incidentally noted that these move operators are blind to the constraints, in the sense that when applied to feasible individuals in the current generation, they may not produce feasible individuals in the offspring generation. Therefore, there has to be a constraint handling technique for any evolutionary metaheuristic algorithms in constrained optimization problems. Following the principle of survival of the fittest, the concept of a 'fitness' function was introduced. Scanning through the individuals in the current generation, examining their feasibility or otherwise, we proceed to the next generation of genetic algorithms. Simulated annealing, tabu search, ant colony algorithms and the like illustrate evolutionary algorithms.

Let us see how alternative solutions (individuals) are developed in successive generations of the widely used genetic algorithms. Genetic algorithms are characterized by a biological representation of the domain of solutions and a fitness function to search this domain for some optimal solutions (individuals). We start with a population of a specified number of candidate solutions to be called chromosomes. Each such candidate should possess some desirable property represented by a code, usually taken as binary, called a gene, so that a chromosome is really like a string of genes. Genes are properties by which individuals (solutions or chromosomes) in the offspring generation can be produced to retain desirable properties of the parent population individuals. Biological operators, namely cross-over, mutation and selection, are used to produce offspring chromosomes. A fitness function is defined for each solution in the current generation to determine if it will be selected as a parent for generating better off-spring (solutions) in the next generation. In fact, the probability of selection depends directly on the fitness score. The procedure is repeated till we come to a stage where new off-spring are generated. The algorithm terminates here.

There can be no unique choice for the fitness function for a given problem. This problem-specific function, computable conveniently for each chromosome (solution), is to indicate how far the solution is from the final desired solution. In order to provide a quantitative measure, it can be possibly taken as the Euclidean or the Manhattan distance in a numerical optimization problem. (However, we cannot expect to know the final solution a priori, and we can at best think of the maximum/minimum attainable value of the objective function.) In the classroom scheduling problem, to minimize class conflicts for most students, the fitness function for any solution (any allocation of rooms to classes/groups of students) can be taken as the inverse of the number of class conflicts. In a simple optimization problem, it could even be the number of 1's in the solution (with the appropriate coding adopted to interpret '1'). In any case, the fitness function should not yield a zero score, nor should it monotonically increase with more and more improved solutions, since in such a case it may reach its highest admissible score ahead of the desired solution. The fitness function should be able to intuitively generate better solutions.

Cross-over plays a vital role in genetic algorithms and traditional cross-over operators select only two parents at a time and produce one or two off-springs which, unfortunately, do not inherit enough information from their parents. This has led to the extension of traditional cross-over operators to multi-parent cross-over operators that improve the quality of solutions to complex combinatorial and numerical optimization problems. Although multi-parent cross-over decisions take genetic algorithms away from biological evolution, computer simulation can easily adopt this operator to tackle complexities in optimization. This has been tried out to solve the quadratic assignment problem, introduced by Koopmans and Beckman (1957) as a mathematical model related to economic activities. It has found many real-life applications, such as typewriter keyboard and control panel design, placement of electronic components on a mother board and hospital planning and scheduling problems. Ahmed et al. (2015)

have successfully applied the sequential multi-parent cross-over operator to solve the quadratic assignment problem. Eiben and Schoenauer (2002) provide a good account of multi-parent recombination in evolutionary computing.

An inherent weakness of genetic algorithms is that the algorithm has a chance of getting concentrated around local optima, without looking at points in the domain which are far away from the local optimum but close to a global optimum. If a local optimum of sufficiently high quality is selected, it will continue to remain present in all successive generations and its solution quality will ensure that it pulls individuals towards itself in successive generations. This led Ghosh (2012) to propose two diversification mechanisms based on the concept of a finite lifespan of an alternative, after which an alternative, even of high fitness, will be dropped and replaced by a new alternative to avoid getting stuck at a local optimum and to improve the search for the global optimum. A poor quality solution will, in any case, be dropped out in the next generation through the 'selection' operation.

In this context, diversity is an important concept. Population management strategies have been investigated to ensure adequate diversity among the offsprings in any generation as well as in the initial population, by considering measure, like the Minkowski distance among the individuals in a generation. Sorensen and Sevaux (2006) discuss the idea of population management.

Xiao et al. (2002) offered some multi-objective evolutionary algorithms for site search in spatial problem analysis which extend across multiple scales, knowledge domains and political perspectives, besides involving multiple and often conflicting objectives. The general goal of a site-search problem is to find a set of contiguous places, like grid cells or polygons, to locate, say, the construction site for a residential complex to meet the requirements of minimizing total cost and also maximizing proximity to some existing facility like a market, school or sports complex. The approach suggested by Brookes (2001) starts with a seed cell which is grown into a region under the control of a region-growing algorithm, in which a set of parameters, such as size, location, number of aims and orientation, guides the growth process. Xiao et al. use an undirected graph to represent a feasible solution and employ a set of operations such as mutation and cross-over to manipulate the shape and location of sites during the search for possible solutions.

11.9. Rules or Procedures as Alternatives

In the context of statistical decision theory as well as in several other decision-making situations, alternatives are different rules or procedures, like those involved in estimating an unknown population parameter, allocating the total sample over the different strata in stratified random sampling, testing some statistical hypothesis, selecting a subset of predictor variables in regression analysis, selecting a subset from a set of models to represent special features of an observed data set, selecting a subset of populations with the best value(s) of some parameter(s) or the like. In most of these situations, alternatives are not initially given and have to be worked out. We may be required to find feasible alternatives which satisfy some constraints or admissible alternatives which are not dominated by other alternatives or optimal alternatives when an optimality criterion is specified.

Ranking and subset selection procedures have interesting applications, both in terms of selecting on the basis of sample data a subset of a given set of populations (with partially specified distributions of some random variable(s) of interest) which have some relative positions in respect of values of some parameter(s), as well as in the context of selecting a subset of data for the purpose of a specified analysis out of a generally large data set. The constraint is often in terms of the size of the subset to be selected not to exceed a given number. The goal is not to maximize or minimize an objective function but to ensure that the subset to be selected includes at least a specified number of elements from the initial set of populations occupying the highest ranks according to values of some unknown parameter(s). The information available is in terms of sample observations arising from the populations in the initial set. Dealing with estimates of parameters (which are random and have their own sampling distributions), the goal cannot be achieved with certainty, and we can only speak of the probability of any decision rule to satisfy the goal. The goal is to ensure that the subset selected through a decision rule has a minimum probability of satisfying the goal.

Such procedures apply even to problems where we have to choose the best or the few best equipment or processes in terms of their performance based on some simulation experiments carried out on the alternative equipment or processes.

Among those who have made notable contributions to ranking and subset selection procedures, mention should be made of Barlow (1969), Gupta (1963), Gupta and Panchapakesan (1984, 1987) and Santner (1976), among others.

Let us consider a simplistic view of this problem, as considered by Hsu and Panchapakesan (2019). Let $\Pi_1, \Pi_2, ..., \Pi_k$ represent $k \geq 2$ normal populations with unknown means $\mu_1, \mu_2, ..., \mu_k$ and a common known variance. Let $\mu_{(k)} \geq, ..., \mu_{(2)}, \mu_{(1)}$ denote the ordered means and let $\Pi_{(i)}$ denote the population associated with $\mu_{(i)}$, $i=1, 2, ..., k$. We assume no prior knowledge about the correct pairing or correspondence between the ordered and the unordered means. Let $\eth \geq 0$ be a given constant such that $S(\eth)$ denotes the set of means in which the smallest difference between any two ordered means is at least $\eth$. Our goal is to select a non-empty subset of the k populations whose size is at most m ($1<=m<=k-t$) so that at least one of the populations associated with t ($1<=t<=k-1$) largest means (called the t best populations) is included in the selected subset with a minimum guaranteed probability P^* whenever the means belong to the set $S(\eth)$ as defined earlier. Any rule R makes a correct selection of s subset of size at most m that contains one of the t best populations with a probability $P_\mu(CS|R)$ for any configuration of the mean vector μ. Any valid rule (validity corresponding to something like feasibility) is required to satisfy the criterion: $P_\mu(CS|R) \geq P^*$ whenever μ belongs to $S(\eth)$.

The region S is referred to as the preference zone. Hsu and Panchapakesan (2019) proposed the following rule based on independent samples of size n taken from each of the k populations. Let Y_I denote the sample mean from the population Π_I and let $Y_{(k)} \geq Y_{(k-1)} \geq, ..., \geq Y_{(1)}$ denote the ordered sample mean. The proposed rule states: Select Π_I if and only if $(Y_I - Y_{(k-m)})/(Y_{(k)} - Y_{(k-m)}) > c$ where $1 > c < 0$ is to be chosen so that the probability of correct solution as indicated earlier satisfies the given requirement. This rule can be written equivalently as: Select Π_i if and only if $Y_I > (1-c) Y_{(k-m)} + c Y_{(k)}$.

Obviously, this rule will always include the population corresponding to $Y_{(k)}$.

Santner (1976) had considered the problem with $t=1$ earlier.

Rules corresponding to non-normal populations, populations characterized by both means and variances, as well as for discrete distributions, have been suggested by various authors.

11.10. Alternatives for Organizational Decisions

Human organizations are complex systems working with people with diverse perceptions, preferences and performance capabilities in environments which change quite often and offer opportunities, on the one hand, and threats, on the other, guided by policies internally developed or inherited from some source or imposed by some externalities, to achieve goals and objectives which are not always unambiguous or clearly stated. Making and implementing decisions pertaining to different activities carried out by the organization is one of the principal tasks of management (in a generic sense). Speaking of decision-making, the first hurdle that an organization may have to face is to identify or/and develop suitable alternatives which are adequate for the purpose of yielding a reasonable choice that can be implemented and can lead to achievement of the goals and objectives, at least to some desired extent. Directly linked with the exercise of identifying or developing alternatives is the one associated with identification or development of criteria which would enable differentiation of one alternative from a second and lead to a choice among the alternatives.

Alternatives relating to policies to be adopted, especially in areas where quantification is not easily done, are quite often not so obvious and, at the same time, may have a long-term impact on organizational performance. Let us consider a few such areas that exist in almost all types of organizations.

Recruitment of employees (including selection and absorption into jobs) is a primary task, and we can immediately think of two alternative policies here, namely direct recruitment or recruitment through an outside agency, with possibly a mixture as the third alternative. Within each of these alternatives are embedded several sub-alternatives. For example, if we decide to recruit directly by ourselves, how do we invite and select candidates and places? Selected candidates for different jobs matching their capabilities are decision problems which throw up many possible alternatives. Depending on the time available and the cost to be incurred, there could be different options for inviting applications or nominations through the news, media or through posters on selected sites or through contacts with employment exchanges or through recommendations from acquaintances and well-wishers, etc. Going further, if we decide to hold a written selection test for each category of candidates corresponding to a specified category of jobs, alternatives could relate to the duration of the test, nature and number of test items, manner of evaluating responses, etc.

Another important activity concerns training programmes for employees at different levels to enhance skills and augment knowledge in relevant areas. Here, alternatives that should be considered by the human resource development department would consist of combinations of the following level factors:

- **Choice of faculty:** External, internal, partly external and partly internal.
- **Duration:** One day, two days, two half-days, etc.
- **Days of the week:** Monday and Tuesday, Friday and Saturday, etc.
- **Location:** Workplace, central facility, outside office premises, etc.

Other factors and other levels for each factor may be thought of, for example, two hours in the evening on Monday to Friday.

Compensation policy choice is a big issue, and the choice has to be made among alternatives such as a fixed consolidated salary or a basic salary plus a performance-related bonus, cost-to-company taking into account expenses incurred on account of complimentary services provided, such as transport, tea and snacks and lunch, as well as training and orientation programmes or a basic pay plus admissible allowances and so on. Marketing decisions, including those concerning possible entry into the export market, cover a wide range of decisions relating to market creation and expansion and consolidation through various means and investment decisions to stay afloat and to grow and excel invite many interesting ideas to generate alternatives which may sound bizarre but are likely to yield substantial benefits.

In applying MCDM methods to arrive at some optimal policy regarding service of customers, location of distribution agents or recruitment of young professionals for the organization, it is often desirable to engage either a professional consultant or a team of internal experts or a blend of the two, to decide on the criteria for comparison of the alternatives, as well as their weights or relative importance measures, and the evaluation of each alternative against each criterion. Alternatives for the last two inputs can be (a) subjective, expressed in linguistic terms, like very good, good, fair, poor and very poor or very high, high, medium, low and very low and (b) quantitative, expressed in terms of scores, which can be normalized in some way. Thus, we have a host of alternatives which are not given a priori but have to be developed in the context of a given decision problem to be solved within the given resources.

11.11. Constraints in Real-life Decisions

In real-life problems, we may not be in a position to even identify the possible alternatives and visualize the constraints and thereafter may not have adequate information about the feasibility or otherwise of an alternative. In situations where we can start with any alternative and want to check its feasibility, lack of prior information may stand in the way of determining its feasibility. For this, we may have to undertake some activities at a cost and with a risk of collecting relevant information. Such efforts cannot be undertaken for more than a countably few alternatives and their feasibility will be determined only after some time. Let us take the example of deciding on the best way to reduce traffic congestion at a road junction that usually witnesses a huge volume of pedestrian and vehicular traffic. Alternatives that can emerge during brainstorming among engineers, traffic police, soil scientists, development planners and other concerned parties include the construction of an underpass to divert pedestrian traffic. To judge the feasibility of this suggested alternative from several considerations, such as expenditure, soil physics to allow digging and holding the roof and time during which traffic has to remain suspended wholly or partly, weighed against the benefits to accrue, is quite a complicated task and may imply some initial data collection. A second alternative to building a road overbridge at the junction may involve considerations not all identical with the ones associated with the underpass construction.

In the case of assigning jobs to some new recruits in an organization, possible alternatives are job-recruit combinations with the objective of maximizing the overall efficiency in operations of the group on the jobs assigned to them. Efficiency can be judged in terms of time to complete some tasks, accuracy in some tasks, total idle time, etc. Whether a particular job allocation is feasible or not, may call for an assessment of the personality make-up of the recruits and their levels of motivation to accept and discharge each of the jobs to be allocated among them. This again invites its own problems.

Straying into problems of social choice or administrative decisions to affect diverse interests of different segments of the population in a country, one critical decision problem faced by the national administration is the progress towards poverty alleviation. Once we get an estimate of the total population below the poverty line L, our task is to estimate the aggregate income gap of the poor, given by $\Sigma(L-y)$, where y is the income per capita in a household below the poverty line, which should be wiped out or at least reduced by either generating additional income and meeting this gap or redistributing the total income of the poor and non-poor (or only rich) people, imposing appropriate taxes on the latter. Each of these two broad alternatives has to be comprehended in terms of various alternatives at several different levels of hierarchy in terms of decisions and actions.

Redistribution to alleviate poverty goes beyond tax collection and has a lot to do with proper policies and plans to benefit the poor. Subsidies announced may again lower the economic activities of the beneficiaries. These constraints should be taken due care of.

A better alternative would possibly to enhance the rates of direct taxes payable by non-poor taxpayers to generate some surplus that may remove the poverty burden, at least to some extent. However, such an attempt may dampen the interest of entrepreneurs in investing in industry and trade and thereby affect the national economy adversely. Whichever way we think of generating possible alternatives, checking their feasibility (implementability in practice) would imply conditional practice of an alternative, assessment of its outcome and subsequent modification or even withdrawal of the alternative, as found necessary.

The problem of checking feasibility or otherwise in any complex optimization problem becomes quite problematic if the constraints are not in terms of explicit functions of decision variables. Evolutionary algorithms—including bio-inspired ones like genetic algorithms or bee-swarm algorithms—are often used to solve such problems. These algorithms usually deal with unconstrained optimization problems and have to be duly modified to deal with constraints. Move operators, such as selection, cross-over and mutation, are usually blind to the constraints.

11.12. Using Infeasible Solutions

In evolutionary algorithms for optimization of complex objective functions using probabilistic search mechanisms, it is not advisable to ignore infeasible solutions altogether. We can either accept them with reduced values of the chosen fitness function or turn the infeasible solutions into feasible ones.

Evolutionary algorithms for constrained optimization have been classified into the following five categories by Takahama and Sakai (2005) depending on how constraints are treated:

1. Constraints are used only to find whether a search point is feasible or not. Approaches in this category are called death penalty methods. Here, generating initial feasible points is difficult and computationally demanding when the feasible region is small.
2. Constraint violation as the sum of violations of all the constraints is combined with the objective function. An important difficulty in the penalty method belonging to this category concerns the choice

of an appropriate value for the penalty coefficient. To overcome this problem, a method wherein the penalty coefficient is adaptively controlled has been suggested.
3. Constraint violation and objective function are separately optimized in a lexicographic order, giving precedence to constraint violation. Venkataraman and Yen (2005) proposed a two-step optimization method, first optimizing constraint violation and then the objective function.
4. Individual constraints and objective functions are treated as independent objective functions and a multi-objective optimization approach is adopted. This is sometimes computationally more complex than the earlier methods.
5. Some of the above four methods are combined into a hybrid approach.

Powell and Skolnick (2007) proposed a method for deriving feasible from infeasible solutions, which was modified as the penalty-parameter-less method by Deb (2000). From the objective function and constraint function values, a fitness function is derived, such that (a) every feasible solution is better than any infeasible solution, (b) between two feasible solutions, the one with a better objective function value is better and (c) between two infeasible solutions, the one with a lesser constraint violation is better. Another method suggested by Angantyr et al. (2003) runs as follows:

1. If no feasible individual exists in the current population, the search should be directed towards the infeasible region.
2. If the majority of the individuals in the current population are feasible, the search should be directed toward the unconstrained optimum.
3. A feasible individual closer to the optimum is always better than a feasible individual if the number of feasible individuals is high.
4. An infeasible individual might be a better individual than a feasible individual if the number of feasible individuals is high.

In complex optimization problems involving search across a parent population of candidate solutions and their offsprings generated through mutations or other possible modifications, we come across three phases, namely (a) Phase 1—no feasible solution, (b) Phase II—at least one feasible solution and (c) Phase III—combined parent–offspring population has more feasible solutions than the size of the next generation parent population. Different constraint handling techniques perform differently during each of these three phases, as pointed out by Mallipeddi et al. (2015).

In the superiority of feasible solutions approach (Deb, 2000), infeasible solutions with low constraint violations are selected in Phase I. In Phase II, first all the feasible solutions are selected and then infeasible ones with low overall constraint violations are selected. Only feasible ones with the best values of the objective function are selected in Phase III.

Even after a sufficient number of feasible candidate solutions have been obtained, one would like to examine the infeasible ones to see if any of them can achieve a better value of the objective or 'fitness' function with a penalty for constraint violation. A self-adaptive penalty function method was proposed by Tesema and Yen (2006). Two types of penalties are added to each individual infeasible solution to identify the best infeasible individuals in the current population. The amount of the added penalties is controlled by the number of feasible solutions in the current combined population. In the case of only a few feasible individuals, a higher penalty is added to infeasible individuals with a higher number of constraint violations. Per contra, if there are several feasible individuals, then infeasible individuals with higher fitness values will be given smaller penalties added to their fitness values. The final fitness values based on which the population members are ranked are given by $F(X) = d(X) + p(X)$ where p stands for penalty and d stands for distance defined as:

$$d(X) = v(X) \quad \text{if } r_f = 0$$

$$= [f''(X)^2 + v(X)^2]^{1/2} \quad \text{otherwise}$$

Here, r_f is the fraction of feasible individuals in the current population and $v(X)$ is the overall constraint violation, $f''(X) = [f(X) - f_{\min}]/[f_{\max} - f_{\min}]$, the maximum and minimum values of the objective function f in the current combined population. The penalty value is taken as:

$$p(X) = (1-r_f) M(X) + r_f N(X) \text{ where}$$

$$M(X) = 0 \qquad \text{if } r_f = 0$$

$$= v(X) \qquad \text{otherwise}$$

$$\text{and } N(X) = 0 \qquad \text{if } X \text{ is a feasible individual}$$

$$= f''(X) \qquad \text{if } X \text{ is an infeasible individual.}$$

Thus, there is a chance for an individual with a lower overall constraint violation and higher fitness to be selected over a feasible individual with lower fitness, even in Phase III, when there are enough feasible solutions to form the parent population using only feasible solutions.

When active constraints are present, solving the problem becomes a tedious exercise and Takahama and Sakai (2006) proposed an € constraint handling method to obtain high quality solutions. The € level is updated until the generation counter G reaches the control generation T_c. After the generation counter exceeds T_c, € level is set at zero and solutions with no constraint violations are obtained. € levels are fixed as follows:

$$€(0) = v(X_r)$$

$$€(k) = €(0) [1 - G/T_c]^{cp} \; 0 < G < T_c$$

$$= 0 \; T_c \geq G$$

Where X_r is the top rth individual and $r = (0.05 \times \text{NP})$. The recommended ranges for T_c and cp are respectively $(0.1\, T_{max}, 0.8\, T_{max})$ and $(2, 10)$. In this approach, a solution is regarded as feasible if its overall constraint violation is lower than $€(G)$.

To work out a balance between the objective function and the overall constraint violation, a stochastic ranking method was introduced by

Runarsson and Yao (2000). A probability factor P_f is used to determine whether the objective function value or the constraint violation extent determines the rank of each individual. The principle can be summed up by the following:

If no constraint violation or rank $< P_f$, then the rank is based on the objective function value only. Otherwise, rank is based on constraint violation only. Thus, infeasible solutions with better objective function values have a chance of being selected in all three phases of evolution. Some authors argue against a constant value of P_f. For example, some have allowed it to decrease linearly from 0.475 in the initial generation to 0.025 in the final generation.

11.13. Figuring out States of Nature

Checking the feasibility of an alternative is sometimes an exercise linked with figuring out the constraints in terms of certain values or relations, which may not be known exactly or uniquely right now. The same problem arises with determining the states of nature and, hence, the pay-offs associated with an alternative or a strategy corresponding to the different states of nature. A simple example that effectively brings out this point is the classical product-mix problem, which maximizes the total profit from a basket of different product types. The total profit depends on the profit per unit of each product type and is to be computed by assigning values to these profit/unit figures, right now, much before products are turned out and marketed. One way to make a robust decision is to assume a set of such figures for each product type, reflecting different market reactions. To work out figures within each such set, one may examine the trends in these figures and make necessary adjustments. In the case of a new product, market intelligence has to be analysed to work out profit/unit figures. Going beyond simply arriving at several likely values of each ratio, one can attempt to assign chances or probabilities (which may reflect subjective degrees of belief) to the different values and thus work out a probability distribution which may be incorporated into a stochastic programming formulation of the problem. In situations where a lot of uncertainty exists about possible states of nature and the associated probabilities of realization, we can take recourse to experts and scenario-writing exercises. In fact, technological forecasting techniques may find interesting applications in this context.

11.14. Post-implementation Feasibility Check

There are situations in decision-making, especially in the context of socio-economic or political decisions, where the outcomes of different alternatives can be assessed only after the concerned decisions have been translated into actions. It may not be possible to check the feasibility or otherwise of a decision alternative right at the time of decision-making. Feasibility of an alternative can be established or negated only during implementation of the decision. Infeasibility may arise from the fact that some resources required to put the alternative into action—may be a safety measure or an emergency control device or the need for a handful of extremely skilled workers—were not duly considered at the time of identifying or generating the alternative. Similarly, the fact that implementation of a project alternative may face resistance from some segments of the population likely to be affected by the project or the fact that cost of implementation turns out to be prohibitively large or the fact that the alternative when completely implemented will yield benefits that will be overshadowed by corresponding benefits from some other alternatives, as can be revealed through a competent technological forecasting exercise, illustrate constraints that may render some initially chosen alternatives(s) eventually infeasible. The safeguard against such possibilities is to develop a comprehensive brainstorming or similar exercise to come up with possible alternatives. In fact, the feasibility of long-term investment strategies or portfolios should be better examined in the light of appropriate technological forecasts as well as decisions to make significant investments in production diversification or expansion plans. A technological forecast is not required to provide an accurate or near accurate prediction of future possibilities. However, it is always better to have a technological forecast as long as it offers some relevant information not available otherwise, and as long as the cost involved does not exceed the value of the information it provides.

CHAPTER 12

Generation of Criteria

12.1. Introduction

The development and use of some criterion or criteria for assessing and comparing the alternatives in relation to the objective(s) of the decision-making process, eventually leading to the choice of some alternative(s) as better than others, is of paramount importance. If the criterion or criteria generated fail to differentiate among the alternatives in terms of their ability to meet the objective(s) of decision-making, our purpose gets lost. Whether to use a single criterion or multiple criteria is to be decided from the point of view of the emerging decision being able or not to account for all possible differences among the alternatives when judged from different perspectives.

In some decision-making situations, we have formulated some goals or objectives that we would like to achieve by taking appropriate decisions. In such a case, criteria to facilitate a choice among the alternatives reflecting their distinct abilities to meet the defined goals and objectives have to be chosen keeping in mind the goals and objectives. There are other situations where the goals and/or objectives are defined only after some criteria are taken into consideration. Thus, in a decision to purchase a particular brand or grade of a product or equipment, we first visualize criteria such as acquisition cost, expected performance quality, guarantee norms, user-friendliness, ease of maintenance and resale value, before we specify our objective, such as maximizing user-friendliness and expected quality of performance subject to an upper limit for acquisition cost or price.

In both a choice problem and a general optimization problem, it is quite important to identify attributes or features associated or associated with the alternatives which can provide an accepted, though not necessarily unique, measure of the extent to which any alternative achieves or can achieve any of the objectives behind the decision problem. Apart from the need for multiple attributes even to take care of a single objective, situations arise where any attribute evades a direct or single value or level. Miller and Starr (1973) observe that out of the eight areas listed by Peter Drucker that require objectives to be specified by an organization, there are four which do not admit of obvious pay-off for any strategy or alternative. These are innovation, managerial performance and development, worker performance and attitude, besides public responsibility. Considering the objective of improving worker attitudes and satisfactory labour relations, we can think of several possible attributes, such as high turnover, work stoppages and strikes, poor performance and low morale. For any strategy to achieve any of these objectives, we can possibly have satisfactory measures of performance, or work stoppages and strikes, turnover rate and the like. However, employee morale and the state of labour relations usually defy any such convenient measures.

Summing it up, one may accept a criterion as a principle, guideline or requirement involved in making a choice—among alternatives or even among methods of evaluation of an alternative in terms of the associated pay-off or a method of ranking among the alternatives. Detailed specifications, including scoring systems (on numerical or semantic scales), may also be treated as criteria in some cases.

12.2. Criterion versus Objective Function

Phrases, such as 'measure of effectiveness', 'objective function', 'criteria' and the like, need not be strictly distinguished, one from the other. They have large overlapping connotations and, used with a bit of care, are not likely to stand in the way of comprehending a decision problem, from its formulation to resolution. In fact, criteria and effectiveness measures or objective functions have often been used interchangeably.

Strictly speaking, the value or level of an objective function or the measure of effectiveness of an alternative may vary from one state of nature to another. On the other hand, the value of a criterion is based on all the states of nature taken together. In decision-making under risk, the expected value of the objective function or the effectiveness measure using state probabilities can be taken as the value of a criterion. If these probabilities are unknown, one may consider some summary like the maximum (minimum) value of the objective function (effectiveness measure) may serve the purpose of being a criterion. Thus, a criterion is defined over the space of alternatives, while the objective function is defined over the (Alternative X state) space.

In decision-making under risk, the criterion could be some property of the probability distribution of objective function values, like the standard deviation or the coefficient of variation or the probability of exceeding a specified value. Incidentally, a measure of effectiveness may not involve all properties or consequences of an alternative, for example, properties which remain the same across alternatives.

Some decision theorists differentiate between criteria and objective functions, even when dealing with decisions under certainty. To carry forward the distinction, it has been argued that different criteria highlight different perspectives in looking at goals and objectives and in judging alternatives in respect of their merits and limitations. It is possible and also relevant that different stakeholders in the decision problem represent different perspectives. On the other hand, some decision problems may justify consideration of several objective functions while concentrating on one perspective only. This leads to MCDM being an exercise distinct from multi-objective optimization. However, the scope of multi-objective optimization incorporating different perspectives cannot be ruled out.

As an illustration from the national development scenario, one of the broad goals for preparing the national budget, particularly focusing on allocations for different state projects, could be 'poverty alleviation'. Alternatives could vary all the way from the disbursement of allowances to the poor, through enhanced allocation of funds for self-employment schemes, to the reservation of some proportion of jobs in public and private enterprises for the poor or economically backward people. The first perspective could be to reduce the head count ratio of poor people; the second could be to increase the rate of employment, and the third could be an enhancement of public services provided free to poor people. It must be remembered that to assess any alternative in relation to others using some criteria, we need to compile information to enable us to compute the criteria values for each alternative. It is also to be noted that different criteria could be interrelated and need not be mutually exclusive. However, different objective functions can also reveal dependencies among them.

One differentiation between objective function and criteria has been generally accepted, in which a criterion is a principle that is adopted by a decision-maker to make a choice among the alternatives, based on the value of some criterion variable (since it varies from alternative to alternative). A criterion variable can be looked upon as derived from the objective function(s) considered against the goals and objectives. In this sense, we speak of the minimax criterion, which can be applied to a criterion variable like pay-off or regret or risk, as distinct from the Bayes criterion based on the expected risk (using a prior) maximum expected utility criterion in general choice problems, based on some measure of utility.

12.3. Alternative–Criterion Interaction

Once the goals/objectives have been more or less concretely formulated and the criteria have been identified, in an interchangeable order, we have to seek information about various alternatives for their properties or attributes that can be assessed against each of these criteria. In fact, we have to identify alternatives which will not be rejected outright for not meeting any of the criteria. Thus, we have to recognize the interaction between criteria and alternatives. Looking at the simple LP algorithm involved in finding the optimal solution to a wide variety of decision problems, we start with a simple and easily identified feasible solution and proceed to find the next better solution, guided by an evaluation criterion. In general, optimization problems, especially the more complex problems that are treated in terms of evolutionary algorithms, alternatives are generated during the search, keeping in mind the criterion like fitness of an alternative defined suitably. In situations where we deal with a hierarchy of criteria, from the one with the least importance to the one with the highest, one may seek alternatives that first meet the criteria at the lowest level and gradually go upwards to identify alternatives which satisfy higher level criteria. Dynamic interaction between criteria and alternatives underlies several MCDM methods.

It is rather common to find situations and procedures where the alternatives are identified and chosen for consideration based on the value of some criterion variable or the corresponding value(s) of some objective function(s). This applies to both decisions regarding concrete entities, like parts to be chosen or systems to be developed to achieve some stated objective(s) as well as to decision-making with abstract entities as are often involved in, say, statistical decision theory.

When a criterion is a principle, like minimax regret or maximum expected utility, any outcome or pay-off variable and, in that way, corresponding objective function can be judged by such a criterion to enable a choice among the decision alternatives which are not circumscribed by the criterion in any manner. However, a criterion in terms of a requirement for some property or aspect of an alternative, like cost, time, user-friendliness or reliability, may indirectly work as a constraint and delimit the choice of feasible alternatives to be assessed.

12.4. Criterion versus Rule for Choice

In relatively simple decision-making situations, a criterion directly leads to the choice of an optimal or a reasonably good (satisficing) solution. For example, in a decision-making under certainty problem represented by a decision matrix, maximum (minimum) pay-off is the criterion that directly identifies the 'best' alternative. One can go from pay-off to 'regret' in decision-making under uncertainty as the objective function and use the minimax regret criterion to directly identify the 'best' alternative. We have referred to several such criteria that directly yield the best alternative. The term 'best' has an obvious connotation of being the maximum or the minimum.

On the other hand, there exist many different decision problems where we have to adopt some 'optimality principle' and use implicitly or explicitly some choice functions on the values of the criterion (or criteria, as in MCDM), apply some rules and involve—if necessary—some computation to find out (and not simply identify) the optimal alternative. Right here comes another feature of a criterion not shared by an objective function. In social choice theory or in group decision-making, involving multiple agents or decision-makers, the criterion for comparing alternatives would require pairwise comparison of the objective function values (which could be just the pay-offs or some qualitative assessments) that reveal the preferences of the decision-makers. The result could be a preference profile for each agent, and this could be considered as the criterion. We have as many criterion values as the number of decision-makers. Consequently, we need some method or rules to aggregate these preference profiles to come up with some yardstick for comparison among the alternatives. And we have a plethora of rules for this aggregation task.

Optimality principle and the use of choice functions runs through the entire gamut of decision theory. There are several versions of optimality like Pareto optimality or Nash equilibrium, umpteen choices of the choice function—many of them binary, quite a few properties like dominance or admissibility, many rules for processing of criteria and for choosing the optimal alternative(s) and the consequence is the opening up of a vast field of research.

12.5. Characteristics of a Criterion

Let us attempt a characterization of a criterion in DMP.

A criterion must take into explicit account the objective or even the multiple objectives behind the decision.

A criterion should duly reflect the attitude of the decision in converting direct monetary or other material consequences or 'pay-offs' to their 'utility equivalents' as well as in avoiding or accepting risks. Different decision-makers preferring different forms of utility functions work in terms of different criteria and may end up with different decisions to resolve the same decision problem.

It should be based on some perspective of the decision-maker in solving the decision problem, like a short-term versus a long-term resolution, a resolution reflecting only the decision-maker's concerns and ignoring those of others interested in the decision versus one that duly incorporates concerns of all stakeholders, a resolution based primarily on commercial considerations versus one that also takes into account social or environmental issues, etc. A narrow perspective prompts a simple criterion, while a broader one calls for either several different criteria or a somewhat involved 'composite' criterion.

A criterion should admit determination for each alternative under consideration. Direct determination may not be needed in some problems, but determinacy is important.

It should be sensitive to the decision-making environment, situation or externalities likely to impact the decision-making process. Whenever multiple states of nature are anticipated by the decision-maker, the value or level of the criterion should change from one state to another. It may be desirable to assign some properly assumed prior probabilities to the states and the corresponding criterion values or levels. Finally, we have a probability distribution of criterion values or levels within the decision-making framework. It is quite pertinent to introduce a continuous distribution in appropriate cases.

A criterion should relate each of the alternatives to the objective(s), indicating the extent to which any alternative achieves the objective(s).

A criterion should be able to bring out differences among the alternatives in terms of their ability to satisfy the objective(s) of the decision-making process. If no such differences are revealed, leaving the decision-maker confused about which alternative(s) to choose, the reasons could point to an inadequate choice of the alternatives or a choice that does not align the alternatives with the objective(s) or an improper choice of the criterion.

Some typical decision criteria, especially in the context of business decision-making, are as follows:

- Ease of implementation—within the given environment
- Cost, taking into account different components, and across categories, for example, opportunity costs (which are sometimes invisible) and indirect costs
- Ease of modification, scalability and flexibility (during implementation of the decision)
- Levels of perceived risks
- Impact on employee morale, including acceptability and commitment
- Cost savings that can be convincingly accepted by all stakeholders
- Increase in sales and in market share, including exploration of new markets
- Return on investment, taking a wholesome view of 'return' not just restricted to monetary gains but stretched to accommodate non-monetary gains also
- Increase in customer satisfaction, with particular reference to customers who might have some problems with customer services
- Time required to implement a decision and to realize the outcome or impact thereof

Some of these criteria apply equally well in other decision-making situations also. To repeat again, the requirement of the criterion or criteria reflecting properly the goals and objectives on the one hand and taking cognizance of the alternatives or options that are to be evaluated or can be conveniently generated.

12.6. Aggregate as a Criterion

In many decision-making situations, a single perspective relating to the objective(s) and the alternatives will suffice. Thus, in most inventory problems, the quantity to be ordered or produced, along with reorder or intra-production run intervals, are the decision variables defining the alternatives and the objective is to maximize profit (net revenue earned) or to minimize loss (cost incurred) given demand behaviour and, if relevant, lead-time consideration, focusing on costs, for the sake of illustration, different types of costs do arise—some directly determinable, like the cost of purchase or production per unit and holding cost and some to be indirectly worked out in situation-specific ways, like the cost of shortage or the cost of excess. In any case, these costs are summable, and one can conveniently find out the total cost associated with a given alternative. If some cost component remains invariant of the alternative, it can be dropped and the total cost can be offered as the criterion.

Consider the problem of managing a service system where management has to decide on the number of customers and, that way, of servers. The lower this number, the higher the expected time an incoming customer has to wait for service, leading to possible reneging of customers and customers balking at other service systems. The higher this number, the greater the expected proportion of time a server will remain idle. The costs of lost customers due to long waiting time is situation-specific and only indirectly estimable, while the cost of idle time of a server can be more objectively estimated. The cost of engaging a number of servers is certainly known. In such a case, it may be suggested that the cost of servers be treated as one criterion while probability of a customer reneging or balking and the probability of a server remaining idle be taken as two other criteria. The two probabilities are not summable. However, one comes across attempts to reduce this decision problem to a single criterion problem with probabilities converted into costs (based on some experience and some assumptions) and consider the total cost associated with a given number of servers as the only criterion.

With opposite signs given to benefits and costs or to profits and losses, an aggregate of such financial consequences, like the net benefit or the net gain, may be an obvious choice as a criterion. In several situations, the different cost (gain) components may not be equally important and we may consider weighted aggregates as criteria. Of course, assignment of weights becomes a problem, introducing an element of subjectivity, unless determined endogenously in terms of data collected within the system.

Like aggregates, ratios of related consequences or pay-offs, with or without weights, can also be considered as criteria.

In situations involving more than one state of nature giving rise to more than one set of consequences for each alternative, we should take into account the expected values of the aggregates or ratios to form criteria.

12.7. Criteria in Group Decision-making

Collective decision-making by a group of stakeholders or agents or decision-makers, involving usually but not necessarily a leader, is amply illustrated by MCDM, in social choice problems and in organizational decision-making. In this context, it may be pointed out that social choice and organizational decision problems generally involve more than one criteria of evaluating the alternatives. Of course, MCDM methods can be used by a single decision-maker as well. As noted earlier, there could be significant and dynamic interactions between alternatives and the criteria.

In many contexts, such groups are called upon to take up and resolve decision problems on repeated occasions. On each occasion, all the members may not be equally satisfied with the decision ultimately reached and there could be conflicts among members on the way. Members also expect and derive some knowledge and skills to structure, analyse and solve decision problems as they go on.

When alternative methods for ranking or weighting other forms of analysis have been developed and are available to any group, they can think of some criteria for choosing one method in preference to others. Against this background, Rubin (1976) proposed six quality indicators for group decision-making to address both achievement and maintenance goals. These are efficiency, careful development and analysis of alternatives (options under consideration in the given decision problem), fairness, member satisfaction and morale, leadership effectiveness and growth over time. Systematic and comprehensive development of alternatives implies that the group must now view a problem from a scope too narrow to ensure a meaningful solution, nor too broad to ensure controllable actions. A set of distinct alternatives has to be identified at a level of abstraction that is adequate for the group.

The criterion of scope for conflict resolution means that the method (here, an alternative) must provide a way for each conflicting party to evaluate the costs and benefits of giving up some of what it has to secure what it wants from the other party. The fairness criterion—important in resource allocation decisions—may even involve stakeholders who may be affected by the implementation of a decision.

Some research workers emphasize the criterion of validity and generality, which may require a formal mathematical representation of the logic and reasoning behind a method and sparsity of assumptions required to ensure generalization. Validity of the outcome concerns the accuracy of prediction of a future state or situation. Thus, validity as a post-implementation criterion differs from the criteria to be followed during the decision-making process.

To compare alternative methods for group decision-making, wherever available, several criteria have been proposed, and we will briefly describe only a few of those.

1. **Leadership effectiveness:** To assess the extent to which a particular method enhances leadership effectiveness, assuming the role of a leader as a facilitator. A method is rated low if it is highly technical or does not involve much interaction, rendering it unnecessary, medium if it provides nothing more than a structure to facilitate group leadership, and high if it also provides other collaborative tools and the necessary control mechanisms to help the leader in pursuing the group's achievement and maintenance goals.
2. **Learning:** To find out the extent to which a given method enhances the capacity of members to make use of objective knowledge in successive decision-making situations. A medium rating implies that the method improves understanding with regard to cause–effect relation in a problem (but actions may not be clear). A high rating corresponds to a situation where both single-loop and double-loop learning (leading to action) are facilitated. A low rating implies that the method advances technical knowledge that has no bearing on the members' subjective values.

3. **Scope:** Not applicable or voting. A method is rated low on this count if it fails to propose a specific technique and does not involve problem analysis that enhances the scope of abstraction; the rating is medium if it provides a technique that creates boundaries that limit group thinking or if it does not provide a specific technique but involves problem analysis that serves as a feedback to broaden problem abstraction, and the rating is high if double-loop learning is explicitly addressed. It must be added here that a group of top executives would generally view a problem from a higher level of abstraction than would a group of operational managers, because they have a much wider choice of space from which to draw controllable alternative courses of action. Thus, the requirement of 'scope' could be relative to the level of decision-makers.
4. **Development of alternatives:** Not applicable in the case of voting where the alternatives are pre-specified. A low rating corresponds to the method's inability to provide a specific technique to identify alternatives, a medium one to a free-wheeling environment without group interaction or coming up with incremental alternatives only, and high if the free-wheeling environment incorporates group interactions with no requirement that the alternatives identified have to possess certain specified properties and a very high one if it is based on challenged assumptions and throws up alternatives systematically.
5. **Fairness—cardinal separation of alternatives:** Applicable to methods which involve aggregation of judgements of individual members. A method is evaluated according to its conformity with the impossibility problem intrinsic to ordinal group aggregation. An aggregation method using an ordinal scale of measurement is rated low and high if it uses an interval scale, a ratio scale or an absolute scale.
6. **Scientific and mathematical generality:** Applicable when the method involves analysis. The method is rated low if it does not involve any mathematics, medium if the mathematics used is not axiomatized or multidimensional concepts have been used which can be axiomatized differently by different researchers leading to diverse results, high if mathematics used is axiomatized with a

more or less unified conceptualization and very high if its results are axiomatized and can be generalized without needing any new assumptions by way of a natural extension.

Among other criteria are structure, breadth and depth of analysis, psychophysical applicability, usefulness in conflict resolution and the like.

Not all these criteria for judging the quality of a decision-making method (as distinct from the ability of an alternative to meet some criteria or even from the quality of the criteria themselves in reflecting achievement and maintenance of the goals and objectives behind the decision-making exercise) apply in all cases, and the rating schemes indicated in the foregoing paragraphs need not be strictly applicable. These may need modifications to suit the requirements of a problem, as judged by those who posed the problem, rather than those who analysed it and attempted a solution.

12.8. Points to Ponder

We have tried to differentiate among alternatives or options available to the decision-maker (single individual or group), outcome or pay-off associated with an alternative in a given state of nature (whenever a unique state is certainly known, cannot be taken for granted) and an objective function for each alternative based on the outcome variable(s) and a criterion. Such a differentiation may appear to some as a redundant exercise in semantic differentiation. And such an observation is not totally uncalled for. We may come across decision problems where the pay-off is itself the objective function as well as the criterion for a choice. Defending the differentiation attempted here, one may put forth the interpretation of a criterion as a principle that may be invoked in a choice problem or even in a general optimization problem to decide whether we go by a 'strict optimizing' approach involving a complete search of the option space directly or otherwise or 'a satisficing' approach restricting the exercise to some 'seed' and playing with it for possible improvement. A somewhat similar issue arises when a problem like a competitive or co-operative game admits different equilibrium solutions with different alternatives and different pay-off pairs, each with a justification for adoption, may be under different assumptions in some cases where it may be difficult to accept one set of assumptions as more realistic than another.

All this is a pointer to the 'fact' that any decision problem involves in its resolution another decision problem. We are possibly in a 'back-to-square one' situation.

CHAPTER 13

Paired Comparisons, Ranking and Scaling

13.1. Introduction

Decision-making does (as it should) reflect the preferences (and indifferences) of the decision-makers or agents—explicitly or otherwise—based on available information and their individual perceptions. Decision-making tools—mostly quantitative—are meant to provide logical support in order to arrive at defensible decisions. These preferences may be revealed through pairwise comparisons, through direct ranking of the possible alternatives, options, their outcomes, the criteria guiding such preferences or the objective functions (if more than one is involved). Ranking of alternatives done directly or derived from pairwise comparisons can identify the best or the most preferred alternative straightaway. Sometimes, multiple criteria are compared pairwise or ranked to find out their weights or measures of relative importance. When a multiplicity of voters or agents is involved, aggregation of results of paired comparisons and of ranks invites non-uniqueness in methods. Building a consensus ranking has been quite a challenging problem computationally.

While paired comparisons or rankings are quite often used, they do not reveal the magnitude of difference between alternatives within pairs presented severally or among all the successive rank holders. To take account of such differences, one can think of developing scale values, say on a continuum for the inherent magnitude of some property. To find out such scale values as weights for different criteria, say, one can elicit responses from the decision-makers in categories, such as very important, important, moderately important, slightly important and not important, and then derive scale values from the observed frequencies of responses in the different categories. We will get numerical values (including negative ones, which can be easily converted to positive integers by changes in origin and scale) to indicate the relative importance of each criterion as the proportion of responses in one particular category, like 'very important', or in a few consecutive categories, like 'very important' or 'important'. We can also present pairs of criteria to each agent and eventually find out the proportion of agents who prefer one criterion I over the second j. From these proportions, we can work out scale values for the criteria which can be accepted as weights.

Scaling of alternatives and/or of their outcomes or pay-offs becomes a necessity to make them comparable. For example, investment amounts, the number of machines and men, export earnings from various countries, etc., may not be comparable among themselves because of differences in units of measurement or, may be, in the mean values or in dispersions. In such cases, we need to scale the alternatives and their outcomes to establish comparability.

The aim of this chapter is to briefly explain the roles of paired comparisons, ranking and scaling in the context of decision-making. Thurstone's method of paired comparisons and the development of product scales have been discussed. Problems of aggregation of results of pairwise comparisons and of ranking in the case of multiple voters have been taken up. Building a consensus ranking obviously has a place. The difficulty posed by rank reversal has been hinted at. Methods of scaling with special reference to Likert scaling have been touched upon.

13.2. Paired Comparison

Pairwise comparisons among several entities (alternatives, outcomes, criteria, objective functions, etc.) may lead to the choice of one or a few in preference to the others or to assigning ranks to such entities which can reflect their relative importance. Thus, in a multi-objective optimization problem, such a comparison may help us to prioritize the objective functions in terms of importance. Paired comparisons may arise when a pair of entities, say (A, B), is presented to a judge or voter who is required to indicate which one is preferred to the other, judged in terms of a given criterion. This can be repeated over several judges and even with several criteria. In the most general case, a pair is presented to each of several judges and each of them is required to prefer one over the other separately in respect of each criterion.

Paired comparisons have been studied over a long period of time by various scientific workers, including psychometricians, economists and statisticians, in different contexts. This fact is reflected in a bibliography on paired comparison methods as early as 1976 by Davidson and Farquahar (1976), in which they consider the contents of 350 articles bearing on the topic.

In the case of a single decision-maker or voter involved, the expected yield is a choice among the alternatives or a complete ranking of the alternatives, using a table with the alternatives listed along the rows as well as along the columns, with all diagonal cells blocked out. Once we compare an alternative in row k with the alternative in Column 1, the cell for Row 1 and Column k is blocked out. This ensures that each pair is considered once only. In each open cell, the alternative preferred is noted and the difference in importance as perceived is recorded as 0 for no difference, 1 for a slight difference, 2 for a moderate difference and 3 for a major difference. Finally, for each alternative preferred, the total difference score is obtained. The entities can now be ranked according to these scores.

Usually, results of paired comparisons made by a number of voters or judges are considered to develop a complete ranking, and this aggregation problem is being considered in the section that follows.

13.3. Aggregating Paired Comparison Results

Among the models used to aggregate results of paired comparisons among alternatives to obtain a complete ranking of the alternatives (or just to choose the most preferred or the most important one) are the Bradley–Terry model and the Thurstone model. Both these models have undergone several modifications and extensions and have laid the foundation stone for some fundamental results in choice theory and its applications.

Starting with alternatives, each of the possible $n(n-1)/2$ pairs is presented to each of m judges, sometimes on each of several occasions, and one element within a pair is preferred to the other. The relative frequency or the proportion of judges who prefer alternative i to alternative j is taken as p_{ij}, so that $1-p_{ij}$ is the proportion of judges preferring j to i. These proportions are converted to scores, their averages worked out for each alternative and then suitably normalized to yield scaled scores for the alternatives. These scores can be obviously taken to yield measures of relative importance or weights or to provide a ranking of the alternatives.

Three possible situations may arise in practice, in recognition of the observed variations in preferences of any judge or decision-maker over occasion. These are as follows:

- A separate pair is considered on each occasion. In particular, one pair of alternatives may be considered by each of the judges on one occasion only.
- The same pair is presented on several occasions to each of several judges or, in particular, to a single judge only.
- Each pair is presented to each judge on several occasions.

Mukerjee (1980) provides complete derivations of scale separations among the alternatives in each of these three cases, under appropriate assumptions. We consider the third situation here, where each pair is presented to each of m judges and the proportions p_{ij} are noted with $p_{ii}=0$ (sometimes taken as 0.5). Evidently, $p_{ji}=1-p_{ij}$.

In each model, we implicitly assume that each alternative i has a worth or utility λ_i, which may be constant or may vary randomly over judges or across occasions even for the same judge. Analysis involves the Bernoulli random variable:

$X_{ij} = 1$ if alternative i is preferred to alternative j
       $= 0$ if alternative j is preferred to alternative i with y
$P_{ij} = \text{Prob}\,[X_{ij}=1] = F(\lambda_I - \lambda_j)$

Here, F is the cumulative distribution function of a continuous distribution. This distribution has been assumed to be normal in the case of the Thurstone model, logistic for the Bradley–Terry models, gamma for the Stern model and the like. Aggregating data on X_{ij} over judges, we estimate the parameters in F usually by the method of maximum likelihood to get estimates of scale separations. Finally, scale values for different alternatives are obtained by introducing a constraint, like $\Sigma \lambda_I = 0$ or $\lambda_k = 0$ for some reference point k.

These utility values are referred to as scale values or scaled scores for the alternatives, as estimated from the data on p_{ij} = proportion of judges preferring alternative i to alternative j.

In the Bradley–Terry model (which really followed up the work of Zermelo [1929] working on a chess tournament where each player met each of the others), we assume, in some sense, a constant utility λ_I for alternative i and postulate that:

$P_{ij} = P_I/(P_I + P_j)$ with $P_I = \exp \lambda_I$ (Bradley–Terry condition)

In the Thurstone model (1927), the standard deviation of the difference is taken as the unit for the scaled scores. Good reviews of the literature on the subject are by Bradley (1976) and Luce (1977), as well as by Bargagliotti (2009).

Many modifications of these models have been developed to widen their applicability in real-life situations and to take care of certain assumptions in the simpler models which may not always be warranted by facts. For example, the distributions of scale separations are assumed to be independent, ties (within pairs) have been excluded and strong stochastic consistency of paired comparisons has been assumed. Methods have been worked out to account for deviations from these assumptions (in the case of aggregated data from paired comparison, we expect that if $p_{ij}>0.5$ and $p_{jk}>0.5$, then $p_{ik}>0.5$. In fact, this is the requirement for weak stochastic consistency. Moderate stochastic consistency would imply $p_{ik} \geq \min(p_{ij}, p_{jk})$, while strong consistency mandates $p_{ik} \geq \max(p_{ij}, p_{jk})$. These models are all characterized as unstructured models, while those which incorporate explanatory covariates are referred to as structured models with $\lambda_I = Y_I' \beta$ where Y is a vector of covariates and β is the vector of regression coefficients.

For a simple illustration of the principle behind Thurstone's method, suppose 25 judges or voters were asked to indicate their preferences for different criteria A, B, C and D, such as cost, out-reach effect, timeliness and impact for choosing the medium of advertisement for a new producer or service out of several possible media. Proportions p of judges preferring the row criterion over the column criterion are given in the following table with the convention that:

$$p_{AA} = p_{BB} = p_{CC} = p_{DD} = 0.5$$

	A	B	C	D
A	0.500	0.770	0.878	0.892
B	0.230	0.500	0.743	0.845
C	0.122	0.257	0.500	0.797
D	0.108	0.155	0.203	0.500

Assuming that the distribution of differences in preferences is normal with mean S like $S_B - S_C$ and standard deviation $\eth_{B-C}$, which we take as the unit of the scale, we get the matrix of scale separations like $S_A - S_B$ as follows:

	A	B	C	D
A	0	0.739	1.165	1.237
B	−0.739	0	0.653	1.015
C	−1.165	−0.653	0	0.831
D	−1.237	−1.015	−0.831	0
Column mean	−0.785	−0.232	0.247	0.771

With origin as the mean of scale values, the column means give us scale values for the four categories. With S_A as the origin, the scale values would become 0, 0.553, 1.032 and 1.556 respectively for the criteria types A, B, C and D, and it is apparent that criterion D is the most preferred criterion.

Davidson and Farquahar considered a stochastic model for paired comparison. They extended the Bradley–Terry model to incorporate the effect of ordering of the entities within a pair when they are presented to a judge. They use both the method of maximum likelihood and the method of weighted least squares for estimating the parameters.

13.4. Ranking of Units

In many research studies, we deal with ranks assigned to a set of n units or individuals by some experts or judges. These may be based on several criteria or features possessed by the units. In some applications of ranking, we may decide to choose the best or the few better than all the rest. The reverse could also be the case, for example, when the ranks are used to identify the poorest and the worst units, units which are poorer or worse than the remaining, so that these units may be removed from further consideration or be referred to some 'recovery treatment'. It is possible that ranks are first obtained in respect of each criterion or feature and then the average ranks are considered. All the units could be presented before an expert or judge to be ranked from 1 (the best) to n (the worst), avoiding ties. When the number of units to be ranked is somewhat large, it may be difficult for the judge to discriminate among all the units, and the judge could be indifferent between two or more units perceived to be very close to one another in respect of the criterion used. In such cases, ties may not be avoidable. It is also possible that the judge may not rank all the units, pleading inability to discriminate. In fact, in some research, the judge is required to take a random sample of units from the totality of units to be compared and to rank only the units selected in the sample. Thus, partial ranking and the presence of tied ranks are both genuine possibilities and methods have been developed to take care of both in preparing a complete rank ordering.

13.5. Aggregation of Ranking Data

The most common case of multiple rankings takes place when each of the entities is ranked by each of several judges, acting independently of one another, according to a single criterion, usually qualitative. It is also possible to think of a situation where a single judge ranks n alternatives according to each of several criteria. Even so, different methods of assessing the performance of some individuals or enterprises may be construed as different judges coming up with multiple rankings. It has been generally argued that in cases of different criteria or different methods getting involved in producing multiple rankings, these rankings should not be aggregated or combined, and no consensus ranking should be attempted. However, differences among the different rankings may be highlighted and explained, whenever possible.

Nonparametric procedures are frequently used to rank order alternatives. Often, information from several data sets must be aggregated to derive an overall ranking. When using nonparametric procedures, Simpson-like paradoxes can occur in which the conclusion drawn from the aggregate ranked data set seems contradictory to the conclusions drawn from the individual data sets. Extending previous results found in the literature for the Kruskal–Wallis test, this paper presents a strict condition that ranked data must satisfy in order to avoid this type of inconsistency when using nonparametric pairwise procedures or Bhapkar's V procedure to extract an overall ranking. Aggregating ranked data poses further difficulties because there are numerous ways to combine ranked data sets. An upper bound for the number of possible ways that two ranked data sets can be combined has also been provided.

Ranks assigned by different judges may be tested for their agreement by calculating the coefficient of concordance, and if this measure is high, we can justifiably average the ranks for each unit. However, these averages may not really represent the consensus or largely agreed ranking. Rankings by nature are peculiar data in the sense that the sample space of m objects can be only visualized in $a(m-1)$ dimensional hyperplane by a discrete structure that is called a permutation polytope. For example, the space considering three objects with all possible ties is a truncated hexagon and with four objects, a truncated octahedron, etc. The polytope is completely determined by the number of objects to be ranked. Data only add information on which rankings occur and with what frequency.

The aggregation of individual rankings of the same set of entities could imply a ranking obtained through ranks assigned to each entity as the arithmetic or geometric mean or the median of the ranks obtained by the entity in the individual rankings (sometimes called the base rankers). This aggregate ranking (also called the aggregate ranker) may not be looked upon as a consensus ranking. A consensus ranking is a ranking that has to be developed by minimizing its distance from each of the base rankers, with some agreed definition of the distance between the two rankings. The development of consensus ranking is discussed in Section 14.7.

13.6. Concordance in Multiple Rankings

As indicated earlier, there could be different methods for dealing with the feature variables in MCDM problems. Thus, in comparing the efficiencies of different DMUs using multiple inputs to turn out multiple outputs, the efficiency of a DMU has been studied through different versions of DEA. The following material attempts to illustrate such a situation.

Dimitrov (2014) does an interesting study of DEA analysis and human rankings of DMUs, using an online survey to elicit the DMU rankings of 399 individuals from India. He considers four data sets, namely (a) a hospital data set with 12 DMUs, two inputs and two outputs, (b) data relating to the United Kingdom Accounting Departments with 12 DMUs, three inputs and seven output variables, (c) airline data with 6 DMUs involving six inputs and five output variables and (d) power generation data from 6 DMUs with three inputs and one output variables.

Dimitrov makes use of the following several DEA methods:

- The super-efficient DEA approach by Anderson and Peterson
- The bounded adjusted measure of efficiency defined by W.W. Cooper, L.M. Seiford and K. Tone
- The canonical correlation analysis—DEA approach defined by Friedman and Sinuany-Stern
- The aggressive cross-efficiency model defined by Doyle and Green
- The benevolent cross-efficiency DEA model proposed by Doyle and Green
- Charnes, Cooper and Rhodes DEA model
- The additive DEA model proposed by Charnes, Cooper and Rhodes
- The benchmark DEA model proposed by Torgerson, Forsund and Kittelsen
- The principal component analysis DEA Model as proposed by Adler and Golany
- The symmetric weight assignment technique proposed by Dimitrov and Sutton (2013)

For the first data set with only two inputs and two outputs, it is expected that each participant in the survey selected from persons with collegiate education would be able to rank the 12 DMUs, may use tied ranks in some cases. The authors quote the ranks of the first 10 participants and these are found to have some tied ranks. It is worthwhile to examine the extent of agreement among these 10 respondents, and for this, we may calculate Kendall's coefficient of concordance W essentially based on ANOVA of the ranks between and within participants using the formula:

$$W = 12S/[n(n^2-1)k^2]$$

Here, S stands for the sum of squared deviations of rank totals of the DMUs from their mean, n is the number of DMUs, namely 12 in this case, and k is the number of participants. We have to replace each tied rank with the mid-rank and adjust the ranks of other DMUs accordingly.

Table 13.1 Ranks Assigned to 12 DMUs by 10 Participants

Participant	DMU											
	A	B	C	D	E	F	G	H	I	J	K	L
1	11	8	6	9	3	2	1	7	12	4	5	10
2	10	12	11	8	9	1	5	7	6	3	2	4
3	6	12	8	1	7	2	9	11	5	3	4	10
4	10	12	11	8	9	2	5	6	7	1	3	4
5	4	5	5	2	1	3	6	7	8	8	11	10
6	11	11	9	8	10	6	4	3	5	7	1	2
7	1	5	5	1	2	5	4	4	2	2	3	4
8	10	10	9	7	9	6	5	8	4	3	1	2
9	2	1	5	4	2	2	3	3	3	6	5	3
10	8	9	10	11	12	5	4	7	6	2	1	3
Totals	73	85	74	59	64	34	46	63	58	39	36	52

Table 13.1 gives the ranks assigned to the 12 DMUs by the first 10 participants as reported by the authors.

It is amply clear that the participants differ a lot in the ranks they assign to a particular DMU, primarily because of differences in the way they combine the output and input values to arrive at a measure of efficiency. In fact, the same DMU has received the lowest and also the highest rank in quite a few cases. Further, some of the participants cannot distinguish between two or more DMUs, so we have many tied ranks. In fact, no ties are observed in the ranks assigned by participants 1, 2, 3, 4 and 10. The formula for computing the coefficient W in the case of tied ranks is given by:

$$W = [12S' - 3k^2 n (n+1)^2] / [k^2 (n^3 - n) - kT]$$

Here, T is a correction factor for tied ranks given by $T = \Sigma(m_j^3 - m_j)$ summed over the g groups of ties, in which m_j is the number of tied ranks in each (j) of the g groups. S' is the sum of squares of total ranks received by the DMUs. In the above case, $S' = 41,733$, $T' = 1$. Hence, the value of W comes out as $W = 0.1853$ and the corresponding value of chi-square with 11 degrees of freedom is 19.883, which is highly significant, implying significant differences among the 12 DMUs in regard to their ranks as given by the 10 participants. This really indicates that ranks assigned by the different participants for any DMU should not be averaged.

13.7. Consensus Ranking

The question of defining and determining a consensus ranking does arise whenever we have multiple rankings of a group of entities (objects or subjects, or more generally, alternatives) generated in different ways by several criteria. Development of a consensus ranking is a complex issue, particularly in cases of weak ranking where ties can exist among units which a judge cannot distinguish on the basis of the properties or aspects initially accepted or when only some of all the units have to be ranked. The term 'consensus ranking', sometimes also known as 'median ranking', is a generic term that implies a ranking that summarizes a set of individual rankings in some defensible way. We can take recourse to subjective negotiations and compromises to arrive at an 'induced' consensus to identify at least the 'best' candidate interviewed. Otherwise, we can develop a consensus ranking logically from the given individual rankings without influencing or modifying any of them.

In such situations, there have been two broad approaches, namely (a) an ad hoc approach which can be divided into elimination (e.g., the American voting method, the pairwise majority rule, etc.) and non-elimination (e.g., Borda's method of marks, Condorcet's method, etc.), (b) distance-based approach in which we try to define a measure of the distance between the consensus ranking and the individual rankings.

In the first approach, we first consider the total rank of each unit to get the consensus ranking, as suggested by Borda. This was criticized by Condorcet (1785) who proposed the use of a majority rule on all possible pairwise comparisons among alternatives. To construct a support table, consider pairwise preferences and then assuming transitivity of preferences, work out the consensus ranking. The support table of

Table 13.2 Frequencies of Ranks

No. of Judges	Alternatives		
	A	B	C
12	2	1	3
5	1	2	3
7	3	2	1

Condorcet is very similar to the matrix of proportions considered by Thurstone (1927) to develop his 'product scales' based on the normality assumption. The two methods may not always yield the same consensus ranking, as illustrated in Table 13.2.

As expected, with 24 judges and only 3 alternatives, there will be differences among the 24 rankings. The total ranks given to the 3 alternatives are 50, 36 and 58 respectively, and the consensus suggested by Borda would be (BAC). We can now construct the support table by Condorcet as given in Table 13.3. to find that $B > A > C$, resulting in the same consensus ranking, namely (BAC).

However, as the number of alternatives increases, greater divergences among the individual rankings are more likely to arise, and the two methods may not yield the same consensus, as for the following case, indicated in Table 13.4.

In this case, Borda's method would lead to (ABCD) as the consensus, while Condorcet's method would yield (ACBD) as the consensus.

In the second approach, Kendall (1938) treated the problem as one of estimation and proposed ranking items according to the mean of

Table 13.3 Frequencies of Pairwise Preferences

	A	B	C
A	–	5	17
B	19	–	17
C	7	7	–

Table 13.4 Frequencies of Ranks

No. of Judges	Alternatives			
	A	B	C	D
4	1	3	2	4
2	2	4	1	3
5	1	2	3	4
1	2	3	1	4

the ranks obtained, a method more or less similar to that of Borda. Moreover, he suggested considering the Spearman rank correlation coefficient given two preference rank vectors R and R^* defined as:

$$1 - 6 \, \Sigma d_i^2/(n^3 - n)$$

Here, $d^2(R, R^*) = \Sigma_j (R_j - R_j^*)^2$ is the squared distance between rankings R and R^*.

Kendall also defined his own correlation coefficient by introducing ranking matrices, by associating to a rank vector of m objects a matrix of order $m \times m$ with elements a_{ij} as $a_{ij} = 1$ if unit i is preferred to unit j; $a_{ij} = 0$ if units i and j are tied, and $a_{ij} = -1$ if unit j is preferred to unit i.

Given another ranking R^* which can now be converted to a matrix $((b_{ij}))$, one can define the generalized correlation coefficient between R and R^* as:

$$\mathrm{Tau}(R, R^*) = \Sigma_i \, \Sigma_j \, a_{ij} \, b_{ij} / [(\Sigma_i \, \Sigma_j \, a_{ij}^2) \, (\Sigma_I \, \Sigma_j \, b_{ij}^2)] 1/2$$

It may be noted that in both the above correlation coefficients, ranks have been taken as scores, and either of the coefficients can be used as a measure of 'similarity' between two rankings.

Kemeny and Snell (1962) proposed and proved an axiomatic approach to finding a unique distance measure between two rankings for the purpose of developing a consensus ranking. They introduced the four axioms stated as follows and also proved the existence of a distance metric which satisfies all these axioms, known as the Kemeny distance, and its uniqueness. The following spell out the Kemeny–Snell axioms:

1. $d(R, R')$ satisfies the three standard properties of a metric for distance, namely (a) positivity $d(R, R') \geq 0$, (b) symmetry $d(R, R') = d(R, R')$ and (c) triangular inequality $d(r, R') \leq d(R, R'') + d(R', R'')$ for any three rankings R, R' and R'' with equality holding if and only if ranking R' is between R and R''.
2. Invariance $d(R, R') = d(R^*, R'^*)$ where R^* and R'^* result from R and R' respectively, by the same permutation of the alternatives.
3. Consistency in measurement if two rankings R and R' agree except for a set S of k elements, which is a segment of both, then $d(R, R')$ may be computed as if these k objects were the only objects being ranked.
4. The minimum positive distance is 1.

The Kemeny distance between the rankings R and R^* (converted into matrices as in Kendall's approach) is now defined as $d(R, R^*) = 1/2 \, \Sigma_I \, \Sigma_j \, |a_{ij} - b_{ij}|$. Kemeny and Snell then suggested the median ranking, which shows the best agreement in the ranking space indicated by the set of input rankings as the median ranking.

We now define a consensus ranking as given by a matrix S such that $\Sigma_i \, d(R_i, S)$ is a minimum, R_i being the ith individual run vector. To find S is an NP-hard problem. When we have n alternatives, there are $n!$ complete rankings. In case tied ranks arise, the analysis gets more complex as the number of possible rankings becomes approximately $1/2 \, (1/\ln 2)^{n+1} \, n!$

In fact, the complexity of the problem directly depends on the number of alternatives. Bogart (1973) generalized the Kemeny–Snell approach to consider both transitive and intransitive preferences. Cook and Shaipe (1976) proposed a branch-and-bound algorithm to determine the median algorithm, deriving a solution from adjacent pairwise optimal rankings. Emond and Mason (2002) pointed out that this method does not ensure that all solutions are found and, in some examples, yields only local optima. Cook et al. (2007) presented a branch-and-bound algorithm in the presence of partial rankings but did not allow for ties. Emond and Mason (2002) proposed a new rank correlation coefficient that is equivalent to the Kemeny–Snell distance metric. In the matrix representation of a ranking, they took $a_{ij}=1$ if alternative i is either ranked ahead or tied with alternative j and $a_{ij}=0$ only if $i=j$. Their correlation coefficient becomes Tau'$=\Sigma\Sigma a_{ij}\ b_{ij}/n\ (n-1)$, which is equivalent to Kendall's coefficient when ties are not allowed. A branch and bound algorithm was suggested by Emond and Mason (2002) based on this correlation coefficient to deal with the median ranking problem when the number of alternatives does not exceed 20 in a reasonable computing time. Two computationally more efficient algorithms have been proposed by Ambrodio et al. (2014) to find out S.

Another distance-minimizing consensus ranking is based on Spearman's foo-rule measure, in which the distance between a pair of rankings is the number of swaps needed (in a bubble sort algorithm) to make one ranking identical with the other. While the problem of determining the consensus to minimize the Kemeny–Snell (or Kendall's tau) distance is NP-hard, the problem with the Spearman footrule distance involves a polynomial time algorithm to solve.

Several other methods for developing a consensus ranking have been suggested over the years, including the MC approach, the boosting approach and the Bayesain approach. To take care of issues like the base rankers being not all complete, not being equally credible or important or when we suspect noises are affecting the ranking of the relevant entities. The MC approach requires one to construct a transition probability matrix $P=((p_{ij}))$ for a transition from entity i to entity j and to work out the stationary distribution (vector of ranks) $\prod$ such that $\prod P = \prod$ and to treat this stationary distribution as the consensus ranking. Several rules have been proposed to build up P.

Suppose the current state of the MC in entity i, then some of the rules state:

- **Rule MC 1:** The next state is generated uniformly from the set of all entities that are ranked higher than (or equal to) i by some base rankers.

- **Rule MC 2:** The next state is generated by first picking a base ranker at random from the set of such rankers and then picking entity j at random from that base ranking with a higher rank.
- **Rule MC 3:** A base ranker is chosen at random from all such rankings containing entity i and entity j is chosen at random from all entities ranked by the selected base ranker and the next state is set at j if j has a higher rank or stay at i otherwise.

In the Bayesian approach, we assume that base rankers are independent, and that the set of such rankers can be divided into two non-overlapping subsets, one containing the relevant entities and the other containing the noisy backgrounds. Further, a uniform distribution is assumed for the relative ranks of the background entities, while a power law distribution is assumed for the relative ranks of the relevant entities. Posterior probabilities, given the base rankers, are then used to develop the consensus ranking. For a detailed study, one can refer to Li et al. (2014).

13.8. Scaling of Alternatives

Situations in which the outcomes or pay-offs for various options or alternatives involve amounts of money or some other benefit like accommodation or transport facilities, extended to some beneficiaries, which may be expressed in units and may not be the same for all options, are not infrequent in decision-making. Even when the units are the same, the amounts could vary widely over the states of nature for one alternative, while these could be more or less concentrated for another or when the mean values across states of nature are widely different, we need to establish comparability of the alternatives by scaling the outcomes appropriately. Similar is the case with criteria. Further, if the outcomes of the alternatives or the criteria judged by their relevance or importance are put into several categories by each of several judges, we should introduce scaling.

In the first case, we can simply normalize the amounts or values or numbers y considering deviations from the mean and dividing them by the standard deviation to get what are usually called z-scores. To avoid negative z-scores, we can change the origin and the scale to make all the scale values positive. This is what is known as T-scores where the z-value is added to 50 and multiplied by 10. The mean and the standard deviation relate to amounts or values under different states of nature for each of the alternatives separately.

Consider the problem of determining numerical weights for several criteria (to evaluate alternatives) based on categorical response data when each criterion is presented to each of several judges or experts who are required to indicate their perceived importance of the criterion in one of several categories. We will get frequencies of responses in each of the response categories, such as not so important, moderately important, quite important, very important and critically important. We assume a continuous distribution for the underlying trait, namely perceived importance, to lie in a continuum $[a, b]$ and consider each category as an interval over this continuum with boundaries determined by equating cumulative relative frequencies to cumulative probabilities under the assumed distribution. Thus, with five categories, the intervals corresponding to these categories may be taken as $[a, x_1]$, $[x_1, x_2]$, $[x_2, x_3]$, $[x_3, x_4]$ and $[x_4, b]$ and the scaled scores for the five categories will be the mean values for the five truncated distributions, truncated on both sides by the boundaries. In the case of Likert scaling (1982) which is used a lot in social science research, the underlying distribution is assumed to be normal with 0 mean and unit standard deviation, and the scale values are the means of the truncated distributions which can be conveniently calculated in terms of the ordinates and tail areas under the standard normal distribution. The following example is self-explanatory.

Let A, B, C and D represent four criteria which are presented to each of 15 judges to rate their importance as indicated by five levels, namely (a) not so important, (b) moderately important, (c) quite important, (d) very important and (e) critically important and the frequencies of responses in different categories for each of the four criteria appear in the following table.

Criterion	1	2	3	4	5	Total
A	1	4	5	3	2	15
B	1	3	7	3	1	15
C	1	3	6	4	1	15
D	0	4	8	3	0	15
Total	3	14	26	13	4	60

Upper-class boundaries under the $N(0, 1)$ assumption for perceived importance become $-1.65, -0.58, 0.55, 1.48$ and infinity. Thus, scale values are $-2.06, -1.04, 0.01, 1.02$ and 1.90. If we take an arbitrary mean of 3 and an s.d. 1, these values stand at $0.94, 1.96, 3.01, 4.02$ and 3.90 respectively. If we are justified assuming a uniform distribution over $[0, 5]$ the scale values would become $0.25, 0.83, 2.50, 3.45$ and 4.67 respectively.

To find the weight for each criterion, we can take the mean of the scaled values with frequencies for the criterion or we can even take the mode of the scale values. These work out as follows (taking the second set of Likert scores):

Criterion	Mean score	Modal score
A	2.98	3.01
B	2.99	3.01
C	3.09	3.01
D	2.93	3.01

Thus, criterion c has the highest weight if we take the mean score, while going by the modal score, all the criteria have the same weight. (This is just for this particular example and is not generally true.) Results could differ from the uniform distribution assumption.

13.9. Rank Reversal

In decision-making,[1] rank reversal is a phenomenon that occurs when a decision-maker, in the process of selecting an alternative from a set of choices based on ranking of the alternatives according to some criterion, is confronted with some new alternative(s) which was (were) not considered when the decision-making process was initiated or when some such alternative(s) turns out to be irrelevant and should be dropped. The consequence of this phenomenon is a likely change in the rank ordering of alternative possible decisions. In fact, the consequence depends on the relationship between the new and the existing alternatives and, in the extreme case, can result in the alternative originally regarded as the best turning out to be the worst or just the reverse, with the entry of some new or exit of some existing alternatives. The issue of rank reversals lies at the heart of many debates on decision-making and MCDM,[2] in particular.

Unlike most other computational procedures, it is hard to tell if a particular decision-making method has derived the correct answer or not. Such methods analyse a set of alternatives described in terms of some criteria. They determine which alternative is the best one, or they provide relative weights of how the alternatives perform or just how the alternatives should be ranked when all the criteria are considered simultaneously. This is exactly where the challenge of decision-making exists. Often, it is hard, if not practically impossible, to determine whether a *correct* answer has been reached or not. With other computational methods, for instance, with a job scheduling method, one can examine a set of different answers and then categorize the answers according to some metric of performance (for instance, a project's completion time). But this may not be possible to do with the answers derived from most decision-making methods. After all, determining the *best* decision-making method leads to a decision-making paradox.[3]

[1] https://en.wikipedia.org/wiki/Decision-making
[2] https://en.wikipedia.org/wiki/Multiple-criteria_decision_analysis
[3] https://en.wikipedia.org/wiki/Decision-making_paradox

Thus, the following question emerges: How can one evaluate decision-making methods? This is a very difficult issue and may not be answered in a globally accepted manner.

The rank reversal phenomenon violates the invariance principle of utility theory that runs through the decision-making process. In this context, one of the fundamental axioms in the theory of choice, namely 'independence of irrelevant alternatives' has to be revisited. As stated first, it reads as: 'If an act is non-optimal for a decision problem under uncertainty, it cannot be made optimal by adding new acts to the problem.' While this statement may continue to be true, it may not be so if some existing acts (alternatives) are removed.

Several types of rank reversal arise in different situations. We came across the following:

- **Type I:** When identical or near-identical copies of non-optimal alternatives are introduced and we check if the best alternative changes or not.
- **Type II:** When we replace a non-optimal solution with a worse one and check if the initially best alternative changes or not.
- **Type III:** When we decompose the original problem into small problems with two alternatives at a time with the same criteria for preference and check if the ranking of the smaller problems conflicts with the ranking of the original multi-alternative problem.
- **Type IV:** When we try the above decomposition and check if the rankings of the smaller problems are in conflict with one another.
- **Type V:** When all the previous types are faced in a problem.

Unfortunately, some of the commonly used MCDM procedures, such as AHP, TOPSIS, ELECTRE and PROMETHE, suffer from consequences of rank reversal. However, certain procedures to overcome the consequences have also been attempted in some of the MCDM methods. Cascales and Lamata (2012) discuss the problem with TOPSIS and takes up the problem in general.

CHAPTER 14

Role of Information

14.1. Introduction

Any decision, or any recommendation that leads to or aids a decision, involves—explicitly or otherwise—processing some relevant information. This information may already exist and be conveniently accessed for the purpose; alternatively, information as needed may be collected as a part of the decision-making process, employing appropriate methods and tools. Existing information or even information collected for the purpose will have to be examined for relevance, first, and then for credibility as well as adequacy. Information, in this context, may well go beyond 'data' in the usual sense and may include processed data by way of summaries or reports or quantitative measures or images and the like. Information that is eventually available for decision analysis may be processed simply by the use of logic without any computation or may be through discussions with peers or experts. Besides this mental processing, we may use tools of analysis to process information and derive knowledge required in the decision-making process. Whenever necessary, we can use quantitative tools and take the help of relevant software to extract as much information from the available data as possible and as much knowledge from the available information as we can. The adequacy of data and/or information depends—at least to some extent—on resources that can be committed.

Information is required for some or all of the following purposes:

1. Developing alternatives or options, if these are not already given, and identification/enumeration of known alternatives.
2. Identifying constraints imposed on the alternatives by exogenous factors to find out which alternatives are feasible, as well as penalties to be paid (and incorporated into the outcome(s)) if some of the constraints are violated during implementation.
3. Selecting features possessed by each alternative which are relevant to the problem of choosing some of them. We may also need information about the relative importance of different features and functions thereof, whenever the situation so demands.
4. Determining or estimating or guessing the value or level of each feature or criterion for each of the alternatives, to indicate the extent to which an alternative satisfies (performs in respect of) the criterion.
5. Developing an appropriate way of aggregating the different features or criteria to come up with the final objective function(s) or the yardstick(s) of comparison.

In many cases, the decision-maker has access to some information about the decision-making situation and possibly some information about what was done in previous situations of a similar nature. The important question is: Do we need some more or additional information that can help us to make a better decision than what we can get in the absence of such additional information?

As against inadequate information being available initially to be augmented by an information-gathering exercise (with some cost consequences, explicitly or implicitly involved), situations may arise where the decision-maker may be confused by a deluge of accessible information. In the latter case, a part of the decision-making process is to sieve out a subset of the information available which contains most of the useful items needed for the present purpose. A lot of research has been motivated by incomplete information, inaccurate information, doubtful information and the like. Information may be available in different forms, some intuitionistic, some probabilistic, some interval-valued, some crisp and some others fuzzy, making it difficult to incorporate all of them into solving a problem.

In this context, it may be worthwhile to mention a possible conflict of interests, which itself poses an important decision-making problem and has to be resolved before proceeding further. Between the two options, namely (a) collecting and processing information before taking a decision with costs associated with both the tasks and (b) taking a decision with no information processing, either ignoring available information and not processing it or not taking the trouble of collecting information if no information is in sight. Which one is 'better'? It should be remembered that additional information will be available only after some time, and the situation may be changed by the time this information is acquired. Additional information is worthwhile only when it is likely to alter a decision taken in its absence. To answer this crucial question, we must assess the value of information in decision-making and weigh it against the cost of information gathering and processing.

14.2. Search for Information

Information is possibly the most important input in making decisions and even in forming opinions. Of course, the quality of decisions will depend not only on the quality of information accessed but also on the way information has been processed to provide desired inputs for the decision-making process. The quality of decisions, the quality of information and the quality of information-processing and information-using activities are concepts which defy straightforward operationalization. Notwithstanding this serious problem, these constructs have been gaining wider and wider implications. It is worthwhile to attempt reasonably good operational definitions and measures of these three entities, since the ultimate objective is to improve the quality of decisions and since, without appropriate measures, improvement cannot be ascertained.

Three basic quality parameters to comprehend the quality of information can be identified as accuracy, adequacy or completeness and contemporaneity or timeliness (besides, being up-to-date or current). Relevance to the need or purpose (as envisaged by the user) is taken for granted as a parameter. Even high quality information may be irrelevant to a particular purpose or need, and it should be the responsibility of the user to look out for and obtain relevant information. Accuracy is a requirement not to be stressed much, rather consistency or comparability across alternatives is important. Many information quality parameters have been suggested in different contexts, some of them depending on the sources of information tapped and the checks and balances applied before accepting information as is available. For example, if information about prices for several automobile brands is sought, one may go by the price lists in current usage along with discount regimes offered. However, information about fuel cost per km or carbon dioxide emissions per litre of fuel used may not be that easy to get. Whether to accept figures claimed by the manufacturers or declared by some accredited testing agency or even generally given out by current users of respective brands has to be decided. Information about constraints imposed by some custodian(s) of the public interest by way of some legislation may undergo changes over time and figures readily accessible may not be up-to-date. It is quite likely that partial information is accessed or processed and not the full information needed for logical analysis.

Deviating slightly from the somewhat regimented need for information in each of the recognized steps in decision-making, we can take the real-life case of a contractor willing to bid on a public work project. Also, suppose that this contractor is somewhat of a new entrant, particularly in relation to the type of projects they like to bid for currently. They need two basic information items to maximize the probability of winning the contract. The first is the estimated cost of executing the project, and the second is the lowest bids for similar projects submitted earlier. Together, these two information items will help the contractor to submit a bid in a sealed envelope, with no chance to alter the amount before bid offers from all participating contractors are opened to find the lowest bid. While the second information involves a single item, may be for several similar projects, the first requires estimates of procurement and deployment costs in respect of materials and utilities, machines and men and some contingent expenses.

A search for information is an important component in the decision-making process and has to be properly designed to provide the desired inputs to decision-making at a reasonable cost, within the time available for the purpose. In fact, the process of search may be considered by itself as a decision-making process with all its steps. There are agencies which are engaged in such search processes to provide information at a cost to decision-makers in need of information. Thus, search problems constitute a class of decision problems. Reconnaissance and scouting are familiar terms in the context of military intelligence gathering. Incidentally, a search for information and an exercise in data collection are not synonymous terms.

Search situations have been classified as qualitative versus quantitative and distributive versus collective. There are other dichotomies as well.

The cost of a search process that must be reckoned with in designing the process consists of two components, namely the cost of the search itself and the cost of errors contained in the information provided by the search for decision-making (consequent upon such errors leading to wrong decisions). These errors could be observational errors and errors involved in sampling. If resources available for search are limited, the larger the sample size to reduce errors due to sampling, the lesser the resources allocated to observing the sampled units and the greater the observational errors.

14.3. Value of Information

Taking a high-value or strategic decision may well justify a non-trivial piece of research to provide inputs into the decision-making process as well as to evaluate the ultimate consequences or outcomes. Too often, such decisions have to be taken in the face of uncertain situations and/or consequences. In fact, decision-making exercises are carried out in several distinct situations, namely: (a) Under certainty, when the consequence or outcome of any possible action is exactly known and the only problem is to find out which action results in the 'best' outcome, and the search may have to be taken up in a 'large' space of all possible and, in most cases, numerous actions. (b) Under uncertainty, where we have to recognize several (finitely or infinitely many) environmental conditions or 'states of nature' and each possible action has a distinct outcome for each such state of nature, giving rise to a decision matrix with rows as possible actions and columns as possible states of nature. Here, we require some optimality criterion to identify the best action. (c) Under risk, where the different states of nature are likely to be realized with known probabilities. The set of probabilities associated with the possible states of nature, given prior to deciding on any action, defines what may be called a prior distribution. It should be remembered that states of nature represent the set of values and/or relations that determine the outcome of any possible action.

In the foregoing discussion, we have considered decisions and actions as synonymous and the decisions are terminal. It is conceivable that a decision-maker takes the initial decision to collect some more information before taking a terminal decision. A similar differentiation is made in the context of stochastic programming (mentioned in Chapter 7) between the 'here and now' approach and the 'wait and see approach'. Against this backdrop, we need to discuss the 'value of information' and the associated measures of opportunity costs. To begin with, we differentiate between immediate and terminal decisions and consider both situations (b) and (c) as 'under uncertainty'. We realize that one has to pay for uncertainty and even reduce the cost of uncertainty through an immediate decision to gather additional information before reaching the terminal decision.

Let us define the expected cost of immediate terminal action as the expected cost of the 'best' terminal action under the given prior distribution. The cost of uncertainty is the irreducible loss due to action taken under uncertainty or the expected loss associated with the best decision for the given probability distribution. The difference between the expected cost of uncertainty and the cost of the best decision under certainty about the state of nature is taken as the value of perfect information. This would depend on the particular state of nature being true or realized. Averaged over the set of possible states, we get the expected value of perfect information (EVPI).

Given a very high EVPI, a decision-maker would tend to gather information about the true state of nature. But this implies some additional costs with two components, namely the cost of gathering information and the cost of processing the information gathered to make the terminal decision. Both these activities may proceed sequentially. Short of gathering a lot of information adequate to remove uncertainty about the true state of nature completely at a relatively large cost (which in some adverse cases may exceed the value of perfect information), one may think of gathering sample information using a proper sampling procedure to get some reasonable idea about the true state of nature. The cost of sampling will depend on the sample size as well as the way sample information is processed to yield the desired information about the true state of nature. The excess of the cost of uncertainty over the cost of an immediate decision to gather sample information and to use it for reaching the terminal decision is the gain due to sampling. Averaging over possible sample sizes, we can define ENGS. In fact, this ENGS may be examined to work out the optimum sample size.

It may be interesting to note how consideration of ENGS can yield 'good' solutions to decision problems which otherwise would involve some complex optimization. Looking back at the secretary selection problem, let us define EVSI in a slightly different manner.

If we do not interview any candidate and randomly select any of the n candidates, the selected candidate will have an expected rank (in the entire population of n candidates) given by $E(r)=(n+1)/2$. The regret for failing to select the best candidate, assumed to be linear in the difference between this expectation and 1 (rank of the candidate we wanted to select), stands at $c(n-1)/2$, where c is an assumed constant to convert the rank difference to regret. Once we decide to interview i candidates selected at random, the EVSI can be considered as the difference between the two regrets—with and without sampling—and this comes out as: $c\ [(n+1)/2-(n+1)/(i+1)]=c(n+1)\ (i-1)/(i+1)$. Thus, the expected net gain due to sampling ENGS comes out as:

$$E=c(n+1)\ (i-1)/(i+1)-k\cdot i$$

As expected, this quantity increases with n and depends on the cost ratio c/k. E is negative for $i=1$ since a sample of one candidate (who is to be selected) which has a non-zero cost adds no information over the situation where no candidate is interviewed and any one of the n candidates is selected. Values of ENGS for some selected sets of parameter values (n, k, c) are presented in the following table.

i	2	4	5	6	8	10	12	16
$n=10, k=c=1$	−0.17	−0.7	−1.3					
$n=10, c=2, k=1$	1.67	2.6	2.3	1.86				
$n=10, c=1, k=2$								
$n=20, c=2, k=1$	8.4	9.0	9.0	8.3	7.1			2.5
$n=20, c=k=1$								
$n=20, c=1, k=2$								

It is evident that, in some cases, ENGS turns out to be negative. However, whenever the cost of regret c exceeds the cost of interview, we get clear ideas about the behaviour of ENGS and can find out the optimum value of i.

Incidentally, treating i as a continuous variable for an approximate solution for the optimum, we find that the optimizing value of i is $[c\,(n+1)/k]^{1/2}-1]$, and it can be verified to corroborate the findings from direct computation of ENGS.

In case the cost of regret is more than proportional to the expected rank difference of the selected candidate (between no sampling and sampling) and involves squared difference, the expression for ENGS becomes:

$$\text{ENGS} = c\,[\{(n+1)/2\}\{(I-1)/(i+1)\}]2 \; k \cdot i$$

In this case, we require a larger number of candidates for the best ENGS, unless the cost of interview is substantially high. With $c=k=1$ and $n=10$, ENGS increases monotonically with i.

Some experts argue in favour of using a pre-posterior analysis, making use of the sample information to calculate posterior probabilities and working out the 'bet' possible terminal decision under the posterior probability distribution. This, of course, will need some assumptions and some additional computations.

A word of caution must be added here. Whatever we are branding as 'perfect information' is in terms of the quality of information or rather the ability of information to indicate the true state of nature (as will usually be realized later), and there could well be a gap between what such information can reveal and what transpires later. The qualifier 'perfect' should lead to the 'correct' decision.

For a detailed and simplified as well as exhaustively illustrated discussion on the subject, one may refer to Schlaifer (1959). What should be taken as a caution in all this exercise is the failure of even 'perfect' information (in the sense of information quality) to reveal the 'true' state of nature (as will usually be realized later) and, hence, to aid in taking the correct decision, in all cases.

14.4. Decisions in Fuzzy Environments

We have thus far assumed complete information about states of nature and hence about the outcomes of different alternatives and the extent to which they satisfy the objective(s) behind the decision-making process, as well as about the constraints to be met by the alternatives. This was referred to as 'decision-making under certainty'. In reality, information available about states of nature or about constraints or about both may be incomplete, giving rise to uncertainty about whether a given alternative is feasible or not and to what extent an alternative meets the objective(s). Uncertainty may be better represented by fuzziness in some cases, for example, where the actual state of knowledge about the constraints or the goal may be put in vague or linguistic terms.

By decision-making in a fuzzy environment, it means a process in which the goals (objectives and/or the constraints) are fuzzy in nature. However, the system under control that bears upon implementation of decisions reached in such an environment is not usually fuzzy: It could be deterministic or stochastic. 'The cost of A should not be substantially higher than a' is a fuzzy constraint, where a is a specified constant. Similarly, 'the solution in terms of a vector X should be close to X_0 (specified)' illustrates a fuzzy goal. Classical Dodge–Romig sampling inspection plans provide another interesting illustration of a fuzzy constraint. These plans require the 'customer's risk' or the probability of accepting a poor quality lot (with a fraction defective equal to or more than the lot tolerance proportion defective) to be approximately equal to 0.10. (This is in recognition of the fact that this probability is discrete.)

Such goals and constraints can be formulated as fuzzy sets in the space of alternatives. Fuzzy environments created through ambiguous information about constraint(s) and objective(s) may immediately attract what may be called 'fuzzy' decisions. 'Fuzzy' decisions pose problems of implementation, and thus, one would look for 'crisp' decisions even in fuzzy environments. It is important to remember that although goals and objectives are not much differentiated in the usual decision-making problem, we need a sharp distinction between 'objective function' and goal in the present context. The objective function provides the outcome value or utility of an alternative, while the goal is a statement involving such values or utilities along with the constraints. The objective functions could be crisp, but the goals statements may contain vagueness that can be represented by fuzzy sets. Similarly, the constraints are relations connecting alternatives (constituent decision variable values) and some coefficients and, hence, such relations could be fuzzy.

In an approach to fuzzy decision-making, goals and constraints can be defined by different universal sets. For example, fuzzy constraints can be defined on the set X and fuzzy goals on the set Y such that:

$$\mu_C: X-[0, 1] \text{ and } \mu_G-[0, 1]$$

A function f can then be defined as a mapping from the set of actions (alternatives) X to the set of outcomes Y such that a fuzzy goal G defined on set Y induces a corresponding fuzzy goal G' set X:

$$\mu_{G'}(x) = \mu_G(f(x))$$

A fuzzy decision D can then be defined as the choice that satisfies both the goals G and the constraints C. If this is taken as logical, we can model D with the intersection of the fuzzy sets G and C as $D = G\ C$.

In this case (which can be easily extended to any number of goals and constraints), the fuzzy set can be specified by the membership function:

$$\mu_D(x) = min\ [\mu_G(x), \mu_C(x)]$$

One should note that this formulation involving 'intersection' rules out any interdependence, interaction, or trade-offs between the constraints and the objectives under consideration. On the other hand, full compensation represented by the 'union' operation corresponding to the max operator may be inappropriate in many cases. Thus, some alternative mode of aggregation should be found to allow some positive compensation among the constraints and especially among the objectives. The relative importance of various constraints and of the several objectives, if present, can be taken into account by introducing weighting coefficients and taking the fuzzy decision as a convex combination of the weighted objectives and of the weighted constraints.

Once a fuzzy decision has been developed, it becomes necessary to choose the 'best' single crisp alternative from the fuzzy set. The alternative that attains the maximum membership grade of D is a natural choice. Sometimes, the mean or the median of the median of the membership function may lead to a good choice.

The example cited in Klir and Folger (1993) is quite interesting and is considered in the following. Suppose we have to choose one out of four job offers a, b, c and d with salary offers $f(a) = 30,000$, $f(b) = 25,000$, $f(c) = 20,000$ and $f(d) = 15,000$, such that the salary should be high, given the constraints that the job should be interesting and the driving distance to the job location should be small. We should note that the so-called objective function or the outcome of any alternative 'job' is certainly known. However, the goal is fuzzy and the two constraints, one related to 'interest' and the other related to 'driving distance', are also fuzzy. In fact, the extent to which any job meets the fuzzy goal (depending on the state of nature) is itself fuzzy.

The first constraint of 'interest' value is taken as a fuzzy set defined over the universal set of alternatives by the membership function:

$$C_1 = 0.4/a + 0.6/b + 0.8/c = 0.6/d$$

The second constraint relating to driving distance was taken in terms of the membership function:

$$C_2 = 0.1/a + 0.9/b + 0.7/c + 0.1/d$$

Defined over the set of jobs, the authors take the following membership function to represent this fuzziness:

$$\mu_G(x) = \begin{array}{l} 1 \text{ for } x > 40,000 \\ ->00125\,(x/1000-1)2+1 \text{ for } 40,000 \geq x \geq 13,000 \\ 0 \text{ for } x < 13,000 \end{array}$$

Hence, the goal G' induced on the set of alternatives is given by the membership function:

$$G' = 0.875/a + 0.7/b + 0.5/c + 0.2/d$$

Taking the standard fuzzy set intersection of these three fuzzy sets, we obtain the fuzzy decision function:

$$D = 0.1/a + 0.6/b + 0.5/c + 0.2/d$$

Finally, the maximum of this set corresponding to the alternative b is chosen. No real distinction is made between a goal and a constraint.

Group decisions in a fuzzy environment in which different members of the group may have different preference orders among the alternatives pose problems. A fuzzy model for group decision was proposed by Blin (1974) and Blin and Whinston (1973). Recourse is taken to the theory of social choice where the choice function corresponds to a membership function to indicate individual preferences and then an appropriate aggregating mechanism is offered in terms of the 'majority voting' principle to come up with the group membership function.

There have been several interesting applications of multi-attribute LP to sole group decision-making problems in fuzzy environments.

14.5. Information to Identify Feasible Options

In a theoretical discussion on the choice of some alternative(s) as 'optimal' or 'better than others' or even 'satisfactory' in achieving the goals and objectives set for the decision-making problem, one may just start with the set of 'feasible' solutions identified or identifiable to meet constraint requirements. Usually, we do not bring in the concept of partial satisfaction of a constraint, though in some cases we do not regard all the constraints as inviolate. In fact, a constraint may relate to a scarce material or energy resource not normally available beyond a specified limit or some restriction that should not be normally ignored or bypassed. In a manufacturing set-up, engaging the workforce for more than the stipulated time per day, a violation to meet exigency may attract some penalty imposed by the competent authority; there could be a cap on the procurement of some particular material from the market, and the consequence of procuring more could invite some penalty. In some problems, the constraints are such that determining the feasibility or otherwise of an alternative is an extremely difficult task and may call for appropriate algorithms. Thus, in a sequencing problem involving five jobs, each to be processed through each of five machines according to prescribed machine sequences for the five jobs (which may not be all identical), there are $(5!)^5$ or approximately 25×10^7 possible job sequences on the five machines (which are the alternatives), and to find out which of these satisfy the given technological orderings of machines for each of the jobs, we badly need algorithms which are still to be developed in cases of medium numbers of machines and jobs. In this case, for an alternative job sequence for each of the machines to be feasible, we have to check whether at any stage the job is free (waiting for processing on the next machine as prescribed by the technology), the machine is free (it is not currently processing any jobs), the job is next for the machine and (according to the alternative) the machine is next for the job. When technology prescribes different machine sequences for different jobs, checking the feasibility of an alternative is really a complex job.

In real-life problems, we may not be in a position to even identify the possible alternatives and visualize the constraints and, thereafter, may not have adequate information about the feasibility or otherwise of an alternative. In situations where we can start with any alternative and want to check its feasibility, lack of prior information may stand in the way of determining its feasibility. For this, we may have to undertake some activities at a cost and with a risk of collecting relevant information. And such efforts cannot be undertaken for more than a countably few alternatives. Feasibility will be determined only after some time. Let us take the example of deciding on the best way to reduce traffic congestion at a road junction that usually witnesses a huge volume of pedestrian and vehicular traffic. Alternatives that can emerge during brainstorming among engineers, traffic police, soil scientists, development planners and others concerned include the construction of an underpass to divert pedestrian traffic. To judge the feasibility of this suggested alternative from several considerations, such as expenditure, soil physics to allow digging and holding the roof and time during which traffic has to remain suspended wholly or partly, weighed against the benefits to accrue, ultimately, is quite a complicated task and may imply some initial data collection. A second alternative to building a road overbridge(s) at the junction may involve considerations not all identical with the ones associated with the underpass construction.

In the case of assigning jobs to some new recruits in an organization, possible alternatives are job–recruit combinations with the objective of maximizing the overall efficiency of operations of the group on the jobs assigned to them. Efficiency can be judged in terms of time to complete some tasks or accuracy in some tasks, total idle time, etc. Whether a particular job allocation is feasible or not, may call for an assessment of the personality make-up of the recruits and their levels of motivation to accept and discharge each of the jobs to be allocated among them. And this again invites its own problems.

14.6. Information in Social Choice Problems

Straying into problems of social choice or administrative decisions that affect the diverse interests of different segments of the population in a country, one critical decision problem faced by the national administration is the progress towards poverty alleviation. Once we get an estimate of the total population below a poverty line L, our task is to estimate the aggregate income gap of the poor $\Sigma(L-y)$ which should be wiped out or at least reduced by either generating additional income and meeting this gap or redistributing the total income of the poor and non-poor (or only rich) people, imposing appropriate taxes on the latter. Each of these two broad alternatives has to be comprehended in terms of various alternatives at several different levels of hierarchy in terms of decisions and actions.

Redistribution of the total national income is easier said than done. Any such effort may also dampen entrepreneurial activities and thus depress the national income. Redistribution to alleviate poverty goes beyond tax collection and has a lot to do with proper policies and plans to benefit the poor. Subsidies announced may again lower the economic activities of the beneficiaries. These constraints should be taken due care of.

A better alternative would involve targeted assistance to the identified poor to engage them in productive activities which can even be limited to producing goods and services meant for their own consumption. This may mean an increase in national income and no extra tax burden on the rich.

A judicious blend of these two approaches may be tried out to alleviate poverty.

Towards a redistribution of the total national income (or the component of 'returns to labour' and 'returns to capital'), we may consider a revision of the income tax structure as an alternative. We start with the quantiles (deciles or quintiles) of the income distribution—or in its absence—of the distribution of final consumption expenditure. For each of the higher income groups, we assume a direct tax policy and estimate the total tax revenue. For each group of consumer and capital goods, we assume a policy for indirect taxes and quantify the total receipt. We may use some discounting factors in the revenue figures to allow for some tax evasion. For any policy for enhanced direct tax, the likely impact of the consequent lowering of economic activity on national income has to be worked out. The total revenue expenditure on subsidies to the poor and to some sectors of the economy has to be calculated. For all such computations, some variations in the parameters involved have to be allowed. The decision variables in such an exercise will include the choice of income groups and commodity/service groups and the choice of the tax rates to be imposed on the different groups. Certain desirable caps on the rates should be considered. The objective function could be the total tax revenue income penalised for the possible negative impact of slowed economic activity. The exercise of finding the optimal tax regime will be a somewhat complex problem that will admit only a heuristic solution.

The final problem of further penalizing the tax income by the cost of distributing this income among the poor effectively gets more complicated in terms of the existing distribution mechanism possibly needing a revamp, with a huge social cost difficult to quantify.

The second approach towards poverty amelioration—and definitely the blend of these two—will still admit some formulation in terms of the decision variables, the given variables and the consequence variables. It is likely that the constraints involved or even the objective function may not admit clear and unambiguous statements.

CHAPTER 15

A Peep into Gray Areas

15.1. Are There Gray Areas?

Is it not just natural to expect that in a subject like decision analysis, there will remain—at any stage of development of the subject—some gray areas? In some cases, these arise from simplistic assumptions made in the process of decision-making and incorporated into the corresponding models, methods and techniques. Some of these have continued to remain, possibly through oversight. Some others have been examined and removed to the extent possible without affecting the desirable features of the procedures based on such assumptions. Some of these assumptions were introduced in 'good faith' in the absence of any contra-indications or to achieve so me sort of simplicity in the procedures. True, some of these assumptions have been found not to hold ground in some applications or not to meet some theoretical (read mathematical) niceties. In the other category, we have some assumptions which are really tricky and difficult to remove or modify. In fact, not absorbing such assumptions would not allow us to generalize some procedures across applications or situations.

Decisions made by individuals and groups are admittedly influenced by their intuitions and emotions, besides their intellectual capabilities and experience. While intuitions are more or less stable attributes of decision-makers, emotions are generally context-specific and are less stable and can have different impacts on decisions on the same problem on different occasions. The theory, however, assumes that every decision-maker is characterized by 'rational behaviour' (which may not necessarily be ethical) that guides them to make choices that best satisfy their self-interests only. Also assumed is the existence of stable preference relations among admissible choices for a decision-maker. It is not completely unexpected that a decision-maker, placed against a second in such a way that the outcomes of actions taken by the other depend on the first decision-maker's move, may co-operate with the second. We also assume that a decision-maker can identify all the information items which are needed in the decision-making process and has access to all of them. In reality, it may be a difficult task to identify all relevant information items and to have convenient access to them. The assumption that follows in theory is that the decision-maker is capable of effectively analysing the available information to get the right input to make a 'good' decision. (For the time being, we ignore the knowledge gap existing with the decision-maker about the methods and techniques to be applied for such an analysis.) This is a matter of serious concern when we face complex optimization problems even in seemingly innocent real-life situations. Intuitions are often developed from experience, and we must not take it for granted that all decision-makers possess adequate experience of the decision problems currently faced by them. Added to this remains the fact that only a small number of decision-makers are adequately equipped with strong computational facilities or possess unusually strong power to make mental calculations and comparisons to work out the 'best' solution, and more and more real-life decision-making situations, including those wherein traditional algorithms for mathematical programming fail to produce desirable results.

15.2. Impact of Uncertainty

Let us first consider the simple case of decision-making under uncertainty, illustrated by an extension of the resource allocation problem (usually solved by the simplex algorithm for LP problems) to the situation where for each possible allocation we have several (finite) states of nature. In this case, formulation of the problem in terms of a suitable objective function to be optimized becomes a problem. Let us denote by $C_{p \times n} = ((c_{ij}))$ the matrix of coefficients c_{ij} (profit per unit of product j under the ith state of nature; $j = 1, 2, ..., n$ and $i = 1, 2, ..., p$). We can possibly make use of Wald's maximin criterion to formulate this problem. Thus, the problem can be formulated as to find $X = (x_1, x_2, ..., x_n)$ subject to m linear constraints $AX < b$ so that $z = \min C_j$, $X = \min \Sigma_j c_{ij} x_j$ is a maximum over i. Possibly, an easier formulation will require maximization of the average value of total profit, averaged over states of nature. While the problem can be computationally tackled, no efficient algorithm appears in the literature.

The point to be emphasized in this section concerns the assumption that the identified set of p states of nature is exhaustive. Since states of nature are generally beyond the decision-maker's control, the possibility of some other state(s) of nature existing cannot be ruled out. There is every possibility of a new state disturbing the entire problem formulation and solution. We must bear in mind that the examination of such a possibility is not covered in the usual post-optimality or sensitivity analysis where we would examine the impact of likely changes in the coefficients c.

The above problem has been to some extent handled as a problem of decision-making under risk by assigning probabilities to the various states of nature and working in terms of the expected profit from each allocation. In fact, we have considered such a situation as being modelled by a stochastic linear program. Going beyond expectations, we also referred to other formulations of this problem in stochastic optimization in terms of the V-rule to minimize the variance of pay-off or the P-rule to optimize the quantile of a given order in the pay-off distribution (or even its converse, where we try to optimize the area under/above a specified value in the pay-off distribution).

Here again, we face and possibly tend to shy away from a situation where the probabilities assigned initially to the various states of nature can change subsequently. As can be easily understood, these probabilities are most often not determined objectively using probability calculus but represent 'degrees of belief' of the individual decision-maker, based on intuition augmented by relevant experience, if any. Hence, these probabilities are more likely to change than to remain stable. In this case, of course, it is possible to examine the dependence of the optimal solution based on the initially assigned probabilities of such deviations. With the subjectivity attached to probabilities attached to states of nature not based on relevant evidence, the applicability of solutions to stochastic optimization problems remains a big question.

In the above problem of decision-making under risk, the difficulty of assigning probabilities to very unlikely states of nature never experienced earlier, which justify inclusion because of their large impacts on the final solution, continues to haunt research workers in the field. Small probability estimation methods, including the use of event tree analysis, have been tried out in some applications.

15.3. Concern for Computational Complexity

Computational simplicity and elegance of results often tempt analysts to make assumptions that may not be warranted in all applications. Just to illustrate, we refer to the oft-cited sampling inspection plan and its Bayesian extension. Usually, a beta prior is assumed for the fraction of defective p in the lot (essentially a binomial probability), and this is a natural conjugate prior. However, prior information definitely restricts the support of the prior to (p_L, p_U) where p_L is a value close to 0, while p_U should not exceed a small value like 0.10 or a slightly higher value. Thus, the prior should better be taken as a truncated beta over such a support. This would obviously make the computation somewhat involved and specific to each case. One simple way out could be to choose the beta-distribution parameters (hyperparameters) in such a way that at least the probability under the prior of exceeding p_U is negligible.

Most decisions have to be made under uncertainty. In fact, some authors consider 'certainty' as just a special case of 'certainty', and 'risk' is, no doubt, a fall-out of 'uncertainty'. Usually, the implications of certainty, uncertainty and risk have been related to information available about likely realizations of different states of nature. Of course, decision-making under certainty usually considers only one state of nature or, in a sense, ignores the consideration of 'state of the nature'. It must be noted, however, that the outcome of any alternative (decision, strategy or action) for a given state of nature has been generally taken to be exactly known. Herein lies the problem. Even in the so-called 'certainty' situation where we do not explicitly bring in a 'state of nature', this outcome may not be known to us exactly for all the possible alternatives. Thus, in the LP problem, the contribution of a decision variable x_j to the objective function $C'X$ may not continue to be proportional to its value below or beyond a certain level. Either we need to incorporate some constraint(s) on values of the decision variables based on adequate knowledge of these levels or we remain uncertain about the outcome of any alternative X. In the case of multiple states of nature, granting that we do not assign any probabilities to those or that the probabilities we assign in a 'decision under risk' framework, we have assumed values of the outcomes for any decision/action alternative as certainly known. This may not fit into real-life situations, and all that we are able to do is to make 'good' guesses about these outcomes. Guessing or formal prediction is a non-unique exercise and errors of varying magnitudes and consequences (on choice) are inevitable. General optimization problems try to handle such situations in various ways, like the use of fuzzy sets or of interval numbers or of gray numbers. A synoptic review of relevant procedures in use may be found in Keith and Ahner (2021). Some reference should be made to the classification of randomness associated with the states of nature, as done by Taleb (2007), in terms of the tail behaviour of the probability distribution over states of nature, treating thin tails as distinct from true fat tails, which cause concern about the predictability of the outcomes.

15.4. Information Overload and Option Deluge

It is better not to be a nihilist right from the outset but to be critical rightfully, if so needed, at the end. We now come to some concerns about the decision-making process expressed by some philosophers, psychologists and futurists in recent times. The basic question that comes up is which one of the following statements is true? 'The "end" justifies the "means" and the "means" will take care of the "end".' 'Do we seek an answer or simply avoid a definitive answer and take it as something context-specific and decision-maker-oriented? Not to betray the hollowness of comprehension, we consider only two essential and sometimes intriguing inputs into the decision-making process, namely the role of information and the identification/generation of options/alternatives. To put matters bluntly, we take up briefly the viewpoints of a few thinkers on two perplexing and interlinked issues, namely 'information overload' and 'option deluge'.

With the exponential growth in science and technology over the last few decades, affecting almost all aspects of our individual and collective lives as reflected in our behaviours and actions, we are literally flooded with options or alternatives in any situation where we have to make a decision. In this connection, we are reminded by Schwartz (2004) that 'learning to choose is hard, learning to choose well is harder and learning to choose well in a world of unlimited possibilities is harder still, perhaps too hard'. Growth in knowledge and the zeal to utilize knowledge to enrich (in some sense) life have led to umpteen alternatives being available to us—be it for buying a particular consumer item (coming to the market in various brands), enrolling for study in an educational institution (for which inducements come from a wide array of mechanisms), selecting a partner in life (for which some portals provide numerous options) or adopting some method of measuring some property of a material (for which several methods along with corresponding equipment are appearing over time). We are literally flooded with options, and we are either unable to assess the relative merits and deficiencies of the options by ourselves or are misled by information supplied by those offering the options not always scrupulously or are forced to pay for a dependable assessment by an 'independent' agency. In short, we are not in a comfortable situation.

Let us try to visualize the different possible situations in respect of options or alternatives in the context of optimization or choice theory. The range of possibilities includes, on the one hand, a situation where options are sparse and demand a lot of effort to be generated and an unimaginably huge set of options (may be infinite in number), all of them easily identifiable though not necessarily to be enumerated, on the other. In the latter case, it may so happen that quite a few available options need not be considered at all in our search for an optimum. This is illustrated by the problem of LP, say, with continuous decision variables constituting a convex set. The theory tells us that the optimal solution must be one of the vertices or an edge connecting two adjacent vertices (the supporting hyperplane with infinitely many optimal solutions). Our search is confined only to the few vertices in the simplex algorithm. There could be other optimization problems where the many possible alternatives have to be identified with some effort. (We are referring to feasibility checks as in scheduling or sequencing problems.)

Faced with the 'option deluge', a decision-maker may have to first take a stand—and this is an overarching decision—between two positions: start with an ambitious expectation about the outcome of the final decision, confront the deluge, work out an optimal solution with a lot of conceptual difficulties and computational complexity and minimize 'regret'. As one, start with modest expectations about the decision outcome, work with a few reasonably good alternatives to work out a 'satisficing' solution that may involve a larger 'regret'. Regret remains in either case. This regret has to be absorbed against high expectations and considerable effort in the first case and against sober expectations and modest effort in the second. Psychologists argue—and not for the wrong reasons—that regret in the first case creates disappointment and even despair, while the second may only have a mild sense of dissatisfaction. Now, this super-decision problem lies in the domain of human behaviour, captured by the phrase 'vectors of the human mind' and is not quite amenable to conventional decision analysis.

It has been argued by some that abundance of choice is a prerequisite for individual freedom, and freedom of choice leads to contentment and happiness. On the other hand, Schwartz (2004) sounds differently by saying, 'We would be better off if we embraced some limits on choice, instead of rebelling, by speaking "good enough" rather than the "best", by lowering our expectations about our decisions, by making our decisions non-reversible, and not comparing ourselves to others.'

15.5. Infirmities in Decision-making

Infirmities and drawbacks in decision-making are not all attributable to limitations or deficiencies in logical or analytical tools for aiding decision analysis or to constraints imposed by the context or situation in which the decision-maker is placed. In fact, one can conveniently think of three sets of factors contributing to fallibilities in decisions. These are (a) situational or contextual constraints on the availability of and access to relevant information, (b) limitations inherent in logical or analytical tools involved in the decision-making process and (c) intellectual inadequacy, cognitive biases and mental instability. It may be incidentally noted that the 'information overload', mentioned earlier, is also a constraint rather than an advantage and can pose a hindrance to effective decision-making.

The second set of factors may be generically characterized as being 'objective'; the second should be taken as 'subjective' in the same spirit, and the first reflects a combination of both. The normative theory behind decision-making takes advantage of developments in the objective set of factors to remove limitations inherent in concepts. Models, methods and techniques are used in decision analysis. The behavioural theory stresses the role played by the third set of factors, does not 'give up' to subjectivity and proceeds to extract as much objective input from this set to decision-making as possible. Literature refers to the prescriptive theory, which is supposed to take into account all the sets of factors, yielding a decision to be prescribed to the decision-maker.

The second set of factors and its contribution to decision-making has been widely discussed; the third lags behind, and the first stands in between. Let us briefly touch upon the third set of factors that reflect differences in aptitudes, attitudes and aspirations of different individual decision-makers, acting independently by themselves or acting jointly as members of a group—may be a society or an organization. It is only to be expected that larger differences will surface as the group becomes large-sized and heterogeneous.

An important factor in the third set is 'intellectual inadequacy', which bears on decision-making. General intellectual capability may not always suffice for the purpose of grappling with a somewhat difficult choice problem. Lack of situational alacrity coupled with required intellectual ability may stand in the way of correctly comprehending the given decision problem. Sometimes, the major concerns or issues to be resolved in a decision problem may not be fully appreciated and sometimes wrongly substituted by others, to the effect that a solution reached to the problem as understood fails to address the real concerns or major issues behind the decision problem. A second negative element is 'impulsiveness' to commit more than what can be ensured and to underestimate any time constraint or to face some problem of escalation of commitment on the part of all concerned in checking feasibility, carrying out some trials and implementing a solution. A much greater problem is created by a sense of 'overconfidence' about the desirability of the outcome. This can be traced backwards to 'overconfidence' in one's ability to comprehend the problem, to identify and access the pertinent information adequately, to take advantage of the 'best' available logical and analytical aid, including the corresponding software and, finally, to interpret the results of decision analysis in terms of an 'implementable' decision. We have to bear in mind that all of us are decision-makers all the time and not all are equipped with the requisite knowledge and skills involved in the decision-making process. In melee, we have people who do not own their knowledge and skill deficiencies and avoid dependence on external advice or support but exhibit a lot of overconfidence, testifying to the phenomenon referred to by psychologists as the Dunning–Kruger effect.

Added to the above are cognitive biases, revealed in preference relations as well as in indifferences. Individuals tend to be guided in their manifest behaviour by leanings towards or affections for some properties or features or characteristics, caused sometimes by volition to 'stand out from the crowd'. If this behaviour becomes context specific, an unfortunate consequence like 'rank reversal' cannot be ruled out, and a robust decision will evade us.

In a good variety of decision-making situations tackled by a wide array of decision-makers, we find applications of 'heuristics', which are essentially mental shortcuts or rules of thumb used in making judgements (as in ordering within a pair or ranking within the entire set or within a truncated set). Recourse to different heuristics is defended by practitioners as well as researchers, particularly in situations where the convenience of treating a structured decision problem does not exist.

15.6. The Paradox of Choice

In the context of Western developed societies offering a bewildering host of choices for consumer goods and services to promote—in their understanding and arguments—freedom of choice and welfare, Schwartz (2004) in his famous book, entitled *Paradox of Choice: Why More is Less?*, came up with the idea, short of a warning, that too much choice, difficult to digest, may—at least in some cases—cause less satisfaction and less happiness and can, on the other hand, lead to 'decision paralysis'. This paradox has been recognized as a major source of confusion, brought about by the mass customization of products and services available online. Schwartz continues to say that if, in the process of a choice among choices accessed by the decision-maker, the latter looks for more of one property or feature they consider more important, less will be available in respect of some other feature or property regarded as less important.

As pointed out in previous section, limitless choices may not necessarily imply a confusing situation or cause decision paralysis. The decision-maker can conveniently steer clear of most irrelevant or not-so-useful options and remain engaged with a handy number. There exist decision problems in real life where options or alternatives have to be generated or searched for and the question of 'option deluge' does not arise.

Back to mass customization and the paradox of choice, it is worthwhile to note the re-definition of the paradox offered by Riasecki and Hanna (2010). According to them, it is not the overwhelming amount of choice itself that may cause customers' dissatisfaction and lead to greater regret but the lack of meaningful choice, which lies at the root of the problem. They further argue that, since users themselves are not often able to make out what constitutes a meaningful choice, the task they face belongs to the category of ill-posed problems. Two computational approaches have been suggested for solving problems related to the re-defined paradox of choice. The first is based on a recommended system and the other involves the implementation of artificial selection in genetic algorithms. Their findings in an empirical study reveal that genetic algorithm tools allow users to move through the solution space to recognize meaningful options rather than their definitions.

15.7. Can We Conclude?

With all this told to us and a major part assimilated by us, can we reach a conclusion that some questions are better not answered or no questions should be put under the carpet and should motivate us to search for a reasonable answer that may not be right now? What should we do till a reasonable answer to a vexing question is worked out? Should we avoid choosing among alternatives and accept any one that appeals to us (our innate abilities to recognize, assess, discriminate and order alternatives)?

Sanity will not argue in favour of giving up 'choice' or decision-making'. It may, however, hold the brief for an appreciation by the decision-maker about the fallibilities of decision-making, leading to 'mellowed' expectations about the decision outcome. Decisions with all the limitations pointed out by wise persons may turn out to be true or valid and infuse a sense of satisfaction or happiness. Decisions may also turn out to be wrong and may cause a lot of disappointment and even regret. Both are aspects of reality.

References and Suggested Readings

Aarts, E., Aarts, E. H., & Lenstra, J. K. (1997). *Local search in combinatorial optimization*. John Wiley & Sons.

Ackoff, R. L., & Sasieni, M. W. (1968). *Fundamentals of operations research*. Wiley.

Ahmed, M., Karagiorgou, S., Pfoser, D., & Wenk, C. (2015). A comparison and evaluation of map construction algorithms using vehicle tracking data. *Geoinformatics*, *19*(3), 601–632.

Ali, A. J., & Seiford, L. M. (1990). Translation invariance in data envelopment analysis. *Operations Research Letters*, *9*(6), 403–405.

Anand, P. (1991). *Fundamentals of rational choice under risk*. Clarendon Press.

Andersen, P., & Petersen, N. C. (1993). A procedure for ranking efficient units in data envelopment analysis. *Management Science*, *39*(10), 1261–1264.

Andtonove, A. A., & Pontryagin, L. S. (1937). Robust systems. *Reports of Academy of Sciences of the USSR*, *14*, 350–359.

Angantyr, A., Andersson, J., & Aidanpaa, J. O. (2003). Constrained optimization based on a multiobjective evolutionary algorithm. Proceedings of Congress on Evolutionary Computation, 1560–1567. "IEEE Xplore".

Arrow, K. (1950). A difficulty in the concept of social welfare. *Journal of Political Economy*, *58*(4), 328–346.

Arrow, K. J., Sen, A. K., & Suzumura, K. (1997). *Social choice re-examined*. Springer.

Arrow, K. J., & L. Hurwicz. (1972). Optimality criteria for decision-making under ignorance. In C. F. Carter & J. L. Ford (Eds.), *Uncertainty and expectation in economics* (pp. 1–11). Basil Blackwell.

Arrow, K. J., & Raynaud, H. (1986). *Social choice and multi-criteria decision-making*. MIT Press.

Aumann, R. J. and Dreze, J. H. (1974). Co-oopeative games with coalition structures. *International Journal of Game Theory*, *3*, 217–237.

Aziz, H. H., Brandt, F., Elkinf, E., & Skowran, P. (2019). Computational social choice: The first ten years and beyond [Lecture notes on computer science]. Computing and Software Science, 48–65, Springer.

Azzopardi, P. V. (2016). *Behavioural technical analysis*. Harrison House.

Baldwin, J. F. and Guild, N. C. F. (1979). Comparison of fuzzy sets on the same decision space. *Fuzzy Sets and Systems*, *2*(3), 213–231.

Banker, R. D. and Morey, R. C. (1986). Use of categorical variables in Data Envelopment Analysis. *Mgt. Science, 32*(12), 1613–1627.

Bard, J. F. (1998). *Practical bi-level optimization: Applications and algorithms.* Kluwer Academic Publishers.

Bardhan, I., WF, B., WW, C., & Sueyoshi, T. (1996). Models for dominance in data envelopment analysis Part I: Additive models and MED measures. *Journal of the Operations Research Society of Japan, 39*, 322–332.

Bargagliotti, A. E. (2009). Aggregation and decision-making using ranked data. *Mathematical Social Sciences, 58*(3), 354–366.

Barlow, R. E., & Gupta, S. S. (1969). Selection procedures for restricted families of probability distributions. *The Annals of Mathematical Statistics, 40*(3), 905–917.

Barron, J. T. (2017). A general and robust adaptive loss function. arXiv: 1701 03077 cs.cv]

Barto, A. G., Sutton, R. S., & Watkins, C. J. C. H. (1989). *Learning and sequential decision-making.* University of Massachusetts.

Basadur, M. (1995). *The power of innovation: How to make innovation a way of life and put creative solutions to work.* Financial Times/Prentice Hall.

Bass, S. M. and Kwakernak, H. (1977). Rating and ranking of multiple-aspect alternativesusing fuzzy set theory. *Automatica, 13*, 47–58.

Bauerle, N., & Reider, U. (2011). *Markov decision processes with applications in finance.* Springer.

Bazerman, M. H., & Moore, D. A. (2008). *Judgment in managerial decision-making.* Wiley.

Bechhofer, R. E., Santner, T. J., & Goldsman, D. M. (1995). *Design and analysis of statistical experiments for selection, screening and multiple comparisons.* John Wiley.

Bellman, R., & Zadeh, L. A. (1970). Decision making in a fuzzy environment. *Management Science, 17*(4), 144–164.

Ben-Haim, Y. (2001). *Information-gap decision theory.* Academic Press.

Ben-Haim, Y. (2006). *Info-gap decision theory* (2nd ed.). Elsevier.

Ben-Haim, Y. (2019). Info-gap decision theory. In V. A. W. J. Marchau, W. E. Walker, P. J. T. M. Bloemen, & S. W. Popper (Eds.), *Decision making under deep uncertainty* (pp. 93–115). Springer.

Benjamini, Y., & Hochberg, Y. (1995). Controlling the false discovery rate: A practical and powerful approach to multiple testing. *Journal of the Royal Statistical Society: Series B, 57*(1), 289–300.

Ben-Tai, A. (1979). Characterization of Pareto and lexicographic optimal solution. Technical Report #157, Technion. http://www.cs.technion.ac.il/users/wwwb/cgi-bin/tr-get.cgi/1979/CS/CS0157.pdf

Bentham, J. (1989). *An introduction to principles of morals and legislation.* Clarendon Press.

Berger, J. O. (1980). Statistical decision theory and Bayesian analysis. Springer Verlag.

Berger, J. O. (1993). An overview of robust Bayesian analysis. *Test*, *3*(1), 93–53.
Bergstrom, T. (2012). Notes on uncertainty and expected utility. UCSB Economics Research Report 210A. https://www.yumpu.com/en/document/read/7183413/notes-on-uncertainty-and-expected-utility-ucsb-economics
Berkeley, D. et al. (1991). *Aiding strategic decision-making: Derivation and development of ASTRIDA in Environment for Supporting Decision processes.* Vecsenyi, Y. and Sol, H. (eds), North Holland, Amsterdam.
Bernardo, J. M. (1979). Reference posterior distributions for Bayesian inference. *Journal of the Royal Statistical Society: Series B (Methodological)*, *41*(2), 113–147.
Bernardo, J. M., & Smith, A. F. M. (1994). *Bayesian theory*. Wiley.
Bernoulli, D. (1738). An example of a new theory on the measure of lot Commentaries on the Imperial Academy of Sciences. *Petropolitanae*, 5, 175–192.
Bickel, D. R. (2004). Error rates and decision theoretic methods of multiple testing. https://arxiv.org/ftp/math/papers/0212/0212028.pdf
Birnbaum, M. H., Coffey, G., Mellers, B., & Weiss, R. (1992). Utility measurement: Configural-weight theory and the judge's point of view. *Journal of Experimental Psychology: Human Perception and Performance*, *18*(2), 331.
Biswas, A., & Kumar, S. (2019). Generalization of extent analysis method for multi-criteria decision-making problems involving intuitionistic fuzzy numbers. *OPSEARCH*, *56*(4), 1142–1166.
Black, D. (1948). On the rationale of group decision-making. Jour. Pol. Econ., *56*(1), 23 34.
Blackwell, D., and Girscick, M. A. (1954). *Theory of games and Statistical Decisions.* John Wiley, New York.
Blin, J. M. (1974). Fuzzy relations in group decision theory. *Jour. Cybernetics*, $. 17–22.
Blin, J. M., and Whinston, A. B. (1973). Fuzzy sets and social choice. *Jour Cybernetics*, *3*, 28–36.
Bohachevsky, I. O., Johnson, M. E., & Stein, M. L. (1986). Generalised simulated annealing for function optimisation. *Technometrics*, *28*(3), 209–217.
Bonissone, P. P. (2008). Research issues in multi-criteria decision-making (MCDM): The impact of uncertainty in solution evaluation. Proc. IPMU Conference, Malaga.
Bookenholt, U. (2007). Thurstone-based analysis: Past, present and future utilities. *Psychometrika*, *71*(4), 615–829.
Borda, J. C. (1781). Mempie sur les electionsau scrutiny. In Histoire de l'Aademie Toyale des sciences, Paris.
Borgart, K. P. (1975) Preference structures II: distance between asymmetric relations. *SIAM Jour. App. Maths.*, *29*, 254–262.
Boyd, J. R. (1995). *The essence of winning and losing*. Daniel Ford Books.
Bradley, R. A., & Terry, M. E. (1952). The rank analysis of incomplete block designs. *Biometrika*, *39*, 324–345.

Bradley, R. A., (1976). Science, Statistics and paired comparisons. *Biometrics*, *32*(2), 213–239.

Brandt, F. et al. (2016). *Handbook of Computational Social Choice*. Cambridge University Press, U.K.

Brans, J. P. (1986). How to select and how to rank projects. *Euro. Jour Oper Res.* *24*(2), 228–238.

Brams, S., & Fishburn, P. (2004). Voting procedures. In K. Arrow, A. K. Sen, & K. Suzumura (Eds.), *Handbook of social choice and welfare*. Elsevier.

Brandstätter, E., Gigarenzer, G., & Hertvig, R. (2006). The priority heuristics: Making choices without tradeoffs. *Psychological Review*, *11*(2), 409–432.

Branke, J., Chick, S. E., & Schmidt, C. (2007). Selecting a selection procedure. *Management Science*, *53*(12), 1916–1932.

Brauers, W. K. (2007). Normalisation in multiobjective optimisation: A general overview. *International Journal of Management and Decision-making*, *8*(5/6), 445–460.

Brazdik, F. (2004). Stochastic data envelopment analysis: Oriented and linearized models [Unpublished].

Brooks, S. J., and Stein, D. J. (2014). Unconsciuos influences on decision-making: neuro-imaging and neuro-evolutionary perspectives. *Behavioral and Brain Sciences*, *37*(1), 23–24.

Brown, L. D. (2000). An essay on statistical decision theory. *Journal of the American Statistical Association*, *95*(452), 1277–1281.

Buckley, J. J. (1985). Fuzzy hierarchical analysis. *Fuzzy Sets and Systems*, *34*, 187–195.

Buffon, G. L. L. (1835). Life expectancy probabilities. In Oeuvres completes de Buffon, Tome III, New Edition (1829) 338–405.

Camerer, C., & Weber, M. (1992). Recent developments in modeling preferences: uncertainty and ambiguity. *Journal of Risk and Uncertainty*, *5*(4), 325–370.

Caraco, T., Martindale, S., & Whittam, T. S. (1980). An empirical demonstration of risk-sensitive foraging preferences. *Animal Behaviour*, *28*(3), 820–830.

Carlin, B. P., & Louis, T. A. (1996). *Bayes and empirical Bayes methods for data analysis*. Chapman and Hall.

Casella, G., & Strawderman, W. E. (1981). Estimating a bounded normal mean. The *Annals of Statistics*, *9*(4), 870–878.

Cayley, A. (1875). Mathematical questions with their solutions. *The Educational Times*, *23*, 18–19.

Cenkov, N. N. (1982). *Statistical decision rules and optimal inference*. American Mathematical Society.

Chakraborty, T. K. (1992). A class of single sampling plans based on fuzzy programming. *OPSEARCH*, *29*(1), 11–20.

Chang, D. Y. (1996). Applications of the extent analysis method on fuzzy AHP. *European Journal of Operational Research*, *95*, 649–655.

Chen, S., Liu, J., Wang, H., & Augusto, J. C. (2013). Ordering-based decision-making: A survey. *Information Fusion, 14*(4), 521–531.

Chen, S.H. (1985). Ranking fuzzy numbers with maximizing set and minimizing set. *Fuzzy Sets and Systems, 17*(2), 113–129.

Chevaleyre, Y., Endriss, U., Lang, J., & Maudet, N. (2005). A short introduction to computational social choice. In *International conference on current trends in theory and practice of computer science* (pp. 51–69). Springer. https://eprints.illc.uva.nl/id/eprint/230/1/PP-2006-55.text.pdf

Chick, S. E., & Inoue, K. (2001). New procedure to select the best simulated system using common random numbers. *Management Science, 47*(8), 1133–1149.

Chinneck, J. W., & Ramadan, K. (2000). Linear programming with interval coefficients. *The Journal of the Operational Research Society, 51*(2), 209–220.

Cho, D. J., Abad, P. L., & Parlar, M. (1996). A Markov decision process approach to repairable item inventory problem. In A. C Borthakur & H. Choudhury (Ed.), *Probability models and statistics*. New Age International.

Chu, T. C., & Lin, Y. (2009). An extension to fuzzy MCDM. *Computers and Mathematics with Applications, 57*(3), 445–454.

Clayton, D., & Kaldor, J. (1987). Empirical Bayes estimation of standardised relative risks for use in disease mapping. *Biometrics, 43*, 671–681.

Clyde, M. et al. (1996). Model uncertainty, *Statistical Science, 19*, 87–94.

Condorcet, M. D. (1785). Essay on the analysis at the probability of decisions rendered to the plurality of voices. Paris

Constantinou, A. C., & Fenton, N. (2018) Things to know about Bayesian networks. *Significance, 15*(2), 19–23.

Cook, W. D., & Kress, M. (1990). A data envelopment model for aggregating preference rankings. *Management Science, 36*(11), 1302–1310.

Cook, W. D. et al. (2006). Distance-based and ad hoc consensus models in ordinal preference ranking. *Euro. Jour. Oper. Res., 172*, 369–385.

Cook, W. P> and Shaipe, A. L. (1976). Committee approach to priority planning: the median ranking method. *Cahiers du Centre d' Etudes de Recherche Operationnelle, 18*(3), 337–351.

Copeland, A. H. (1951). *Seminar on mathematics in social science*. University of Michigan.

Cotta, C., Mathisen, L., & Moscato, P. (2017). Memetic algorithms. In R. Martí, P. M. Pardalos, & M. G. C. Resende (Eds), *Handbook of heuristics* (pp. 1–32). Springer.

Cox, D. R., & Hinkley, D. V. (1974). *Theoretical statistics*. Wiley.

Cramer, H. (1956). A theorem on ordered sets of probability distributions. *Theory of Probability & Its Applications, 1*(1), 16–21.

D'Ambrosio, A., Aria, M., & Siciliano, R. (2012). Accurate tree-based missing data imputation and data fusion within the statistical learning paradigm. *Journal of Classification, 29*(2), 227–258.

D'Ambrosio, A., and Turore, V. A. (2008) Kemeny's axiomatic approach to find consensus ranking in tourist satisfaction. *Statistica Applicata*, *20*(1), 21–**.

Dalal, S. R., & Hall, W. J. (1979). Most economical robust selection procedures for location parameters. *The Annals of Statistics*, *7*(6), 1321–1328.

Dantzig, G. B., & Ramser, J. H. (1950). The truck dispatching problem. *Management Science*, *6*(1), 80–91.

Davidson, R. R. and Farquhar, P. H. (1976). A bibliography on te method of paired comparisons. *Biometrics*.

Deb, K. (2000). An efficient constraint handling method for genetic algorithms. *Computer Methods in Applied Mechanics & Engineering*, *186*(2–4), 311–338.

DeGroot, M. (2004). *Optimal statistical decisions*. Wiley Classics library.

DeGroot, M. H. (1986). *Probability and statistics*. Addison Wesley.

Dekkers, A., & Aarts, E. (1991). Global optimisation and simulated annealing. *Mathematical Programming*, *50*, 367–393.

Deming, W. E. (1986). *Out of the crisis*. Cambridge University Press.

Derman, C. (1970). *Finite state Markov decision processes*. Academic Press.

Dickhaus, T. (2012). Simultaneous statistical inference in dynamic factor models. SFB Discussion paper 649. Humboldt University.

Dickhaus, T. and Stange, J. (2013). Multiple point hypothesis test problems and effective number of tests for control of the family-wise error rate. *Cal Stat. Assoc. Bull.* *65*, (257–260) 123–144.

Ding, X., & Wang, C. (2012). A novel algorithm of stochastic chance-constrained linear programming and its application. *Mathematical Problems in Engineering*, *10*, 1–16.

Dimitrov, S. (2014). Comparing Data Envelopment Analysis and human decision-making unit rankings: A survey approach. *Economic Quality Control*, *29*(2), 129–141.

Dodge, H. F. and Romig, H. G. (1959) *Sampling Inspection Tables*. John Wiley, New York.

Dodgson, C. L. (Lewis Carroll). (1884). *The principles of parliamentary representation*. Harrison and Sons.

Donoho, D. L. (1994). Statistical estimation and optimal recovery. *The Annals of Statistics*, *22*, 238–270.

Doyle, J. (1984). Reasoned assumption and Pareto optimality. IJCAI.

Doyle, J. R., & Green, R. (1994). Efficiency and cross-efficiency in data envelopment analysis: Derivatives, meanings and uses. *Journal of the Operational Research Society*, *45*(5), 567–578.

Draper, D (1995). Assessment and propagation of model uncertainty. *Jour. Royal Stat. Soc. B*, *57*(1), 45–70.

Dumaldar, M. N. (2015). On efficient solutions of 0–1 multi-objective linear programming problems. *OPSEARCH*, *52*(4), 861–869

Easley, D., & Kleinberg, J. (2010). *Networks, crowds and markets: About a highly connected world*. Cambridge University Press.

Ebrahimnejad, A. (2012). A new approach for ranking of candidates in voting systems. *OPSEARCH*, *49*(2), 103–115.

Efron, B. and Morris, C. (1973). Stein's estimation rule and its competitors—An empirical bayes approach. *Jour. Amer. Stat. Assoc. 68*(341), 117–130.

Efron, B., & Tibshirani, R. (2002). Empirical Bayes methods and false discovery rates for micro-arrays. *Genetic Epidemiology*, *23*(1), 70–86.

Ehrgott, M. (2008). *Introduction to applied optimization*. Chapter One, 47–57.

Eiben, A. E., & Schoenauer, M. (2002). Evolutionary computing. *Information Processing Letters*, *82*(1), 1–6.

Ellsberg, D. (1961). Risk, ambiguity and the Savage axioms. *The Quarterly Journal of Economics*, *75*(4), 643–669.

Elster, J. (1979). *Ulysses and the Sirens: Studies in rationality and irrationality*. Cambridge University Press.

Emond, E., & Mason, D. (2002). A new rank correlation coefficient with application to the consensus ranking problem. *Journal of Multi-criteria Decision Analysis*, *11*(1), 17–28.

Emrouznejad, A., & Marra, M. (2017). The state of the art development of AHP (1979–2017): A literature review with a social network analysis. *International Journal of Production Research*, *55*(22), 6653–6675.

Faigle, U., & Kern, W. (1992). Some convergence results for probabilistic tabu search. *ORSA Journal on Computing*, *4*(1), 32–37.

Fan, W., Hong, L. J., & Nelson, B. L. (2016). Indifference-zone free selection of the best. *Operations Research*, *64*(6), 1499–1516.

Farcomeni, A. (2008). A review of modern multiple hypothesis testing, with particular attention to the false discovery proportion. *Statistical Methods in Medical Research*, *17*(4), 347–388.

Figueira, J., Greco, S., & Ehrgott, M. (ed.). (2005). *Multiple criteria decision analysis: State of the art surveys*. Springer.

Fishburn, P. C. (1972). *The theory of social choice*. Princeton Legacy Library.

Fishburn, P. C. (1973). *The Theory of Social Choice*. Princeton University Press.

Flanders, N. E., Brown, R. V., Andre'eva, Y., & Larichev, O. (1998). Justifying public decisions in Arctic oil and gas development: American and Russian approaches. *Arctic*, *51*(3), 262–279.

Fouskakis, D., & Draper, D. (2002). Stochastic optimisation: A review. *International Statistical Review*, *70*(3), 315–349.

Fox, B. L. (1993). Integrating and accelerating tabu search, simulated annealing and genetic algorithm. *Annals of Operations Research*, *41*, 47–67.

Garcia-Cascala, S., & Lamata, M. T. (2012). On rank reversal test and TOPSIS method. *Mathematical and Computer Modelling*, *56*(5–6), 123–132.

Gardenfors, P., & Sahlin, F. E. (1982). Unreliable probability, risk-taking and decision-making. *Synthese*, *53*, 361–386.

Geisser, S. (1993). *Predictive Inference*. Chapman & Hall, London and New York.

Gelfand A. E. et al. (1992). Bayesian analysis of constrained parameter and truncated data problems using Gibbs sampling. *Jour Amer. Stat. Assoc. 87*(18).

Gelman, A. et al. (1995). *Bayesian data Analysis*. Chapman and Hall.
Gen, M., & Cheng, F. (1999). Genetic algorithms. John Wiley.
Genzon, Y. (1977). Pareto optimality in multi-objective problems. *Applied Mathematics and Optimization*, 4(1), 42–59.
Ghosh, D. (2012). A diversification operator for genetic algorithm. *OPSEARCH*, 49(3), 299–313.
Ghosh, J. K., & Samanta, T. (2002). Towards a non-subjective Bayesian paradigm. In J. C. Misra (Ed.), *Uncertainty and optimality* (pp. 1–70). World Scientific.
Gibbard, A. (1973). Manipulation of voting schemes: A general result. *Econometrica*, 41, 587–601.
Gibbons, J. D., Olkin, I., & Sobel, M. (1979). An introduction to ranking and selection. *The American Statistician*, 33(4), 185–195.
Gilboa, I. (2011). *Making better decisions: Decision theory in practice*. Wiley-Blackwell.
Gilboa, I., & Schmeidler, D. (1994). Case-based decision theory. *The Quarterly Journal of Economics*, 110(3), 605–639.
Gilboa, I., & Schmeidler, D. (1995). Case-based decision theory. *The Quarterly Journal of Economics*, 110(3), 605–639.
Ginevicious, R., & Podovezko, V. (2007). Some problems in evaluating multi-criteria decision methods. *International Journal of Management and Decision-making*, 8(5–6), 527–539.
Glover, F., & Laguna, M. (1997). *Tabu search*. Kluwer Academic Publishers.
Gogodze, J. (2019). Ranking-theory methods for solving multi-criteria decision-making problems. *Advances in Operations Research*. https://doi.org/10.1155/2019/3217949
Goldberg, D. E. (1989). *Genetic algorithms in search, optimization and machine learning*. Addison Wesley Professional.
Goldratt, E. (1970). What is this thing called Theory of Constraints and How should it be Implemented? Google books.
Grandi, U. (2017) Social choice and social networks. In Trends in Computational Social Choice. Ed. Endriss, U. Chapter 9, 169–184.
Granger, C. W. J., & Machina, M. J. (2006). Forecasting and decision theory. In G. Elliott, C. W. J. Granger, & A. Timmermann (Eds.), *Handbook of economic forecasting* (pp. 82–98). Elsevier.
Gstach, D. (1998). Another approach to data envelopment analysis in noisy environments: DEA+. *Journal of Productivity Analysis*, 9(2), 161–176.
Gunnantara, N. (2018). A review of multi-objective optimization. *Cogent Engineering*, 5(1). https://doi.org/10.1080/23311916.2018.1502242
Guo, J. E., Levina, E., Michailidis, G., & Zhu, J. (2011) Joint estimation of multiple graphical models. *Biometrika*, 98(1), 1–15.
Gupta, S. S. (1963). On a selection and ranking procedure for Gamma populations. *The Annals of Mathematical Statistics*, 14, 199–216.

Gupta, S. S., & Panchapakesan, S. (1984). Subset selection procedures: A review and assessment. Technical Report #84-4. Purdue University. https://www.stat.purdue.edu/docs/research/tech-reports/1984/tr84-04.pdf

Gupta, S. S., & Panchapakesan, S. (1987). Statistical selection procedures in multivariate models. In A. K. Gupta (Ed.), *Advances in multivariate analysis* (pp. 141–160). D. Reidel Publishing.

Hafezalkotob, A. et al. (2019). Interval multi-MOORA method integrating interval Borda rule and interval best-wrst-method–basedweighting model: Case study on hybrid vehicle engine selection. IEEE Transactions on Cybernetics, PP (99), 1–13.

Hajdukova, J. (2006). Coalition formation games: A survey. *International Game Theory Review*, 8(4), 613–641.

Hald, A. (1981). *The theory of sampling inspection plans by attributes* (Parts I and II). Academic Press.

Hammond, J. S., Keeney, R. L., & Raiffa, H. (2002). *Smart choices: A practical guide for making better decisions*. Crown Business.

Hansen, L. P., & Sargent, T. J. (2008). *Robustness*. Princeton University Press.

Hashimoto, A. (1997). A ranked voting system using a DEA/AR exclusive model: A note. *European Journal of Operational Research*, 97, 600–604.

Hladik, M. (2009). Optimal value range in interval linear programming. *Fuzzy Optimization and Decision Making*, 6(3), 283–294.

Hladik, M. (2012). Interval linear programming: A survey. In Z. A. Mann (Ed.), *Linear programming: New frontiers in theory and applications*. Nova Science Publishers.

Holmes, C., & Watson, J. (2014). Robust statistical decisions under model misspecification. https://www.newton.ac.uk/files/seminar/20140424091510151-153985.pdf

Holt, C. A., & Roth, A. E. (2004). The Nash equilibrium: A perspective. *Proceedings of the National Academy of Sciences*, 101(12), 3999–4002.

Holtzman, S. (1988). Intelligent decision systems. Addison-Wesley.

Hommel, G. (1988). A stage-wise rejective multiple test procedure on a modified Bonferroni test. *Biometrika*, 75(2), 383–386.

Howard, N. (1966). The theory of meta-games. *General Systems*, 11, 167–200.

Howard, R. (1960). *Dynamic programming and Markov processes*. MIT Press.

Hu, J., & Yang, L. (2011). Dynamic stochastic multi-criteria decision-making method based on cumulative prospect theory and set-pair analysis. *Systems Engineering Proceedia*, 1, 432–439.

Hull, J., Moore, P. G., & Thomas, H. (1973). Utility and its measurement. *Journal of the Royal Statistical Society: Series A*, 136, 226–247.

Hume, D. (1999). *An enquiry concerning human understanding* (T. L. Beauchamp). Oxford University Press (Original work published 1748).

Hurson, T. (2007). *Think better: An innovator's guide to productive thinking*. Tata McGraw-Hill Education.

Hsu and Panchapakesan (2019).
Huber, P. J. (1964). Robust estimation of a location parameter. *Ann. Math. Statistt. 35*(1), 73–101.
Hwang, C. L., & Yoon, K. (1981). Multiple attribute decision making. Lecture Notes on Econometrics and Mathematical Systems 186, Springer-Verlag.
Ikeziri, L. M., Souza, F. B. D., Gupta, M. C., & de Camargo Fiorini, P. (2019). Theory of constraints: Review and bibliometric analysis. *International Journal of Production Research, 57*(15–16), 5068–5102.
Inuiguchi, M., & Sakawa, M. (1995). Minimax regret solution to linear programming problems with an interval objective function. *European Journal of Operational Research, 86*(3), 526–536.
Ishizaka, A., & Labib, A. A. (2011). Review of the main developments in the analytic hierarchy process. *Expert Systems with Applications, 38*(11), 14336–14345.
Iwamura, K., & Liu, B. (1996). A genetic algorithm for chance constrained programming. *Journal of Information & Optimisation Sciences, 17*(2), 409–422.
Jackson, M.O. (2008) Social and Economic networks. Princeton University Press, USA.
Jain, P., & Sharma, P. (2014). *Behind every good decision.* AMACOM.
Jayalakshmi, B., & Singh A. (2017). A hybrid artificial bee colony algorithm for the p-median problem with positive/negative weights. *OPSEARCH, 54*(1), 87–93.
Jeffrey, R. C. (1983). *The logic of decision.* University of Chicago Press.
Jensen, E. V. (1996). An introduction to Bayesian networks. UCL Press.
Johnson, J. E., Cheng, L., & Rabinovi, A. (2007). Adjusting batch effects in micro-array expression data using empirical Bayes methods. *Biostatistics, 8*(1), 118–127.
Johnson, R. A. and Mouhab, A. (1996). A Bayesian decision theory approach to classification problems. *Journal of Multivariate Analysis, 56*(2), 232–244.
Kacelnik, A. and Bateson, B. (1996). Risky theories—The effects of variance on foraging decisions. *Integrative and Comparative Biology, 36*(4), 402–434.
Kahneman, D., & Tversky, A. (1979). Prospect theory: An analysis of decision under risk. *Econometrica, 47*(2), 263–291.
Kahneman, D., & Tversky, A. (1984). Choices, values and frames. *American Psychologist, 39*(4), 341–350.
Kalashnikov, V. V., Dempe, S., Pérez-Valdés, G. A., Kalashnykova, N. I., & Camacho-Vallejo, J. F. (2015). Bilevel programming and applications. *Mathematical Problems in Engineering.* https://doi.org/10.1155/2015/310301
Karaboga, D. D., Gorkemli, B., Ozturk, C., & Karaboga, N. (2014). A comprehensive survey: Artificial bee colony (ABC) algorithms and applications. *Artificial Intelligence Review, 43*(1), 21–57.
Kaufmann, A. (1968). The science of decision-making. World University Library.
Keeney, R. L. (1982). Decision analysis: An overview. *Operations Research, 30*(5), 803–838.

Keeney, R. L., & Raiffa, H. (1976). *Decision with multiple objectives: Preferences and value trade-offs*. John Wiley.

Keith, A. J., & Ahner, D. K. (2021). A survey of decision-making and optimization under uncertainty. *Annals of Operations Research*, *300*(2), 319–353.

Keller, K. L., & Staelin, R. (1987) Effects of quality and quantity of information on decision effectiveness. *The Journal of Consumer Research*, *14*, 200–223.

Kemeny, J. G., and Snell, J. L. (1962). Mathematical models in the social sciences (vol. 9). Kepner.

Klaes, M., & Sent, E. M. (2005). A conceptual history of the emergence of bounded rationality. *History of Political Economy*, *37*(1), 27–59.

Klein, G. A. (1999). *Sources of power: How people make decisions*. MIT Press.

Klir, G. J., & Folger, T. A. (1993). *Fuzzy sets, uncertainty and information*. Prentice Hall of India, New Delhi.

Koopmans, T. C., & Beckman, M. (1957). Assignment problem and the location of economic activities. *Econometrica: Journal of the Econometric Society*, *25*(1), 53–76.

Kou, G., Meittenen, K., & Shi, Y. (2011). Multi-criteria decision making: Challenges and advances. *Journal of Multi-criteria Decision Analysis*, *18*(1–2), 1–4.

Kreprs, D. M. (1988). *Notes on the theory of choice*. Westview Press.

Kundakci, N. (2016). Combined multi-criteria decision-making approach based on MACBETH and multi-MOORA methods. *Alphanumeric Journal*, *4*(1), 17–26.

Laarhoven, V., & Pedrycz, P. J. M. (1983). A fuzzy extension of Saaty's priority theory. *Fuzzy Sets and Systems*, *11*(1–3), 229–241.

Lahdelma, R, Hokkanen, J., & Salminen, P. (1998). Stochastic multi-criteria acceptability analysis. *European Journal of Operational Research*, *106*(1), 137–143.

Lahdelma, R., Miettinen, K., & Salminen, P. (2003). Ordinal criteria in stochastic multi-criteria acceptability analysis. *European Journal of Operational Research*, *147*(1), 117–127.

Lahdelma, R. et al. (2007) Treating dependent uncertainties in multi-criteria decision problems. In Operational Research and Its Applications Ed. Rao, M.R. and Puri, M.C.

Lahiri, P., & Maiti, T. (2002). Empirical Bayes estimation of relative risks in disease mapping. *Calcutta Statistical Association Bulletin*, *53*(3–4), 211–224.

Laplace, P.S. (1812). *Analytic Theory of probability*. Britannica.

Larichev, O. (2000). *Theory and methods of decision making, complete with the fairylands chronicle*. Logos.

Leamer, E. (1978). Spec. John Wiley, New York.

legislation.nsw. (2012). *Sydney local environment plan 2012*. New South Wales legislation. https://legislation.nsw.gov.au/view/pdf/asmade/epi-2012-628

Li, X. et al. (2019). A computer study of rank aggregation methods for partial and top-ranked lists in genomic application. *Bio-Informatics*, *20*(1), 178–189.

Likert, R. A. (1982). *A technique for the measurement of attitudes* [PhD dissertation, Columbia University]. Series: Archives of Psychology, 140.

Lim, C. P. (ed.). (2010). *Handbook on decision making: Techniques and applications* (Vol. 4). Springer Science & Business Media. Liu, B. (1998). Stackelberg–Nash equilibrium for multi-level programming with multiple followers using genetic algorithms. *Computers & Mathematics with Applications, 36*(7), 79–89.

List, C. and Goodin, R. E. (2001). Epistemic democracy: generalizing the Condorcet Jury Theorem. *Jour. Pol. Phil.* 277–306.

Liu, B., Zhao, R., & Wang, C. (2003). *Uncertain programming with applications.* Springer.

Loan, P. V. D., & Vertdooreen, L. R. (1989). Selection of populations: An overview and some recent results. *Biometrical Journal, 31*, 383–420.

Loridan, P. (1984). ε-solutions in vector minimization problems. *Journal of Optimization Theory and Applications, 43*(2), 265–276.

Luce, R. D., & Raiffa, H. (1958). *Games and decisions.* John Wiley.

Luce, R. D. (1977). The choice axiom after twenty years. *Jour. Math. Psychol., 15*, 215–233.

Luo, J. J., & Li, W. (2013). Strong optimal solutions of interval linear programming. *Linear Algebra and Its Applications, 439*(8), 4156–4265.

Mabin, V. J., & Balderstone, S. J. (1999). *The world of the theory of constraints.* CRC Press.

Mahamunulu, D. M. (1967). Some fixed sample ranking and selection problems. *The Annals of Mathematical Statistics, 38*(4), 1079–1091.

Makarov, I. M. (1987). *Theory of choice and decision-making.* Mir Publishers.

Mallipeddi, R. et al. (2015) Ensemble of constraint handling techniques for single objective constrained optimization. In Evolutionary Constrained Optimization. Ed. Datta, R. and Deb, K. Springer. 231–248.

Manski, C. F. (1977). The structure of random utility models. *Theory and Decision, 8*(3), 229–254.

Manski, C. F. (2004). Measuring expectations. *Econometrica, 72*(5), 1329–1376.

Manski, C. F. (2019). Treatment choice with trial data: Statistical decision theory should supplant hypothesis testing. *The American Statistician, 73* (Special 1), 296–304.

Mareschal and Brans, J. P. (1988). Geometrical representations of PROMETHEE for MCDA, the GAIA module. *Euro. Jour. Oper. Res., 34*, 69–77.

Mardani, A., Jusoh, A., & Zavadskas, E. K. (2015) Fuzzy MCDM techniques and applications: to decades review from 1994–2014. *Expert Systems with Applications,* 12, 1126–1148.

Maritz, J. S., & Lwin, T. (1989). *Empirical Bayes methods.* Chapman and Hall.

Markovic, V., Stajić, L., Stević, Ž., Mitrović, G., Novarlić, B., & Radojičić, Z. (2020). A novel integrated subjective-objective model for alternative ranking in order to achieve business excellence and sustainability. *Symmetry, 12*(1), 164.

Marshall, K. T., & Oliver, R. M. (1995). *Decision-making and forecasting: With emphasis on model-building and policy analysis*. McGraw Hill.

Marshall, R. J. (1991). Mapping disease and mortality rates using empirical Bayes estimators. *Journal of the Royal Statistical Society: Series C (Applied Statistics)*, 40, 283–294.

Melendez, J. R., Zoghbe, Y. A., Malvacias, A. M., ALmeida, G. A., & Layana, J. (2018). Theory of constraints: A systematic review from the management context. *Revista Espacios*, 39(48).

Miller, D. W., & Starr, M. K. (1973). *Executive decisions and operations research*. Prentice Hall of India.

Mishra, S. (2014). Decision-making under risk: Integrating perspectives from biology, economics and psychology. *Personality and Social Psychology Review*, 8(3), 280–307.

Morris, C.N. (1983). Parametric Empirical bayes Inference: Teory and appliocations. *Jour. Amer. Stat. Assoc. 78*(381), 47–85.

Moulin, H. (1980). On strategy proof-ness and single peakedness. *Public Choice*, 35(4), 437–455.

Moulin, H. (1994) Theory of Social Choice. In Handbook of Game Theory with Economic Applications, 2, Chapter 31, 1091–1125.

Mukherjee, R. (1980). A generalized procedure for product scaling. *IAPQR Transactions*, 2, 71–83.

Mukherjee, R. (1984). Optimal randomised decision rule in univariate stochastic optimisation. *OPSEARCH*, 21(3), 179–182.

Mukherjee, S. P. (1980). Mixed strategies in chance-constrained programming. *Journal of the Operational Research Society*, 31, 1045–1047.

Mukherjee, S. P. (2009). Dodge–Romig plans revisited. *Journal of Quality Management & Analysis*, 5(1), 1–8.

Mukherjee, S. P., & Dasgupta, B. (1992). An inventory problem revisited. *Calcutta Statistical Association Bulletin*, 42, 103–110.

Mukherjee, S. P., & Mandal, A. (1992). A new solution of the block replacement problem. *Economic Quality Control*, 7(1), 56–62.

Mukherjee, S. P., & Mandal, A. (1994). Secretary selection problem with a chance constraint. *Journal of the Indian Statistical Association*, 32, 29–34.

Muller, P., Xu, Y., & Thall, P. T. (2007). Clinical trial design as a decision problem. *Applied Stochatic Model in Industry and Business*, 33(3), 296–301.

Nash, J. F. (1950). Equilibrium points in n-person games. *Proceedings of the National Academy of Sciences*, 36(1), 48–49.

Nash, J. F. (1951). Non-cooperative games. *Annals of Mathematics*, 54, 286–295.

Nelson, B., & Banerjee, S. (2001). Selecting a good system: Procedures and inferences. *IEEE Transactions on Knowledge and Data Engineering*, 33(3), 149–166.

Neumann, V., & Morgenstern, O. (1944). *Theory of games and economic behaviour*. Princeton University Press.

Nezhad, M. S. F., & Nasab, H. H. (2012). A new Bayesian acceptance sampling plan considering inspection errors. *Scientia Iranica*, 19(6), 865–869.

O'Brien, G. C., & Wu, L. (2004). Generalized DEA model: Alternative transformation and duality of linear fractional programming. In M. R. Rao & M. C. Puri (Eds.), *Operational research and its applications*. Allied Publishers.

Olesen, O.B. and Petersen, N.C. (2016) Stochastic data envelopment analysis: A review. *Euro. Jour. Oper Res.*, *251*(1).

Olmeda, H. G., & Aguilar, M. J. R. (2015). Compromise programming. *Agricultural and Resource Economics*, *15*(1), 113–119.

Pan, S. J., & Yang, Q. (2010). A survey on transfer learning. *IEEE Transactions on Knowledge and Data Engineering*, *22*(10) 1345–1359.

Parikh, R. (2002). Social software. *Synthese*, *132*(3), 187–211.

Parkan, C. (1994) Operational competitiveness ratings of production units. *Managerial and Decision Economics*, *15*, 201–221.

Parkan, C. (2002). Measuring the operational performance of a public transit company. *International Journal of Operations & Production*, *22*(6), 693–720.

Pearly, J. (1988). *Probabilistic reasoning in intelligent systems: Networks of plausible inference*. Morgan Kaufman.

Peniwati, K. (2007). Criteria for evaluating group decision-making methods. *Mathematical and Computer Modelling*, *46*(7–8), 935–947.

Perfia, E. A., Habiger, J. D., & Wu, W. (2011). Power-enhanced multiple decision functions controlling family-wise error and false discovery rates. *Annals of Statistics*, *39*(1), 556–583.

Perfia, E. D., Habiger, J. D., & Wu, W. (2015). Classes of multiple decision functions for strongly controlling FWER and FDR. *Metrika*, 78(5), 563–595.

Pintea, C. M., Pop, P. C., & Chira, C. (2017). The generalized travelling salesman problem solved with ant algorithms. *Complex Adaptive Systems Modeling*, 5. https://doi.org/10.1186/s40294-017-0048-9

Pisinger, D., & Ropke, S. (2005). A general heuristic for vehicle routing problems. *Computers & Operations Research*, *34*(8), 2403–2435.

Powell, D. and Skolnick, M. (1993). Using genetic algorithms in engineering design optimizationwith non-linear constraints. Fifth Int. Conference on Genetic Algorithms, San Mateo, California.

Pratt, J., Raiffa, R., & Schlaiffer, R. (1965). *Introduction to Statistical decision theory*. McGraw Hill.

Pritsker, A. A. B. (1966). *Graphical evaluation and review technique*. RAND Corporation Research Memorandum RM 4973—NASA. https://www.rand.org/content/dam/rand/pubs/research_memoranda/2006/RM4973.pdf

Pritsker, A. A. B. (1979) *Modelling and Analysis using Q-GERT Networks*. Wiley, New York.

Pritsker, A. A. B., & Happ, W. W. (1966). GERT: Graphical evaluation and review technique: Part I, fundamentals. *Journal of Industrial Engineering*, *17*(6), 267–274.

Puranam, P., Stieglitz, N., Osma, M., & Pillutla, M. M. (2015). Modelling bounded rationality in organizations: Progress and prospects. *Academy of Management Annals*, *9*(1).

Raftery, A. E., Tanner, A. E. and Wells, M. T. (2002). Statistics in the 21st Century. Chapman and Hall, London.
Rahman, S. (1998). Theory of constraints: A review of its philosophy and its applications. *International Journal of Operations & Production Management*, 18(4), 336–355.
Raiffa, H. (1968). *Decision analysis*. Reading, Mass: Addison Wesley.
Rakus-Anderssen, E., Yager, R. R., Ichalkaranje, N., & Jain, L. (ed.). (2009). *Recent advances in decision-making*. Springer
Rao, C. R. (1973). *Linear statistical inference*. Wiley.
Regenwetter, M., Grofman, B., Popova, A., Messner, W., Davis-Stober, C. P., & Cavagnaro, D. R. (2009). Behavioural social choice: A status report. *Philosophical Transactions of the Royal Society B: Biological Sciences*, 364(1518), 833–843.
Regenwetter, M., Gropman, B., Harley, A. A. J., & Tsetlin, R. M. (2006). *Behavioural social choice: Probabilistic models, statistical inference and application*. Cambridge University Press.
Regenwetter, M., Ho, M. H. R., & Tsetlin, I. (2007). Sophisticated approval voting, ignorance priors and plurality heuristics: A behavioural social choice analysis in a Thurstonian context. *Psychological Review*, 114(4), 994–1014.
Riasecki, M., & Hanna, S. (2010). A redefinition of the paradox of choice. In S. Gero (Ed.), *Design computing and cognition*. Springer.
Rivaz, S., & Yaghoobi, M. A. (2015). Some results in interval linear programming for recognizing different solutions. *OPSEARCH*, 52(1), 75–85.
Rizun, N., & Taranenko, Y. (2014). Simulation models of human decision-making process. *Management Dynamics in the Knowledge Economy*, 2(2), 241–264.
Robbins, H. (1951). Asymptotically subminimax solutions of compound decision problems. In Proceedings of the second Berkeley symposium on mathematical statistics and probability (pp. 157–163). University of California Press. https://digitalassets.lib.berkeley.edu/math/ucb/text/math_s2_article-10.pdf
Robbins, H. (1977). Prediction and estimation for the compound Poisson distribution. *Proceedings of the National Academy of Sciences of the United States of America*, 77, 2382–2383.
Robert, C. P. (1994). *The Bayesian choice*. Springer Verlag.
Roberts, B. J. (1960). Decision-making: An illustration of theory building. *Health Education and Behaviour*, 1(9), 20–44.
Romero, C., Tamiz, M., & Jones D. F. (1998). Goal programming, compromise programming and reference point method formulation: Linkages and utility interpretations. *Journal of the Operational Research Society*, 49(9), 986–991.
Rosati, A. G., & Stevens, J. R. (2009). Rational decisions: The adaptive nature of context-dependent choices of rational animals, irrational humans. Keio University Press.
Rosenhead, J., Elton, M., & Gupta, S. K. (1972). Robustness and optimality as criteria for strategic decisions. *Operational Research Quarterly*, 23(4), 413–431.

Rosing, J. (1970). The formation of groups for co-operative decision-making under uncertainty. *Econometrica, 38*(3), 430–448.
Roy, B. (1990). Paradigms and challenges. In G. Salvatore, E. Matthias, & F. José Rui (Eds.), *Multi-criteria decision analysis: State of the art surveys* (pp. 3–24). Springer.
Roy, B. (1996). *Multi-criteria methodology for decision-aiding*. Kluwer Academic Publishers.
Rubin, D. B. (1976). Inference and missing data. *Biometrika, 63,* 581–592.
Rubinstein, A. (1998). Similarity and decision-making under risk. *Journal of Economic Theory, 46,* 145–153. http://www.dklevine.com/archive/refs47637.pdf
Ruggerio, J. (2004). Data envelopment analysis with stochastic data. *Journal of the Operational Research Society, 55*(9), 1008–1012.
Runarsson, T., & Yao, X. (2000). Stochastic ranking for constrained evolutionary optimization. *IEEE Transactions on Knowledge and Data Engineering, 4*(3), 284–294.
Saaty, T. L. (2004). Fundamentals of the Analytic Network Process—depencence and feedback in decision-making with a single network. *Jour. System Sci. Engg. 13,* 129–157.
Saaty, T. L. and Takizawa, (1986). Dependence and independence: From linear hierarchies to non-linear networks. *Euro. Jour. Oper. Res. 26*(2), 229–237.
Sahoo, B.K. (2007). Scale, scope and capacity in DEA: A reconsideration. *Jour. App. Econ. And Econometrics, 15*(4), 298–328.
Salehi, S., Amiri, M., Ghahramani, P., & Abedini, M. (2018). A novel integrated AHP-TOPSIS model to deal with big data in group decision-making. Proceedings IEOM Conference, Washington DC, USA.
Sandhu, M. S., Rashid, T., & Kashif, A. (2019). Modelling of linear programming and extended TOPSIS in decision-making problems under the framework of picture fuzzy sets. *PloS One, 14*(8), e0220957.
Santner, T. J. (1975). A restricted subset selection approach to ranking and selection problems. *The Ann. Statist., 3*(2) 334–349.
Saocheng, T. (1994). Interval number and fuzzy number linear programming. *Fuzzy Sets and Systems, 66*(3), 301–306.
Sarkar, S. K. (1998). Some probability inequalities for ordered MTP_2 random variables: a proof of the Simes conjecture. *Ann. Statist. 26,* 494–504.
Savage, L. J. (1954). *The foundations of statistics*. Wiley.
Schafer, G. (1976). *A mathematical theory of evidence*. Princeton University Press.
Schaffer, J. P. (1995). Multiple hypothesis testing. *Annual Reviews of Psychology, 46,* 561–584.
Schaik, J. W. J. (1985). *Bradley–Terry models for paired comparisons incorporating judge variability* [Doctoral dissertation, Iowa State University].
Schlaiffer, R. R. (1967). *Analysis of decisions under uncertainty*. McGraw Hill.
Schwartz, B. (2004). *Paradox of choice: Why more is less?* Harper Collins.

Schwartz, B. (2002). Maximizing versus satisficing: Happiness is a matter of choice. *Journal of Personality and Social Psychology*, *83*(5), 1178–1197.

Scutari, M. (2016). *Bayesian network modelling*. Oxford University Press.

Seiford, L. M., & Zhu, J. (2002). Classification invariance in data envelopment analysis. In J. C. Misra (Ed.), *Uncertainty and optimality* (pp. 331–342). World Scientific.

Sen, A. (1971). Choice functions and revealed preference. *Review of Economic Studies*, *38*(3), 307–317.

Sen, A. (1976). Social choice theory. In K. Arrow & M. Intriligator (Ed.), *Handbook of mathematical economics* (Chapter 22). Elsevier.

Sen, A. (1987). Rational behaviour. In J. Eatwell, B. Eatwell, M. Milgate, & P. K. Newman (Ed.), *The new Palgrave dictionary of economics* (pp. 198–216). MacMillan.

Sengupta, A., & Pal, T. K. (2009). *Fuzzy preference ordering of interval numbers in decision problems*. Springer.

Sengupta, J. K. (1998). Stochastic data envelopment analysis: A new approach. *Applied Economics Letters*, *5*, 287–290.

Shaocheng, T. (1994). Interval number and fuzzy number linear programming. *Fuzzy Sets and Systems*, *66*, 301–306.

Simaan, M., & Cruz, J. B. Jr. (1973). Additional aspects of the Stackelberg strategy in non-zero-sum games. *Journal of Optimization Theory and Applications*, *11*(6), 613–626.

Simes, R. J. (1986). Applications of statistical decision theory to treatment choices: Implications for the design and analysis of clinical trials. *Statistics in Medicine*, *5*(5), 411–420.

Simon, H. A. (1957). *Models of man: Social and rational*. John Wiley.

Simon, H. A. (1982). *Models of bounded rationality*. MIT Press.

Singh, R. S. (1978). Sequence-compound estimation in scale-exponential families and speed of convergence. *Journal of Statistical Planning and Inference*, *2*(1), 53–62.

Singh, O. P. and Chand, S. (2007). Ranking of decision-making units: a review and development of new model using Data Envelopment Analysis. *Opsearch*, *3*(3).

Sinuany-Stern, Z., Mehrez, A., & Barboy, A. (1994). Academic departments' efficiency via data envelopment analysis. *Computers & Operations Research*, *21*(5), 543–556.

Smith, J. Q., & Thwaites, P. (2008). *Encyclopedia of quantitative risk analysis*. Wiley.

Sniedovich, M. (2006). What is wrong with info-gap: An operations research perspective [Working paper MS 1–06]. Presented at the ASOR mini conference. https://citeseerx.ist.psu.edu/viewdoc/download?doi=10.1.1.125.4010& rep=rep1&type=pdf

Sniedovich, M. (2016). From statistical decision theory to robust optimization: A maximin perspective on robust decision-making. In M. Doumpos, C.

Zopounidis, & E. Grigoroudis (Eds.), *Robustness analysis in decision aiding, optimization, and analytics*. Springer.

Soloman, M. et al. (2008). Consumer Behavviour: A European Perspective. Pearson Education Ltd., Essex, U.K.

Somerville, P. N. (1985). A new subset selection method for Normal populations. *Journal of Statistical Computation and Simulation, 22*(1), 27–30.

Sonnemann, E. (2008). General solutions to multiple testing problems. *Biometrical Journal: Journal of Mathematical Methods in Biosciences, 50*(5), 641–656.

Sorensen, K., & Sevaux, M. (2006). MA|PM: Memetic algorithms with population management. *Computers & Operations Research, 33*(5), 1214–1225.

Srinivas, T., & Baker, R. C. (2002). A multiphase mathematical programming approach for effective supply chain design. *European Journal of Operational Research, 141*(3), 544–558.

Stallard, N. (1998). Sample size determination for phase II clinical trials based on Bayesian Decision Theory. *Biometrics 54*, 279–294.

Stallard, N. (2003). Sequential designs for phase III clinical trials incorporating treatment selection. *Statistics in Medicine, 22*(5), 689–703.

Stansu-Minasian, I. M. (1984). *Stochastic programming with multiple objective functions*. Reidel.

Stewart, T. J. (1997). Future trends in MCDM. In J. Climaco (Ed.), *Multicriteria analysis* (pp. 590–595). Springer-Verlag.

Sun, D., & Berger, J. O. (1998). Reference priors with partial information. *Biometrika, 85*(1), 55–71.

Taakahama, T. and Sakai, S. (2006). Constrained optimization by the constrained differential evolution with gradient-based mutationa IEEE Congress on Evolutionary Computation, Vancouver, Canada. nd feasible elites.

Taha, H. (1999). *Operations research: An introduction*. Prentice Hall.

Takahama, T. and Sakai, S. (2005). Constrained optimization by the €-constrained hybrid algorithm of particle swarm algorithm and genetic algorithm. Advances in Artificial Intelligence, 389–400 (Australasian Joint Conference on Artificial Intelligence)

Takahama, T. and Sakai, S. (2006). Constrained optimization by the constrained differential evolution with gradient-based mutation and feasible elites. IEEE Congress on Evolutionary Computation, Vancouver, Canada.

Takahama, T., & Sakai, S. (2009). Solving differential constrained optimization problems by the €-constrained differential evolution with gradient-based mutation. In E. Mezura-Montes (Ed.), *Constraint handling in evolutionary computation* (pp. 51–72). Springer.

Taleb, N. N. (2007). *Anti-fragile: Things that gain from disorder*. Random House Publishing Group.

Talluri, S. et al. (2003). Vendor evaluation with performance variability: A maximin approach. *Euro. Jour. Oper. Res., 146*(3), 543–552.

Tessema, G. and Yen, G. G. (2006). A self-adaptive penalty function based aalgorithm for constrained optimization. Paper presented at the IEEE Congress on Evolutionary Computation.

Thaler, R. H. and Sunstein, C. (2008). Nudge: Improving Decisions about Health, Wealth and happiness. Yale University Press. New haven, USA.

Thanassoulis, E., Dyson, R. G., & Foster, M. J. (1987). Relative efficiency assessments using data envelopment analysis: An application to data on rates departments. *Journal of the Operational Research Society, 38*(5), 397–411.

Tone, K. (2000). Slacks-based measure of efficiency in DEA. *Euro. Jour. Oper. Res.*

Thomas, J. A., & Thomas, M. C. (2006). *Elements of information theory.* John Wiley.

Thompson, M. L. (1978). Selection of variables in multiple regression, Part I: A review and evaluation. *International Statistical Review, 46,* 10–19.

Thompson, N., & Thompson, S. (2008). *The critically reflective practitioner.* MacMillan Education.

Thompson, R. G., Singleton Jr, F. D., Thrall, R. M., & Smith, B. A. (1986). Comparative site evaluations for locating a high energy physics lab in Texas. *Interfaces, 16*(6), 35–49.

Thurstone, L. L. (1927). A law of comparative judgment. *Psychological Review, 34,* 273–286.

Todd, P. M., & Miller, G. F. (1999). From pride and prejudice to persuasion: Satisficing in mate search. In P. Carruthers (ed.), *The innate mind: Culture and cognition.* Oxford University Press.

Toffler, A. (1970). *Future shock.* Bantam Books.

Toth, P., & Vigo, D. (ed.). (2002). *The vehicle routing problems: Monographs on discrete mathematics and applications.* SIAM.

Tsetlin I. and M. Regenatter et al. (2003). On the probabilities of corrector incorrect majority preference relations. *Social Choice and Welfare, 20*(2), 283–306.

Tversky, A., & Kahneman, D. (1992). Advances in prospect theory: Cumulative representation of uncertainty. *Journal of Risk and Uncertainty, 5,* 297–323.

Tzeng, G. H., & Huang, J. J. (2011). *Multi-attribute decision-making: Methods and applications.* CRC Press.

Urena, R., Chiclana, F., Morente-Molinera, J. A., & Herrera-Viedma, E. (2015). Managing incomplete preference relations in decision-making: A review and future trends. *Information Sciences, 302,* 14–32.

Vansnick, I. C. (1986). On the problem of weights in multiple criteria decision making (the non-compensatory approach). *European Journal of Operational Research, 24,* 288–294.

Varian, H. R. (1975). A Bayesian approach to real estate assessment. In *Studies in Bayesian Econometrics and Statistics,* Fienberg, S.E. and Zellner, A. (eds), North-Holland, Amsterdam, 195–208.

Vehtari, A., & Ojanen, J. (2012). A survey of Bayesian predictive methods for model assessment, selection and comparison. *Statistics Surveys, 6,* 192–228.

Venkataraman, S., & Yen, G. (2005). A generic framework for constrained optimization using genetic algorithms. *IEEE Transactions on Evolutionary Computation*, 9, 80–92.

Vercelli, A. (1999). The recent advances in decision theory under uncertainty. In L. Luini (ed.), *Uncertain decisions* (pp. 237–260). Springer.

Verma, A. K., Srividya, A., & Gaonkar, R. S. P. (2007). Fuzzy set solutions for optimal maintenance strategy selection. *OPSEARCH*, 44(3), 261–276.

Virine, L., & Trumper, M. (2008) *Project decisions: The art and science.* Management Concepts.

Vroom, V., & Yetton, P. (1973). *Leadership and decision-making.* University of Chicago Press.

Vroom, V., Yetton, P., & Jago, A. (1988). *The new leadership: Managing participation in organizations.* Prentice hall.

Wald, A. (1950). *Statistical decision functions.* Wiley.

Wald. A. (1945). Statistical decision functions which minimize the maximum risk. *Annals of Mathematics*, 46(2), 265–280.

Walsh, T. (2020). *Trends in computational social choice.* IILC University.

Wang, H. F., & Wang, M. L. (2001). Decision analysis of the interval-valued multi-objective linear programming problems. In M. Koksalan & S. Zionts (Eds), *Multiple criteria decision making in the new millennium* (Vol. 507, pp. 210–218). Springer.

Wang, N., Yi, R., & Liu, D. (2008). A solution method to the problem proposed by Wang in voting systems. *Journal of Computational and Applied Mathematics*, 221, 106–113.

Wang, Y. M. (2007). Three new models for preference voting and aggregation. *Jour. Oper. Res. Soc.*, 58, 1389–1393.

White, D. J. (1966). Forecasts and decision making. *Journal of Mathematical Analysis and Applications*, 14, 163–173.

White, R. E. (1986). Generic business strategies, organizational context and performance: An empirical investigation. *Strategic Management Journal*, 7(3), 217–231.

Whyte, G. (1993). Escalating commitment in individual and group decision-making: A prospect theory approach. *Organizational Behaviour and Human Decision Processes*, 54(3), 430–455.

Wilrich, P-Th. (2010). A new approach to Bayesian sampling plans. In H. J. Lenz, P. Th. Wilrich, W. Schmid (Eds.), *Frontiers in statistical quality control* 9. Springer Verlag.

Wu, W., & Pena, E. A. (2013). Bayes multiple decision functions. *The Electronic Journal of Statistics*, 7(1), 1272–1300.

Xiao, N., Benett, D. A., & Armstrong, M. P. (2002). Using evolutionary algorithms to generate alternatives for multi-objective search problems. *Environment and Planning A*, 34(4), 639–656.

Xu, Y., Thall, P. F., Muller, P., & Mehran, R. J. (2017). A decision-theoretic comparison of treatments to resolve air leaks after lung surgery based on non-parametric modeling. *Bayesian Analysis, 12*(3), 639–652.

Yazdani, M., Zaraté, P., Zavadskas, E., & Turskis, Z. (2019). A combined compromise solution (CoCoSo) method for multi-criteria decision problems. *Management Decision, 57*(9), 2501–2529. https://core.ac.uk/download/pdf/335470898.pdf

Yenjay, O. (2015). Penalty function methods for constrained optimization with Genetic Algorithms. *Mathematical and Computer Applications, 10*(1), 45–56.

Zarmelo, E. (1929). On the concept of defniteness in Axiomatics. In Collected Works of Zarmelo, 352–367.

Zavadskas, E. K., & Turskis, Z. (2010). A new additive ratio assessment (ARAS) method in multi-criteria decision-making. *Technological and Economic Development of Economy, 16*(2), 159–172.

Zavadskas, E. K., Kaklauskas, A., Turskis, Z., & Tamošaitienė, J. (2009). Multi-attribute decision-making model by applying grey numbers. *Informatica, 20*(2), 305–320.

Zavadskas, E. K., Tsuskis, Z., & Kildiene, S. (2014). State of art surveys of reviews of MCDM/MADM methods. *Technological and Economic Development of Economy, 20*(1), 165–179.

Zeleny, M. (1982). *Multiple criteria decision making*. McGraw Hill.

Zellner, A. (1986). Bayesian estimation and predictionusing asymmetric loss functions. *Jour Amer. Stat. Assoc. 81*(394), 446–451.

Zhang, C. H. (2003). Compound decision theory and empirical Bayes methods. *Annals of Statistics, 31*(2), 379–390.

Zimmermann, H. J. (2000). An application oriented view of uncertainty. *European Journal of Operational Research, 122*(2), 190–198.

About the Author

Shyama Prasad Mukherjee is a former centenary professor of statistics (1982–2004) and former dean of the faculty of science (1987–1991) at the University of Calcutta. As an author of three books and several edited volumes, he has been a Fellow of the National Academy of Sciences and is currently Chairman of the Board of Directors of the International Statistical Education Centre. Dr Mukherjee was previously president of the Indian Society of Probability and Statistics; the Operational Research Society of India; the Calcutta Statistical Association, and the Indian Association for Productivity, Quality and Reliability. He has guided many researchers in statistics, mathematics, management and engineering. Dr Mukherjee received the prestigious P. C. Mahalanobis Birth Centenary Award from the Indian Science Congress Association; the P. V. Sukhatme National Award in Statistics from the Government of India, and the Distinguished Teacher Award from the University of Calcutta.

Index

absolute error loss, 165–166
action learning sets, 256
adaptive loss functions, 167
admissibility, 160–162
alpha-inflation rate, 181
alternatives, 29, 179
   checking feasibility, 311
   criterion interaction, 316–317
   desiderata, 288–289
   development, 289–291
   domain knowledge in designing, 294–296
   evolutionary algorithms, 297–301
   organizational decisions, 303–305
   scaling, 343–346
analytic hierarchy process (AHP), 204–207
analytic network process (ANP), 207–208
appreciative inquiry, 256
arcs, 60
Arrow's theorem, 238
   independence of irrelevant alternatives, 239
   no dictator, 239
   Pareto optimality, 238
   transitivity, 239
average run length (ARL), 187
average sample number, 187

BADIR framework, 256, 270–272
base rankers, 335
Bayesian Paradigm, 164
Bayesian paradigm
   prolongation, 175–179

Bayesian Paradigm
   use of priors, 173–175
binary cross entropy loss, 168
bounded rationality, 11
Bradley–Terry model, 330
BRAIN, BRAN and brand analysis, 255, 259–260
buffer, 277

case-based decision theory (CBDT), 20–25
   act similarity, 23
   concepts, 22
   memory-dependent similarity, 23
ceratainty effect, 110
chance-constrained programming, 102–104
choice compensation policy, 304
choice criteria, 34–36
choice function, 42
choice problem, 314
chromosomes, 286
classical optimization problems, 286
classical statistics, 143–144
clearly and consistently defined, 289
co-operative games, 135–137
CoCoSo model, 216
compensation policy, 304
completeness, 162–163
computational complexity, 367–368
computational simplicity, 367
computational social choice theory, 249
constant, 88
constraints, 89, 287
   real-life decisions, 305–307

control, influence and accept model, 255
control, influence and adapt model, 260–261
criterion, 35
criterion versus rule for choice, 317–318
criterion
   aggregate, 320–322
   characteristics, 318–320
   development of alternatives, 324
   group decision-making, 322–325
   leadership effectiveness, 323
   learning, 323
   objective function vs, 314–316
   scientific and mathematical generality, 324
   scope, 324
   ultimate analysis, 35
cross-over, 299
Cynefin framework, 256

data envelopment analysis (DEA), 208–212, 335
   limitation, 209
decision alternatives, 142
decision analytic network (DAN), 69
decision criteria, 197
decision environment, 55–57
decision matrix, 57–59
decision problems, 90
   quality management, 8
decision rule, 117, 147, 160
   classes, 162
decision space, 41
decision theory, 4, 25
   descriptive and normative, 18–20
decision trees, 62–67
decision variables, 29
decision-maker, 23
decision-making, 4, 25
decision-making theories, 252
decision-making units (DMUs), 208
decision-making

approaches to under risk, 96–97
Bayesian approach, 162
evidence theory, 113
infirmities, 371–373
meta-level, 14
problem-solving, 17–18
process, 28, 32
prospect theory, 111
rank reversal, 337–346
real-world problems, 197
situations, 312
under certainty, 78, 88–90
under uncertainty, 55, 79, 80–83
decisions, 2
decisions-making processes (DMPs), 45
decisions
   actions, 4
   fuzzy environments, 356–360
   games, 116–117
   hierarchy, 12–15
   operational, 14
   post-implementation, 3
   preceding implementation, 3
   robustness, 53
   social choice, context, 16–17
   tactical, 13
   ubiquity, 5–9
decision–action pair, 26
demand, 98
design of clinical trials, 189–192
dirichlet process prior, 173
diversity, 300
drum, 277
drum, buffer and rope (DBR), 276
dynamic decision-making, 52
   control of dynamic systems, 53

efficiency, 244
empirical Bayes (EB) method, 176–179
   SMR, 179
equalizer rule, 158
evidence theory, 113

evolutionary (dynamic) games, 129–132
evolutionary algorithms
  alternatives, 297–301
  features, 298
evolutionary operations, 279
expert opinions, pooling, 291–294

false discovery proportion (FDP)
  defined, 181
feedback loops, 60
fitness function
  defined, 298
four-step innovative process, 256
framework, 253
frequenist approach, 155
fuzzy decision-making, 105–108
fuzzy MCDM, 228–230

game theory, puzzle, 127
games, decisions, 116–117
Gantt charts, 69–71
gene, 298
general entropy loss function, 168
general optimization problem, 314
genetic algorithms, 298
  inherent weakness, 300
geometric analytic interactive aid (GAIA), 220
Graphical evaluation and review technique (GERT)
  drawback, 74
  logical operators, 75
  queueing, 75
  R&D project, 77
gray areas, 364–365
group decisions, 15–16
growing attention, 20

hierarchical Bayes analysis, 175
hinge loss, 169
human organizations, 303

Hurson's productive thinking model, 256
Hurwicz criterion, 82

implementation, 26
inertia, 280
infirmities, decision-making, 371–373
influence diagram, 59–62
  chance events/uncertainty nodes, 59
  comparing with decision tree, 67
  decision nodes, 59
  outcome/value nodes, 59
info-gap decision analysis, 83–86
information
  defining, 348
  identify feasible options, 360–361
  overload and option deluge, 368–371
  purposes, 349
  search, 350–352
  social choice problems, 361–363
  value, 352–356
interval linear programming, 86
interval programming, 80
interval programming models
  decision problems, 86
intrinsic loss functions, 166

Kepner–Tregoe
  approach, 267–269
  four-step matrix model, 256

leader, 137
linex loss function, 166
loss function, 180
  adaptive, 167
  choice, 164–169
  general entropy, 168
  intrinsic, 166
  linex, 166

M-MACBETH software, 222, 224
marketing decisions, 304

mathematical programming, 79
matrix games, 117–120
  solving, 120–124
maximin pay-off criterion, 81
maximum average pay-off criterion, 81
Measuring attractiveness by a categorical-based evaluation technique (MACBETH), 220–223
memory
  defined, 23
meta-games
  analysis, 132–135
methodology, 253
methods and techniques, 254
minimal classes of rules, 162
minimal complete class, 162
mixed strategy, 117
model, 254
Monte Carlo methods, 180
Monte Carlo simulation, 74
multi-attribute decision-making (MADM), 198
multi-criteria decision-making (MCDM), 42, 198, 199, 315
  challenges, 222
  classification, 200–201
  essentials, 201–202
  fuzzy, 228–230
  methods, 305
  problem-solving methods, 199
multi-objective decision-making (MODM), 198
multi-objective optimization, 315
Multi-objective optimization based on a ratio analysis (MOORA), 223–226
multi-output decision-making units (DMUs)
  ranking, 210–212
multiple decision functions, 179–185
multiplicative exponential weighting, 200

mutri-criteria decision aids
  GAIA, 217
  PROMETHEE, 217

Nash equilibrium, 120
national statistical agency, 293
network defined, 72
network diagrams, 71, 74
non-randomized binary decisions, 179
non-subjective prior, 170
non-zero-sum games, 117
Nudge theory, 247–249

OODA loop model, 255, 262–264
operational competitiveness rating (OCRA), 215, 217
operational decisions, 14
operational research, 46
optimal rule, 155
optimality principle, 40–43, 119–120, 155–158
optimized production scheduling (OPS), 276

paired comparison, 328, 329–330
  aggregating results, 330–333
  analysis, 257, 274–276
parameter estimation, 141
Plan-do-check-act Model, 256
Poliheuristic theory (PHT) of decision-making, 19
polymatrix games, 124–126
preference aggregation, 236–238
preference zone, 302
prior
  choice, 169–175
  dirichlet process, 173
  non-subjective, 170
  uniform, 171
  use in non-Bayesian framework, 173–175
priority heuristic, 112–113
Prisoners' dilemma, 126–129

probabilistic dynamic programming, 105
probabilistic social choice functions, 244
problem-solving
 models, 272–274
problem
 classification, 152–153
 prediction, 153–154
 ranking and selection, 154–155
 single sampling inspection, 150–152
prospect theory, 108–112
 additivity, 109
 advancement, 112
 asset integration, 110
 risk aversion, 110
puzzle, game theory, 127

quality management
 decision problems, 8

random decision variables, 104
random dictatorship, 244
 Gibbard's theorem's statement, 245
random objective function, 100–102
rank reversal, 337–346
rankings
 aggregation of data, 334–335
 concordance in multiple, 335–338
 consensus, 338–343
 nonparametric procedures, 334
 units, 334
rationality, 10
 concept in context of human behaviour, 10
 assumption, 10
recognition-primed decision process, 256, 269–270
reference ranking organization method for enrichment of evaluation (PROMETHEE)
 six versions, 217

regret, 38–40
relevance diagram influence diagram, 59
robust decision-making, 192–181
rope, 277
Russian roulette wheel, 129

satisficing
 criticism, 11
 principle, 11
savage
 minimax regret criterion, 82–83
sequential decision theory, 185–187
 optimal stopping problem, 187–189
sequential decision-making, 52
 objective, 52
simplex process, 256, 264–265
Six-Sigma methodology, 256
skew-symmetric matrix, 122
social choice functions
 axioms, 238
 consistency, 240–241
 probabilistic, 241–245
social choice mechanism, 246
social choice problems
 information, 361–363
social choice theory
 aggregation of preferences, 236
 controversies and counter-examples, 234
 dealing, 233
 preference aggregation, 236–238
social choices
 features, 235–236
social networks, 245, 246
soft systems methodology, 255, 261–262
squared error loss function (SELF), 164
Stackelberg equilibrium points, 138
Stackelberg games, 137–139
standard deviation, 2
states of nature, 33–34, 179

states of reality, 179
statistical decision process, 144–150
statistical decision theory, 48, 141
   developed from, 142
   element, 146
   examples, 150–155
   problem in, 145
stochastic linear programming, 100–104
stochastic multi-criteria acceptability analysis (SMAA), 226–228
stochastic optimization, 95, 97–100
stock-building operation, 98
stopping rule problems, 187
strategies, 29, 31–32
   constraints, 32–33
Strawman concept, 256
Strawman framework, 265–266
super-efficiency ranking model, 211

tactical decisions, 13
TDODAR decision model, 256, 266
technical efficiency
   defined, 208
technically sound, 289
Technique for order preference by similarity to ideal solution (TOPSIS), 212–214
theory of choice in mathematics, 42
theory of constraints (TOC), 256, 276
   measures system, 277
   principles, 278
   steps, 274–276
theory of social choice, 233
Thurstone model, 330

TOC international certification organization (the Theory of Constraints International Certification Organization [TOCICO]), 278
trade-offs
   establishment, 43–45
tree diagram representation, 66
triangular fuzzy numbers (TFNs), 230

uncertainty
   impact, 365–367
   third form, 91
undesirable effects (UDEs), 279
uniform prior, 171
units
   ranking, 334
upper approximation of the class, 149
utility
   concept introduced by Neumann and Morgenstern, 95
   function, forms, 37
   measurement, 36–38

value-focused, 289
VIKOR, 202–204
Vroom–Yetton and Vroom–Jago models, 255, 258–259

Wald's theory of statistical decision functions, 140

zero-sum game, 118
ϵ-efficiency methods, 12